Thomas D. Carlson
Martin J. Erickson
Editors

Spirituality and Family Therapy

Spirituality and Family Therapy has been co-published simultaneously as *Journal of Family Psychotherapy*, Volume 13, Numbers 1/2 and 3/4 2002.

Pre-publication REVIEWS, COMMENTARIES, EVALUATIONS . . .

"ONE OF THE BEST BOOKS I HAVE READ ON THIS TOPIC. . . . Provides an excellent mix of theoretical, clinical, and research chapters. I strongly recommend this text for clinicians and students alike. . . . A first-rate piece of scholarship."

Joseph Wetchler, PhD
Professor and Director
Marriage and Family Therapy Program
Purdue University Calumet
Editor, Journal of Couple & Relationship Therapy

More pre-publication
REVIEWS, COMMENTARIES, EVALUATIONS . . .

"A RICH FEAST OF CLINICAL PERSPECTIVES on spiritual and family therapy. . . . UNIQUE CROSS-CULTURAL FOCUS. . . . Something for novices and experienced therapists alike. . . . Takes the step beyond consciusness-raising by delving into what therapists can do in their practices."

William J. Doherty, PhD
Professor of Family Social Science
University of Minnesota
Author, Soul Searching

The Haworth Press, Inc.
New York

Spirituality and Family Therapy

Spirituality and Family Therapy has been co-published simultaneously as *Journal of Family Psychotherapy*, Volume 13, Numbers 1/2 and 3/4 2002.

The *Journal of Family Psychotherapy* Monographic "Separates" (formerly the *Journal of Psychotherapy & the Family* series)*

For information on previous issues of the *Journal of Psychotherapy & the Family* series, edited by Charles R. Figley, please contact: The Haworth Press, Inc., 10 Alice Street, Binghamton, NY 13904-1580 USA.

Below is a list of "separates," which in serials librarianship means a special issue simultaneously published as a special journal issue or double-issue *and* as a "separate" hardbound monograph. (This is a format which we also call a "DocuSerial.")

"Separates" are published because specialized libraries or professionals may wish to purchase a specific thematic issue by itself in a format which can be separately cataloged and shelved, as opposed to purchasing the journal on an on-going basis. Faculty members may also more easily consider a "separate" for classroom adoption.

"Separates" are carefully classified separately with the major book jobbers so that the journal tie-in can be noted on new book order slips to avoid duplicate purchasing.

You may wish to visit Haworth's website at . . .

http://www.HaworthPress.com

. . . to search our online catalog for complete tables of contents of these separates and related publications.

You may also call 1-800-HAWORTH (outside US/Canada: 607-722-5857), or Fax 1-800-895-0582 (outside US/Canada: 607-771-0012), or e-mail at:

getinfo@haworthpressinc.com

Spirituality and Family Therapy, edited by Thomas D. Carlson, PhD, and Martin J. Erickson, MS (Vol. 13, No. 1/2 and 3/4, 2002). *"One of the best books I have read on this topic. . . . Provides an excellent mix of theoretical, clinical, and research chapters. I strongly recommend this text for clinicians and students alike. . . . A first-rate piece of scholarship." (Joseph Wetchler, PhD, Professor and Director, Marriage and Family Therapy Program, Purdue University Calumet; Editor,* Journal of Couple & Relationship Therapy*)*

Multi-Systemic Structural-Strategic Interventions for Child and Adolescent Behavior Problems, edited by Patrick H. Tolan, PhD (Vol. 6, No. 3/4, 1990). * *"A well-written, informative, practical guide for clinicians interested in utilizing multi-systemic, structural-strategic interventions for child and adolescent behavior problems and for dysfunctional family patterns." (Journal of Marital and Family Therapy)*

Minorities and Family Therapy, edited by George W. Saba, PhD, Betty M. Karrer, MA, and Kenneth V. Hardy, PhD (Vol. 6, No. 1/2, 1990).* *"A must for those who are interested in family therapy and concerned with handling the problems of minority families. A particularly thought-provoking book for the novice who knows little about the area." (Criminal Justice)*

Children in Family Therapy: Treatment and Training, edited by Joan J. Zilbach, MD (Vol. 5, No. 3/4, 1989). *"The range of clinical material presented in this volume provides a powerful and vivid addition to an important and often neglected area of family therapy. . . . Lively, illustrative, and convincing." (Carol C. Nadelson, MD, Professor and Vice Chairman of Academic Affairs, Department of Psychiatry, Tufts University School of Medicine)*

Aging and Family Therapy: Practitioner Perspectives on Golden Pond, edited by George A. Hughston, PhD, Victor A. Christopherson, EdD, and Marilyn J. Bonjean, EdD (Vol. 5, No. 1/2, 1989).* *Experts provide information, insight, reference sources, and other valuable tools that will contribute to more effective intervention with the elderly and their families.*

Family Myths: Psychotherapy Implications, edited by Stephen A. Anderson, PhD, and Dennis A. Bagarozzi, PhD, MSW (Vol. 4, No. 3/4, 1989).* *"A marvelous international collection of papers on family myths–their development, process, and clinical implications." (American Journal of Family Therapy)*

Circumplex Model: Systemic Assessment and Treatment of Families, edited by David H. Olson, PhD, Candyce S. Russell, PhD, and Douglas H. Sprenkle, PhD (Vol. 4, No. 1/2, 1989).* *"An excellent resource for the Circumplex Model." (The Family Psychologist)*

Women, Feminism, and Family Therapy, edited by Lois Braverman, ACSW (Vol. 3, No. 4, 1988).* *"Get the book, have it at your fingertips, and you will find it hard to put down." (Australian Journal of Marriage & Family Therapy)*

Chronic Disorders and the Family, edited by Froma Walsh, PhD, and Carol M. Anderson, PhD (Vol. 3, No. 3, 1988).* *"An excellent text, for it thoughtfully explores several of the critical issues confronting the field of family systems medicine. . . . It should have a long shelf life for both clinical and scholarly work." (Family Systems Medicine)*

The Family Life of Psychotherapists: Clinical Implications, edited by Florence W. Kaslow, PhD (Vol. 3, No. 2, 1987).* *"A first in the field, these innovative contributions by outstanding therapists/trainers will enable family therapists to understand and explore the reciprocal influences between the therapist's personal family system and professional life." (Jeannette R. Kramer, Assistant Professor of Clinical Psychiatry and Behavioral Science, Northwestern University Medical School)*

The Use of Self in Therapy, edited by Michele Baldwin, PhD, MSW, and Virginia Satir (Vol. 3, No.1, 1987).* *"Recognized masters share insights gathered over decades on how the person the therapist is the fulcrum around which therapy succeeds. Thirty-six masters, from Kierkegaard to Buber to Satir and Rogers . . . this collection of scholarly work imparts lasting information." (American Journal of Family Therapy)*

Depression in the Family, edited by Arthur Freeman, PhD, Norman Epstein, PhD, and Karen M. Simon, PhD (Vol. 2, No. 3/4, 1987).* *Here is the first book focused on treating depression through the family system.*

Treating Incest: A Multiple Systems Perspective, edited by Terry S. Trepper, PhD, and Mary Jo Barrett, MSW (Vol. 2, No. 2, 1987).* *"Both theoretical and clinical aspects of intrafamily sexual abuse are covered in this important book which stresses the need for a systemic approach in working with incestuous families." (Journal of Pediatric Psychology)*

Marriage and Family Enrichment, edited by Wallace Denton, EdD (Vol. 2, No.1, 1986).* *"A practical book. A good introduction to the history, philosophy, and practice of this group-based approach." (The British Journal of Psychiatry)*

Family Therapy Education and Supervision, edited by Fred P. Piercy, PhD (Vol. 1, No. 4, 1986).* *"Written by authors who are well-known and well-represented in the family therapy literature (Beavers, Duhl, Hovestadt, Kaslow, Keller, Liddle, Piercy, and Sprenkle) . . . individual chapters are well-presented and offer valuable, concrete guidelines." (Journal of Family Psychology)*

Divorce Therapy, edited by Douglas H. Sprenkle, PhD (Vol. 1, No. 3, 1985).* *"While focusing on the specific area of divorce, the book in fact adds richly to a more general knowledge of family dynamics." (The British Journal of Psychiatry)*

Computers and Family Therapy, edited by Charles R. Figley, PhD (Vol. 1, No. 1/2, 1985).* *"An ideal resource for clinicians who have a systemic orientation in their practice and who are intrigued with how recent developments in home computers might be applied as an adjunct to their clinical work." (Canada's Mental Health)*

∞ ALL HAWORTH BOOKS AND JOURNALS
ARE PRINTED ON CERTIFIED
ACID-FREE PAPER

Spirituality and Family Therapy

Thomas D. Carlson
Martin J. Erickson
Editors

Spirituality and Family Therapy has been co-published simultaneously as *Journal of Family Psychotherapy*, Volume 13, Numbers 1/2 and 3/4 2002.

The Haworth Press, Inc.
New York • London • Oxford

Spirituality and Family Therapy has been co-published simultaneously as *Journal of Family Psychotherapy*™, Volume 13, Numbers 1/2 and 3/4 2002.

Cover design by Marylouise Doyle.

Library of Congress Cataloging-in-Publication Data

Spirituality and family therapy / Thomas Carlson, Martin J. Erickson, editors.
p. cm.
"Co-published simultaneously as Journal of family psychotherapy, volume 13, numbers 1/2 and 3/4 2002"–P.
Includes bibliographical references and index.
ISBN 0-7890-1960-4 (hard) – ISBN 0-7890-1961-2 (pbk.)
1. Family psychotherapy. 2. Spirituality. I. Carlson, Thomas (Thomas D.) II. Erickson, Martin J., MS.
RC488.5 .S72 2002
616.89′156–dc21

2002013254

Indexing, Abstracting & Website/Internet Coverage

This section provides you with a list of major indexing & abstracting services. That is to say, each service began covering this periodical during the year noted in the right column. Most Websites which are listed below have indicated that they will either post, disseminate, compile, archive, cite or alert their own Website users with research-based content from this work. (This list is as current as the copyright date of this publication.)

Abstracting, Website/Indexing Coverage . . . . Year When Coverage Began

- *Biology Digest (in print and online)* **1992**
- *CNPIEC Reference Guide: Chinese National Directory of Foreign Periodicals* **1995**
- *Educational Research Abstracts (ERA) <www.tandf.co.uk>* **2002**
- *EMBASE/Excerpta Medica Secondary Publishing Division <URL: http://www.elsevier.nl>* **1992**
- *e-psyche, LLC <www.e-psyche.net>* **2001**
- *Family Index Database <www.familyscholar.com>* **2002**
- *Family & Society Studies Worldwide <www.nisc.com>* **1996**
- *Family Violence & Sexual Assault Bulletin* **1992**

(continued)

- *FINDEX <www.publist.com>* **1999**
- *FRANCIS.INIST/CNRS <www.inist.fr>* **2000**
- *Gay & Lesbian Abstracts <www.nisc.com>* **2002**
- *Index Guide to College Journals* **1999**
- *Index to Periodical Articles Related to Law* **1992**
- *National Clearinghouse on Child Abuse & Neglect Information Documents Database <www.calib.com/nccanch>* **2001**
- *PASCAL <www.inist.fr>* **1999**
- *Psychiatric Rehabilitation Journal* **1996**
- *Psychological Abstracts (PsycINFO) <www.apa.org>* **1992**
- *Referativnyi Zhurnal (Abstracts Journal of the All-Russian Institute of Scientific and Technical Information–in Russian)* **1992**
- *Sage Family Studies Abstracts (SFSA)* **1992**
- *Social Services Abstracts <www.csa.com>* **1992**
- *Social Work Abstracts <www.silverplatter.com/catalog/swab.htm>* **1992**
- *Sociological Abstracts (SA) <www.csa.com>* **1992**
- *Special Educational Needs Abstracts* **1992**
- *Studies on Women Abstracts* **1992**
- *SwetsNet <www.swetsnet.com>* **2002**
- *Violence and Abuse Abstracts: A Review of Current Literature on Interpersonal Violence (VAA)* **1995**

(continued)

Special Bibliographic Notes related to special journal issues (separates) and indexing/abstracting:

- indexing/abstracting services in this list will also cover material in any "separate" that is co-published simultaneously with Haworth's special thematic journal issue or DocuSerial. Indexing/abstracting usually covers material at the article/chapter level.
- monographic co-editions are intended for either non-subscribers or libraries which intend to purchase a second copy for their circulating collections.
- monographic co-editions are reported to all jobbers/wholesalers/approval plans. The source journal is listed as the "series" to assist the prevention of duplicate purchasing in the same manner utilized for books-in-series.
- to facilitate user/access services all indexing/abstracting services are encouraged to utilize the co-indexing entry note indicated at the bottom of the first page of each article/chapter/contribution.
- this is intended to assist a library user of any reference tool (whether print, electronic, online, or CD-ROM) to locate the monographic version if the library has purchased this version but not a subscription to the source journal.
- individual articles/chapters in any Haworth publication are also available through the Haworth Document Delivery Service (HDDS).

Spirituality and Family Therapy

CONTENTS

SPIRITUAL APPROACHES TO WORKING WITH SPECIFIC POPULATIONS

ABOUT THE EDITORS

Thomas D. Carlson, PhD, is Assistant Professor in the Marriage and Family Therapy Program at North Dakota State University. He has published numerous articles and book chapters related to narrative therapy and spirituality, narrative therapy, feminist theory, and MFT training. He is especially interested in exploring how therapists' spiritual lives and beliefs can be used as a resource in developing a relational ethic in their work with clients.

Martin J. Erickson, MS, is a PhD candidate in the Marriage and Family Therapy Program at Iowa State University and currently works as a family therapist for the Anasazi Foundation in Mesa, Arizona. He has published articles on religion and spirituality, narrative therapy, marriage and family therapy and family life course, and morality and value exploration in therapists' lives. He is interested in poststructural inquiry, narrative therapy, relationalism, and the centrality of the moral domain in both helpers' lives and the helping professions.

Preface

Terry S. Trepper

The *Journal of Family Psychotherapy* has now completed 12 years of publishing case studies, reports on novel and innovative treatment programs, and strategies in clinical practice in the broad areas of family therapy and psychotherapy. We are most proud that we are often the first source for novel ideas and intervention, usually developing "from the field," which then can lead to further refinement and eventually empirical investigation. We also are proud that the *Journal*, because of its strong clinical orientation, was chosen by the International Family Therapy Association to become its official journal. This allowed family therapists from all over the world to participate in the process of sharing exciting new clinical ideas and interventions.

Occasionally, the *Journal* has published thematic issues. These allow us to focus on one topic in more depth than could be attained through a single article. When Thomas Carlson and Martin Erickson came to me with the idea of a special volume on Spirituality and Family Therapy, I was intrigued. This topic has had relatively little formal focus in the professional press or in our academic journals. At the same time, conference workshops on spirituality and family therapy are often the best attended and best reviewed. The books that have been published on this topic are big sellers. And students in marriage and family therapy and related fields have been telling us for years that they wanted more training in how to incorporate spirituality and religion in their clinical practices.

Why, then, has such an important topic, one in which practitioners are clearly interested, been almost absent from the literature? There are probably many answers to this question, but I think one answer may come from how therapists view religion and God; that is, with *embar-*

[Haworth co-indexing entry note]: "Preface." Trepper, Terry S. Co-published simultaneously in *Journal of Family Psychotherapy* (The Haworth Press, Inc.) Vol. 13, No. 1/2, 2002, pp. xix-xx; and: *Spirituality and Family Therapy* (ed: Thomas D. Carlson and Martin J. Erickson) The Haworth Press, Inc., 2002, pp. xv-xvi. Single or multiple copies of this article are available for a fee from The Haworth Document Delivery Service [1-800-HAWORTH, 9:00 a.m. - 5:00 p.m. (EST). E-mail address: getinfo@haworthpressinc.com].

rassment. As a sex therapist who has been in practice for over 25 years, I see a parallel with how sexuality and therapy was viewed back in the '70s. Therapists knew it was important to assess client's sexuality and how it affects their lives and relationships, but were often embarrassed to bring it up. Cultural changes and improved training, for the most part, changed that, and today most marriage and family therapists can and do talk about sexuality as easily as any other aspect of their clients' lives. But the same therapists who can discuss sexuality with ease have trouble bringing up God, religion, or spirituality. It is, for some, more taboo than sex or death (another topic therapists often avoid). Clearly, clinicians desire and need more training and exposure to spirituality.

To contribute to the beginning of this process, I happily accepted Carlson and Erickson's offer to guest edit a special edition of the *Journal of Family Psychotherapy* focusing on spirituality and family therapy. Apparently, many others were as excited by the prospect as I. What was going to be a single, special issue, grew as more and more academic and professional marriage and family therapists wanted to contribute. What finally came to my desk was a much larger and better-than-expected set of articles covering the full range of this important topic. What should have been one issue had grown to cover an entire volume! The publisher and I had to decide what to do. Should we cut some of the articles? Should we spread them out over four issues? We finally agreed that the topic was so important as to warrant special considerations and departure from our usual format.

Therefore, what you will receive are two double issues of the *Journal of Family Psychotherapy* this volume year, *Spirituality and Family Therapy, Parts I and II*. This special edition will also be published as a book for non-*Journal* subscribers. This two-part volume covers the whole range of issues relating to religion and spirituality and family therapy: (1) the relationship of spirituality and family therapy theory; (2) research in spirituality, ethics and spirituality; (3) training therapists in spirituality issues; and (4) spiritual approaches to working with specific populations. I think you will agree that this is a very exciting set that Carlson and Erickson have put together, one that is particularly timely given the sad events in the world today, and our clients' apparent reconnecting with their spirituality to help to understand and cope with major life struggles.

INTRODUCTION

A Conversation About Spirituality in Marriage and Family Therapy: Exploring the Possibilities

Thomas D. Carlson
Martin J. Erickson

The importance of addressing both religion and spirituality in marriage and family therapy (MFT) has been a theme in many recent articles, and books (i.e., Chubb, Gutsche, & Efron, 1994; Doherty, 1995; Harris, 1998; Patterson, Hayworth, Turner, & Raskin, 2000; Prest, & Keller, 1993; Prest, Russell, & D'Souza, 1999; Sperry, & Giblin, 1996; Stander, Piercy, Mackinnon, & Helmke, 1994; Walsh, 1999; Watson 1997). MFTs seem to be addressing spirituality and religion more and more as we collectively have come to understand that for most peoples throughout the world, religion and/or spirituality occupy a very central aspect of culture on both macro and micro levels. This growing trend

Thomas D. Carlson is Associate Professor of Marriage and Family Therapy, North Dakota State University.

Martin J. Erickson is a doctoral candidate, Marriage and Family Therapy Program, Iowa State University, and is affiliated with Anasazi Foundation, Mesa, Arizona.

[Haworth co-indexing entry note]: "A Conversation About Spirituality in Marriage and Family Therapy: Exploring the Possibilities." Carlson, Thomas D., and Martin J. Erickson. Co-published simultaneously in *Journal of Family Psychotherapy* (The Haworth Press, Inc.) Vol. 13, No. 1/2, 2002, pp. 1-11; and: *Spirituality and Family Therapy* (ed: Thomas D. Carlson, and Martin J. Erickson) The Haworth Press, Inc., 2002, pp. 1-11. Single or multiple copies of this article are available for a fee from The Haworth Document Delivery Service [1-800-HAWORTH, 9:00 a.m. - 5:00 p.m. (EST). E-mail address: getinfo@haworthpressinc.com].

has allowed us to bring together this current special collection. Our field is definitely not as disconnected from discussing the sacred of persons', couples', and families' lives as we have been in the past. The process of being guest editors for this special double volume on spirituality and family therapy has been a unique and positive experience for us. By way of introduction we were unsure what we could write that would appropriately capture both the topic at hand as well as the approach we have taken in bringing this volume together. We decided because spirituality is such a personal experience that a personal introduction may be a way of keeping in the spirit of our theme. Therefore we decided on presenting an e-mail dialogue we had with each other as an introduction. In this dialogue we sent one another questions and invited ourselves to personally and critically reflect on the questions, hopefully in a way that helps us situate the genesis and guiding thoughts of this special collection as well as the theme itself. In doing so, our questions and responses hopefully reach beyond our personal interchange, and address readers by addressing some of the most important questions about this important theme as well as this particular special volume.

Marty: Tom, when you had the option presented to you from Terry Trepper (*Journal of Family Psychotherapy* Chief Editor) for us to do a special issue on spirituality and family therapy, what inspired you most as you thought about this special issue? What do you personally feel is so important about addressing spirituality in MFT?

Tom: As I thought about doing a special issue on spirituality and family therapy, I was inspired by two things in particular. The first was that it symbolized to me that the field is finally embracing the value and importance of spirituality in the lives of clients and our clinical work. I also felt inspired about the possibility of developing an issue that would purposefully bring forth multiple voices related to spirituality and its implications for the field. While there have been a number of articles that address the importance of spirituality as a topic for therapy, I envisioned this special issue as a means to further explore ways that spirituality can enhance our understanding and experience of therapy, training and supervision, and ethics. Besides the fact that spirituality is at the heart of who I am I have always believed change or transformation in persons' lives takes place as they transform their beliefs about who they are as persons. I have found it virtually impossible to enter into meaningful conversations with persons about their beliefs without talking about their spirituality. For most people, their spiritual beliefs are at the core of who they are. Spiritual beliefs form the lens through which most people experience the world and their place in it. A therapy that is centered in a beliefs focus cannot avoid conversations about spirituality. As persons have shared their spiritual lives with me, I have noticed that it has opened up our conversations to topics such as beauty, love, compassion, forgiveness, mercy, etc. These experiences have led me to consider how the spiritualities of persons' lives can serve as the foundation of their ethical and relational involvements with others.

Marty: I couldn't agree with you more. I'm also glad that you mentioned the need for multiple voices concerning spirituality and our field. I've noticed that this has been a significant aspect of this issue as it has come together and I would like to say a bit about that. We have tried to represent a small sample of differing spiritual, religious, philosophical, and theoretical views with the assortment of articles selected for this issue. Of course we have not adequately represented *all* the different voices who may have quite important thoughts and ideas to share on this important theme, but we hope that the multi-vocal nature of the articles as a whole does show the diversity and plurality we are dealing with when we speak of spirituality and family therapy.

In order to bring some continuity to the issue as a whole we did invite a number of authors to contribute who are informed by postmodern, social constructionist, and/or poststructuralist perspectives. We felt this important for two reasons, first our work has been influenced primarily by narrative therapy ideas and practices and we have found these ideas to be quite amenable to discussions of spirituality in family therapy, and in addition we have found that narrative therapy ideas have positively influenced our own personal spiritualities. We simply hoped to be able to share that in a formal way through this issue. Second, there has not been a great deal written concerning postmodernism and spirituality, particularly as it relates to MFT. We hoped that this special issue could be an important formal platform for authors interested in both postmodernism and spirituality, something which is as yet only beginning to be articulated in our field.

Tom, what intrigues you most about the possible relationships between spirituality and postmodernism? Share some about your experience with both your interests in narrative therapy (and all attendant ideas) and your own spirituality. How does this all relate to this special issue for you?

Tom: While some people might consider a connection between postmodern ideas, such as social constructionism, and spirituality to be odd, I personally have found that social constructionist ideas have opened up many possibilities for me in understanding and experiencing my own spirituality. Some people see social constructionism as offering a relativist position in regard to values, ethics, and morals.

My experience of social constructionism has been quite different from this. I have experienced social constructionist ideas as encouraging me to enter into a moral and ethical experience with myself and others. This has led me to believe that morality and ethics really are at the heart of social constructionism. Let me explain. Social constructionism proposes a view of the self that is *in relationship* with others. There is no self without others. Social constructionism also proposes that the self is constantly being created in our relationships with others. Every new encounter with an "other" participates in bringing forth a new self. The self is emergent in relationships with others. As I consider the implications of this view of the emergent self, it becomes impossible to escape considerations of morality and ethics in our relationships with others. It has invited me to enter into an *intimate* experience of accountability. As I have entered into social constructionism in these ways I have begun to see every encounter as an ethical encounter where I become accountable for how my way of being and actions participate in the shaping of the self of "the other." The social constructionism that I have experienced shares much with spirituality. In connection to my relationship with God, when I think of spirituality I think of love, ethics, connection, unity, beauty, communion, accountability, etc. I think social constructionism offers in-roads to many of these very same experiences.

While spirituality has always been at the center of my life I believe that as I have entered into social constructionism in these ways my experience of spirituality has been enriched. While spirituality has always been a source of personal meaning in my life as I have embraced narrative therapy and social constructionist ideas I have experienced a more *relational* spirituality. By that I mean a spirituality that encourages me to see the connections between spirituality and social justice. I have been able to see how the stands that I take for social justice in my life, family, and community are an expression of my spirituality. This has led me to really consider how the spiritualities of therapists' lives can become foundational to their ethical and relational preferences for their work with others.

In reading through this question, I am curious to know what inspired you to ask this question of me. What has been the connection between narrative ideas and your own experience of spirituality?

Marty: As you know, I share the very same sentiments you expressed. When I thought of this question, I was thinking a lot about the many discussions we have had over the past few years exploring the ideas of narrative therapy, postmodernism, social constructionism, etc. in terms of our own spiritualities and spiritual experiences. These conversations have so often been very generative for me. They have been conversations marked by feelings of wonder, enthusiasm, beauty, and connection; and for me this speaks to the heart of spirituality, those times of excited clarity and wondrous love when we see and feel in ways we haven't before, or haven't for awhile. And I really think that I wanted us to explore this question because I want to try and share a bit of our excitement and wonder for some of the possibilities and connections between postmodern thought and spirituality, as well as to share a bit of the transformative experiences of spirituality in and of itself. I hope this desire to share is not just one of wanting to proselytize. I was very recently reading Brenda Ueland (1938), and was moved by her thought that to write or produce art or whatever is most meaningful when the purpose is not to show off, or get money, etc. but rather out of sincere generosity and gratitude. That is what spirituality encourages and invites me toward, and that is what my take on postmodern, social constructionist, and poststructuralist thought invites me toward as well–to generously share my experience because I have felt so grateful to have been moved in these ways. Granted there are many different takes on both spirituality and postmodern ideas that would be antithetical to my experience, but I hope that the great diversity inherent in both allow room for the wonder I've felt.

Marty: To switch gears some now, I want to ask you what has this experience of guest editing this special issue been like for you? What has been most meaningful to you in this experience working with authors and reading their work, and discussing these things with me?

Tom: My involvement with this special issue and my experience reading and interacting with the authors have shaped my life in a powerful way. While spirituality has always been an important part of my work, it was largely through this issue that I have been able to more fully reflect upon how my own spirituality can be a sustaining influence in my work with others. For the past few years you and I have been interested in and written about the importance of considering the spiritual lives of clients as a resource for therapy (i.e., Carlson & Erickson, 2000). While this is becoming more widely accepted in our field, there has been little discussion about the importance of therapists using *their own* spirituality as a help in their own work. This experience has further encouraged me to see the spiritual lives of therapists as relevant and meaningful to our work with clients, which has led me to believe that therapists' spiritual beliefs do not need to be kept separate from their professional lives.

Marty: I'm really curious to know what it was specifically about doing this special issue that so encouraged you to more fully reflect on how your own spirituality can be a sustaining influence in your work with others?

Before you answer, I'll answer this question too. I'm amazed at how our lives have significant themes that ebb and flow, I'm particularly amazed when I notice these themes in my life and especially when I'm able to see those themes that are positive, encouraging, and hopeful. During the time that we have be working on this special issue, there has been an important theme of spirituality emanating through my day to day life, and there has even been a significant *denouement* or spiritual turning point that has been a blessing to my life and is proving to have an important influence in all my relationships. A number of things have influenced this spiritual theme in my life during this time from being more alone as I have been adjusting to new social environments after a recent move to Arizona, a new experience for me teaching 6 year olds in Sunday School, attending a fascinating religion class taught from a unique perspective, my in- depth involvement with philosopher Terry Warner's (Warner, 1985; 1997) ideas through my work (I find his ideas spiritual and deeply relational), feeling called to both forgiveness and repentance in a way I have not before felt, and of course reading and reviewing great articles for this issue. I want so much for my spiritual life to be a sustaining influence in my work as a family therapist, and my life experiences of this past number of months have really confirmed the importance of this in a dramatic and moving way for me.

Tom: I think working on this special issue has really allowed me to share in a sense of community with others who are intentional about the place of spirituality in their lives and work. In my every day work setting, others don't share this same desire and so I have often felt a sense of isolation in my work. We have had many conversations about how important it is to belong to a community of persons who share our beliefs about the importance of narrative ideas. This is not to say that it is not important to belong to a community of diverse voices, but when the ideas that we embrace are somewhat at odds with the dominant ways of thinking in our field, sharing in a community helps to keep those ideas alive. Working on this special issue and reading the thoughts and beliefs of the other authors has brought me into a community experience with them. This experience has allowed me to keep my preferences for a spiritually informed practice (both therapy and supervision) closer to me. I really believe that being part of this community of authors has allowed my ideas about the importance of spirituality as a source of relational ethics for therapists to emerge in a way that could not have taken place without such a community. It is my belief that belonging to and participating in a community of persons who embrace similar ways of being in the world is generative and life giving. It allows for the generation of ideas and thinking that would not be possible when this community is not present. For me, community is generative. This has been one of the main blessings of being a Co-Guest Editor of this issue with you. It has allowed us to experience a greater sense of community together. The other authors worked mostly in isolation from one another, but we had the privilege of being influenced by their writings and experiences and this experience has strengthened me in many ways. I want to let the authors know that they have each influenced my life and work in many powerful ways. They have shaped my experience of the importance of spirituality in ways that I could not have predicted and for that I am grateful.

Marty, how do you hope the readers of this issue might in some small ways be encouraged to think and feel about: their work and relationships with their clients, the field of MFT, and their personal lives and relationships from any of their readings from this issue? Not just what they might learn intellectually, but rather what you hope they might feel inside, even spiritually?

Marty: I think this is an important question first of all because you are asking me to reflect on the relational accountability with readers we both are invited into by virtue of being guest editors of this issue. Hmm . . . first and foremost, it is my hope that readers may feel an inspiration toward exploring the spiritual lives of their clients. When I was first becoming an MFT and especially when I worked for a church run therapy clinic, I noticed that I held off to some extent addressing spirituality and religious things in my work. I would address it, but sometimes not on a deep personal level that I could have. I thought maybe it would be better for clients to speak with their ecclesiastical leaders about such things and that I shouldn't share my feelings. Upon reflections, and some important conversations that you and I had, I realized that I was making some distinctions and drawing some dichotomies between my clients' (as well as my own) spiritualities and their day to day lives, presenting problems, and relationships that were really unnatural and arbitrary. These were not distinctions and dichotomies that my clients were necessarily drawing, but rather were most often imposed by me. The conversations you and I had and especially some really moving experiences discussing spiritual things in-depth in therapy with others were really inspiring to me and created in me a genuine curiosity and wonder about the spiritual in the lives of my clients that had me quite excited to explore with them. This also was the genesis for me really exploring the place and influence of my own spiritual feelings and beliefs in my professional work and relationships. This was all very encouraging and it is simply my hope that as readers explore any of the ideas in these articles that they will feel a similar encouragement to somehow bring and invite the spiritual into their work in whatever ways they may be inspired to do.

With regard to the field of MFT, I'm hopeful that readers may in kind be excited and enthusiastic about the fact that this special issue represents another drop in the MFT literature sea that is calling for spirituality to be much more relevant and even more central to the practice of MFT. Granted, MFTs who value spirituality and/or religion in their lives will likely be grateful for this issue, but I also hope that MFTs who would not consider themselves particularly religious or spiritual might be encouraged to, to use a Christian Biblical phrase, "come and see" the significance and importance of this theme in their own work.

Lastly, it is my hope that readers will see these articles representing a call for their work to be more integrated, sustained, influenced, and comprehended in terms of all that they may value that would fit under the broad term "spirituality." I really believe that spirituality lies at the heart of persons' lives, and therefore at the very heart of the nature of change. Change is a transformative experience; who has comprehended it all? Who knows exactly how to bring it about? Who doesn't marvel at the experience of a person, or a couple, or a family, or a community experiencing a change for the better? I say these are spiritual experiences, in this world we will never comprehend them in full. Infusing our work with the spiritual will do much to turn the tide of our field away from the medical model, mechanistic and merely scientific descriptions of therapy, and all such practices that actually serve to squelch the spiritual and leave no room for the never ending wonder it has to offer us in this work.

Tom: Marty, as I read through what we have written I am curious to know how others will experience our conversation. Since we have had so many conversations like this together and we know the desires and intents of one another's hearts it is hard for us to be critical about what we have written. As you look back on what we have written are their any concerns you might have about what we have said?

Before you answer this question, I will share a thought with you. As I look back on what we have written I noticed that we don't speak about some of the struggles of bringing spirituality and therapy together. This is a very delicate issue and many people are concerned about the potentially negative ethical implications of this. This of course is a real concern and has been something that we both struggled with for some time and continue to struggle with. As therapists we are in such a powerful position in regard to clients that bringing spirituality into the therapy process without a critical reflection of that power could be disastrous. While we both believe that spirituality is so often at the heart of our work, we are cautious about our positions as therapists and strive to place the spiritualities of *clients'* lives at the center of these conversations. However, we have recently acknowledged that it is impossible for our own spiritualities to not influence our work. As with issues of gender, culture, race, etc., rather than trying to remain objective (i.e., keep our spirituality separate from our work), which is impossible, it is essential that we undertake a purposeful exploration of our spiritual lives and our moral preferences for how we hope our spiritualities will influence our work and relationships with others. We want to be clear that we are not simply encouraging therapists to share their spiritual beliefs with clients, rather we are calling for therapists to reflect upon how their spiritual beliefs call them *to be in relationship* with others. This is a constant struggle.

And in this struggle there have been moments that I have doubted how much of an influence spirituality should have in my work. These tensions, I think, are related to my consciousness of the position of power that I hold as a therapist. I also think, however, that these doubts are related to the dominant notions of therapy that constantly call for therapists to separate their personal lives from their work. While I do not believe in or want to participate in such a discourse, I am constantly influenced by it.

Marty: I think that is really helpful noting the struggles of bringing spirituality and family therapy together. Although I don't really have any stats, I'm convinced many, perhaps a vast majority of family therapists struggle with this integration. It is a critical aspect to our field, and one that has yet to be clearly and adequately articulated in our literature.

As I read over our conversation, I do have a couple additional concerns. I fear that this introduction, both its style and what we have said, could sound a bit pretentious, as if we are trying to speak for the field on the issue of spirituality. We in no way want to speak for the field of MFT, but we did want to offer our own thoughts and perspectives in a way that hopefully will be *experience near* for readers. I hope that we have captured, even just in part, a bit of what is complex and difficult to articulate about spirituality and MFT. I'm also concerned that there are perhaps some very salient issues with regard to this theme that we have not addressed at all. I'm sure there are some ideas and perspectives on what we have said here that would be very thought provoking and important. One of our purposes of this dialogic introduction has been to invite readers *into* the dialogue. To be sure, this printed dialogue only represents a starting off point to many generative conversations that could be and we hope will be had among MFTs. And with this in mind, I think it is important for us to acknowledge that many readers may object in part or in whole to what we have attempted to articulate. We welcome this, we value continued discussion and genuine dialogue about this important theme; in fact we feel the importance of spirituality in MFT practice demands that we take a closer and harder look at the field, and perhaps more importantly at our individual practices. In the end, for me the importance for each of us as MFTs to take a critical, reflexive stance on the role of spirituality in family therapy is the most salient point. Not just a critical academic look at our field, but a self-reflexive approach to finding out what this means for those who consult us, as well as what this means for our own spiritualities that indeed cannot be kept neutral in our work. As we reflect on the necessity, the messy complexity, and the wonder of possibilities in this coupling of spirituality and MFT, what are we being called to?

REFERENCES

Carlson, T. D., & Erickson, M. J. (1999). Recapturing the person in the therapist: An exploration of personal values, commitments, and beliefs. *Contemporary Family Therapy, 21* (1), 57-76.

Carlson, T. D., & Erickson, M. J. (2000). Re-authoring spiritual narratives: God in person's relational identity stories. *Journal of Systemic Therapies, 19 (2)*, 65-83.

Chubb, H., Gutsche, S., & Efron, D. (Eds.). (1994). Spirituality, religion, and world view. Introduction to the special issue (editorial). *Journal of Systemic Therapies, 13* (3), 1-16.

Doherty, W. J. (1995). *Soul searching: Why psychotherapy must promote moral responsibility*. New York: Basic Books.

Harris, S. M. (1998). Finding a forest among trees: Spirituality hiding in family therapy theories. *Journal of Family Studies, 4* (1), 77-86.

Patterson, J., Hayworth, M., Turner, C., & Raskin, M. (2000). Spiritual issues in family therapy: A graduate-level course. *Journal of Marital and Family Therapy, 26* (2), 199-210.

Prest, L. A., & Keller, J. F. (1993). Spirituality and family therapy: Spiritual beliefs, myths, and metaphors. *Journal of Marital and Family Therapy, 19* (2), 137-148.

Prest, L. A., Russell, R., & D'Souza, H. (1999). Spirituality and religion in training, practice and person development. *Journal of Family Therapy, 21* (1), 60-77.

Sperry, L., & Giblin, P. (1996). Marital and family therapy with religious persons. In E. P. Shafranske (Ed.), *Religion and the clinical practice of psychology* (pp. 511-532). Washington, DC: American Psychological Association.

Stander, V., Piercy, F. P., Mackinnon, D., & Helmke, K. (1994). Spirituality, religion and family therapy: Competing or complementary worlds? *The American Journal of Family Therapy, 22* (1), 27-41.

Ueland, B. (1938, reprinted 1987). *If you want to write: A book about art, independence, and spirit.* St. Paul, MN: Graywolf Press.

Walsh, F. (1999). *Spiritual resources in family therapy*. New York: Guilford.

Warner, C. T. (1985). Anger and similar delusions. In R. Harré (Ed.), *The Social Construction of Emotion* (pp. 135-166). Oxford, England: Basil Blackwell.

Warner, C. T. (1997). *Oxford papers*. Salt Lake City, UT: Arbinger.

Watson, W. H. (1997). Soul and system: The integrative possibilities of family therapy. *Journal of Psychology and Theology, 25* (1), 123-135.

SPIRITUALITY AND THEORY

Spirituality: The Heart of Therapy

Harry J. Aponte

SUMMARY. Today's society speaks with conflicting voices about values, morality, and faith–in a word, about spirituality. Consequently, therapists are having to consider with their clients the values and morality upon which to base the therapy, and having to aid clients in utilizing their belief systems and faith communities to help themselves. *Spirituality* is treated here in terms that are inclusive, applying both to secular and religious spirituality. We suggest three general ways in which *spirituality enhances the power of therapy.* The first relates to making *moral choices* the heart of issues clients present. The second involves assisting clients in becoming emotionally and spiritually *grounded.* The third has to do with including *spiritually enriched resources* among people's options for solutions. *[Article copies available for a fee from The Haworth Document Delivery Service: 1-800-HAWORTH. E-mail address: <getinfo@haworthpressinc.com> Website: <http://www.HaworthPress.com> © 2002 by The Haworth Press, Inc. All rights reserved.]*

Theresa Romeo-Aponte contributed to the development of this paper.

[Haworth co-indexing entry note]: "Spirituality: The Heart of Therapy." Aponte, Harry J. Co-published simultaneously in *Journal of Family Psychotherapy* (The Haworth Press, Inc.) Vol. 13, No. 1/2, 2002, pp. 13-27; and: *Spirituality and Family Therapy* (ed: Thomas D. Carlson, and Martin J. Erickson) The Haworth Press, Inc., 2002, pp. 13-27. Single or multiple copies of this article are available for a fee from The Haworth Document Delivery Service [1-800-HAWORTH, 9:00 a.m. - 5:00 p.m. (EST). E-mail address: getinfo@haworthpressinc.com].

KEYWORDS. Spirituality, family therapy, morality, values

In an era of intense interest in and controversy about values in our society, spirituality has moved into the forefront of therapy. What stands out about how we deal with spirituality in therapy today is that we consciously attend to and talk about it. Therapy has always been practiced within the framework of a society's values and its structure. Contemporary society, however, is particularly uneasy and contentious about its values. The civic leaders and parents of yesterday spoke with a more or less single voice. Society now speaks with many and conflicting voices about values and morality. It is a society that has evolved from valuing consensus to esteeming individual difference and choice. From expecting people to cooperate and be interdependent, contemporary society looks for people to be self reliant and learn to decide for themselves.

Clients now come to therapy asking questions about the appropriateness of their thinking and the morality of their choices (Aponte, 1994, pp. 168-185). They are having to ask questions that were not questions in past generations, for example, about the connection between sex and commitment (Wilson, 1993, pp. 230-237), about abortion as contraception (Hoge, 1996, p. 37), about suicide as a solution to declining "quality of life" in terminal illness (Peck, 1997). Therapists working with adolescents are forever dealing with questions about the dangers and potential consequences of sex outside of marriage. Therapists working in hospice increasingly confront issues related to the purpose and meaning of pain, illness, and death. New science and new attitudes toward sex, love and babies have added heretofore unheard of issues and challenges to therapy. Therapists are having to assess people's values behind their clinical issues, and to determine within themselves and with their clients values and morality upon which to base their therapy. These developments drive today's debates and exploration about values and spirituality among therapists.

With this radical change of attitude towards values, morality and spirituality in the real of therapy, clinicians now hardly pretend to be value neutral as they were expected to be yesteryear. Whether because of their schools of therapy or because of their personal values, therapists everyday introduce their philosophies and values into the therapy they do (Aponte, February, 1998). They may speak from a feminist perspective (Goldner, 1993) and advocate a politically determined ideal by which to judge a healthy marriage, such as equality and sameness of power between marital partners. From a postmodern perspective (Becvar,

1997) they may emphasize a subjective spin on experience over an objective reality, creating greater room for difference and disagreement about moral issues among family members. A Christian therapist (Bardill, 1997) may present definite moral standards as the basis for assessing right behavior, setting a single moral pennant around which to set the goals of therapy. From their professional training, political affiliations, and personal belief systems, therapists bring their idiosyncratic opinions about the link between morality and psychological health into their work.

All therapists hold their own personal opinions about what makes for better living, whether it is about the benefits and drawbacks of punishing children, staying and escaping a difficult marriage, or the usefulness and dangers of religion for our mental health. Therapists vary in their ideas not only about how good values contribute to good mental health and felicitous relationships. They also come with differing thoughts about whether spirituality in the form of prayer and worship ritual may serve as proper and effective resources for healing for their clients (Tan, 1996). Clients themselves challenge therapists with their own views about values and spirituality. Clients' issues, by their very nature, bear some degree of moral, value or spiritual valence. Therapists react overtly or subliminally to the spirituality of clients and their issues with their own endorsements, disapprovals or recommendations.

The media promulgates the new moral and ethical dilemmas that eventually creep into the agenda of our therapy. 20/20 only recently interviewed a man who spoke of his intention to clone his aging mother. How is that for a solution to the pain of separation from a parent? We already face questions of donor sperm where the male cannot produce healthy sperm. New scientific possibilities present novel potential forms of extra-marital conception. We read about moral and legal dilemmas for therapists today that have to do with greater public acceptance of non-traditional life styles. Child welfare workers are embroiled in controversies about adoptions by gay couples. Suicide is publicly debated and dramatized into ever greater acceptability. Therapists working with terminal AIDS patients are likely to face requests for assistance to terminate life through various forms of suicide. The trivialization of extra-marital sex in the media presents therapists who counsel marital couples with an amorphous social environment for addressing how seriously to treat the occurrence of a sexual liaison outside of a marriage. The media presents an ambiguous morality that influences society's moral sense, and leaves therapists to figure out for themselves the moral standards by which to advise clients about what is appropriate and healthy.

WHAT IS SPIRITUALITY IN THERAPY?

In this paper we are using a treatment of spirituality that is inclusive, that is, a definition that can apply both to secular and religious spirituality, that has validity and usefulness whether or not it includes formal organization, doctrine, ritual or God. Spirituality is a universal dimension of life that lends a meaning to our existence, sets a moral standard for living, and assumes some sense of moral connection among people at the very heart of our humanity. Some spirituality is based on ethics and philosophy. Other spirituality sees its source and end in the supernatural realm of a deity, and is most often expressed in formal religion. Both forms speak to morality, meaning, and the nature of the individual's relationship to the world, whether or not it is supernatural.

This definition of spirituality has certain implications for a therapy that would be sensitive to the spiritual in the lives of clients. It supposes that to gain a fuller understanding of clients, therapists consider not only the family history and psychological dynamics of client issues, but also the world view and moral contexts of their struggles. In the pursuit of solutions, therapists also consider spirituality as a potential resource for support and direction.

Whatever difficulties clients face, therapists who are spiritually sensitive themselves bring a philosophy of life and moral perspective to bear on their interpretation and view of the hurts and conflicts clients present in therapy. The meaning and purpose therapists bring to clients' issues set the course of the therapy. For example, infidelity in marriage can be viewed simply as acting out on an unsatisfactory relationship that needs psychological repair. However, it can also be seen as an opportunity for a couple to reach more deeply within their relationship for a love that is both emotional and spiritual to build something more meaningful over the failings of the past. A patient's depression because of a chronically debilitating illness can be treated simply as grief over the loss of vitality, or as a chance to turn a frenetic pursuit of "success" into a more contemplative spiritually purposed life.

A spiritual perspective also implies that there are moral components to the issues people present. Morality connotes standards of behavior that distinguish good from bad. Staying with the question of infidelity, sexual betrayal in marriage can be treated simply as a sign of a breakdown in the emotional bonds between marital partners, or can also be viewed as a violation of a moral obligation that is integral to the commitment of marriage. In the latter instance, the moral implication is that whatever the emotional problems contributed to the betrayal, the nature of the commitment calls for some form of remorse, apology, and repair that reaches for a love fortified by a spiritual bond that transcends the human failings and trials of the marital relationship. Morality adds a contractual component to the emotional relationship. The concept of morality also necessitates the consideration of free will, the ability to make a moral choice. Ensconced somewhere in the heart of what people may need to do in order to achieve the desired change or solution of a problem is a moral decision that goes beyond feelings. In the infidelity example, the straying husband may have to decide whether to endeavor to give up the extra-marital relationship in his heart, not just in his behavior, and the wife whether to forgive to the point of reopening her heart to her husband. Such decisions form the moral foundation upon which the work of emotional repair is begun.

Spirituality also implies that the issues of clients take place within a context of the ties among people that lend a social meaning to life. In other words, people and their problems exist in the context of relationships. However personal an issue may be, its existence and solution touch on the lives of others. These ties, with all of their social and moral implications, exist at the levels of marriage, family and community. They may also be viewed as potentially transcending everyday relationships, entering the realm of the spiritual world of publicly celebrated church ritual, or the prayerful relationship with their God. In this sense an individual's act of infidelity has profound implications about betrayal not just of another individual but also to the institutions of marriage, family and community-living social entities. An act of marital infidelity also has its own implications for the religious person's relationship to a faith.

Spirituality is also a possible resource for healing. Spirituality lends added options for solutions to clients' struggles. As a source of meaning, it signifies ways of thinking about the human experience that offers answers to difficult conundrums of life. Spirituality gives meaning and provides motivation to remain committed to love in the face of that very human every-partner's flaws. Spirituality gives purpose and significance to the passage of a loved one's death, giving significance to that earthly separation. Moreover, spirituality offers a well articulated and consistent morality that can serve as a self defining stabilizer and guide to people in a morally murky and inconstant world. A married couple torn apart emotionally by infidelity may discover clarity of perspective and direction for the choices confronting them in the moral principles of their religious beliefs. Spirituality also provides a sense of belonging and very personal support for people who feel alone and not understood in the alienation of a betrayal. They experience support and nurturance in the comradery of a faith community, and may view God, however they relate to the deity, as a source of strength and love in a lonely time.

In other words, spirituality represents a whole other dimension to life that gives another level of meaning, morality and community to the search for solutions in therapy. It can provide hope in despair, motivation in discouragement, clarity in confusion, strength in weakness, and companionship in loneliness.

HOW THERAPISTS CAN WORK WITH SPIRITUALITY

There are three general ways in which *spirituality enhances the power of therapy.* The first relates to making *moral choices* the heart of issues clients present. The second involves helping clients become *grounded*, that is, taking control of the solutions of their problems from within their own inner beliefs and motives. The third has to do with adding *spiritually enriched resources* to people's recourses. These resources support the transcendent bonds, especially of love, that people have to other humanity and the supernatural. These general principles of a spiritually sensitive therapy translate into specific interventions for specific issues.

When it comes to solving *specific issues,* the basic steps are:

1. Identify the key decisions vis-a-vis the focal issue that are necessary for people to begin turning their lives around;
2. Set the value platform that is to serve as the moral standard upon which these decisions are to be made;
3. Place the decisions within the key relationships in people's lives, from human to divine, that will support their critical life-changing choices.

Identifying key moral judgments vis-a-vis clients' *specific issues* implies that whatever people contend with, they always have a free will choice, with at least "a residue of freedom" (Frankl, 1967, p. 67). For example, a lonely, divorced woman in her seventies, after repeated "slips" in her outpatient therapy, wants to try yet one more time to lick her alcoholism without entering a residential drug and alcohol rehabilitation program. Confronting her weakness to the addiction will take great moral courage. A determination to enter the rehab center will not solve the alcoholism, but will overcome the immediate hurdle to her recovery. Of course, there will be other decisions to make at each stage of the trek on the road to recovery. Identifying that key personal decision at each stage allows clients to take charge of that step of their transformation. A family as a whole as well as each individual member come up against the challenge of key choices that determine whether they move ahead on the road to change and growth.

Setting the value platform for that decision simply means helping clients determine the philosophy and the particular moral values within which they will make the choices that are key to changing their lives. The woman dependent on alcohol would have to acknowledge that her addiction is wrong for whatever reasons her morality supports. She has to decide on the kind of obligation she owes herself and her family to stop the drinking. She also considers her philosophy about the importance of depending upon others, including her God, for help when contending with her flaws.

Placing that decision in the context of relevant human and/or spiritual relationships implies electing how to engage in the solution with others who are affected by the the person's difficulty. For the woman addicted to alcohol, this may mean as a first step not only admitting the problem to herself and her therapist, but also to her family. From the point of view of therapy, the most critical aspect of this decision making process is including those who can help a person make and carry out the determination to change. With addictions, Alcoholics Anonymous recognizes that people cannot solve problems alone. AA builds into its structure the need to reach out to others in the program, but also to God "as we understand him" for the support and help to change.

All these steps in the process of trying to solve specific issues add a spiritual element to therapy whatever the therapeutic model employed. Spirituality affixes a dimension to therapy that lends people a new source of empowerment to people's efforts to make life-changing choices when feeling emotionally embattled. Spirituality supplies meaning and motivation to their efforts to change, and a connection with others, natural or supernatural, who can help in the loneliness of the human struggle (Aponte, 1999).

The Spirituality of Therapists: The Person of the Therapist

Of course, an essential element to working with the spiritual as integral to therapy is the spirituality of the therapist. Therapists can exercise their ability to recognize spirituality in the life struggles of their clients, only if aware of the place of spirituality in their own lives. This is the same reasoning that expects therapists to know their own psychology and families of origin in order to relate to the psychology of their clients and to their families (Aponte & Winter, 2000). The relevant question here is what it means for clinicians to connect to their own spirituality in ways that enhance their performance as therapists.

The overarching issue for therapists when it comes to their spirituality is the extent to which they are knowledgeable about the spiritual in their own lives. Spirituality is inherent in the human struggle of everyman/woman. The act of reaching for remedies in times of turmoil and hardship speaks to people's looking for a better life. In that struggle to improve and change is ensconced people's search for meaning and purpose, morality, and a link to another who will serve as caring companion and helper. Spirituality is part of everybody's life, be it a secular or religious spirituality. Therapists who do not consider the legitimacy of a spiritual perspective, or who are personally at war with their own spirituality, or who do not tolerate spirituality alien to their own, limit their ability to see and relate to the spirituality of their clients.

All therapists must know themselves with their unique history along with current dynamics of their lives, be able to access this self awareness within the context of conducting therapy, and develop the skills to actively and purposefully utilize themselves in the interest of relating to clients and their stories. Their knowledge of self, access to their inner self, and mastery of their psychological forces are essential to therapists' ability to understand clients, relate empathically to them, and utilize their life experience and life forces to impact the lives of their clients. There is a spiritual dimension to all aspects of their use of self.

For therapists to know themselves signifies that they can identify the key personal struggles of their lives, specifically places within their psychology that are vulnerable and habitually cause them difficulty. This includes insight into the history that led to these difficulties, and how their particular vulnerabilities present them with challenges today. To complete this perspective on their key human struggles, therapists would need to be conscious of how and to what degree they are engaging with these personal issues of theirs. They would need to have an understanding of the nature and process they use to meet the daily challenge of their individual issues. The spiritual dimension of their unique themes encompasses the choices they face around their issues, the values they hold in making these decisions, and where they go outside of themselves for support and guidance, including their faiths and deity.

For therapists to be able to access their own story and emotional life in the context of doing therapy means that while relating to clients and their themes, they allow to come to the surface and track the thoughts, memories and emotions aroused about their own related themes. They aim to "know" their clients through their own pain and struggle with life, including of course the moral and spiritual dimensions of the battle. To the extent these therapists are grounded in their contention with their own difficulties, they will discover the ability to feel, remember and think about these struggles without being flooded with memories and emotions. They will be able to connect to their own issues without losing a sense of the boundaries between their issues and those of their clients.

For therapists to have the skills to use themselves actively and purposefully in their roles as clinicians means that they can more effectively engage the relationship with clients in strategically therapeutic ways, as well as more empathically understand and address issues with clients. The judicious personal integration of their spirituality with their professional role enables them to use aspects of themselves to relate to the spiritual in their clients' stories without having to impose their own values or religious convictions on their clients. They can afford the personal closeness to the client necessary to understand and impact the client without infringing upon the boundaries of the client, and not allowing their own boundaries to be trespassed.

A Case Example

To give this discussion of spirituality in therapy a human face, the following account of a session with a family represents one type of therapeutic interaction that touches on spirituality. This is a young African American couple who volunteered to be interviewed for a workshop. They did not participate as patients, but were asked to present on some family issue they would like to discuss with a therapist and get some feedback. They offered a dilemma about teaching their young son, Perry, to be assertive, even ready to defend himself physically, just as they were teaching him the principles of peace as learned from Gandhi, Martin Luther King, and the New Testament. Behind this discussion of principle also lay the social milieu and psychological dynamics of the parents who grew up in very different circumstances. Father took for granted his African American identity, while mother had to strive for hers. Moreover, the father, because of his early life experience with his own relatively absent, hard working father, was strongly motivated to be both a positive influence and loving parent to his children. Both parents wanted to reconcile the apparently contradictory principles of peace seeking, with the survival instinct, especially of a minority in America, to be ready to stand up for one's self. Moreover, from an emotional standpoint mother had little trouble being tough with the kids, but father did. The interviewer hoped to give them something they could take home that would draw on their strengths as individual parents as well as a couple.

At the beginning of the session, the father put the paradox of the principles in the context that most concerned them–of raising an African American son in America, while wanting their son to conduct himself according to their strongly held Christian beliefs.

Father: We have a five-year-old son and two-and-a-half year old little girl, and in August our little boy will be going to kindergarten, and I think there is a little bit of . . . anxiety that we face about sending him off to school . . . Raising an African American male child in America is, I think, another major fact of concern. In light of the fact that we are looking into a private Christian school setting, and more than likely he will be one of only a few African American children in the classroom, that is important to us. And at home we definitely teach not only Christian values, but pride and respect and honor for where we have come from in the past. And so it is, there is an anxiety that we deal with concerning that and him.

Mother: Well, I think Ben basically summed up how I feel. Also in discussing my anxiety, it is a probably a lot stronger than Ben's . . . Ben was taught his African heritage compared to where I wasn't. I grew up in a predominantly white environment, starting all the way from elementary school all the way through high school, college . . .

Therapist: Why do you emphasize male?

Father: There is a lower expectation of all kinds that society has placed on African American men . . . We want to teach our children to live with and converse with all types of people. A lot of times we find that the doors of opportunity in America especially tend to not swing open as wide for black men. It is something that I've experienced over the last eight or nine years of being a business person.

Therapist: How do you see the challenge for yourself? You know. It is one thing to know what it is you want to accomplish. But, it's another thing to know . . . [as a parent] "I can't go to school with Perry. I can't sit next to him or behind him. How do I do this?"

Father: Exactly.

Mother: I think I have to add that my anxiety has calmed some from when we were here for the weekend at a family life marriage counseling . . . In [a] session they dealt with raising our children in a Christian environment, raising our children according to God's plan. When I got finished with that session, it eased my anxiety a lot because I got the tools that I needed to help calm the anxiety . . .

Therapist: There are going to be a couple of things that you are going to be dealing with. One is that you [mother and father] are . . . different people.

Mother: Yes, that is true, but because I am the mother and Ben is the father, . . . that just makes us totally different.

Therapist: I believe it is important to be able to say, "Okay, where are we going to find our particular difficulties?" . . . Peculiar to us.

Here the therapist was looking for the differences in their approaches to their children based not so much on their religious values, which were virtually identical, but on the differences of their life experiences, including gender. All the while, the therapist was tracking their stories with his own experience as a Puerto Rican raised in New York's Harlem and South Bronx while also attending the Irish Catholic Schools his mother enrolled him in because of her wish for him to absorb values different from what he would learn in the streets. The therapist's early enthrallment with boxing resonated with the story the father goes on to tell.

Father: I remember when there was a period when Perry was about two years old, and we had him in day care . . . When I got him to the top of the stairs to take his coat off, two of the other kids came up to him and one of the children pushed on him, and the other kid, which one of them was smaller than Perry, started just kind of pounding on his head . . . He [Perry] began to cry . . . I was upset because he didn't defend himself. And so that afternoon, I stopped by my parents' home, and I picked up my little projector . . . with a lot of reel to reel films of Joe Louis and Muhammad Ali . . . I told Perry . . . now this is what you call "dukes up." And we started watching the films, and I said, "You see how the guy is fighting, he is defending himself?" And so after that I would kind of get rough with him and we would kind of wrestle around . . . I'm kind of concerned about him letting people take advantage of him, letting people pick on him. I've never been a big fighter type. I've always considered myself a peacemaker type of person. And I have talked my way out of many situations.

Therapist: This is a fascinating topic that you are bringing up because it raises so many issues . . . Society teaches you two things that don't particularly come together . . .

Father: The only way that I can retaliate against evil, against aggression, is kindness. It is a principle that Mahatma Gandhi and Dr. King took from his learning, but it is [also] a biblical principle . . . However, I think it is important that growing up as a young person you have to understand you have to know how to protect yourself . . . And so it is important I think that our children, Perry and Laura, understand that there is a measure of physical confrontation.

Mother: Perry wants to please. Now Laura is the challenge because she is fire on two legs . . . She is a fighter.

Therapist: The question is, how are you going to bring out that part of him [the fighter] without sacrificing your values.

Father: I try to, we spend a lot of time, Perry and I. We engage a lot physically. We wrestle. We play football . . . So we engage in that type of fashion. He [also] attends bible study. I teach bible study for the young people's department at my church. He is right there with me . . . [In a recent incident Perry] broke down crying . . . when [the teacher] didn't want to listen to him, and she didn't want him to help and he was a little hurt.

Mother: Which we handle totally different . . . Ben handles that that way. And when Perry came in and Ben told me about the incident . . . I started to talk about it, and I said, "Who are you?" He said, "Perry King," and I said, "Say your name again." He said "Perry King." I said, "Don't cry, Perry King," and he just got stronger, and stronger, and stronger with it and we talked and I explained to him that it doesn't matter if someone laughs at you as long as you feel comfortable and confident with knowing who you are. Maybe you were not chosen to be the helper this time, but at least you know that you can help. . . . He's like,

"You are right, mommy. I can do it. I can." So I let Ben handle it the way he wanted to, and then when it was Perry and I . . . We have different styles . . . He will give in, and I will not.

Therapist: You have different styles, and are just going to deal with [your] kids in different ways.

Mother: What I'm tuning into is part of what I am feeling for Ben, is . . . to know when to assert yourself naturally, and not to be so easy going that you let too many things go by. Because people often misinterpret easygoing for weakness.

Father: Sure, which is something that I deal with personally. That's how a lot of times as a manager, as a business owner, a lot of my employees mistake my kindness or my easygoingness as weakness. And they end up finding themselves on the outside [fired] . . .

Therapist: Your strength is a quiet strength . . . I don't know if you take that same strength home with Perry and Laura . . .

Father: I think what happens [is that] I wish I could have spent more time with my father . . . so [it's] important for me when my children see me at home, I want them to see first of all a man that loves God, man that loves his wife, and a man that loves them . . .

Therapist: This is the one thing that I think might be worth taking home with you, that you have a strength about you, a toughness about you that is so much a part of you that you don't have to make a big deal of it. But that you are talking about raising your son to be this strong man who is proud of himself, that he needs to experience both sides of his father, the loving soft, generous part of him and also the strong part of him . . . It's different kind of toughness that you [two] have. And I think both the toughness that you [father] have and the toughness that you [mother] have, both [are] important, and one cannot substitute for the other . . . Thank you for coming.

The therapist concluded that the best gift he could offer this father was to place his accommodating nature in a light where both parents could see the quiet strength that was there. It brought together both ideals of his being a man of peace, while also showing him to be a strong man of principle. In his business, he expected his employees to follow orders. He would not argue. However, when they gave him a hard time, he would fire them. At the same time, the mother had a lively and assertive personality, and had no trouble being the disciplinarian at home. She also had some definite ideas about how to teach her son pride in himself that seemed to be getting some results. The therapist chose to draw out the value of both styles of the parents, even if different. This was a loving couple who were disposed to be supportive of each other and who tried diligently to find ways of working out their differences without hurting the relationship.

In many ways this couple typified the family of today. As parents, they want to raise their children by their values. Yet, today's society presents them with contradictions they cannot ignore. Parents who ask therapists for guidance with the care of their children contend with conflicting values within themselves, between each other, and with society. Layered over their emotional life and relationship dynamics are the difficult value choices that family, church and society presents. Their priorities and life principles are at the very heart of their personal identity and sense of self worth, and at the core of what defines the values they hope will shape their children's personality. In today's world, therapists cannot deal with the character formation and emotional development of children without also dealing with the values and spirituality of the family.

CONCLUSION

Spirituality is the heart of therapy, addressing the transcendent bonds to human and supernatural resources, along with the moral values and ideals undergirding the decisions that determine the course of people's solutions. This is a materialistic and secular society in which there is a growing thirst for values and meaning beyond money, power, and personal gratification. In our contemporary society therapists find themselves having to raise and draw out questions about spirituality in relation to clients' efforts to solve life's problems. They are more frequently reaching out to the spiritual resources in people's lives, including assistance from their faith communities. Therapists are challenged to become knowledgeable and skillful about values, morality, and religion, and learn to listen to and speak to spirituality as integral to their clients' lives.

REFERENCES

Aponte, H. J. (1994). *Bread & spirit: Therapy with the new poor*. New York: Norton.

Aponte, H. J. (February, 1998). Love, the spiritual wellspring of forgiveness: An example of spirituality in our therapy. *Journal of Family Therapy (U. K.), 20*(1), 37-58.

Aponte, H. J. (1999). The stresses of poverty and the comfort of spirituality. In F. Walsh (Ed.), *Spiritual resources in family therapy*. New York: Guilford.

Aponte, H. J., & Winter, J. E. (2000). The person and practice of the therapist: Treatment and training. In M. Baldwin (Ed.), *The use of self in therapy* (2nd ed.). (pp. 127-166). New York: The Haworth Press, Inc.

Bardill, D. R. (1997). The spiritual reality: A Christian world view. In D. S. Becvar (Ed.), *The family, spirituality and social work* (pp. 89-100). New York: The Haworth Press, Inc.

Becvar, D. S. (1997). Soul healing and the family. In D. S. Becvar (Ed.), *The family, spirituality and social work* (pp. 1-11). New York: The Haworth Press, Inc.

Frankl, V. E. (1967). *Psychotherapy and existentialism*. New York: Washington Square Press.

Goldner, V. (1993). Power and hierarchy: Let's talk about it! *Family Process, 32,* 157-162.

Hoge, D. R. (1996). Religion in America: The demographics of belief and affiliation. In E. P. Shafranske (Ed.), *Religion and the clinical practice of psychology* (pp. 21-42). Washington, DC: American Psychological Association.

Peck, M. S. (1997). *Denial of the soul*. New York: Harmony Books.

Tan, S. Y. (1996). Religion in clinical practice. Implicit and explicit integration. In E. Shafranske (Ed.), *Religion and the clinical practice of psychology* (pp. 365-387). Washington, DC: American Psychological Association.

Wilson, J. Q. (1993). *The moral sense*. New York: The Free Press.

Spirituality: Lives and Relationships in Family-Therapy Concepts and Practices

Adam D. Coffey

SUMMARY. Scholarly literature continues to address spirituality and family therapy. Yet, spirituality has not gained a foothold for many researchers and, hence, has struggled to define itself in peer-reviewed literature. As scholars learn more about recognizing spirituality and its place in family therapy, perhaps results from this learning will honor spirituality in humans' relationships and lives. Then researchers, educators, and practitioners may add to their dialogue about how spirituality influences what they do. Hopefully, this dialogue will lead to two things: (a) a collective action that provides better service to readers of research, students, and clients; and (b) a collective action that allows professionals to better care for themselves. *[Article copies available for a fee from The Haworth Document Delivery Service: 1-800-HAWORTH. E-mail address: <getinfo@haworthpressinc.com> Website: <http://www.HaworthPress.com> © 2002 by The Haworth Press, Inc. All rights reserved.]*

KEYWORDS. Spirituality, family therapy, relationships, interconnection, realities

---

Adam D. Coffey, PhD candidate, runs an independent practice and is Co-Founder of Systemic Consulting Associates, LLP.

Address correspondence to: 8351 Santa Clara Drive, Dallas, TX 75218-4343 (E-mail: cofflind@flash.net).

The author thanks his life partner, Christy Lindsay, JD, for her editorial assistance.

[Haworth co-indexing entry note]: "Spirituality: Lives and Relationships in Family-Therapy Concepts and Practices." Coffey, Adam D. Co-published simultaneously in *Journal of Family Psychotherapy* (The Haworth Press, Inc.) Vol. 13, No. 1/2, 2002, pp. 29-52; and: *Spirituality and Family Therapy* (ed: Thomas D. Carlson, and Martin J. Erickson) The Haworth Press, Inc., 2002, pp. 29-52. Single or multiple copies of this article are available for a fee from The Haworth Document Delivery Service [1-800-HAWORTH, 9:00 a.m. - 5:00 p.m. (EST). E-mail address: getinfo@haworthpressinc.com].

INTRODUCTION

In contrast to a statement suggested by Worthington, Kurusu, McCullough, and Sandage (1996), this article assumes that all humans live as spiritual beings. Such spirituality acts as a basis from which humans' existence flows. Due to spirituality's presence in humanity, clients sometimes present to marriage and family therapists (MFTs) with spiritual concerns. In fact, about half of the MFTs in Winston's (1991) study noted that clients struggle with spiritual concerns about 50-100% of the time. Considering such struggles, some clients may prefer to discuss spiritual concerns in therapy as these relate to their lives (see Rose, 1998). Apart from therapy, clients' lives can provide clues to MFTs about transformation and maintaining the status quo.

Humans possess an amazing capacity to persevere as they access the competence in their lives. Humans as clients arrive in MFTs' work settings with competency areas that sometimes allow clients to make progress before seeing an MFT. Further, some clients make progress despite their having had an unsatisfactory experience with their MFT. Still other humans never become MFTs' clients, advancing their lives by relying on other areas of competence. Such progressive elements suggest that humans can travel toward their goals by organizing around competence. Accordingly, Lambert (1992) suggested that about 40% of positive outcome in psychotherapy results from factors outside of the therapeutic experience. Hence, MFTs' learning about such factors or life experiences could improve therapeutic efficacy.

Along with these extratherapeutic factors, the relationship between practitioners and clients (about 30%), therapeutic techniques (about 15%), and client's expectancy (about 15%) account for the remaining contribution to positive outcome (Lambert, 1992). In considering these four areas that lend to positive therapeutic outcome, one may consider how spirituality emerges from each of them. First, some clients' extratherapeutic factors or life experiences inextricably are linked to spirituality (see, e.g., Boyd-Franklin & Bry, 2000; Red Horse, 1982; Semans & Fish, 2000). Other clients may do activities (e.g., meditating) and/or have beliefs (e.g., "I have no use for bitterness in my life") that relate to their spiritual existence. Further, some clients may experience spirituality as an ineffable state of bliss (see Pahnke & Richards, 1990), a resource (see Walsh, 1999a), and/or a dimension that gives new meaning to their troubling experiences (see Frankl, 1988).

Second, clients' relationships with their practitioners necessarily involve spirituality. Spirituality does not require any doing between people. It is part of all relationships. However, MFTs and clients may recognize spirituality more easily through shared experiences of acceptance, connection, and/or a meeting of the minds. Such experiences can transcend theoretical distinctions, revealing the significance of the therapeutic relationship as a common notion. As part of this relationship, many psychotherapy scholars have noted the use of spiritual techniques or interventions, the third factor that contributes to positive therapeutic outcome (see, e.g., Boyd-Franklin & Bry, 2000; Prest & Keller, 1993; Richards & Bergin, 1997; Watson, 1997; Worthington et al., 1996). Such research has highlighted what practitioners can do to address spiritual concerns stated by their clients. By using techniques, practitioners can enter their clients' worldviews and potentially connect with them based on a shared understanding. Further, clients can create their desired changes from such techniques.

Fourth, expectancy or the placebo effect may add to positive therapeutic outcome by clients believing in the possibility of something different. This difference may emerge from spirituality, or the cybernetic concept of "Mind" between two or more people (see Bateson, 1972). As examples, a client may believe that transcendent spirituality influences the way a practitioner listens and responds to a client (see Anderson & Worthen, 1997). Additionally, clients may believe that transformative spirituality (see Wilber, 2000) reveals itself through hope, prayer, forgiveness, healing, and/or anything that honors the process of well being. Although not explicitly noted by Lambert's (1992) research, other members within the client system may expect positive therapeutic results related to spirituality. As examples, practitioners may believe that spirituality represented by love can help clients transform their lives (see Aponte, 1998; Becvar, 1997; Johnson, 2001). Extended family members, friends, and other social support may believe that a spiritual interconnection can encourage clients to make their desired changes. Thus, spirituality can play a significant role in how individual and relational expectation lead to desired outcomes.

In summary, spirituality arises through clients' lives (apart from therapy), their relationships with their practitioners, spiritual techniques, and individual and shared expectations. Each of these four areas, which have contributed to positive therapeutic outcome, combines data from much research. Of course, many things besides spirituality constitute these four areas (e.g., gender, emotion, narrative techniques, the perceived "authority" of a therapist, respectively). Due to the diversity of things that may contribute to positive therapeutic outcome, it is important to note an abridged list of what spirituality is not.

SPIRITUALITY DISTINCTIONS

First, spirituality is not emotion/feeling. Associations may exist between spirituality and emotion/feeling, but they remain different due to the relational nature of spirituality. Recognition of spirituality requires an awareness of the relationships one has with oneself, others, and/or a Presence of something within and outside of human bodies (Coffey, 2001). Hence, one can recognize spirituality individually and/or with others, but for humans, spirituality always involves relationships. Second, spirituality is not quantitatively different among humans because it is not a quantitative construct; albeit, spirituality can have qualitative differences. As examples, humans may recognize spirituality through their experiences, activities, and/or beliefs (see Miller & Thoresen, 1999). Additionally, humans may recognize spirituality beyond such domains, in states that do not merit anthropomorphic description. So, one's level of recognition about her/his spirituality does not suggest that different people have more or less spirituality. Rather, such recognition levels relate to factors outside the scope of this article.

Finally, transformative spirituality is not an individual's sacred journey. Rather, such spirituality requires humans to go beyond an individualistic experience, go into one of a collective consciousness, and then beyond that into the aesthetic or sacred (Bateson, 1980). The compassion and generosity of the aesthetic state extinguishes an individual's pride inherent in making a "me, not-me" distinction (see Trungpa, 1987). As humans move toward the Sacred, they see ostensible differences less and see spirituality more through a broadening perspective. Of course, due to a bodily nature with sensory input, humans' capacity to recognize the aesthetic or sacred state constantly is challenged.

The above three distinctions may help to limit how one conceptualizes spirituality. By creating limits, one may operationalize spirituality for the sake of clarity and viability, needed characteristics for spirituality to undergo continued research (see Doherty, 1999). Moreover, these distinctions join many definitions of spirituality already existing in family-therapy literature (see, e.g., Adams, 1995; Anderson, 1987; Aponte, 1998; Haug, 1998a; Prest, Russel, & D'Souza, 1999).

PURPOSE AND OUTLINE

This article will examine spirituality as it relates to family-therapy concepts and practices. Many of these concepts and practices will highlight life experiences and relationships that organize around competence. The purpose of this article is to evoke continuing dialogue/action about the research, practice, and education of spirituality, family therapy, and more generally, psychotherapy. To accomplish this purpose, an abridged literature review will provide a basis from which to understand what scholars already have written. (The author selected all references within this article as thematically representative of the many citations not included.) Then, a theoretical model built on this review will act as a lens to examine examples of clinical usage. A discussion of the theoretical model will follow. As a conclusion, the author will recommend how professional dialogue and activities may continue to recognize spirituality both conceptually and practically.

SPIRITUALITY AND FAMILY-THERAPY THEORY

Although many scholars have defined it differently, spirituality as distinct from yet including religion has received a broadening emphasis in the psychotherapeutic field, including family therapy. Four texts that recently have emphasized spirituality include: *Integrating Spirituality into Treatment*, edited by William Miller (1999a); *Spiritual Resources in Family Therapy*, edited by Froma Walsh (1999b); *A Spiritual Strategy for Counseling and Psychotherapy*, by P. Scott Richards and Allen Bergin (1997); and *Soul Healing: A Spiritual Orientation in Counseling and Therapy*, by Dorothy Becvar (1997). From these texts, one may see how significant spirituality has become in not only the psychotherapeutic field, but also in the broader area of health care, including the medical and nursing disciplines. This multidisciplinary context has involved MFTs, especially in their recognition and/or conscious integration of spirituality into their practices (see Kahle, 1997).

In the process of such integration, certain family-therapy scholars have noted a possible link between family therapy and spirituality (see, e.g., Anderson, 1987; Harris, 1998; Walsh, 1999a; Watson, 1997). Seminal family-therapy scholars, like Virginia Satir (1988) and Gregory Bateson (1972), sought to examine both implicitly and explicitly additional connections between spirituality and family therapy. Other scholars have offered various ideas about spirituality and family therapy. These ideas have included how social constructionism can aid practitioners in acknowledging in-session spirituality (Thayne, 1997), how barriers have hindered a connection between spirituality and family therapy (Adams, 1995), and how practitioners' strategies/techniques can assist in addressing clients' traditional and nontraditional beliefs (Prest & Keller, 1993). Further, Berenson (1990), like Anderson (1987), noted that MFTs' relational focus inevitably involves spirituality. Berenson suggested that this relational spirituality can occur between an individual(s) and a Presence, a person and another person, and/or the gender conceptions of feminine and masculine (or Jung's anima and animus [see Hopcke, 1989]), hence potentially synthesizing human experiences.

RESEARCH

Some scholars have posed a partial affront to Adams' (1995) barriers in mixing spirituality and family therapy by conducting quantitative and qualitative research. Two examples of such research will follow. Prest et al. (1999) explored family-therapy graduate students' perspectives on spirituality, training, and practice. Their results included these ideas:

1. Participants valued spirituality and religion in humans' lives and considered these dimensions in their work.
2. Such valuing manifested by participants' identification with spirituality and their holistic understanding and development of it.
3. Most participants believed in a transcendent dimension.
4. Participants felt reluctant to talk about spirituality in professional contexts.
5. Participants honored, valued, and supported their clients' spirituality when appropriate.
6. Despite participants' willingness to work with clients on spiritual concerns, a minority of them had received training on how to do so, and a majority felt uncertain about their skills in this area.

In a qualitative study, Joanides (1997) hoped that his religious participants would provide interpretive perspectives on religion and spirituality. Further, he wanted to learn about their perception of interconnection between their religious and spiritual perspectives. He concluded that in addition to assisting his participants in their connection with past and present concerns, religion also contained moral guidelines, gave structure to their spiritual experience and development, and helped form their worldviews. Also, his participants viewed spirituality as inextricably connected to their religious tradition, and their relationship with God gained nurturance through their religious involvement.

In reviewing family-therapy literature, one may note the lack of research on spirituality as distinct from religion. Religion, as a more easily identifiable construct, serves researchers well as they seek to examine a phenomenon and offer pragmatic, useful results (see, e.g., Worthington et al., 1996). Even though some scholars have examined spirituality and religion in therapeutic practice (see, e.g., Kahle, 1997; Rose, 1998; Winston, 1991), neither spirituality nor religion has undergone repeated examinations as they relate to therapy experiences. This shortcoming provides researchers opportunities to learn more about practitioners' and clients' experiences, as well as how these experiences shape the process and outcome of therapy. Of course, examining the topic of spirituality requires that both researchers and practitioners consider ethical and risk management areas.

ETHICS

MFTs recognizing spirituality in their practice have a duty to protect their clients, acknowledge and monitor therapeutic influence, and maintain fitting levels of knowledge to serve their clients. Most MFTs also devote some energy regarding how to protect themselves from possible liabilities. Haug's (1998a) article addressed both ethical and risk management concerns regarding the spiritual dimension. First, she suggested that practitioners examine their own spirituality, especially related to their relationships with clients, gender/cultural contexts, and theoretical positions. Doing so may increase the likelihood of practitioners making ethically sound decisions in their clinical practice. Second, practitioners may open space for spiritual discussions (including those involving interventions), refer clients when appropriate, and neither impose their beliefs upon clients nor ignore their beliefs (see also Becvar, 1997). Third, practitioners may connect through their language with clients' worldviews (see also Doherty, 1999), respect ethnic/cultural rituals, acknowledge and honor clients' roles, and gain training to assure standard levels of competence.

In each of the above instances whereby practitioners extend a protective choice to their clients, they also may consider ways to protect themselves. As examples, by monitoring, edifying, and developing their subjective experiences, practitioners might add to their vitality and health while reducing their personal/professional risks. Also, practitioners might seek out training in spirituality to serve better a diversity of clients and to supplement practitioners' potential levels of competency. A brief examination of such training may provide additional ideas about how practitioners may edify and develop their lives.

TRAINING

Haug (1998b) gave three stages that support certain goals of spiritual training. In the first stage, teachers and supervisors will gain comfort in and model spiritual self-examination such that they may teach these behaviors to their students and supervisees (see Patterson, Hayworth, Turner, & Raskin, 2000). The second stage will involve a more thorough self-examination through a spiritual genogram (see Frame, 2000) and scholarly exposure to spiritual traditions (Stander, Piercy, MacKinnon, & Helmeke, 1994). Third, supervisors will address how their supervisees and their clients experience spirituality in therapy. Through these stages, educators, supervisors, and students may become more adept at handling spirituality in the practice of therapy.

PRACTICE

Practitioners have implemented numerous interventions to discuss spirituality in therapy. As examples, Frame (2000) showed how practitioners might use spiritual genograms to give a broader understanding of clients' troubling experiences. Frame, like Haug (1998b), noted that therapy participants (including practitioners) evaluate their comfort levels about spirituality before constructing a spiritual genogram. Similarly, Hodge (2000) presented a spiritual ecomap based on an anthropological view that all humans are spiritual and hence have spiritual dimensions (cf. Frankl, 1988). In contrast to the genogram's emphasis on time, Hodge stated that ecomaps depict humans in space. He offered ideas on how practitioners might use ecomaps in their assessments and interventions. Further, he noted ethical concerns that could discourage practitioners from using spiritual ecomaps, instead recommending traditional ecomaps and/or genograms. Such concerns resemble the above considerations made by Haug (1998a). Both Frame and Hodge offered family examples of how practitioners might use their spiritual genogram and ecomap tools, respectively.

Other approaches to spirituality in therapy involve fewer structural guidelines and a different type of personal commitment from practitioners. As examples, Aponte (1998) used unconditional forgiveness and love as spiritual illustrations in therapy. Due to his assumption that spirituality is part of therapy, he mentioned the importance of recognizing *how* spirituality influences practitioners' professional and personal lives rather than *if* spirituality has an influence. After providing a clinical encounter, he suggested that unconditional love encourages responsibility, autonomy, and motivation, things identified as trans-theoretical. Anderson and Worthen (1997), like Aponte, amplified the importance of love or activities requiring acceptance, forgiveness, and compassion. They offered three assumptions that support their spiritual orientation, just as other theoretical models contain embedded assumptions. Then, they examined how practitioners might listen and respond to couples in helping them with their troubling experiences. Anderson and Worthen concluded that spiritual assumptions held by therapy participants act as a basis from which to understand spirituality in therapy.

In summary, many scholars have added to the links between spirituality and family therapy. Three statements about these links follow:

1. Four creative activities have helped challenge particular barriers in combining spirituality and family therapy:

   a. postmodern theories like social constructionism,
   b. assumptions held by therapy participants about a Presence in therapeutic relationships,
   c. research,
   d. ethical guidelines.

2. Scholars offering training guidelines and programs have responded to the voices of students and clients.
3. Therapists have created tools to learn about spiritual contexts and bind relational benevolence with recognizing and/or assuming spirituality in therapy.

Dialogue about an interconnection between spirituality and family therapy continues to expand, pushing conceptual and practical limits and considering multiple realities. Clients' extratherapeutic lives and practitioners' relationships with clients can assist in directing such dialogue. Additionally, these lives and relationships serve as a reminder to researchers, educators, and practitioners about what contributes most significantly to positive therapeutic outcome. As an expansion to professional dialogue, the author now will offer a model of four realities or ways by which humans may understand their world.

THEORETICAL MODEL

First, one may review a family-therapy conceptual context that partially parallels Wilber's (1997; 2000) four realities. Denton (2001), a well-known psychiatrist and family therapist, reviewed MFTs' three revolutions in his keynote speech, and these revolutions neatly corresponded with three of the four realities offered by Wilber. Anderson's (1997) and Gergen's (1994) social-constructionist writings recently have represented the first of these realities identified as intersubjective. The intersubjective reality emerges from language and is recognized by how people share interpersonal understandings.

For example, intersubjectivity occurs in your ability to understand this sentence due to shared interpersonal understandings between you and the author. As another theoretical example addressing the intersubjective reality, Hare-Mustin (1978) offered concerns about gender and culture that some MFTs then minimized in their conceptual and practical activities. Denton stated Hare-Mustin's article acted as the first revolution in changing how MFTs think and act. This change occurred in part due to a broader understanding of the intersubjective reality.

Denton (2001) continued by saying that family therapy's second revolution involved many MFTs re-visiting the individual subjective nature of humans (e.g., Nichols, 1987). This subjective reality arises from how individuals make sense of their inner experiences. Of course, the subjective reality would cease to exist without the intersubjective reality (Wilber, 2000) because the subjective reality depends upon one's ability to create meaning through language. The writings of depth psychologists like Piaget and Jung would land in this theoretical understanding of reality.

Further, Denton noted that the third revolution, represented prominently by the medical sciences, continues to influence many MFTs' concepts and practices. This revolution, identified by some as an objective reality, has an ongoing influence on empirically-based research and practice. For example, some MFTs correspond with insurance companies that require a substantiation of "medical (individual) necessity" in order for clients to continue receiving services. Such correspondence exemplifies an objective reality, one wherein the amount of hours a person sleeps everyday (e.g., as reported symptoms of insomnia or hypersomnia) matters. Hence, MFTs appear to have at least three realities that may influence their concepts and practices:

a. an intersubjective reality,
b. a subjective reality,
c. an objective reality.

However, one of these realities is integral to and sustaining of the other realities. This one, identified as the intersubjective reality, merits humans' continued attention, for it helps humans form relational meanings that allow them to harmoniously exist (Gergen, 1994). Further, humans cannot have language or signifiers without intersubjectivity. Additionally, Wilber (1997) suggested that humans could not perceive the objective reality without the intersubjective reality. Again, without language, humans would lack a capacity to make perceptual sense. Hence, the intersubjective reality is arguably most significant for an understanding of all four realities.

In addition to the above three realities, Wilber's (1997; 2000) integral approach included a fourth one: an interobjective reality. (This is the reality in which Wilber placed von Bertalanffy's [1968] *General System Theory*, an outgrowth of part of MFTs' theoretical origins.) This reality deals with functional fit or how people do things based on their intersubjective understandings. In short, Wilber suggested that the subjective, objective, and interobjective realities inevitably influence and constrain the intersubjective reality clearly articulated by Anderson (1997) and Gergen (1994). For example, one could not "find a shared worldview where apples fall upward or men give birth . . ." (Wilber, 1997, p. 25). By offering these distinctions through an appeal to the interobjective reality (i.e., seeing apples fall and not seeing men give birth), Wilber has neither sided with some empiricists who report observably knowing reality, nor has he dismissed scholarly constructivist views (see, e.g., Maturana & Varela, 1992). Rather, Wilber seemingly has integrated the realities in which humans exist by recognizing somewhat predictable happenings, regardless of whether such happenings as we perceive them have any factual correspondence to Reality, whatever this is. Accordingly, Wilber's integral approach is simply that, a *metaphorical* movement that includes the old and something new.

Due to the interrelationships between the four above realities, most MFTs already consider such realities in their practices. First, MFTs often will learn about the individual meaning that each client gives to her/his experiences. This represents the subjective reality of psychodynamic therapy to which many MFTs historically responded. Second, MFTs generally consider the individual objective reality. For instance, if a client underwent limb amputation and/or threatened to kill her/himself, most MFTs would accept this as something objective and act accordingly. Third, MFTs attend to the collective activities between family members. For example, when clients talk simultaneously and/or sit close to each other, many MFTs consider this in how they interact with clients (see Bateson's [1972] ideas on analog communication). This is the interobjective reality. Fourth, MFTs participate in the collective meaning-making in families, or the intersubjective reality. For instance, if a couple speaks of happiness in their relationship, most MFTs will seek to understand how the couple shares this view.

Wilber's (1997; 2000) model of four realities may give MFTs another way to attend to different forms of understanding without compromising a relational/systemic emphasis. Many MFTs already feed this emphasis by extending their vision of systems through, for example, Mead's (1968) cybernetics of cybernetics and/or Dallos' and Urry's (1999) third-order cybernetics. Further, MFTs continue to humanize the sometimes rigid and automated structures found within some systemic understandings. In a similar vein, Wilber's primary criticism of systems theories (not only von Bertalanffy's [1968] work) has revealed that despite their holistic emphases, they theoretically miss those who do not fit in a functional web. So, instead of an all-inclusive holism, one can find some rather monologic ideas about how everything has its interobjective place. In fact, Hare-Mustin's (1978) article addressed the exclusivity of this interobjective fit: what have systemic and cybernetic theories partially led MFTs conceptually and practically to miss? Hence, some family-therapy scholars have helped MFTs advance by offering ideas about culture, race, gender/sex, dialogue, postmodernism bound closely to poststructuralism, etc. Such ideas have challenged some of the interobjective understandings promoted by systems theories.

A theoretical understanding of these four realities is central to this article's conceptual model for two reasons. First, Wilber's ideas assist in strengthening the link between spirituality and family therapy and provide a way for MFTs to enhance their practical activities with clients. As an illustration, spirituality or transformative spirituality requires humans to acknowledge and honor all sentient perspectives (Wilber, 1997). Wilber's four realities (e.g., as represented by the writings of Hare-Mustin [1978], Nichols [1987], medical scholars, and von Bertalanffy [1968]) have added a needed difference in the way that MFTs acknowledge and honor multiple perspectives. Hence, MFTs' origins and revolutions potentially have added to a more recognized spirituality in what MFTs do. For instance, MFTs may ask about how culture and gender influences therapeutic process and outcome and/or how it helps/hinders clients in attaining what they want in their lives. MFTs may give tasks that focus on an individual's phenomenological experiences, especially as such experiences relate to language, others, perceptions, actions, emotions, etc. MFTs may assess potential areas of dangerousness and intervene in less flexible yet more ethical ways. MFTs structurally may influence (and be influenced) by the interactive processes occurring in session. In each above action, MFTs reveal an honoring of multiple perspectives and hence a recognition of a spiritual requirement by attending to others in four realities. Further, each action may increase the likelihood of interconnection between self and others and/or a Presence within and outside human bodies (Coffey, 2001).

Second, such a theoretical understanding helps form a basis in order to understand two more of Wilber's seminal ideas (i.e., holons and consciousness). "Holon," a word coined by Koestler (1976), has extensive implications in the practical linking of spirituality with family therapy. Holons represent steps of development or differentiation in people, places, and/or things that go beyond and include previous steps. Wilber (2000) conceded that holons occur in both linear and non-linear ways as well as in all four realities. He suggested the conceptual utility of holon rather than hierarchy due to the latter's etymological and historical origins (i.e., hierarchy literally means "sacred governance" as used by Saint Dionysius and later modified by the political sovereignty of Catholicism).

Such utility also fits more appropriately into linking spirituality and family therapy. For instance, MFTs and their clients have assumptions about how change occurs. The "how change occurs" spectrum may range from Nike's "just do it" slogan to leading someone into the experience of her/his mother's and/or past life wombs. Assumptions, as things, have undergone some level of development or a holonic process, even if humans have no awareness of such development. When discussing how change occurs with clients, MFTs may use the conceptual idea of holons to experience a desired outcome in therapy. This idea of holon resembles Bateson's (1972, pp. 271-272) "a difference which makes a difference," for holons are a difference that makes a difference in how people, places, and things function. MFTs attending to this idea will experience something with their clients fitting for the moment, not too unfamiliar and not too familiar. In contrast, an MFT working with a "just do it" client in a regressive fashion has disregarded her/his holonic development, potentially dishonored her/his perspectives, and hence has diminished the recognition of interconnective spirituality. As one may see, holons have conceptual and practical implications throughout MFTs' activities.

Holons, in their linear, non-linear, and four-reality forms can contribute to knowledge, understanding, and consciousness, Wilber's final seminal idea (for this article). "The agency of each holon establishes an opening or clearing in which similar-depthed holons can manifest to each other, for each other" (Wilber, 2000, p. 570). As an example, continuing with the theory of change example, MFTs form intersubjective understandings with their clients based in part on mutual relationships and their progression in therapy, which includes and goes beyond what happened before. The holonic process of having done some level of assessment may allow MFTs to know, for example, their clients' name(s), to know what their clients want, to know what is troubling to them, and to know how their clients think change occurs.

With this holonic knowledge, therapy participants establish a space wherein additional information can emerge from and assimilate with previous knowledge. As such knowledge and understanding occurs, MFTs and clients can create a mutual and functional theory of change that is aimed toward benefiting the client without eradicating the former theories held by either MFTs or clients. In so doing, MFTs and clients may add to their individual and collective consciousness. In other words, therapy participants can have some shared understandings about how clients' lives, their relationships with MFTs, clients' hope regarding therapy, and MFTs' techniques contribute to positive therapeutic outcome. These understandings or levels of consciousness necessarily acknowledge and honor therapy participants' perspectives, hence fulfilling some recognition of spirituality. Further, this level of consciousness diminishes spiritual materialism (Trungpa, 1987), adds to "Mind" or "Epistemology" (Bateson, 1972; 1981, respectively), and leads to the aesthetic/sacred (Bateson, 1980) or the Nondual (Wilber, 2000). Hence, consciousness ideas, as offered by Wilber, have the potential to strengthen the link between spirituality and family therapy, both conceptually and practically.

CONCEPTUAL SUMMARY

The author will offer the following ideas as a conceptual summary, suggesting some similarities between Wilber's and MFTs' concepts. First, Wilber's (1997; 2000) integral approach attempted to interconnect multiple disciplines, from systems theory to philosophy to spirituality. Like Wilber, family therapy's origins arose from the multiple contexts and disciplines that influence MFTs' concepts and practices. Second, Wilber emphasized transformation in his writings about spirituality, like both Anderson (1997) and Gergen (1994). Accordingly, MFTs continue to include spirituality in their concepts and practices so that they may embrace the contextual elements in clients' lives and relationships. Such a spirituality inclusion aims to promote further transformation in the family-therapy field and in those clients whom MFTs serve.

Third, Wilber depicted four realities (or the above three revolutions by Denton [2001] plus the GST reality) as a conceptual schema for understanding different theoretical positions. Likewise, scholars in the family-therapy field have accentuated multiple realities or multiplicity (e.g., Anderson, 1997; Becvar, 1997; Doherty, 1999; Gergen, 1994; Stander et al., 1994; Walsh, 1999b). Fourth, due in part to Wilber's transpersonal studies, he advanced an understanding of spirituality that might allow his readers to create profound conclusions. Through the explicitly spiritual writings of Satir (see, e.g.,1988) and the implicitly spiritual writings of Bateson (see, e.g., 1972, 1980, 1981), some MFTs have challenged the conceptual and practical activities of the psychotherapeutic field. From this challenge, some researchers, educators, and practitioners radically have changed their professional activities. The following section will offer a look at MFTs' activities using Wilber's integral lens.

CLINICAL USAGE

Extratherapeutic Lives

Humans as spiritual beings have numerous life experiences that may help them create well being and health. As MFTs encounter these humans as clients, therapy offers opportunities to amplify such life experiences. Like Anderson and Worthen (1997) and Berenson (1990), the author assumes that the interconnective process with others inevitably involves a Presence both within and outside of human bodies (Coffey, 2001). Hence, spirituality as an interconnective process and therapy reside together.

MFTs may link spirituality to their practice by seeing, thinking, and acting with clients in their four realities while recognizing holonic processes and consciousness. Clients who experience their lives spiritually, for example some African-Americans (Boyd-Franklin & Bry, 2000), Native Americans (Red Horse, 1982), and people of the Jewish faith (Semans & Fish, 2000), likely will offer numerous opportunities for MFTs to interconnect with them. For instance, African-American clients may talk about the grace of God, or Native American clients may talk about their connection with Nature. From each disclosure, MFTs may select fitting language (see Doherty, 1999) to co-create clients' four spiritual realities and see how these realities influence therapeutic process and outcome. Additionally, these realities provide MFTs and clients various ways to explore their experiences. MFTs may conduct this exploration through inquiry, self-disclosure, and/or whatever language or non-language ways that seem appropriate. Examples of questions might include:

1. How does the grace of God influence our work together?
2. What does your connection with Nature offer you?
3. When you experience grace or connectivity, how does that change the problem with which you are struggling?

Other clients may not experience their lives spiritually, but they believe or do things identified as spiritual. As examples, some clients may meditate, believe they have no use for bitterness in their lives, and/or experience spirituality as ineffable, a resource, or a meaningful dimension. Again, each of these activities and meanings correlate with Wilber's four realities. For these clients, MFTs could briefly disclose of themselves for the purpose of becoming more human to their clients. For example:

1. When you talked about your 'no use for bitterness,' I thought about how you could help others learn what your life has been like without it.
2. When I experienced racism growing up, I wondered about how I could learn from others treating me poorly. I am wondering now, how have you grown from others judging you by the color of your skin?

While some clients recognize spirituality in their lives, others do not. Further, some clients do not see relationships as spiritual, do not want to experience spiritual interventions, and/or have no use for expectancy in their lives. MFTs respectfully and curiously may explore how such clients add to their sense of well being and health without spirituality.

Therapeutic Relationships

Relationships with clients provide MFTs additional ways to explore spirituality with them. As MFTs relationally practice trans-theoretical experiences like acceptance and warmth, clients may experience a transcendent dimension or a building upon consciousness within relationships. Such experiences highlight the intersubjective reality of relational meaning (Gergen, 1994). Further, therapeutic relationships formed with an assumption of spirituality may lead to different individual and collective meanings and actions. Examples of the MFTs' dialogical part might include:

1. I am honored that you feel "connected" with me. How have you managed to share yourself so freely with me?
2. I appreciate your knowing that I accept you. As a couple/family, you have helped me learn how easy it is to accept others.
3. I enjoy laughing with you. I could be wrong, but our minds seem to be on the same page.

Techniques

Spiritual interventions provide an additional way MFTs may link spirituality and family therapy. These interventions include structural tools like genograms (Frame, 2000) and ecomaps (Hodge, 2000). Spiritual tools land in Wilber's objective and interobjective realities, dependent on whether participants complete them individually or collectively (of course they have subjective and intersubjective components). Further spiritual interventions may include subjective and intersubjective experiences of love, forgiveness, acceptance, and compassion. Additionally, some spiritual interventions represent objective and/or interobjective realities that happen in clients' lives. These interventions might include rituals (e.g., prayer, exercise, fasting, etc.), going to public services, and/or volunteering to promote women's equality. All of these techniques require MFTs to know about their therapeutic holonic processes so that what they say/do seems meaningful to their clients. Additionally, these techniques seem most effective once having considered levels of individual and collective consciousness.

Expectancy

Finally, expectancy begins with subjective and intersubjective realities. However, as many MFTs know, clients often will change their individual and collective "doings" as their subjective and intersubjective realities or holons evolve. Expectancy linked to spirituality may arise from pre-session change, healing, hope, and systems of influence (e.g., friends, family, gender, culture, sexual orientation, etc.). Examples to highlight expectancy might include:

1. How did you manage to see the problem differently before you came to see me?
2. What has given you hope throughout our work together?
3. How has your understanding of womanhood allowed you to make progress?

In each of the four areas that contribute to positive therapeutic outcome (i.e., extratherapeutic lives, relationships, interventions, and expectancy), MFTs have the privilege of highlighting clients' competencies. Further, MFTs may respond appropriately to clients who do not see their competency. Using Wilber's integral approach is one way that MFTs may continue to recognize spirituality in therapy to expand client competency. His overlapping models of four realities, holons, and consciousness provide MFTs avenues to participate in both individual and collective experiences. Also, his realities allow MFTs respectfully to explore the internal meanings and external doings of their clients. Both this participation and exploration can lead to an experience of transformative spirituality, wherein human perspectives are heard, honored, and valued.

DISCUSSION

Family therapy works for many clients struggling with life experiences, although no data suggests that one conceptual model works any better than another model (Pinsof & Wynne, 1995). Thus, practitioners who recognize spirituality as embedded in the therapeutic process do not have any data that supports their having better therapeutic outcomes. However, when practitioners examine the empirical data offered by Lambert (1992) and the others who joined him previously (see, e.g., Lambert, Shapiro, & Bergin, 1986), they may confront the importance of two premises:

1. Most people handle their troubling meanings/experiences by organizing around competency, either revealed through recognized spirituality, resiliency, and/or strengths. Such a life organization may keep them from ever seeking psychotherapeutic assistance.
2. Those people who do seek psychotherapeutic assistance gain significantly from their already-existing life organization and the relationships they form with their practitioners.

Given such premises, one may ask, "What is it about humans' extratherapeutic lives and their relationships with practitioners that allow them to get what they want from therapy?" This article suggests that one answer to this question is spirituality, recognized in all of its explicit and implicit forms.

Spirituality in the form of spiritual materialism (Trungpa, 1987) has infected the sacred and health-promoting notion of transformative spirituality (Wilber, 2000). Due to this negative association, some researchers, educators, and practitioners do not wish to further their professional and/or personal journey into spirituality. Yet, one may find it difficult to distinguish between spiritual materialism, that which uplifts the self while dismissing others, and transformative spirituality, that which despite humans' embodiment succeeds in recognizing a collective consciousness and leads to the aesthetic/sacred.

Spiritual materialism possesses an attractive lure, touting spirituality as temporary emotion/feeling, deserving quantification, individual enlightenment, and/or other seductive illustrations. Transformative spirituality requires wholeness, what Bateson linked with the sacred or Mind (1980; 1972, respectively) and what Wilber (2000) linked with Nonduality. However, wholeness or nonduality presents a dilemma because humans' language is necessarily dual or constituted by a "sign" made of two parts (i.e., a word and that thing which the word arbitrarily represents [see Saussure, 1959]). Thus, in choosing the word "Presence" associated with spirituality (Coffey, 2001), the author conceded to the restrictions mandated by human language and merely is beginning to understand the nature of such a transformative spirituality.

Regardless of the above conceptual and practical links between spirituality and family therapy (e.g., Anderson, 1987; Harris, 1998; Watson, 1997), family-therapy scholars need not exercise ownership of recognizing therapeutic spirituality (see Pinsof & Wynne, 1995). Numerous scholars from different psychotherapeutic traditions have written about the concepts and practices linking spirituality to what they do. With such a broad array of scholars, perhaps further data will inform researchers, educators, and practitioners in their professional activities. Moreover, as noted in the research section above (Joanides, 1997; Prest et al., 1999), professionals have so much more to learn about spirituality and therapy, especially related to clients' perspectives (see Anderson & Worthen, 1997; Haug, 1998a).

Consciously mixing spirituality and therapy has manifested in many forms. Pastoral and Christian counselors, shamans, spiritual guides, clergy, and others often make spirituality an explicit experience in their service to others. Sometimes these service-providers offer ecumenical and trans-religious assistance, while other times they may give assistance directly attached to a religious tradition (see Richards & Bergin, 1997). As licensed practitioners, many ethical codes prohibit both imposing values upon clients and ignoring their values. Hence, licensed practitioners judiciously choose what to do given therapeutic moments of explicit spirituality. However, practitioners may not make benevolent choices about addressing spirituality due to their lack of spiritual training and a minimization of professional spiritual dialogue. By collaborating with the above professionals, following ethical codes, and encouraging curricula revisions, spirituality may become a more recognized therapeutic dimension.

In the collaborative spirit, this author found that Wilber's integral approach (1997; 2000), from the discipline of transpersonal psychology, helps link spirituality with family therapy. However, his approach contains some conceptual and practical limitations. Conceptually, every theory, regardless of how integral it may be, elevates certain knowledge and subordinates other knowledge. Wilber's grasp of multiple epistemologies initially might suggest that he minimally subordinates other forms of knowing compared to some scholars. This idea is probably not accurate because Wilber's knowledge is much more slippery than his writings appear. As an illustration, he noted that "People shouldn't take it (his work) too seriously . . . It leaves all the details to be filled in any way you like . . . I hope I'm showing that there is more room in the Kosmos than you might have suspected" (1997, p. xi). Hence, due to his metaphorical quality and his allowance for evolution, scholars may struggle to create conceptual integrity from his work. This apparent lack of integrity will leave Wilber's work untouched by some researchers.

Scholars and researchers may see Wilber's writings as meta-theoretical, another potential conceptual dilemma. In considering multidisciplinary connections, many researchers may read Wilber as a philosopher rather than someone who has offered a theory base from which to learn about humans. In fact, using Wilber's integral approach requires researchers to choose an area (like his four realities) that seems most fitting for their study. Because he has combined theories supported by differing assumptions, one must find her/his conceptual usefulness in the parts rather than the whole. Of course, every theory requires its promoters to find usefulness in the parts, but most theories do not attempt to combine numerous disparate parts. Because his approach does combine disparate conceptual parts, finding a forum for its use is challenging.

Finally, humans have begun to apply Wilber's integral approach in ecological and political areas, but such application lags in therapeutic practice due partially to the above conceptual dilemmas. Likewise, his four realities do not fit with some practitioners' theoretical models and hence do not enter into their practice. Even though his approach lacks practical usage, it potentially could influence therapeutic practice, especially regarding spirituality. Yet, despite the hot debate surrounding his approach, many professionals reluctantly do not accept it for practical purposes. All of these areas may contribute to dilemmas faced by practitioners as well as psychotherapeutic researchers and educators.

RECOMMENDATIONS

This author makes the following recommendations:

1. Agreeing with Anderson and Worthen (1997), Haug (1998a), and Worthington et al. (1996), researchers and practitioners should continue to learn about clients' perspectives on spirituality in therapy.
2. Both researchers and practitioners should learn about how clients' perspectives influence the process and outcome of therapy.
3. Conceptual distinctions between spirituality that promotes health and well being and spirituality that does not need continued development.
4. Collaboration with other psychotherapists, service providers who explicitly include spirituality in their practice, and medical/nursing professionals may legitimize spirituality's place in therapy.
5. Spiritual dialogue between researchers, educators, students, and practitioners may expand current ideas regarding spirituality and ethics, training, and common practices.
6. Practitioners may integrate the spiritual concepts of scholars like Wilber and intersubjectively create ways to use these concepts for clients' benefit.
7. Having given transformative spirituality more energy, researchers, educators, students, and practitioners may begin to see, think, and act more collectively, moving gradually toward the Sacred.

CONCLUSION

As practitioners continue to embrace spirituality in their concepts and practices, lives and relationships may become less taken for granted. Practitioners may care for themselves differently. Further, they may recognize that clients continue to offer knowledge about how practitioners may assist in alleviating clients' troubling meanings/experiences. Along the way to such alleviation, practitioners humbly may participate in their clients' lives through therapeutic relationships. Perhaps this participation will remind practitioners of the collective Mind or Spirit that all humans share.

REFERENCES

Adams, N. (1995). Spirituality, science and therapy. *Australian and New Zealand Journal of Family Therapy, 16*(4), 201-208.

Anderson, D. A. (1987). Spirituality and systems therapy: Partners in clinical practice. *Journal of Pastoral Psychotherapy, 1*(1), 19-32.

Anderson, D. A., & Worthen, D. (1997). Exploring a fourth dimension: Spirituality as a resource for the couple therapist. *Journal of Marital and Family Therapy, 23*, 3-12.

Anderson, H. J. (1997). *Conversation, language, and possibilities: A postmodern approach to therapy*. New York: Basic Books.

Aponte, H. J. (1998). Love, the spiritual wellspring of forgiveness: An example of spirituality in therapy. *Journal of Family Therapy, 20*, 37-58.

Bateson, G. (1972). *Steps to an ecology of mind*. Chicago: The University of Chicago Press.

Bateson, G. (1980). Seek the sacred. Resurgence: *Journal of the Fourth World, 10*(5), 18-20.

Bateson, G. (1981). The eternal verities. *The Yale Review, 71*(1), 1-12.

Becvar, D. S. (1997). *Soul healing: A spiritual orientation in counseling and therapy*. New York: Basic Books.

Berenson, D. (1990). A systemic view of spirituality: God and twelve step programs as resources in family therapy. *Journal of Strategic and Systemic Therapies, 9*, 59-70.

Boyd-Franklin, N., & Bry, B. H. (2000). *Reaching out in family therapy: Home-based, school, and community interventions*. New York: The Guilford Press.

Coffey, A. D. (2001). *Spirituality and couples therapy: Ethnographic perspectives from therapy experiences*. Unpublished doctoral dissertation, Texas Woman's University, Denton.

Dallos, R., & Urry, A. (1999). Abandoning our parents and grandparents: Does social construction mean the end of systemic family therapy? *Journal of Family Therapy, 21*, 161-186.

de Saussure, F. (1959). *Course in general linguistics*. New York: Philosophical Library.

Denton, W. (2001, January). *Family therapy as health care profession*. Paper presented at the meeting of the Texas Association for Marriage and Family Therapy, Dallas, TX.

Doherty, W. J. (1999). Morality and spirituality in therapy. In F. Walsh (Ed.), *Spiritual resources in family therapy* (pp. 179-192). New York: Guilford Press.

Frame, M. W. (2000). The spiritual genogram in family therapy. *Journal of Marital and Family Therapy, 26*(2), 211-216.

Frankl, V. E. (1988). *The will to meaning: Foundations and applications of logotherapy* (Expanded ed.). New York: Penguin.

Gergen, K. J. (1994). *Realities and relationships: Soundings in social construction*. Cambridge, MA: Harvard University Press.

Hare-Mustin, R. T. (1978). A feminist approach to family therapy. *Family Process, 17*, 181-194.

Harris, S. M. (1998). Finding a forest among trees: Spirituality hiding in family therapy theories. *Journal of Family Studies, 4*(1), 77-86.

Haug, I. E. (1998a). Including a spiritual dimension in family therapy: Ethical considerations. *Contemporary Family Therapy, 20*, 181-194.

Haug, I. E. (1998b). Spirituality as a dimension of family therapists' clinical training. *Contemporary Family Therapy, 20*, 471-483.

Hodge, D. R. (2000). Spiritual ecomaps: A new diagrammatic tool for assessing marital and family spirituality. *Journal of Marital and Family Therapy, 26*(2), 217-228.

Hopcke, R. H. (1989). *A guided tour of the collected works of C. G. Jung*. Boston: Shambhala.

Joanides, C. J. (1997). A qualitative investigation of the meaning of religion and spirituality to a group of Orthodox Christians: Implications for marriage and family therapy. *Journal of Family Social Work, 2*(4), 59-76.

Johnson, S. (2001, January). *Couples therapy: The promise of the new millennium*. Paper presented at the meeting of the Texas Association of Marriage and Family Therapy, Dallas, TX.

Kahle, P. (1997). *The influence of the person of the therapist on the integration of spirituality and psychotherapy*. Unpublished doctoral dissertation, Texas Woman's University, Denton.

Koestler, A. (1976). *The ghost in the machine*. New York: Random House.

Lambert, M. J. (1992). Psychotherapy outcome research: Implications for integrative and eclectic therapists. In J. C. Norcross & M. R. Goldfried (Eds.), *Handbook of psychotherapy integration* (pp. 94-129). New York: Basic.

Lambert, M. J., Shapiro, D. A., & Bergin, A. E. (1986). The effectiveness of psychotherapy. In S. L. Garfield & A. E. Bergin (Eds.), *Handbook of psychotherapy and behavior change* (3rd ed., pp. 157-212). New York: Wiley.

Maturana, H. R., & Varela, F. J. (1992). *The tree of knowledge: The biological roots of human understanding* (Rev. ed.). Boston: Shambhala.

Mead, M. (1968). Cybernetics of cybernetics. In H. vonFoerster, J. D. White, L. J. Peterson, & J. K. Russell (Eds.), *Purposive systems: Proceedings of the first annual symposium of the American society for cybernetics* (pp. 1-11). New York: Spartan Books.

Miller, W. R. (Ed.). (1999). *Integrating spirituality into treatment: Resources for practitioners*. Washington, DC: American Psychological Association.

Miller, W. R., & Thoresen, C. E. (1999). Spirituality and health. In W. R. Miller (Ed.), *Integrating spirituality into treatment: Resources for practitioners* (pp. 3-18). Washington, DC: American Psychological Association.

Nichols, M. P. (1987). *The self in the system: Expanding the limits of family therapy*. New York: Brunner/Mazel.

Pahnke, W. N., & Richards, W. A. (1990). Implications of LSD and experimental mysticism. In C. T. Tart (Ed.), *Altered states of consciousness* (3rd ed., pp. 481-515). New York: HarperCollins.

Patterson, J., Hayworth, M., Turner, C., & Raskin, M. (2000). Spiritual issues in family therapy: A graduate-level course. *Journal of Marital and Family Therapy, 26* (2), 199-210.

Pinsof, W. M., & Wynne, L. C. (1995). The efficacy of marital and family therapy: An empirical overview, conclusions, and recommendations. *Journal of Marital and Family Therapy, 21*(4), 585-613.

Prest, L. A., & Keller, J. F. (1993). Spirituality and family therapy: Spiritual beliefs, myths, and metaphors. *Journal of Marital and Family Therapy, 19*, 137-148.

Prest, L. A., Russel, R., & D'Souza, H. (1999). Spirituality and religion in training, practice and personal development. *Journal of Family Therapy, 21*, 60-77.

Red Horse, J. (1982). Clinical strategies for American Indian families in crisis. *The Urban & Social Change Review, 15*(2), 17-19.

Richards, P. S., & Bergin, A. E. (1997). *A spiritual strategy for counseling and psychotherapy*. Washington, DC: American Psychological Association.

Rose, E. M. (1998). Spiritual issues in counseling: Clients' beliefs and preferences (Doctoral dissertation, University of Iowa, 1998). *Dissertation Abstracts International, 59(5-B)*, 2431.

Satir, V. (1988). *The new people making*. Mountain View, CA: Science and Behavior Books.

Semans, M. P., & Fish, L. S. (2000). Dissecting life with a Jewish scalpel: A qualitative analysis of Jewish-centered family life. *Family Process, 39*, 121-139.

Stander, V., Piercy, F. P., Mackinnon, D., & Helmeke, K. (1994). Spirituality, religion, and family therapy: Competing or complementary worlds? *The American Journal of Family Therapy, 22*, 27-41.

Thayne, T. R. (1997). Opening space for clients' religious and spiritual values in therapy: A social constructionist perspective. *Journal of Family Social Work, 2*(4), 13-23.

Trungpa, C. (1987). *Cutting through spiritual materialism*. Boston: Shambhala.

von Bertalanffy, L. (1968). *General system theory*. New York: George Braziller.

Walsh, F. (1999a). Opening family therapy to spirituality. In F. Walsh (Ed.), *Spiritual resources in family therapy* (pp. 28-58). New York: Guilford Press.

Walsh, F. (1999b). *Spiritual resources in family therapy*. New York: Guilford Press.

Watson, W. H. (1997). Soul and system: The integrative possibilities of family therapy. *Journal of Psychology and Theology, 25*, 123-135.

Wilber, K. (1997). *The eye of spirit: An integral vision for a world gone slightly mad*. Boston: Shambhala.

Wilber, K. (2000). *Sex, ecology, spirituality: The spirit of evolution* (2nd ed.). Boston: Shambhala.

Winston, A. (1991). Family therapists, religiosity, and spirituality: A survey of personal and professional beliefs and practices (Doctoral dissertation, The Union Institute, 1991). *Dissertation Abstracts International, 52*(2-B), 1044-1045.

Worthington, E. L., Kurusu, T. A., McCullough, M. E., & Sandage, S. J. (1996). Empirical research on religion and psychotherapeutic processes and outcomes: A 10-year review and research prospectus. *Psychological Bulletin, 119*, 448-487.

Coping with a Child's Death: Spiritual Issues and Therapeutic Implications

Sean E. Brotherson
Jean Soderquist

SUMMARY. This study focused on understanding spiritual issues addressed in parental accounts of losing a child and the therapeutic implications for helping professionals. Qualitative, in-depth interviews were conducted with nineteen parents concerning their experience with having a child die and its effect on their lives. The parents' stories were recorded and the narratives were then explored to develop a better understanding of spiritual themes and issues shared by parents related to the loss of a child. *[Article copies available for a fee from The Haworth Document Delivery Service: 1-800-HAWORTH. E-mail address: <getinfo@haworthpressinc.com> Website: <http://www.HaworthPress.com> © 2002 by The Haworth Press, Inc. All rights reserved.]*

Sean E. Brotherson is affiliated with North Dakota State University.
Jean Soderquist is affiliated with Cornerstone Counseling Services.
Address correspondence to: Sean E. Brotherson, Extension Family Science Specialist, EML 277, North Dakota State University, Fargo, ND 58105 (E-mail: sbrother@ndsuext.nodak.edu).

[Haworth co-indexing entry note]: "Coping with a Child's Death: Spiritual Issues and Therapeutic Implications." Brotherson, Sean E., and Jean Soderquist. Co-published simultaneously in *Journal of Family Psychotherapy* (The Haworth Press, Inc.) Vol. 13, No. 1/2, 2002, pp. 53-86; and: *Spirituality and Family Therapy* (ed: Thomas D. Carlson, and Martin J. Erickson) The Haworth Press, Inc., 2002, pp. 53-86. Single or multiple copies of this article are available for a fee from The Haworth Document Delivery Service [1-800-HAWORTH, 9:00 a.m. - 5:00 p.m. (EST). E-mail address: getinfo@haworthpressinc.com].

KEYWORDS. Spirituality, bereavement, children, parents

Analysis of the parents' personal narratives demonstrated that spiritual issues could be broadly grouped into three categories. These categories were:

a. spiritual beliefs and coping with child loss;
b. spiritual relationships and coping with child loss;
c. spiritual resources and coping with child loss.

Key themes in each category were identified and used to provide insight into how helping professionals can approach dealing with such issues in a therapeutic setting. Spiritual issues are commonly raised as parents face the coping process after a child's death. Helping professionals are encouraged to avoid pathologizing spiritual issues in the therapeutic process and to treat such matters with appropriate care and respect. The study contributed to further development of understanding about spiritual issues related to child loss and identified important patterns in parents' experience that can be used to promote greater therapeutic understanding and appropriate care by helping professionals.

Peggy, a fifty-five year old emergency room nurse and mother of five, was in her home caring for another child when her young son came in and told her to come outside and see her eighteen-month-old daughter because she was "dead." Her daughter did have some health challenges due to a blood disease, but she was inclined to dismiss her son's initial description of the situation. Upon going out to investigate, however, she found that her daughter had fallen from a small climbing structure and was not breathing. Her daughter, Tina, died in the hospital the next day. Peggy described the experience as leaving her overwhelmed with "a sadness, a sadness that hurts; it's like a knife."

The experience of death is a universal feature of human existence. In the process of growing up, we learn to accept the inevitability that all things eventually die and that we will experience loss many times as we progress toward our own end. We may experience death in many forms through the loss of pets and the deaths of older acquaintances, family members, and other loved ones. And yet, death is a topic that is seldom addressed directly through personal conversations in our society (Kalish, 1981). This pervasive reluctance in Western culture to confront death prompted LaRochefoucauld, a seventeenth-century philosopher, to state that "the human mind is as little capable to contemplate death for any length of time as the eye is able to look at the sun" (Choron, 1964, p. 107). Such discomfort with the topic of death becomes particularly apparent when addressing perhaps its most distressing occurrence: the death of a child. Rarely do we pause to consider the possibility that parents may outlive their own children. According to Fitzgerald (1994), this is because "the death of a child seems to defy the laws of nature. It puts things out of order for a child to die before his or her parents" (p. XX). While it is not uncommon to face perinatal or infant loss as a result of miscarriage, birth defects, abortion, SIDS, or illness, seldom do we contemplate the death of a child who has lived beyond the hazards of birth and early infancy. Less seldom do we speak of such thoughts. However, each year in the United States alone there are tens of thousands of children who die and thus set in motion a life change experience of profound magnitude for parents and other family members (Holmes & Rahe, 1967; Knapp, 1986). Researchers on loss and bereavement share nearly universal agreement that a child's death is of greater severity and impact on individuals than nearly any other type of loss (Bernstein, 1997; Edelstein, 1984; Finkbeiner, 1996; Rando, 1985; Sormanti & August, 1997; Weiss, 1988). It is certain that the grief process for bereaved parents typically is intense and long-lasting and requires greater understanding.

Grief has been defined as "an individual's subjective emotional response to loss" (Bernstein, 1997, p. 4), and it typically elicits the onset of the mourning process. The mourning process itself has been studied extensively and is composed of the set of reactions and adaptive processes that take place following a loss. A child's death is a particularly severe type of loss that tends to ignite extreme distress or grief over an extended period of time (Parkes, 1988b). While a number of theoretical descriptions of the mourning process following a loved one's death have been proposed with some distinctive components (Bowlby, 1980; Engel, 1972; Fenichel, 1945; Freud, 1917; Kubler-Ross, 1969; Parkes, 1986; Pollock, 1961; Sanders, 1989; Sullivan, 1956), in general these models overlap and suggest that each person experiences a number of different emotional tasks in the mourning process that take time to resolve (Parkes, 1988a). Lindemann (1944) suggests that such "grief work" includes dealing with the pain of grief, releasing the lost individual, adapting to a new life without the loved one, and establishing a new identity. Worden (1982) defines his "final task of mourning" as the withdrawal of emotional energy and reinvesting it in another relationship. Such traditional approaches to helping persons struggling with grief thus seem to have focused on the person's need to "complete" the emotional tasks of detaching from the lost person and "move on." Those who do not or cannot overcome these strong attachments may be diagnosed as suffering from "delayed grief" or "pathological mourning." Recently, however, the consensus in professional literature has begun to indicate that the death of a child is followed by a grief process, unique to parents, which may be lifelong (Klass, Silverman, & Nickman, 1996; Sormanti & August, 1997).

Both the avoidance of child death as a topic in our cultural conversation and the limitations of our understanding of parental grief contribute to the challenges in helping parents cope with a child's death. The "conspiracy of silence" about the subject creates an atmosphere in which there is little opportunity to develop healthy attitudes about death or to learn and share coping skills for managing grief (Fitzgerald, 1994). It also limits the exploration of experiences and possibilities for coping with grief that might be shared in a culture, so many individuals and professionals are left to develop, find, or stumble across coping mechanisms that may or may not alleviate the difficulty of the mourning process. In addition, if a grieving parent does not follow what is considered to be "normal" progress toward resolution of grief or copes in a manner unfamiliar to some helping professionals, the person may find themselves emotionally isolated or open to criticism from others. Spirituality is a particular coping resource often utilized by bereaved parents, and yet its sensitivity as a topic (combined with the discomfort of death) and little-understood role in the mourning process have limited understanding of its importance.

This study utilized a grounded-theory approach to explore parental accounts of a child's death and generate a greater understanding of spiritual issues raised by parents following a loss and implications for therapeutic practice. Parents were interviewed about their particular experiences in having a child die and its effect on themselves, their relationships with the deceased child, and their relationships with other children. The parents' narrative accounts were examined for particular themes or issues raising the issue of spirituality and the role it plays in the coping process following a child's death. Due to differing definitions of religion versus spirituality and to avoid narrow conceptualization, we have chosen to use Prest and Russell's (1995) broad definition of spirituality as "the human experience of discovering meaning, purpose, and values, which may or may not include the concept of a God or transcendent being" (p. 4). Within this framework, many persons may discuss spiritual issues from a particular psychological, religious, or cultural belief system, and these systems represent the formalized context for spiritual beliefs or practices (Prest & Russell, 1995; Sormanti & August, 1997). Spiritual issues raised by bereaved persons are common and the tendency to search for a meaning that will make sense of a child's death is nearly universal (Knapp, 1986). Therefore, helping professionals need to be sensitive to this tendency and may benefit from a familiarity with key issues related to spirituality and coping with a child's loss. This study addresses particular themes related to spirituality and coping with a child's death and corresponding implications for helping professionals.

LITERATURE REVIEW

Child death is a difficult experience to face and it can also be challenging to study. While the topics of death of a family member and bereavement have been studied for years in the social and behavioral sciences, only a limited number of studies address the topic of a child's death from a qualitative perspective (Bernstein, 1997; Edelstein, 1984; Knapp, 1986; Miles & Perry, 1985; Sanders, 1989). In particular, issues of spirituality and meaning tend to be dealt with primarily from an anecdotal or incidental perspective rather than in a systematic manner, although some research has included a specific focus on spiritual matters involved in grieving for a lost child (Edmonds, 1993; Kalish & Reynolds, 1981; Klass, 1991, 1993; Simon-Buller, Christopherson, & Jones, 1989; Sormanti & August, 1997; Talbot, 1999). The existing literature regarding spirituality and coping with a child's death might be categorized the following way:

a. spiritual beliefs and coping with child loss;
b. spiritual relationships and coping with child loss;
c. spiritual resources and coping with child loss.

Parents who lose a child often search their personal beliefs for meaning in the coping process and may turn to or rely upon particular spiritual beliefs to find comfort and support (Cook & Wimberley, 1983; Klass, 1993; Knapp, 1986; Wheeler, 1994). Kalish (1981) has suggested that "it is the particular beliefs that one holds and the intensity with which they are held" (p. 115) that influences the impact of spiritual beliefs on coping. Some studies show that many parents' religious beliefs tend to become stronger after a child's death, although this occurs primarily with those parents who already had some religious commitment or upbringing prior to the loss (Binger, Ablin, Feurerstein, Kushner, Zoger, & Mikkelsen, 1969; Cook & Wimberley, 1983; Miles & Crandall, 1986). Knapp (1986) interviewed bereaved parents from 155 families and found that 7 out of 10 parents in his study eventually turned to their religious belief systems for answers regarding the loss. Over time as parents search for resolution of their grief they may rely upon particular spiritual beliefs for some comfort and peace, including such theodicies as reunion with the child in an afterlife, the child's death serving a higher purpose, or even death as a punishment for parental wrong-doing (Cook & Wimberley, 1983). The death of a child may serve as a catalyst for change in a parent's spiritual beliefs. Perhaps the most common pattern involves deepened spiritual beliefs through coping with a child's loss. A variety of studies have shown that bereaved persons often describe themselves as "being more spiritual" or having stronger religious beliefs following a family member's death, although this seems more common among women than men (Calhoun & Tedeschi, 1989; Edmonds, 1993; Knapp, 1986; Miles & Crandall, 1986; Shanfield et al., 1984; Videka-Sherman, 1982). Less common but also apparent in the literature is a loss of or confusion regarding spiritual beliefs after a child's death. Talbot (1999) reported that some of her study participants "had experienced a spiritual crisis as a result of their child's death" (p. 173), and that over half of them questioned or changed their spiritual beliefs after the loss. It may not be uncommon for bereaved parents to question such beliefs as the mercy of God or to express anger at others who suggest a belief that a child's death fits some spiritual purpose (Edmonds, 1993; Knapp, 1986). The role of spiritual beliefs in a parent's coping process following a child's death thus may be a strong influence on the course of their grieving.

An oft-reported but little-understood dimension of child loss involves parental accounts of spiritual encounters or experiences related to their deceased children (Klass, 1993; Rando, 1986; Rees, 1975; Shapiro, 1994; Worden, 1982). Although it is not uncommon for bereaved parents to report such spiritual contacts to practitioners who work extensively with bereavement, there has been little research done on such spiritual contacts reported by parents, the beliefs behind them, or the meanings of either in the parents' grief processes. Researchers who analyzed data from a 1980 bereavement study of 500 widows described what they called the "sensing phenomena" (the "experience of feeling the presence of a deceased person") and found that at least half the sample indicated having such an experience (Simon-Buller, Christopherson, & Jones, 1989). Post-death manifestations or similar spiritual connections to the deceased were reported by almost one-third of the participants in another bereavement study by Rubin (1993). Klass (1993) conducted a ten-year ethnographic study of a self-help group for bereaved parents and reported that parents either affirmed or refashioned their worldviews through a "continuing interaction with the inner representation of the dead child" (p. 255). Included in such interactions were a sense of presence, hallucinations in any of the senses, thoughts or memories of the lost child, etc., and the encounters were suggested to occur within the realm of a parent's unconscious or imagination. More recently, Sormanti and August (1997) have studied what they call "the phenomenon of continuing connection between parents and their deceased children" and define this to include "visions, physical sensations, dreams, and a variety of other experiences that ma[k]e the parents feel connected to the children and seem to help them in dealing with their grief" (p. 461). Their exploratory qualitative study of 43 bereaved parents suggests that such experiences foster a continuing sense of connection with the deceased child, impact the mourning process in a positive way, prompt change in spiritual beliefs, and require sensitivity from helping professionals. Thus, it seems that such spiritual connections may play an important role in the coping process but as yet have received only limited study and understanding.

A third genre of research on spiritual issues in coping with a child's death relates to the use of spiritual resources in the coping process. A number of authors have noted the general importance of spirituality and religion in the lives of many Americans (Bergin, Masters, Stinchfield, Gaskin, Sullivan, Reynolds, & Greaves, 1997; Steere, 1997), and it is not uncommon for persons coping with distress to turn to religious or spiritual sources of support for comfort and healing (Larson & Larson, 1992; Prest & Keller, 1993; Watson, 1997). Specific sources of spiritual support utilized may include consultations with clergy or spiritual leaders, engagement in religious rituals or practices, use of prayer or meditation, and discussion with others about spiritual questions (Knapp, 1986; Patterson, Hayworth, Turner, & Raskin, 2000). Knapp (1986) noted in his research that reliance upon spiritual sources of support was a common coping strategy for bereaved parents. However, some research suggests that the effect of support received from clergy, for example, is largely dependent on the willingness of such spiritual leaders to go beyond dogma or religious ritual and reach out to the bereaved in sensitivity and compassion (Bernstein, 1997; Brabant et al., 1995). Due to the plethora of differing spiritual traditions and faith systems, it seems important to note that a wide range of practices and resources may be grouped under the category of spiritual sources of support (Hodge, 2000; Patterson et al., 2000). Although much research remains to be done, it seems that spiritual sources of support can diminish anxiety and enable some bereaved parents to cope more effectively with the traumatic loss they have experienced.

METHOD

This study utilized a qualitative research design in order to allow exploration of parents' own descriptions of their experiences in losing a child. The particular method of study for the project involved conducting in-depth personal interviews with bereaved parents that focused on collecting personal narratives of their experiences. Since specific and detailed study of spiritual issues raised by bereaved parents remains somewhat limited, this study was deliberately exploratory in nature. The exploratory nature of the study focused on uncovering the content and meaning of spiritual issues raised by parents in their response to child loss, allowing for a phenomenological approach to this topic. The phenomenological approach suggests research "data" is like a text that must be read and understood (Nielsen, 1990; Tesch, 1990; Walker, 1996). Following Widdershoven's (1993) assertion that "the meaning of life cannot be determined outside of the stories told about it" (p. 2), the narrative accounts shared by parents were of particular interest. Specifically, *narrative accounts* were defined as "the stories people tell about their own experiences, along with the meanings they attach to those stories" (Dollahite, Hawkins, & Brotherson, 1996, p. 350). These stories and their meanings were explored to further understand spiritual issues raised by the parents and their implications for the practice of therapy.

The sampling processes used in this study included "key informant" sampling and "snowball" sampling. Key informant sampling was accomplished through identifying knowledgeable persons in target communities who were able to provide information on bereavement and also links to other persons. Key persons for the study were identified through contacting local grief support groups, other institutions, and individuals in order to facilitate a request for study participants, and also through identifying bereaved parents who were already known to the researchers. Snowball sampling was then pursued through asking such key persons or volunteer participants to identify other individuals who might be willing to participate in the designed study (Lincoln & Guba, 1985; Miles & Huberman, 1994). Three of the study participants were recruited through contacts made with grief support groups, six were recruited through individual contacts made by the researcher, and ten were recruited through referrals from other study participants. The participants were often very willing to participate and volunteered to assist with referring others for the study. Limitations on potential participants were that the child's death had to have occurred at least two years prior to the interview taking place, and that the child be between the ages of 18 months and 25 years at death. Also, the study included only bereaved parents whose children died as a result of accident or illness. Through these procedures nineteen study participants were eventually contacted and agreed to participate.

Participants consisted of thirteen mothers and six fathers from two mid-sized communities in two Western states. Study participants were all Caucasian and ranged between the ages of 40 and 93 years of age, although most were in their forties or fifties. The average age of mothers in the study was 59 years and the average age of fathers in the study was 56 years. Nine women in the study were married (first marriage for all but one), two were divorced, and two were widowed. All six men in the study were married (first marriage for all but one). Family size for parents in the study ranged between 2 children and 10 children, with the average being 4-5 children per family. Nearly all of the study participants described themselves as having a mid-level socioeconomic status, with four suggesting they were "low to middle," thirteen stating they were "middle," and two saying they were "middle to high." All study participants had completed at least a high school education, with seventeen of the nineteen actually completing a college degree or some college education. Ten of the thirteen mothers in the study identified themselves as being currently active in a faith community, and five of the six fathers in the study also identified themselves as being active in a faith group. Thirteen of the participants in the study experienced the loss of a child quite suddenly through a variety of accidental deaths, most commonly due to a traffic accident. Six of the participants experienced a child's death as a result of disease or illness, usually due to cancer.

Prior to the actual interviews with study participants, interview questions were developed and piloted for use in creating a final interview schedule. It should be noted that the interview questions themselves did not focus on spiritual issues in parental bereavement, but rather encouraged the parents to talk extensively about their experience with child loss. Each interview was conducted at a time and location convenient for the participant and lasted from one to two and a half hours. The interviews were tape-recorded with the permission of the participant on a small, portable standard tape recorder on hour-long, high quality audiocassettes. Nearly all study participants openly welcomed the opportunity to share stories about their deceased child and even the details of their loss experience, although the interview participants were often somewhat emotional when recounting the actual child's death. At these times the interview itself sometimes slowed down as an exchange of thoughts and feelings between the participant and researcher took place. During the interviews some participants took time to show pictures of the child, break for a visit to a deceased child's memorial garden or other important spots, or to simply discuss and share thoughts in a more relaxed setting. All of the recorded interviews were transcribed verbatim and studied systematically by the researchers to discern content and meaning related to spiritual issues discussed by parents in the bereavement process (Glaser & Strauss, 1967; Miles & Huberman, 1994).

FINDINGS

Spiritual elements of child loss seem to play an important role in the coping process for many parents, but have not tended to receive significant attention in the therapeutic literature. The findings from this study on spiritual issues in child loss are discussed here with a focus on implications for therapeutic practice. As was noted earlier, the interview questions did not focus on spiritual issues in parental bereavement. However, each of the participants spontaneously discussed such issues. For bereaved parents, the impact of a child's death appears to be intricately woven with spiritual dimensions, both positive and negative. In therapeutic work with these parents, it would then seem that failing to include or at least address spiritual matters might be detrimental to a fully satisfactory treatment outcome. For this reason, along with the discussion of several of the major spiritual factors found in our study, we will discuss the related treatment issues.

SPIRITUAL ISSUES AND CHILD LOSS

When a child dies, spiritual factors such as a parent's beliefs or relationships with clergy are likely to be involved and to be affected by the loss. These factors may influence parental bereavement in a variety of different ways. Parents in our study discussed the spiritual dimensions of their loss experience in four key areas:

1. struggle with or loss of particular beliefs;
2. spiritual beliefs and practices as a coping resource;

3. a sense of spiritual connection with their child;
4. lack of support for or rejection of these spiritual aspects. Each of these aspects may have a substantial impact on the grieving process and the viability of therapeutic interventions.

Struggle with or Loss of Beliefs

Several of the parents in our study said that the death of their child had caused them to question or reject their religious beliefs. This struggle ranged from wondering why God had "allowed" the death to rejection of God and/or religious convictions. For some, this was a temporary stage, but for others the questioning and rejection had lasted for months or years following the occurrence of the loss. One theme was that the death might have been caused by the sins of the parent. During one interview, a parent commented:

> It also makes you wonder what you have done [to deserve this]. What have I done in my life that would be so horrible that would cause this to happen to my child? Why am I being punished?

Another theme involved spiritual disillusionment when the realities of the death conflicted with a particular belief. One fifty-year old mother identified her three-year spiritual struggle, which developed when her belief in a spiritual connection with her child was disappointed:

> Consequently, I'm struggling with religion and a lot of beliefs that I had. Well, as a mother you always think that you have this instinct and that you're going to know when something happens to your child. Well, I was watching the game at the same time [my child died] and then I went to bed.

Beyond temporary concern about or questioning of beliefs, some bereaved parents reported a breakdown of their belief systems. A mother, fifty-six, found herself unable to resolve her hurt and anger. She questioned, and for the four years following the loss has rejected, her fundamental and long-held religious beliefs, including her concept of God:

> I had a mind-body-spirit connection that was one, and now it's very separate and I can't get it back together no matter what I try. The trust and faith I had in my God is no longer there. I actually had reached a point where I truly had this total blind faith and trust,

> and to have your prayers "answered" . . . what's the point of praying if you're not going to get them answered? . . . it's devastating to find out that you got the absolute opposite of what you prayed for. Your hold on life has been turned down. I feel like God let me down. Well, if God controls everything, then why is my daughter dead?

Therapeutic Implications

Losing a child can raise stark questions for parents and force them to confront their own beliefs about life, death, and meaning. If these questions evolve into challenges to a person's beliefs or even disbelief, then the resulting struggle can become a serious source of personal distress for the bereaved parent. This may be particularly true if the person had a strong religious identity. Issues facing the therapist in such circumstances may include consideration of his or her own level of comfort addressing spiritual concerns, preparation for or experience with this topic in therapy, and approaches to dealing with struggle regarding a client's personal beliefs.

At times faith and other spiritual or religious feelings have been seen by therapists as being "outside" of, or even inappropriate in, the therapeutic relationship (Bergin & Jensen, 1990). Even though recent research has shown that the field seems to be making progress toward dealing with spiritual issues in therapy (Carlson, 1996), many professionals may be inclined to avoid discussion of spiritual issues, even when initiated by their clients. However, our findings suggest that for some parents the questioning of or disappointment in their beliefs or faith is part of their overall experience of loss and grieving. A child's loss, being untimely, may raise particular questions for parents who look for comfort in spiritual beliefs. The experiences and reactions of clients can be expected to be very different for parents who find the comfort they have sought and those who do not. Treatment interventions cannot be completely successful if major aspects of the grieving experience are not addressed or if differing reactions are not considered.

Dealing with a client's spiritual disillusionment may not be a common experience for many professionals. This may be due in part both to some hesitation in exploring explicit spiritual concerns and to a lack of training or expertise in such topics. Dealing with spiritual issues in a therapeutic setting is not a commonly taught element of graduate training in marriage and family therapy or in other counseling programs (outside of seminaries). Carlson (1996) noted that over three-quarters of respondents in his study had not received such training, although many indicated it would be valuable. We suggest that professionals who counsel bereaved parents consider the following:

- Assess your individual comfort level regarding discussion of spiritual matters in a therapeutic setting.
- Consider the importance of spiritually related concerns in the bereavement process with specific clients. The experiences and reactions of clients can be expected to vary widely.
- Determine whether you would like to deal with spiritual issues directly or wish to refer clients to clergy or other spiritual advisors for such discussion.
- If making a referral, ensure that the client and other professional are comfortable with the arrangement. At times a bereaved parent may be feeling angry toward God, clergy, or religious representatives and may wish to discuss their questions with someone outside of the religious or spiritual community.
- Avail oneself of training opportunities related to handling spiritual concerns in the therapeutic setting.

At times particular issues within the therapy context can make it difficult for clients to address the full extent of their grief experiences, which often include questioning of or disappointment with their belief systems and their communities of faith. It is quite possible that both therapists and clients have developed some firmly held general opinions and beliefs about spiritual and/or other religious issues. Such beliefs could include a personal "certainty" in the truth or the impossibility of spiritual and religious experience. To question or even to discuss these issues can quickly bring defenses to the surface, often below the conscious level of interaction. The possibility of imposing one's own beliefs on a client brings up ethical boundaries that therapists should carefully consider as they explore spiritual disillusionment. For example, many therapists feel it is ethically inappropriate to share their own religious or spiritual beliefs in the therapeutic setting with a client. Many of these therapists and others are also uncomfortable with exploring or otherwise including their clients' spiritual or religious beliefs in therapy sessions.

To approach dealing with spiritual disillusionment, professionals should first decide on their own boundaries and then ask the client some questions. Questions to ask might include:

> Are you comfortable talking about the spiritual aspects of your child's loss? Has your child's death affected any religious or spiritual beliefs that you hold? Is the impact of your child's death on your spiritual life something that you would like to discuss?

Such questioning can help in discerning the client's desire to discuss spiritual issues and possible areas of concern or frustration in a spiritual context. For example some people, both therapists and clients, may have previously had negative faith experiences in their lives that are now exacerbated by a child's death. Some issues that clients may wish to explore regarding spiritual struggle or loss of beliefs might include:

- Harsh or difficult experience with religion or religious representatives before, during or after a child's loss.
- Feelings of abandonment or punishment by God.
- Feelings of guilt based on violations of spiritual beliefs after a child's death.
- Discomfort or frustration with spiritual issues and beliefs.
- Loss of spiritual certainty or questioning of spiritual beliefs and practices.

Spiritual Beliefs and Practices as a Coping Resource

Research on spirituality and parental bereavement suggests that spiritual beliefs and practices often serve an important role in helping parents to cope with their grief (Cook & Wimberley, 1983; Knapp, 1986). The influence of such beliefs and practices can range from providing a meaningful framework to understand the child's death to furnishing specific means to remember the child (a worship service in child's honor, etc.). Some patterns of importance from this study include a shift in or deepening of beliefs, the comforting power of specific spiritual ideas or beliefs, and the value of spiritual practices or symbols in the coping process.

In contrast to those who were disappointed in their faith or beliefs, many parents experienced a development or deepening of their beliefs, occasionally after an initial period of questioning. At times it was an already established belief that helped the parent to cope throughout the process of loss, further strengthening their spiritual convictions. For others, experiences before and following the death brought spiritual feelings and beliefs that had not previously been part of their lives. The strength merely to continue to exist through the pain of bereavement often rested on maintaining established religious beliefs. One mother expressed the role of faith as a spiritual resource in her own experience:

> It's been critical. It's been critical. I cannot imagine surviving. I don't mean just surviving emotionally, I can't imagine that I maybe wouldn't have tried to take my life if it had not been for my religious convictions . . . All of those things helped me to be able to release him. Helped me to function again. Helped me not to kill myself.

Religious beliefs also helped some parents find value and meaning in their grief, which in turn seemed to strengthen their beliefs. One mother of Christian belief expressed an increased understanding of her relationship to God as another bereaved parent in these words:

> [My faith was strengthened] through a sense of identifying with deity or what the Lord went through. In fact, that was a parallel through this whole thing. [My daughter] bled from every pore. Our firstborn was taken. It was just . . . those feelings of really identifying with what God must have felt when His Son suffered.

Bereaved parents who find solace or strength in spiritual beliefs thus seem to gain an added coping resource in their grief.

Many parents relied on their belief systems to make sense of death and of the dying process and found comfort in specific spiritual ideas or beliefs. For example, parents often mentioned a comforting belief that the child's death had some meaning as part of a divine plan. This belief recurred throughout the interviews and was actually a combination of intertwined beliefs that there is a "time to die" and a better life beyond the present. One mother stated:

> I knew that it was [my daughter's] time to die, and that she would be fine, and that our faith was not wavering. There was nothing wrong with what we were doing or not doing, and there was nothing wrong with what the doctors were doing. We were all doing our best.

And a father:

> I didn't know what the plan was, but if it's part of a plan and Scott was only going to be here for sixteen years, the fact that we didn't

> know it is irrelevant. But it's part of a plan and my job is to reconcile myself to the plan, not whine about it.

This particular belief that a child's death fits into a spiritual plan with a higher purpose allowed some parents to move beyond feelings of bitterness at the loss. Another aspect of this belief seemed to allow certain parents to conceptualize the timing or form of the child's loss as a merciful event. One father who expressed his view that his young child had gone to a "better place" also suggested that perhaps if his child "could bypass all the stresses and troubles in this life, I would think it would be a blessing." A mother, whose daughter had a brain tumor but died of another illness, considered it an act of divine benevolence that her daughter's death was much less painful and drawn-out than it might have been:

> One of my conclusions has been, and was even at that time in the hospital, that dying from the [complications] saved her the agony of having to die of a brain tumor and I was grateful for that. I always prayed that God would not allow her to suffer, and in a way maybe that was the answer.

This is one example of a specific spiritual concept or idea that is commonly grasped upon by parents seeking to make sense of a child's death and to find avenues for accepting the loss. The belief that a child's passing fits into a greater plan allows some parents to find meaning and acceptance that might otherwise be difficult to achieve.

Another spiritual belief that was almost universally cited by bereaved parents was a certainty that the deceased child was still part of the family, and although absent, would always retain membership in the family. Frequently the family connection was expected to continue as a parent-child relationship after the parents themselves passed away. This spiritual idea seemed to convey reassurance and hope to those who expressed it, rather than a sense that the child was gone forever. For some parents the child's status was nebulous while for others with a more explicit belief system it seemed to be very clear. A father in the study commented that he just "accepts the idea that [his child] is gone and that he's doing something someplace else," a rather general statement of the belief. Another mother stated:

> This probably gets into my own personal religious beliefs, and every family will be different, but I do believe that Laura lives. I believe that I will [see] her again in the resurrection.

This expressed belief in the continuation of a person's existence after death has a strong spiritual component and shapes a parent's view of how they can relate to the experience of a child's death. It leaves the door open for further family connections in a future context. A mother who lost her young adult son said:

> I know that he is around. If I honestly felt that Jeff had ceased to exist, I wouldn't know what to do. I've had to come to the conclusion that I'm not leaving [him] behind . . . we're not leaving Jeff behind at all. I feel Jeff has moved on and has just gone ahead of us. He just went ahead of us.

This spiritual belief was commonly expressed among parents we interviewed and seemed to hold a great deal of comfort for parents who held it. The idea that a child still lived elsewhere and could possibly be seen again was a positive, comforting spiritual concept.

Another avenue through which spirituality acted for some parents as a coping resource was in their involvement in certain spiritual practices. These practices ranged from prayer to meditation to religious worship, but the common theme in the parents' experience was that the practice provided a method by which they could express their emotions and seek comfort or direction in their mourning. One mother whose daughter was in the hospital for several weeks before dying noted how helpful it was for the hospital to provide a room where she or other family members could go to pray at different times. Similarly, another mother instinctively turned to her faith for guidance and found the strength to "let go" as her child was dying. This spiritual act also brought comfort to her through the period following the death:

> It has meant a lot to me in my life since then that in the worst process of my life, my most immediate reaction was to pray for help. It came to me immediately what I should pray for, and I remember that it was striking to me that I should not pray for the life of my son.

The value of a spiritual gift from a friend from another culture was reported by one father as a strengthening influence for him:

> The tribe's spiritual leader made me a medicine bag and he drove all over the reservation and had it in some sort of ceremony where it was blessed . . . He said, "Take this medicine bag and put some-

> thing in there and never tell anyone what it is." . . . For the first time since the accident I felt like I could function. So I still wear it. I still wear it every day. I've added things to it that mean something to me, but it's a very important part of me and it's helped me to cope a lot.

These examples display the vital role that spiritual beliefs and practices can play in the coping process for some bereaved parents. Whether it is the belief in a divine plan or the use of a medicine bag, these spiritual avenues of coping provide an important resource that is available to those who have lost a loved one. Helping professionals need to realize the importance of this resource in the lives of many persons and the role it can play in the healing process.

Therapeutic Implications

A starting point for helping professionals in addressing this topic may be simply to acknowledge the significance of spiritual beliefs and practices for some bereaved parents. A client's spiritual feelings and values have sometimes been overlooked as a factor in treatment. Moules (2000) suggests that "it is a relatively recent development in family therapy that people are asked about their spiritual beliefs and are invited into conversations that explore how these beliefs might contribute to or reduce suffering" (p. 238). Yet when religious faith or beliefs are included in therapy, the role is most likely to be as a coping mechanism. Professionals can begin the process of addressing spirituality as a coping resource for clients by making its discussion an explicit part of their practice.

Including the role of spirituality in therapy when counseling the bereaved can be facilitated through a variety of means. Some suggestions to consider include:

- Suggest that some persons experiencing loss find comfort in their spiritual beliefs and practices. Let the client know if you are open to this topic and, if so, express a willingness to discuss it.
- Ask if a client has particular spiritual beliefs or religious rituals associated with loss of a family member that are meaningful to them. Allow the client to explore the meaning and value of such beliefs or rituals.
- Encourage the client, if they are receptive, to think about their own or others' past experience in using spiritual beliefs and practices

when dealing with loss. Ask what they felt was helpful and what may not have been in this context.

Professionals may open the door to exploration of spirituality as a resource by asking questions that prompt reflection and allow the client to freely choose whether to address the topic. An important consideration may be to help a person explore spiritual beliefs or ideas they may hold that are not necessarily associated with a specific creed or religious system.

Acknowledging the role of spirituality and asking open-ended questions can broaden the range of coping resources available to a client. This can be shown by a specific example. In one family counseling session, a therapist who happened to be a non-observant Jew was working with a Christian family. The therapist knew that prayer in the family setting was important in this family's faith, and so at the end of one session asked if they wanted to join in a prayer together. The family acknowledged they would like to do so. The therapist then asked a family member who was particularly struggling to arrange the family for the prayer in a family "sculpturing" arrangement that was most meaningful to him and to be the voice for the feelings of the prayer. This family later recounted how grateful they were to the therapist for his sensitivity to the importance of their spiritual values and how helpful that particular experience had been in their healing process. This example suggests that skillful professionals can learn to incorporate spiritual beliefs and practices as coping resources for bereaved persons in specific circumstances.

Spiritual Connections with Children

Beyond the comfort and hope expressed by parents who believe that a deceased child is still a family member and that the relationship will continue, many parents reported experiencing a more immediate and consistent spiritual connection with the deceased child. These feelings of parent-child spiritual connection were expressed in different ways and seem to reflect Moules' (2000) suggestion of "a sacred and spiritual unity that ties us to each other as humans and intimately ties us to a world that is greater than or certainly more than human" (p. 229). Klass (1999) has written that understanding the bereaved parent's spiritual relationship with the deceased child is often at the heart of the bereavement process. Study participants often shared stories of spiritual connection as part of, or following, more general discussions of the different things they had done to maintain a parenting relationship or to memorialize the child. This sense of spiritual connection was expressed in varying contexts that included mental dialogue with the child, visiting locations that prompted memories of the child, dreams, and spiritual manifestations of the child to the parent or other family members.

A number of parents described talking to the deceased child and suggested it was a one-way mental conversation by them toward the child that included a feeling of emotional connection. These parents, in essence, continue a dialogue with the departed child in which the child's response is a sense of involvement or a presence. These conversations can occur in any location or for particular reasons, but seem to hold a valuable place for some parents. Some parents merely wanted to reach out to the child while others sought the child's attention to certain issues. One father expressed his sense of connection as a rather constant occurrence:

> I don't know that I do anything necessarily to try to remain connected because it's something that's never too far away from me. There are times when you feel an extra presence that time and experience tell you who it is and what it is. On occasions that are special to the family for one reason or another, you still feel a presence and know that they are aware and part of what is happening. They are still interested in you, just like you are interested in them.

In a somewhat different circumstance, a mother in the study carried on a mental dialogue with her deceased son to prompt his attention to family concerns or needs:

> When my [living] daughter has had some physical problems, such as before she went in to have her baby, I said, "Tell Greg [deceased son] to do such-and-such" and I was telling him, too. Now, that's a head trip but it still is something that makes you feel a little more powerful in a powerless situation. It is comforting. I can't sit here and say it isn't true. So far it's worked. So far those planes have landed okay and we've all survived.

The usefulness of this sense of connection to some parents is embodied in her statement that such dialogue can bring a sense of comfort under conditions of concern.

It is also common for parents to find or create a special or symbolic location where they can feel more directly connected to their child. This seems to allow the parent a convenient source of comfort when grief is strong or when they simply wish to feel close to the departed child. It may involve visiting the cemetery or another spot that recalls the child. One mother who built a memorial garden to her daughter said:

> The memorial garden [we created for her] . . . so that to me is very special because I can go out there and talk to her and really feel her presence when I'm there.

Parents who discussed this type of experience often referred to feeling close to the child and even having a spiritual sense of the child's presence or attention. A father whose son died after being struck by a car later commented on how he felt spiritually close to his son:

> I was never very much a church-oriented spiritual person, but I still felt some sort of spirituality about a person and their presence and their place in the universe . . . I remember asking the earth to take his presence and bless him, and to put it into Oregon so that I could be with him. So when I go to all these wild places I feel like he's right there and I feel like he's got his arms around me. If I'm feeling very depressed and blue, or just stressed at work or around the house, then I know it's time to go and talk to [my son]. I go to some of these wild places and I come back feeling very much refreshed by that sense of being there with him. If you go to the top of Jones Peak on a very windy day with the rain slashing at you . . . that's him. He's right there. To watch the sunset or the seagulls flying along the surf . . . that's [my son]. He's right there. I feel very strongly and passionately about that.

The parents' sense of connection in these descriptions is very focused on feeling the child's presence or influence in a spiritual or metaphysical way. Also, the descriptions suggest that parents visit these locations to achieve a sense of closeness when they are under stress or deeply miss the child and want to re-establish a sense of connection. These patterns can be useful for professionals to understand in discerning how a bereaved parent may approach the post-death relationship with a child.

Dreams represented another means by which parents made a connection with or became aware of the on-going involvement of the deceased child in their lives. Dreams involving deceased children take various forms and one researcher described them as an example of the "parents' continuing interaction with the inner representation of the dead child" (Klass, 1993, p. 255). Parents who felt a dream was significant, however, usually differentiated between memories of the lost child in a dream and dream-state encounters that were more vivid and focused. Such dreams often were described as providing a chance for communication or reassurance from the deceased child to the parent. For example, one mother reported:

> When I was by myself one night I remember dreaming about her and stroking her hair. She was wearing her favorite pajamas. I remember talking to her and saying, "Why don't you go and take a shower and we'll go shopping." She sat up and I remember saying to her, "Oh, by the way, what do you think of the memorial garden I made for you?" It seemed to trouble me that I was mentioning the memorial garden to her when I was going to take her shopping. Then she looked back, and it's the only time she's ever said anything to me, and she said, "Mom, I can't stay. I've got to go." That was it. So I know that she's with me all the time.

In this example, the dream served as a gentle way to combine the seemingly incompatible concepts of the child as both lost and continually present. Such dreams with a strong spiritual component seem to be a common occurrence among bereaved parents (Sormanti & August, 1997).

In addition to the varying means of spiritual connection just described, many parents reported a more tangible, though still spiritual, connection with the child including auditory, visual, or other sensory experiences following the child's death. These experiences were common and involved a feeling of "presence" or extra-sensory awareness of the child. These included both the experiences of parents themselves and of others close to them such as family members. In nearly every case there was a complete belief on the part of the parent that the experience was a tangible and real interaction with the deceased child in some manner. However, many also made reference to the probability that others would not accept their experiences. Whether subjectively real or not, each parent was deeply comforted by the encounters and other manifestations. Receiving sensory input such as hearing the child's voice or laughter, feeling a familiar touch, or recognizing the child's scent, were the most often mentioned forms of manifestation. A mother shared this experience with her deceased daughter:

> Now [talking to her is] not so much a two-way exchange, as much as I'm talking and she's listening. Sometimes if I'm really, really quiet I hear her singing. She loved to sing.

In another circumstance a father described the sense of his son's spiritual presence:

> There was one other specific experience where I knew he had been in the house. In fact, I knew right where he was and where he was standing. I don't know how to explain how I knew as much as . . . it was my senses. I smelled him, in fact, I think it was actually the smell that woke me up. I'm not sensitive with my nose and I would not, for the most part, say that you can identify an individual by his or her smell. Yet we do, we have our own smells that are unique to us, and he did and I knew that he was standing right by me. So there are those times, as well as the times when you feel the presence, the peacefulness, especially at family events and rites of passage, weddings and such things when you know they're there for it.

This type of sensory perception of a departed child's presence furnishes emotional comfort to many parents who describe it and provides a strong linkage to the child.

Some parents described even more vivid visual manifestations that involved the presence of their departed child. The parents always emphasized that these visual contacts were completely distinguishable from dreams in that, without doubt, they had been awake when the visitations happened. It is also notable that none of these accounts, regardless of the length, involved the mixing of reality and unreality common to dreams (i.e., suddenly shifting scenes, becoming aware that the person they were talking to had already died, or any other distortions of probability in addition to the manifestation itself). One mother whose daughter died in a car accident was comforted by this experience shortly after the child's death:

> I was thinking of her and suddenly it was as though she came [through the door]. There was a man with her and he was taller. They came right towards us. She stood there at the side of the bed looking down at me and at my husband. As I reached [toward her], it seemed like the man turned Alice away and they walked off down the hall. I think that experience really gave me a little comfort. We have prayed often in the past that we'll see her again, and even today we do that.

This mother's account notes the comforting nature of the experience and also her prayerful efforts and hope that it might occur again, which is somewhat notable since it had been many years since the child's passing. Another mother told of an extensive and multi-sensory contact with her recently deceased daughter

> So we went shopping . . . and all of a sudden there was Beth. She was pointing at something that she wanted me to buy her. I thought, "Am I dreaming?" I looked at my watch and it was 3:00 in the afternoon. I thought, "No." I remember that she grabbed my elbow. When she and I went shopping we always walked with our arms together. She just enjoyed doing that. I remember that she pulled me and I remember actually stopping. She wanted to put her arm in mine. I remember when she did that feeling that this was really weird, and then there were more tears . . . It was okay. We walked around and Beth was there. In fact, I could smell her perfume. She always had this special brand of perfume that she used, and all of a sudden that perfume was really overpowering and I knew she was there.

Note the mother's self-questioning before she accepted the experience and the strong emotional impact that she described. These manifestations represent distinctive spiritual encounters which may have a substantive influence on a bereaved parent's thoughts and feelings as they deal with grief. Helping professionals should be aware of such potential occurrences and find ways to help bereaved parents address their impact on coping with a child's loss.

Therapeutic Implications

The continuing sense of connection between a parent and a deceased child is a powerful part of many parents' grieving processes. This can also be the most useful and the most difficult part of a therapeutic relationship. The spiritual belief that the deceased child remains a part of the family can give parents comfort in believing that the bonds of love continue beyond death. This sense of connection also provides a feeling that the child is still aware of the words and behaviors of the parents. This awareness makes it possible for the parent to continue the relationship in a variety of important and potentially healing ways. They can talk to the child with a trust that their words are heard, giving them the opportunity to resolve unfinished issues and to keep the child involved in the on-going family process. They can continue to include the child as a participant/witness in meaningful family events and rituals. Perhaps most important to many parents, they can memorialize the child in a way that is tangible to the parent and can feel the child's acceptance of the memorial efforts. Each of these and other forms of connection can mediate the effects of bereavement and aid in resolution of grief. While some models of grief and coping after a loss have suggested that parents must somehow disengage themselves emotionally after a child's loss to move on (Brotherson, 2000), more recent work has suggested that bereaved parents benefit from "saying hello" again to their departed children (White, 1988). It may be that parents who incorporate this attachment into their lives in a new and different way are helped in the grieving process (Klass, Silverman, & Nickman, 1996; White, 1988), and it therefore seems important for therapists or counselors to consider interventions that allow for exploration of such a sense of spiritual connection.

In addition to the general sense of connection described, the actual experiences of feeling, hearing, or seeing a departed child were cited by many parents in our study. These manifestations were credited as a source of strength that helped them to cope better with the loss. Although sensory connection with a child was reported as a positive, healing experience, it is in this area that the continued parent-child connection can become the most difficult part of a successful therapeutic relationship. Many professionals may not have been exposed to this aspect of the grief experience. Also, those who have received any training may have been indoctrinated to the professional belief that such experiences are, at best, "wishful hallucinations" that will go away when they are no longer needed. Such experiences tend to be represented in much research as a "psychological representation" or a "hallucination" of the parent's senses, rather than as an actual interaction with the continuing embodiment of the deceased child (Klass, 1993; Rees, 1975). Parents are often encouraged to realize that these visitations are not actually possible and that a healthy resolution of grief will involve a return to "reality." For example, one mother in the study reported such an experience to her therapist and was told, "Well, you've healed enough that you don't need that any more." The balance between a parent's personal description and belief about an event and a professional's interpretation of such an event can be delicate. In dealing with spiritual matters related to a child's loss, professionals may need to realize that mothers or fathers who report such experiences generally feel they are tangible and real interactions.

It has not been uncommon for bereaved persons who do not "move on" beyond their connections to a deceased family member to be diagnosed as suffering from "delayed grief" or "pathological mourning." Sormanti and August (1997) suggest, however, that bereaved parents may follow a unique grieving process which involves inclusion of such connections. Labeling or treating sensory manifestations as possibly pathological poses at least two immediate impediments to therapeutic intervention. Whether the manifestations are provably real or in fact hallucinatory is not of immediate concern. In either case, the parents are first robbed of the ability to use this form of connection as a coping mechanism in the easing of their grief. At the same time, they are given the message that it is unacceptable for them to express honestly their own experiences with their child's death. Rather than being open and feeling accepted in the therapy process, parents may be guarded about disclosures to avoid making statements that will put their mental health into question and risk rejection, ridicule, or correction. Therapists are taught to treat a variety of client disclosures and confessions with a non-judgmental attitude. When counseling bereaved parents, professionals ought also to treat their clients' spiritual discussions with such deference.

The availability of formal training opportunities for professionals related to dealing with spirituality in therapy is desirable but still limited (Carlson, 1996). But in addition to the limited formal training available, therapists may also be hampered by their involvement in the modern Western culture. Ironically, ours is a culture in which psychics and mediums are openly consulted by people from all social strata, including public figures from movie stars to politicians. Yet, when an individual dies those who are left to grieve often find themselves surrounded by persons who are uncomfortable or dismissive of the emotional trauma surrounding such a loss. Discussion of death and its related emotions, particularly the spiritual elements of the experience, may be hampered in a culture where persons tend to avoid, discount, or otherwise discourage exploration of death in all of its aspects. Also, the culture is outwardly tolerant of an increasingly broad range of spiritual beliefs while continuing to be uncomfortable with spiritual or religious conversations. An oft-repeated maxim states that "to avoid a fight, it's best not to discuss a person's politics or religion." Therapists without sufficient training in the spiritual aspects of grief counseling may be left to rely on their own, often confused and reactive, cultural training. Unfortunately, the major interventions would then be to "avoid or debate" the experiences. The spiritual dimensions of a parent's bereavement experience may have both similarities and differences to those of another person, and professionals need to be sufficiently open to spirituality to provide a safe venue for exploring its role in a person's coping.

Lack of Support or Rejection by Others

The type of support given to parents who have lost a child is a critical factor in the grief and coping process. Various types of formal and informal sources of support are important to bereaved parents, but a concern is that they may often be left without those social and emotional supports desirable for coping with a child's loss (Rando, 1985). Parents who feel victimized by a child's loss often feel even more discouraged if they cannot gain support which is critically needed from friends, clergy or counseling professionals. They may feel that they have to do the hard work of teaching others how to relate to them and their concerns. This can be particularly true when dealing with spiritual issues and bereavement. Two issues that arise for bereaved parents related to this topic are perceived lack of support for their spiritual perceptions about the loss and lack of support by those in the faith community.

Feelings of rejection or lack of support are often expressed by bereaved parents following a child's loss. For many, this takes the form of a relatively typical social reaction to uncomfortable situations. When faced with illness, impending death, or actual bereavement and grief, it is common for people in our society to withdraw by avoiding the topic as much as is possible. Bereaved parents sometimes feel rejected or isolated when others avoid them, chastise them for grieving "too long," or hesitate to discuss a child's death so as not to bring up an uncomfortable topic (Rando, 1985). Parents are often aware that others may feel uncomfortable but still are discouraged when others ignore their child's loss. One mother explained:

> There are those who don't want to [talk about the experiences] and even apologize for bringing it up, but to me it's an expression of them not understanding the experience and they can't. It's something you can't understand if you haven't gone through it.

For some parents the experience of rejection seemed to be more related to what was perceived as a dismissive explanation of spiritual experience. The discomfort people feel related to death is greatly compounded when a spiritual aspect is involved in the grieving process. Discussion of the spiritual facets of experience can be difficult for many people, whether it is related to a religious connection or not. The following excerpt from our study shows the increased expectation of rejection felt by one mother. Even while describing her spiritual experience, she seems to be protesting its validity and value, showing an awareness that others would offer a more psychologically based interpretation. This preoccupation with how others might perceive her spiritual account engendered a kind of subtle defensiveness:

> Every time I went into that room I could feel her presence. I can't explain it . . . I mean, it was a good feeling. It wasn't disturbing to me or anything. I just remember going up . . . one day, and it wasn't there. At that point it felt like I'd walked into a door. So I'm sure that people who don't believe in the spirit would say that was the day I realized she wasn't coming back, except that it wasn't as though I was going there for comfort. I was going there to get a spool of thread! I still had [visitors] downstairs and it wasn't like I could go up there and spend time.

Many bereaved parents worry about whether their grief experiences are "normal," and this seems especially to be important as they consider the spiritual dimensions of their loss experience. Parents may be reluctant to share their reliance on spiritual concepts or experiences in the coping process because they are unsure how others will perceive or react to them.

Another context in which parents sometimes felt lack of support or even rejection was by their clergy or by their communities of faith. This may be especially difficult for those who currently or previously had relied explicitly on such sources of support. Bereaved parents are often caught in a paradox as they question God's mercy or feel anger toward God but also desire to find comfort within a spiritual context. The personal confusion associated with such a paradox can be compounded when they feel unsupported by persons within their spiritual community. Some parents described encounters in which it was implied that the child's death or the parent's extended grief was related to a deficit in the faith of the parent. Rather than motivating or comforting the parents, these contacts were likely to produce anxiety and even anger on the part of bereaved parents. For example, a mother recounted the following experience as her daughter lay dying in the hospital:

> One of her teachers and his wife, who were Christian, came up and felt very strongly that we needed to pray harder. They felt that we

> weren't doing all that we needed to do. The news of her being ill just devastated the school, the community, and the church in our area because she was very well known in a lot of circles . . . so I was real devastated when he left . . . There was nothing wrong with what we were doing or not doing . . . we were all doing our best. In fact, the doctors gave us a little conference room there that we called our "prayer room." We would go in and pray and pray, and our family would come in and pray with us.

While the mother concluded after some reflection that she was not guilty of a "lack of faith," that assertion from a person whom she expected to receive support from was emotionally difficult. Others within a faith community may unrealistically or arbitrarily impose expectations about how the bereaved parent should think or behave during the grief process. A mother commented:

> My church does not understand. They expect me to be able to go down there. That's another change in me. I cannot find one more mask on the wall to take down and put on for other people.

Her feeling that associating with her faith community would require a masking of her emotions and grief reactions demonstrates the sense of isolation she experienced in this context. Such a sense of feeling rejected or unsupported poses a challenge for helping professionals who deal with bereaved parents.

Therapeutic Implications

By the time bereaved parents seek out a therapist, they have likely experienced rejection by some of the people in their various community networks. Often they will have tried to talk through their grief with a number of family members, friends, and others in their lives. These potential sources of support may at times instead give the message that their grief is overly extensive, unnatural, and/or burdensome. It can be even more difficult to find supporters who are willing to allow the grieving parents to talk about the spiritual aspects of their mourning. At this point the parent may seek out therapy, often for depression or failure to adequately adjust to their loss.

Therapists, as members of society, may not be socially comfortable with religious or spiritual conversation outside of a church or a debate. It is also often unlikely that they will have had any training or experience with appropriately including spiritual topics in therapy sessions. Therapists who have not worked through their personal issues related to death, grief, and spirituality–and their place in therapy–may inadvertently add to their clients' experiences of rejection. Parents who have lost a child are sensitive to the response they get from others regarding the spiritual components of their loss. Yet caring professionals can make a genuine difference in providing support to bereaved parents and helping them not feel rejected. Professionals should try to:

- Provide a safe forum for parents to share their feelings.
- Help bereaved parents to understand the commonality of spiritual dimensions of loss and ease any feelings of anxiety.
- Validate clients' spiritual experiences as credible and "normalize" their occurrence in the grief process as a way to help them keep the deceased in their lives.
- Allow them to explore, challenge, redefine, or reject their belief systems in a non-judgmental atmosphere can be helpful as they cope with the loss.
- Avoid negative responses that may interfere with a client's treatment, such as focusing only on the symptomatic factors sometimes associated with spiritual elements of loss, like sleep interference or dysphoria.
- Be careful in labeling spiritual feelings and manifestations as "hallucinations," "defense mechanisms," "denial of reality," or similar terms that may be used to pathologize, and thereby reject, the client's experience.

One way that professionals may avoid their own discomfort has been to make a "treatment boundary" in which they decide that they will treat emotional or relationship issues, but refer "spiritual things" to the clergy, as outside of their scope of practice. It is important to remember that some clients may have already had negative or unsuccessful interactions with clergy prior to entering therapy. They may also have ambivalent or negative feelings toward God and other spiritual factors. Sending clients to clergy for the "spiritual stuff" may, then, be sending them back to a source of discomfort for some persons. Even when there has been little or no contact with the clergy prior to therapy, a client may prefer to discuss their negative spiritual feelings with a more neutral person. It may be extremely uncomfortable to contemplate telling a priest or minister that they have lost their faith and blame God for their loss, or that they feel rejected or misunderstood by their faith community. A referral, which the client might never follow through with, could leave them with virtually no one to talk to about these very upsetting issues. It is also important to remember that a person could very well have spiritual experiences, but have no affiliation with a clergy member. Professionals should take steps to arrange an appropriate setting for bereaved parents to discuss spiritual concerns, either by preparing themselves for such discussion or helping the person to contact a professional who is willing to work with them on such concerns.

CONCLUSION

Coping with a child's loss represents one of the most trying challenges that a parent can face. In this process it is not unusual for parents to encounter and explore varied reactions to the spiritual dimensions of such an experience. While this study did not directly set out to address spiritual dimensions of parental bereavement, the fact that religious or otherwise spiritual experiences were spontaneously reported by all of the participants highlighted many things that must be considered by those who work with such families prior to or following the death of a child. Such issues can include a struggle with or loss of particular beliefs, spiritual beliefs and practices as a coping resource, a sense of spiritual connection with the departed child, or lack of support for or rejection of these spiritual aspects.

The need for someone to understand and let the sufferer express themselves and be vulnerable is nearly universal for those grieving the loss of a loved one. Therapists, grief counselors, clergy, and others who work with the bereaved must be prepared to address spiritual dimensions of loss in addition to other concerns. The therapeutic setting can be a place where the bereaved parent feels they do not need to wear a mask and can safely share their feelings, but only if helping professionals furnish a comfortable arena for such discussion. This can be difficult, however, if the therapist is unprepared to deal with spiritual questions or seems non-receptive due to personal discomfort, a tendency to pathologize, or a lack of openness to spiritual topics. As every therapist is likely, during the course of a career, to encounter at least a few clients who are dealing with grief issues, we suggest it could be beneficial to make whatever preparations are necessary to understand and assist those who wish to explore the spiritual dimensions of their loss experience.

REFERENCES

Bergin, A. E., & Jensen, S. P. (1990). Religiosity of psychotherapists: A national survey. *Psychotherapy*, *27*, 3-7.

Bergin, A., Masters, K., Stinchfield, R., Gaskin, T., Sullivan, C., Reynolds, E., & Greaves, D. (1997). Religious life-styles and mental health. In L. B. Brown (Ed.), *Religion, personality, and mental health* (pp. 120-136). New York: Springer.

Bernstein, J. R. (1997). *When the bough breaks: Forever after the death of a son or daughter*. Kansas City: Andrews and McMeel.

Binger, C. M., Ablin, A. R., Feurerstein, R. C., Kushner, J. H., Zoger, S., & Mikkelsen, C. (1969). Childhood leukemia: Emotional impact on patient and family. *New England Journal of Medicine*, *280*, 414-418.

Bowlby, J. (1980). *Attachment and loss: Loss, sadness and depression* (Vol. 3). New York: Basic Books.

Brabant, S., Forsyth, C., & McFarlain, G. (1995). Life after the death of a child: Initial and long term support from others. *Omega: The Journal of Death and Dying*, *31*(1), 67-85.

Brotherson, S. E. (2000). *Parental accounts of a child's death: Influences on parental identity and behavior*. Unpublished doctoral dissertation, Oregon State University, Corvallis, Oregon.

Calhoun, L. G., & Tedeschi, R. G. (1989). Positive aspects of critical life problems: Recollections of grief. *Omega: The Journal of Death and Dying*, *20*, 265-272.

Carlson, T. D. (1996). *Religion, spirituality, and marriage and family therapy*. Unpublished master's thesis, Purdue University, Calumet, Illinois.

Choron, J. (1964). *Modern man and mortality*. New York: MacMillan.

Cook, J. A., & Wimberley, D. W. (1983). If I should die before I wake: Religious commitment and adjustment to the death of a child. *Journal for the Scientific Study of Religion*, *22*(3), 222-238.

Dollahite, D. C., Hawkins, A. J., & Brotherson, S. E. (1996). Narrative accounts, generative fathering, and family life education. In M. B. Sussmann & J. F. Gilgun (Eds.), *The methods and methodologies of qualitative family research* (pp. 349-368). New York: The Haworth Press, Inc.

Edelstein, L. (1984). *Maternal bereavement: Coping with the unexpected death of a child*. New York: Praeger Publishers.

Edmonds, S. A. (1993). *Perceived changes following bereavement: A comparison of Pan Am Flight 103 parents to college students*. Unpublished doctoral dissertation, Syracuse University, Syracuse, New York.

Engel, G. (1972). Grief and grieving. In L. Schwartz & S. Schwartz (Eds.), *The psychodynamics of patient care*. New York: Prentice Hall.

Fenichel, O. (1945). *The psychoanalytic theory of neurosis*. New York: Norton.

Finkbeiner, A. K. (1996). *After the death of a child: Living with loss through the years*. New York: The Free Press.

Fitzgerald (1994). *The mourning handbook*.

Freud, S. (1917). Mourning and melancholia. In *A general selection from the works of Sigmund Freud*. New York: Doubleday Anchor Books.

Glaser, B. G., & Strauss, A. L. (1967). *The discovery of grounded theory: Strategies for qualitative research*. New York: Aldine de Gruyter.

Hodge, D. R. (2000). Spiritual ecomaps: A new diagrammatic tool for assessing marital and family spirituality. *Journal of Marital and Family Therapy, 26*(2), 217-228.

Holmes, T. H., & Rahe, R. H. (1967). The Social Readjustment Rating scale. *Journal of Psychosomatic Research, 11*, 213-218.

Kalish, R. A. (1981). *Death, grief, and caring relationships*. Monterey, CA: Brooks/Cole Publishing Company.

Kalish, R. A. & Reynolds, D. K. (1981). *Death and ethnicity: A psychocultural study*. Amityville, NY: Baywood Publishing Company.

Klass, D. (1991). Religious aspects in the resolution of parental grief: Solace and social support. *Prevention in Human Services, 10*(1), 187-209.

Klass, D. (1993). The inner representation of the dead child and the worldviews of bereaved parents. *Omega, 26*(4), 25-272.

Klass, D. (1999). *The spiritual lives of bereaved parents*. Philadelphia: Brunner/Mazel.

Klass, D., Silverman, P. R., & Nickman, S. L. (Eds.). (1996). *Continuing bonds: New understandings of grief*. Washington, DC: Taylor & Francis.

Knapp, R. J. (1986). *Beyond endurance: When a child dies*. New York: Schocken Books.

Kubler-Ross, E. (1969). *On death and dying*. New York: Macmillan.

Larson, D., & Larson, S. (1992). *The forgotten factor in physical and mental health: What does the research show?* Arlington, VA: National Institute for Healthcare Research.

Lincoln, Y. S., & Guba, E. G. (1985). *Naturalistic inquiry*. Beverly Hills, CA: Sage.

Lindemann, E. (1944). Symptomatology and management of acute grief. *American Journal of Psychiatry, 101*, 141-148.

Miles, M. S., & Crandall, E. K. B. (1986). The search for meaning and its potential for affecting growth in bereaved parents. In R. H. Moos (Ed.), *Coping with life crises: An integrated approach* (pp. 235-243). New York: Plenum Press.

Miles, M. S., & Huberman, A. M. (1994). *Qualitative data analysis*. Thousand Oaks, CA: Sage Publications.

Miles, M. S. & Perry, K. (1985). Parental responses to sudden accidental death of a child. *Critical Care Quarterly, 8*, 73-84.

Moules, N. J. (2000). Postmodernism and the sacred: Reclaiming connection in our greater-than-human worlds. *Journal of Marital and Family Therapy, 26*(2), 229-240.

Nielsen, J. M. (Ed.). (1990). *Feminist research methods*. Boulder, CO: Westview Press.

Parkes, C. M. (1986). *Bereavement: Studies of grief in adult life* (2nd American ed.). Madison, CT: International Universities Press.

Parkes, C. M. (1988a). Bereavement as a psychosocial transition: Processes of adaptation to change. *Journal of Social Issues, 44*(3), 53-65.

Parkes, C. M. (1988b). Research: Bereavement. *Omega, 18*(4), 365-377.

Patterson, J., Hayworth, M., Turner, C., & Raskin, M. (2000). Spiritual issues in family therapy: A graduate-level course. *Journal of Marital and Family Therapy, 26*(2), 199-210.

Pollock, G. N. (1961). Mourning and adaptation. *International Journal of Psychoanalysis, 43*, 341-361.

Prest, L. A., & Keller, J. F. (1993). Spirituality and family therapy: Spiritual beliefs, myths, and metaphors. *Journal of Marital and Family Therapy, 19*, 137-148.

Prest, L. A. & Russell, R. (1995). Spirituality in training, practice, and personal development. Unpublished paper.

Rando, T. R. (1985). Bereaved parents: Particular difficulties, unique factors, and treatment issues. *Social Work, 30*(1), Jan-Feb, 19-23.

Rando, T. R. (Ed.). (1986). *Parental loss of a child: Clinical and research considerations*. Champaign, Illinois: Research Press.

Rees, W. D. (1975). The bereaved and their hallucinations. In B. Schoenberg et al. (Eds.), *Bereavement: Its psychosocial aspects* (pp. 66-71). New York: Columbia University Press.

Rubin, S. (1993). The death of a child is forever: The life course impact of child loss. In M. S. Stroebe, W. Stroebe, & R. O. Hanson (Eds.), *Handbook of bereavement* (pp. 285-299). New York: Cambridge University Press.

Sanders, C. M. (1989). *Grief: The mourning after*. New York: John Wiley & Sons.

Shanfield, S. B., Benjamin, G. A. H., & Swain, B. J. (1984). Parents' reactions to the death of an adult child from cancer. *American Journal of Psychiatry, 141*, 1092-1094.

Shapiro, E. R. (1994). *Grief as a family process: A developmental approach to clinical practice*. New York: Guilford Press.

Simon-Buller, S., Christopherson, V. A., & Jones, R. A. (1989). Correlates of sensing the presence of a deceased spouse. *Omega: The Journal of Death and Dying, 19*(1), 21-30.

Sormanti, M., & August, J. (1997). Parental bereavement: Spiritual connections with deceased children. *American Journal of Orthopsychiatry, 67*(3), 460-469.

Steere, D. A. (1997). *Spiritual presence in psychotherapy: A guide for caregivers*. New York: Brunner/Mazel.

Sullivan, H. L. (1956). The dynamics of emotion. In H. L. Sullivan (Ed.), *Clinical studies in psychiatry*. New York: W. W. Norton & Company.

Talbot, K. (1999). Mothers now childless: Personal transformation after the death of an only child. *Omega: The Journal of Death and Dying, 38*(3), 167-186.

Tesch, R. (1990). *Qualitative research: Analysis types and software tools*. Bristol, PA: The Falmer Press.

Videka-Sherman, L. (1982). Coping with the death of a child: A study over time. *American Journal of Orthopsychiatry, 52*, 688-698.

Walker, J. A. (1996). Learning to be interpretive: Hermeneutics and personal texts. In M. B. Sussman & J. F. Gilgun (Eds.), *The methods and methodologies of qualitative family research* (pp. 223-239). New York: The Haworth Press, Inc.

Watson, W. H. (1997). Soul and system: The integrative possibilities of family therapy. *Journal of Psychology and Theology, 25*(1), 123-135.

Weiss, R. S. (1988). Loss and recovery. *The Journal of Social Issues, 44*(3), 37-52.

Wheeler, I. (1994). The role of meaning and purpose in life in bereaved parents associated with a self-help group: Compassionate Friends. *Omega, 28*(4), 261-271.

Widdershoven, G. A. M. (1993). The story of life: Hermeneutic perspectives on the relationship between narrative and life history. *The Narrative Study of Lives, 1*, 1-20.

Worden, J. W. (1982). *Grief counseling and grief therapy: A handbook for the mental health practitioner* (1st ed.). New York: Springer.

Spirituality and Meaning: A Qualitative Inquiry with Caregivers of Alzheimer's Disease

Angela L. Smith
Jennifer Harkness

SUMMARY. Alzheimer's disease has been described as a complex chronic illness that is known to cause significant stress for its caregivers. It has created dramatic role alterations in families, has increasingly more biopsychosocial demands as it progresses, and often taxes caregivers to the point of compromising their own health and well-being. This study used qualitative analyses to explore the stories of Alzheimer's caregivers. Of the 45 caregivers interviewed, all but nine mention an expression or significant event related to spirituality, whether religious or secular in nature. Specifically, twelve caregivers described a negative experience with their spiritual community, whereas twenty-four shared positive encounters. Findings supported the incorporation of a biopsychosocial-spiritual model of healthcare to optimize caregiver well-being. Recommendations were given to assist family therapists in including spiritual beliefs and faith communities in the design and delivery of services.

Angela L. Smith and Jennifer Harkness are Assistant Professors, Marriage and Family Therapy Program, Department of Child Development and Family Relations, School of Human Environmental Sciences, East Carolina University.

Address correspondence to: Angela L. Smith, Marriage and Family Therapy Program, 251-C Rivers Building, East Carolina University, Greenville, North Carolina 27858-4353 (E-mail: smithang@mail.ecu.edu).

Portions of this paper were presented at the 1st Annual National Hospice Organization Conference on February 21, 2000, in Nashville, TN.

[Haworth co-indexing entry note]: "Spirituality and Meaning: A Qualitative Inquiry with Caregivers of Alzheimer's Disease." Smith, Angela L., and Jennifer Harkness. Co-published simultaneously in *Journal of Family Psychotherapy* (The Haworth Press, Inc.) Vol. 13, No. 1/2, 2002, pp. 87-108; and: *Spirituality and Family Therapy* (ed: Thomas D. Carlson, and Martin J. Erickson) The Haworth Press, Inc., 2002, pp. 87-108. Single or multiple copies of this article are available for a fee from The Haworth Document Delivery Service [1-800-HAWORTH, 9:00 a.m. - 5:00 p.m. (EST). E-mail address: getinfo@haworthpressinc.com].

KEYWORDS. Spirituality, religiosity, meaning, caregiver, Alzheimer's, resources, family therapy, biopsychosocial

Few life events have a greater impact on a family than a terminal illness. Some might suggest that Alzheimer's Disease is the ultimate of terminal illnesses, whereas others would strongly disagree and state that it is the complications of Alzheimer's that lead to an individual's death. Regardless, the burdens that many primary caregivers have experienced are often uniquely and severely stressful when assisting individuals who struggle with this complex disease (George & Gwyther, 1986; Mace & Rabins, 1981). Several researchers have linked patient symptomatology and complications with caregiver outcome (e.g., Schultz, Biegel, Morycz, & Visintainer, 1989).

In 1994, researchers across the United States reported that Alzheimer's was on the rise (Alzheimer's Disease, 1994). They projected that the 1994 statistic of 4 million Alzheimer's sufferers would turn into 14 million sufferers by 2050. An Alzheimer's sufferer does not stand alone, as each Alzheimer's sufferer has at least one caregiver. Alzheimer's caregivers often experience depression (Harkness, 1997; Schultz & Williamson, 1991) and anxiety, strained relations with family and others, feelings of being overwhelmed, and feelings that life is uncontrollable (Barnes, Raskind, Scott, & Murphy, 1981; Morycz, 1985; Rabins, Mace & Lucas, 1982; Smith, 1999; Zarit, Reeves, & Bach-Peterson, 1980). Without a better understanding of the caregiver's needs or concerns, many may die before their loved one who suffers from this non-discriminating disease. All individuals who have come in and out of their lives must know the needs, concerns, and most importantly the strengths of caregivers.

In 1998, when this study was first designed, several articles existed addressing the deficits or challenges inherent in caring for someone with Alzheimer's disease. Researchers, then, focused mainly on caregiver's struggles in relation to care receiver's needs. They explored various financial (Alzheimer's Disease, 1994; Max, 1993), medical (Family Caregivers Alliance, 1990-1992), legal (Brenton & Larson, 1995), emotional/relational (Alzheimer's Disease, 1996; Gallagher-Thompson & DeVries, 1994), and housing (Mace & Rabbins, 1991) concerns using only quantitative measures to understand issues related to caregiver burden or stress. Few researchers attended to the interaction between caregiver needs, care receiver level of care, and caregiver strengths. Furthermore, an even smaller sample of researchers measured the impact of caregiving from a qualitative approach. The compilation of research was subsequently only half-complete, and the stories and descriptive realities from the perspectives of those directly impacted by Alzheimer's remained largely unknown.

Researchers, who investigated caregiver needs, typically concentrated on only one or two components from either the biological, psychological, or social implications of Alzheimer's (Hooker, Monahan, Bowman, Frazier, & Shifren, 1998; Theesen & Boyd, 1990). Furthermore, the primary research focus was either on the 'patient,' or on the caregiver, not simultaneously on both (Ross, Petrovitch, & White, 1996-1997). However, Alzheimer's disease does not impact a care receiver or caregiver one need, one individual, or one concern at a time. Alzheimer's has a systemic impact on each individual in its path. As with every biomedical, psychological, or social change in the care receiver, a change also occurs in the caregiver, as well as in other family members.

An integrated understanding of caregivers' needs is illustrated in the biopsychosocial approach (Engel, 1980). Engel believed that physicians tend to focus on the biomedical aspects of a patient's health, while social scientists tend to fixate on the psychosocial components of a client's health. Therefore, he suggested that all practitioners become more systemic by looking at the interaction between biological and psychosocial systems in an individual's life.

Family therapists have extensive training in gathering psychosocial information and using this information to work with families in a collaborative, systemic way. As the field grew, professionals in family therapy saw a need to bridge the biomedical system with the psychosocial systems and created an area of expertise in medical family therapy (McDaniel, Hepworth, & Doherty, 1992). Medical family therapists specialize in gathering biomedical and psychosocial information, developing collaborative relationships with the patient, couple, family, and larger systems, and in developing biopsychosocial treatment plans and interventions. Subsequently, the biopsychosocial model has become a guide for assessing impact and providing quality care to those families struggling with illnesses such as Alzheimer's Disease.

The systemic impact of the disease can also be described through an integration of biomedical, psychological, social, and spiritual implications for the care receiver and primary caregiver, especially when the primary caregiver is a relative or close friend of the individual with Alzheimer's. Smith (1999) found that the majority of caregivers tend to be the spouse or daughter of an Alzheimer's sufferer. She also found that while past research had focused on the biological (i.e., difficulty in swallowing and incontinence), psychological (depressive symptoms and agitation), and social (friends tend to withdrawal, more difficult to go to noisy public places) impact of Alzheimer's on the care recipient, less focus had been given to the changes required of caregivers. Smith found in her study that caregivers were more likely than not to live with the care receiver. They were impacted by biological (ulcers, back pain, and asthma), psychological (depressive symptoms, guilt, and anger), social (friends tend to withdrawal, less time to go places, lack of support), and spiritual (inability to go to church, changes in perception of spirituality, and acknowledgement of faith as a resource) implications due to the demands of caregiving.

Spirituality in respect to the current study best fits the definition set forth by Aponte (November, 2000). He stated that spirituality may be experienced as religious (formal and organized) and/or secular (personal, philosophical, and not oriented to God or spirits). Aponte also stated that everyone has a spirituality, a perspective on life, and a personal morality. Recently, spirituality whether religious or secular has received increased attention from health professionals in regard to illness (Wright, Watson, & Bell, 1996).

Researchers have suggested that spirituality or religiosity has an impact on an individual's physical health (Bernstein, 1994). In particular, researchers have linked patients' religiosity with life expectancy (Helm, Hays, Flint, Koenig, & Blazer, 2000), a decrease in risky health behaviors (Brown & Gray, 1994), and psychological well-being (Maltby, Lewis, & Day, 1999). Unfortunately, these researchers have typically assessed the symptoms of the primary patient who struggles with an illness, not the caregiver of the patient.

Even fewer researchers have focused on the impact of spirituality or religious practices of caregivers on the caregiving relationship (Chang, Noonan, & Tennstedt, 1998; Tix & Frazier, 1998). Chang et al. (1998) provided insight into the role of spirituality among caregivers of elderly who were disabled, and suggested that religious/spiritual beliefs promote relationship satisfaction with the care receiver. In addition, Tix and Frazier (1998) assessed the affects of religious coping strategies of patients undergoing a kidney transplant. They also reported relationship improvements when caregivers used religious coping strategies. While these studies were significant, they did not incorporate the demands of a progressive illness that are common to an Alzheimer's caregiver. In fact, Straw, O'Bryant, and Meddaugh (1991) found Alzheimer's caregivers have more unmet needs than do caregivers of other diseases. Therefore, the role of spirituality among caregivers may differ.

The purpose of this article was to report the views of Alzheimer's caregivers on the role of spirituality in the caregiving experience. These researchers used a qualitative approach to data collection, analysis, and reporting of results. Implications for clinicians, researchers, and spiritual advisors who are currently or who may be interested in pursuing this area of work are made at the conclusion of this article.

METHOD

Sample

Participants in this study included forty-five caregivers from mostly rural areas of the Midwestern and Southeastern United States. Whereas some of the caregivers were from urban regions of their state, more of these caregivers currently lived in rural areas. The demographics of these caregivers were similar to statistics of Alzheimer's caregivers from past studies (Family Caregivers Alliance, 1990-1992) in that 39 (87%) were female with the modal age of 65-75. In addition, twelve of the caregivers were 46-55 years old, 10 were 56-75, and 7 were 75 or older. Most of the caregivers 23 (51%) were the spouses of the individual with Alzheimer's. Beyond those who were spouses, 16 (36%) were adult children of the Alzheimer's sufferer, one of which was an adult son. Among all the caregivers, 22 (49%) lived with the individual with Alzheimer's. Not surprising, many (33%) of these caregivers stated that they cared for their loved one 16-24 hours on a typical day.

In addition to the caregiving responsibilities, 40% of the caregivers worked outside of the home. Of these caregivers six worked part-time (5-29 hours per week), three worked regular time (30-35 hours a week) and 9 worked full-time (40 or more hours a week).

The demographic information on Alzheimer's sufferers was descriptive of a typical Alzheimer's patient. Gender of the care recipient was almost evenly split, as 23 were male and 22 were female. The modal age of the individual with Alzheimer's was 75 and older (n = 26). There were two individuals who were 46-55, two who were 56-65, and 15 who were 66-75. Whereas the education level of the caregiver was very diverse with 65% having at least some college up to a terminal degree, 62% of the care recipients had a high school diploma or less.

Furthermore, based on their experience, the caregivers provided an estimate of the current Alzheimer's stage of severity of the care recipient: early, middle, or late (Gwyther, 1985). Of the 45 sufferers, 10 fit within the early stages of the disease, 21 fit in the moderate stage, and 11 fit in the late stage. These stages did not fit for three caregivers, as their loved one died prior to the interview. These caregivers all believed that their loved one was in the late stage prior to their death.

Measure

The process for this study followed the suggestion of Babbie (1983), who advised against an in-depth literature review prior to field work. Babbie believed that an in-depth literature review prior to research would promote the researcher to observe exactly what he or she expected to find. Therefore, a literature search on past research was tallied only to support areas of study on Alzheimer's caregivers that had already become saturated.

With little known about the specific needs of Alzheimer's caregivers prior to the interview process, overly generalized questions were asked of primary caregivers. Interestingly, what came through strongest from the interviews with caregivers would not have been found in any prior literature review search, spirituality and religiosity.

The primary technique in collecting information from the caregivers was the use of a semi-structured intensive interview. Intensive interviewing is a guided discussion with the purpose of gathering rich, detailed material that can be later used in qualitative analysis (Lofland & Lofland, 1984). Within this type of interviewing it is more likely than with a quantitative measure to receive the impromptu stories or descriptions of the caregiver's experiences. Through the use of qualitative measures the researchers approached the interview as exploratory. In this study, the intensive interviewing was used to discover the experiences of caregiver needs, concerns, and strengths.

The interview was considered semi-structured, because a pre-developed interview guide was utilized to capture different components that could be discussed during the interview. Questions were not asked in any particular order with the exception of the first question, 'What has it been like to be the primary caregiver of an Alzheimer's patient?' Questions were sometimes adapted to promote spontaneity and flexibility in the interview process. However, for the most part all questions in Appendix A were answered at some point throughout the interview process. Prompting was given to the interviewee only when more details were necessary to better understand the context of a given answer.

Most questions throughout the interview were straightforward and exploratory in nature. An exception to the typical questions within the interview process, were those that related to meaning-making. When conducting the first interview, it became apparent that meaning making was occurring. According to Nadeau (1998), meaning was defined as "the products of interactions with others and are influenced by the context in which they occur, including the influence of society, culture, and historical time" (p. 14). Therefore, meaning-making in this study included caregivers' stories about how they were influenced by caregiving throughout the history or presence of Alzheimer's, the culture and connections through spirituality, and their family, friends, and spiritual community.

The question related to meaning making was asked in the form of a Milan method of circular questioning (Boscolo, Cecchin, Hoffman, & Penn, 1987). Circular questioning, a systemic family therapy technique, is described as a question that asks an individual to speak or answer for family members who are not currently present. In this case, caregivers were asked 'If you were to ask your mother how she would want to be remembered, what do you think her response would be?' According to Wright, Watson, and Bell (1996), the meanings and beliefs that people hold about an event are a testament to their spirituality and religiosity.

This meaning-making question was critical, as it shared more than just an answer, it shared the caregiver's perspective of how he or she believed that loved one should be remembered and the spirituality in their experience. For many caregivers, a natural connection was made between how their loved one would want to be remembered and being a Christian, a follower of God, or a spiritual person. Perhaps, this question also allowed caregivers a new perspective on how they choose to interact with or perceive the individual who suffers from Alzheimer's.

Procedure

Caregiver participants came from three different venues: support group meetings, adult day centers, and through community functions (i.e., governor's task force meetings on Alzheimer's). Each caregiver established a comfortable meeting place for the interview; this was typically in their home. Each caregiver was given written information about the study's benefits and risks and asked to sign an informed consent for the study and a permission to audiotape.

At the conclusion of each interview, all audiotapes were transcribed. Throughout the study, a journal was kept documenting all research activity including personal reflections on the progress of the study. Furthermore, just as in quantitative research, reliability or dependability is critical to qualitative research. Therefore, a colleague who was not a researcher on this project conducted a dependability audit on randomly selected transcripts, to assess these researchers' interpretations and research methods and to ensure that consistency was maintained. That is, the use of the dependability audit ensured that researcher bias was excluded from phrasing of interview questions or analysis of interview findings to meet researcher expectations.

As the primary researcher reviewed the transcripts, each response was reduced to one or two sentences, creating a summary document. A full transcript of the interview or a summary document was distributed to randomly selected respondents as a member check. The use of respondents as member checks confirmed to the researchers that information that was collected and summarized represented the experience that the caregiver was trying to convey.

From the summary documents, key words or topics were organized, coded, and labeled into two domains:

1. caregiver's needs, concerns, and satisfactions
2. meaning-making. Spirituality made up just one category of information that fit under the domain of caregiver's needs, concerns, and satisfactions.

Other categories under the caregivers' needs, concerns, and satisfaction domain (i.e., financial, legal, housing, medical) will not be discussed in this paper.

RESULTS

Quantifiable Expressions of Spirituality

Of the 45 caregivers interviewed, all but nine mentioned an expression or significant event related to their spirituality, whether religious or secular in nature. In relation to church or religious communities, each caregiver offered different words to express their interpretation of their spiritual community. However, nearly all of the caregivers (36) stated that the clergy or members of the church were 'kind.' The second most common word (24) used to describe the church community was 'friendly.'

Unfortunately, not all caregivers who spoke out about their church community were consistently positive about their experience. An example of a common negative descriptor of clergy or church members was the word 'hypocritical,' which was used by nine of the caregivers. The words 'phony' or 'dishonest' were used by three caregivers.

Furthermore, six caregivers specifically stated that they did not feel that the church clergy or members made time for them. In addition, six other caregivers mentioned that the church clergy or members did not make time for the individual with Alzheimer's. Examples given by caregivers included: 'members of the church never called,' 'the church never brought attention to my bed ridden mother,' 'church members never came by to ask if I needed help,' 'my pastor was not supportive.' In quantitative research, numerical information would have been interesting but would not have included the in-depth responses and experiences. Findings from the interview process are described in more detail in the following sections.

The Caregiver's Voice

Negative Support from Church Community

There were twelve of 36 caregivers that mentioned spirituality in their interview who provided at least one negative description of their church or clergy. Some of the individuals were very brief about their disappointments, frustrations, or interactions. Six caregivers expressed in great detail the negative experience that they encountered. Words such as 'hypocritical,' 'phony,' and 'dishonest' were included in some of the descriptive accounts of the dissatisfied caregiver participants.

JS was a 49-year-old mother of three adult children whose husband was diagnosed with early onset Alzheimer's at the age of 50. JS cared for her husband in the home that they have shared for 16 years. They have been married for close to 27 years. JS's husband, at one time, was a prominent business owner and she was a homemaker. While providing information about her caregiving experience, she began to discuss her disappointment with her pastor. The following was an excerpt from her interview:

> I would encourage churches to be more supportive. I don't feel that the church gave me the support I needed. When I took him (her husband) to an adult day center and he hated it, I went to my

> pastor. So, I went to my pastor and said, 'I have to have help.' The pastor sided with him and decided that he didn't need to go to the adult day center. I said, 'Look I need help. I can't take this.' The pastor's response was, 'You said your marriage vows, for better or for worse, until death do you part. You have had the better, this is the worst and it is your responsibility to take care of him.'

NS was a 58-year-old female, mother, and grandmother. At the time of the interview, she was married and still worked as a self-employed upholstery fabric renovator. NS took care of her mother in her mother's home and had this to say about her experience with the church:

> She's had very few visitors from the church. I've been a little disappointed in the church. It would be nice if someone would make the effort to get to see her. And even now that she recognizes faces, rather she knows who they are, I think our minister could come over a little more often. I hate to downgrade him (the minister). From what I have seen, he doesn't appear as supportive as I thought he would have been.

Two male caregivers, CE, a gentleman in his late 60s, and JM in his early 80s, who both took care of their wives, also made comments. CE stated that his son lived about 60 miles away from him and had very little to do with him or his wife. CE stated that his son is a minister and

> really doesn't seem to realize what a lonely life I have.

JM was one of three caregivers whose loved one had died just prior to the interview. He stated

> I was disappointed in them (the church members), mainly in the people from church. I expected them to do much more than what they did. Many of these people had known her for years and when she died, I expected more from them.

HS, a male in his early 50s, and CG, a female in her late 30s, had very similar comments about what would make the process of being a caregiver easier for them. HS lived with and cared for his brother who was about the same age. CG, on the other hand, cared for her mother but did not currently live in the same home as her mother. HS stated:

> Having the support and help from the church community and others would have made this process easier on me.

CG mentioned that:

> Support from church members would have helped.

Positive Support from Church Community

While most of the caregivers (24) provided at least some positive remarks about their church community, only three provided in-depth experiences. Caregivers who spoke about the positive support from the church were very general and stated that many of the church members or pastors were 'friendly' or 'kind' toward them or the individual with Alzheimer's. In fact, 16 caregivers simply mentioned how loving the members of the church were toward the individual with Alzheimer's. Two caregivers could not elaborate on their statement, but merely stated that,

> my church is very supportive.

AG was a female in her late 80s and cared for her husband in their townhouse until the day that he passed away. AG shared many stories of her visits with her husband to church and his relationships with church members. AG seemed so proud to share:

> We always went to church, every Sunday. We were able to go to church until the day he died.

MP a female in her late 50s who cared for her mother, had this to say about the positive support that her mother received from the church:

> I think the church has been her (her mother's) main support, and her beliefs and her faith. I think we have all learned from her. We know she's in God's hands.

Impact of Spirituality (Religious or Secular) on Caregiving Experience

Seven of the 36 caregivers provided messages on the impact of spirituality on their caregiving experience. Four of these caregivers gave detailed responses, whereas the other three made brief comments about spiritual changes in their lives. Interestingly, some caregivers mentioned negative support from the church but were maintaining or gaining a strong sense of spirituality. JS, the caregiver who earlier stated how difficult it was to receive support from her pastor, also had this to say:

> Before we were married, I was raised in the church and he wasn't. So once we were married, I stopped going because it was just too complicated. My faith is the only thing now that gets me through. It is the only thing that I can depend on. God is the only one I can count on. My faith has grown leaps and bounds. This tragedy has brought me to God and what he teaches, that he is the only one we can count on in life.

JF was a caregiver for her mother. JF was in her late 40s and had this to say about her spirituality:

> Sometimes I get very down, but the Lord has a way of drawing my attention to how fortunate I am that I don't have a young child with a chronic debilitating disease. At least my mom has lived a full life and we have the hope of a better life to come.

PH was a female caregiver in her early 70s, who cared for her husband in their home. Her husband had been struggling with symptoms of Alzheimer's for seven years. In her interview, she mentioned that one of her greatest satisfactions in being a caregiver was her growth in spirituality. She stated:

> I feel I have grown spiritually and have gained strength.

ND was a female caregiver in her late 70s who cared for her husband 21-24 hours a day for nine years, until recently when he was transferred into a nursing home. ND noted changes that occurred in her life throughout the disease process:

> I have come through these nine years from anger and why me to becoming a more caring, more compassionate, and truly different person. I have learned a lot. I have changed, feeling a new purpose in my life. I'm getting my life back. I am not a religious person but now feel God teaching me and leading me, it is a profound experience.

Caregiver Expressions of Meaning-Making

Meaning of Caregiving

Many of the caregivers (34) had expressions of why they thought they were given the role of caring for an individual with Alzheimer's.

Because of the large number of caregivers who offered statements related to the meaning that they attached to being a caregiver, only a few expressions were listed.

ND, a female caregiver for her husband, stated:

> I feel I have made something positive out of this. I am now an Alzheimer's volunteer, give speeches, do some counseling. I am a patient advocate at a care center. These are things I never would have done before or would have dreamed of doing.

PD, another female caregiver for her husband, commented that:

> At this point I don't know why I was given this task. I just know that I am a different person and I do what I have to do and one day at a time I will understand what this is all about.

The Meaning of Legacy

Eight of the caregivers made a statement that related to the care recipient's legacy, at some point within their interview. Most provided their perspective on how they believed their loved one would want to be remembered. Meaning-making occurred as these primary caregivers attached a perception not only of how they thought their loved one would want to be remembered, but possibly how they too will continue to remember their loved one in the future. These statements and the thoughtfulness within these perspectives were so insightful that the caregivers seem comforted just by sharing them.

JL was a female caregiver in her late 40s who along with her husband and children cared for her mother. This caregiver, throughout her interview, shared so many stories of when she was frustrated, scared, upset, and overwhelmed, it was amazing when she ended her interview by saying:

> She would want to be remembered as a loving mother, she loved the kids. She loved us, told us she loved us as kids, and would hug us, and help us if we needed it.

JS, the caregiver whose husband had been diagnosed with early onset Alzheimer's at the age of 50, had a quite different response to how she believed her husband would want to be remembered.

> Of course he would absolutely hate it if he knew some of the things he does and some of the things he says. I am sure that he

> would have lived his life differently if he had realized that he was going to end up like this. I don't think he would have worked as many hours. He wouldn't have put as much emphasis on money. He wanted to save money for retirement. Now he won't even see retirement.

MP, a female in her late 50s who cared for her mother, stated:

> My mom would want to be remembered for her beliefs. Her love of Christ and always wanting to help other people, I think that would be the thing that she would want to be remembered by.

JM, a male in his early 80s who cared for his wife, described so many days of heartache, frustration, and embarrassment, yet stated:

> We have always been a very close and loving couple. She was still the same woman I married, only a little sicker.

The experiences of these caregivers included so many facets of spirituality whether religious or secular. These narratives should prompt practitioners of all fields to question why they have not integrated spirituality into their practice or to reconsider how they are approaching spirituality in their work with caregivers. Perhaps there are practitioners who have integrated spirituality into their work with caregivers but have not conducted research on the interaction between spirituality, faith, or church support and caregiving to find out what is helpful and what is not. The following section provides recommendations for practitioners who plan on considering their level of comfort with spirituality or consider including spirituality in their work with caregivers.

RECOMMENDATIONS

Many of the caregivers who participated in this study offered their perspectives and experiences to the researchers but had not shared these stories with other individuals. As researchers, this information seemed critical to share with those working directly with the caregivers and their families. Family therapists are known for their expertise in helping individuals, couples, and families see the whole picture in relation to a presenting psychosocial concern. Medical family therapy, a specialized sub-area of family therapy, casts an even wider net and focuses on the implication of illness and biomedical concerns as well as the psychosocial implications placed on family systems.

Practitioners in the field of family therapy have oftentimes heard and reflected upon caregivers' spiritual strengths and but may not have considered them in relation to their own level of spiritual/religious understanding, comfort, and bias. Practitioners need to not only understand how to ask questions about faith and spirituality, but also know how to then integrate the roles of faith and spirituality into the treatment process (Dosser, Smith, Markowski, & Cain, 2001).

Since 70% of all patients with diagnosable psychosocial-spiritual complications are never seen by a mental health professional, and are treated only in primary care (Narrow, Regier, Rae, Manderscheid, & Locke, 1993; Schurman, Kramer, & Mitchell, 1985), family therapists may benefit from establishing strong working relationships with those medical professionals that have direct access to Alzheimer's caregivers. Through incorporating spirituality into their practice styles a truly systemic family therapist can then use the biopsychosocial-spiritual approach to assess the caregiver's physical, emotional, social, spiritual concerns, and level of support. This approach, thereby, creates a greater likelihood for maximizing overall well-being for the caregiver rather than focusing exclusively on one aspect of health.

A link should be made between the positive and negative spiritual support, the impact of spirituality, and the meaning attached to caregiving to overall health. If a family stressor can create physical symptoms or physical symptoms can create family stress, then it is also likely that spiritual stressors can also impact physical and emotional health. The following recommendations are given to assist family therapists in the inclusion of spiritual beliefs and faith communities into the design and delivery of interventions and services.

1. Reflect on your own level of spiritual/religious understanding, comfort, and bias. The position of family therapists is not to merely encourage sharing of spiritual beliefs, but to utilize the spiritual resources of the caregiver (Dosser, Smith, Markowski, & Cain, 2001). It is important though that the therapist be aware of how their belief systems may influence, or significantly differ, from those of the caregiver.

2. In promoting and utilizing the biopsychosocial-spiritual approach raise your awareness of practitioners from other fields who may be able to assist you in providing holistic care for the caregiver. Family therapists are experts at gathering and integrating information from the larger systems. At times they need to find creative methods for incorporating the larger system professionals as collaborative resources. These

systemic supports may help reinforce therapeutic goals and interventions, especially if they feel connected to the process. The more that the professionals are working together, the greater the likelihood that the client will be able to initiate and sustain change.

3. Be prepared to discuss with mental, physical, or spiritual health providers your preference in including spirituality or assessing for spirituality needs or concerns among caregivers as well as your expectations/limitations in the inclusion of spirituality. If you intend on using the client's faith or spiritual beliefs in the therapeutic process, it is important to identify that as a part of your model of therapy to your collaborators. Your inclusion of spirituality needs to make sense to your potential collaborators, and clients, or else it will not be supported. If you do not intend on incorporating spirituality into the therapy process, and a collaborator suggests that you do, provide a rationale for why you are declining to address it in session. Perhaps you are aware that your religious beliefs may serve as a barrier, rather than as an asset.

4. When considering how to appropriately address a caregiver's spiritual concerns, you may want to request consent from the caregiver to speak to a member of their clergy or their spiritual advisor. Religious leaders, clergy, and advisors are often an untapped resource in family therapy practices. Many families seek spiritual guidance in addition to family therapy. If the two professionals are offering contradicting information, this could thwart or slow therapeutic progress. Collaborating with the spiritual/religious professional may serve to strengthen the client's trust in the therapeutic process, demonstrate to them your knowledge of their support systems, and increase your network of professionals in the community.

5. Assess and discuss the caregiver's spirituality (religious or secular) with empathy and understanding rather than from an expert stance. Allow the caregiver to share his or her perspective about what spirituality and being a caregiver means to them. As you gather information about your client's support system, inquire about their spiritual/religious supports. For example, even though you and your client may both classify yourselves as Jewish, you want to ask questions about what being Jewish means to him or to her. Provide empathy and understanding regardless of spiritual similarities or differences. Many clients fear being judged by others for their lack of adherence, or strong convictions, to their spiritual or religious practices. If clients understand that they are the co-experts (perhaps shared with their higher power) of their faith and spirituality, their hesitation to share stories based on spirituality will most likely decrease.

6. Talk with the caregiver about possibilities of bringing in internal or external mental, physical, or spiritual health providers into appointments with the caregiver, upon appropriate release documentation. In the event that multiple providers cannot be present at appointments, caregivers could approve consultation among providers to maximize systemic care. Encourage clients to invite everyone that is associated with being a part of the solution into a collaborative dialogue. Although this may initially be intimidating for both the clients and the professionals, most find that this is a wonderful mechanism toward clarifying goals, interventions, and mobilizing additional resources. It is often important that an agreed upon agenda for the session be established prior to meeting. It will take some of the mystery out of the meeting and decrease anxiety so that everyone understands the purpose of the session.

7. Be cognizant of the rules or regulations of your workplace to explore spirituality and at what level spirituality can be discussed. Some clinical environments are strict, and others are liberal, in respect to spiritual/religious beliefs and practices. It is important that you discuss with your supervisor, and perhaps even your colleagues, your clinical model of identifying and incorporating biopsychosocial-spiritual information into the therapy process. This prevents any possible misunderstandings that may occur about your use of spiritual/religious information in the therapeutic setting.

8. Discuss your approach with colleagues, administrators and supervisors, as they may wish to provide biopsychosocial-spiritual care or refer a caregiver to receive this type of care. Sharing your model of therapy with your colleagues may open up doors for referrals. People are innately curious and cautious about a colleague who keeps his or her therapeutic approach secret from others. They are more apt to trust and refer clients to a colleague who puts his or her beliefs before them to discuss and understand. When you explain that you are not questioning nor correcting clients' spiritual/religious practices, but rather utilizing their perceived strengths associated with it, they will be more inclined to see the usefulness in your approach.

9. Understand that some circumstances related to spirituality may be beyond your expertise even when offering biopsychosocial-spiritual care. Simply put, there may be times or situations that are more appropriately served by a minister. Directing a client to discuss an issue or question of spiritual/religious significance with their advisor, minister, priest, or rabbi is oftentimes a necessary referral. For example, family therapists are not in the position of absolving sins or interpreting scripture for clients. They cannot predict how a religious community will re-

spond to a divorce or an admission of sexual orientation. Some therapists are dually trained as family therapists and spiritual/religious professionals, and in those cases their scope of practice may be wider if the client is of the same belief system. However, the issue of having the same spiritual beliefs, versus being from the same church community, is still one to be considered.

CONCLUSIONS

The perspectives of the Alzheimer's caregivers in this study illuminated the importance that the role spirituality/religiosity plays in the caregiving experience. Whether a positive or negative experience, 36 of 45 participants made reference to its impact on the caregiving process. While family therapists attend largely to the biomedical, psychological, and social manifestations of the caregiving experience, they often lack an ability to focus on the importance of spirituality. Perhaps some practitioners fear that discussing spirituality with a caregiver will make the caregiver feel uncomfortable and pressured to adhere to the tenets of one religion or another. Others may have not yet identified what ascribes meaning to their lives and therefore, talking about it with clients would only reveal their own spiritual questions. However, inquiring about a caregiver's relationship with their spiritual beliefs does not mean that a conversation about religious preferences must ensue. Rather, it is asking about the beliefs and meanings that the caregiver has allocated to the experience that gets at their spirituality. In theory, we suggested that it is the beliefs about illness that connect the biological questions with the psychosocial-spiritual answers.

We also suggested that providing opportunities to be curious with caregivers about positive or negative spiritual experiences may facilitate steps toward their clients' well-being. It may also open up resources for the caregiver and the practitioner to use, as the disease progresses and the caregiving demands increase. However, to understand the depth and richness of the experience requires that more qualitative research be done in this area. Within each quote included in this study lies a deeper and richer story. These stories may reveal more explicit needs, relationships, and struggles with spirituality throughout the Alzheimer's caregiving experience. Once we have a more comprehensive understanding of spirituality and the Alzheimer's caregiving experience, then we can return to incorporating quantitative methods of research to statistically measure its impact.

Limitations

The limitations of this study were inherent in its design. Qualitative research was not designed to manage large sample sizes. Therefore, the results were not meant to be generalizable to all caregivers of Alzheimer's disease. The composition of the sample was not representative of the viewpoints of all caregiving experiences, cultures, races, religions, or ages. A more diverse or focused sample may have resulted in different realities, results, and recommendations. Those that find the results relevant legitimize this study.

Another limitation was that this study was not designed to exclusively focus on the spiritual/religious implications of the Alzheimer's caregiving experience. The theme of spirituality arose unexpectedly from the interview process, as it is common for unexpected themes to commence in qualitative research. As mentioned above, the impact of spirituality on caregiving should be further explored in a more focused study.

REFERENCES

Alzheimer's Disease and Related Disorders Association, Inc. (1996). *Understanding difficult behaviors.* Ypsilanti, MI: Alzheimer's Education Program.

Alzheimer's Disease and Related Disorders Association, Inc. (1994). Alzheimer's disease: Statistics. 919 North Michigan Avenue, Suite 1000, Chicago, IL 60611-1676.

Aponte, H. J. (2000, November). *Spirituality Sensitive Therapy.* Paper presented at the meeting of the American Association for Marriage and Family Therapy, Denver, CO.

Babbie, E. (1983). *The practice of social research* (3rd ed.). Belmont, CA: Wadsworth.

Barnes, R. F., Raskind, M. A., Scott, M., & Murphy, C. (1981). Problems of families caring for Alzheimer's patients: Use of a support group. *Journal of the American Geriatrics Society, 29*, 80-85.

Bernstein, A. (1994, Summer). Profiles 1993 diversity award honorable mention Frieda Hopkins-Outlaw and Cary Wright. *American Family Therapy Academy Newsletter*, 45-48.

Boscolo, L., Cecchin, G., Hoffman, L., & Penn, P. (1987). *Milan systemic family therapy.* New York: Basic Books.

Brenton, M. A., & Larson, L. N. (1995). *The gift of peace of mind: For yourself, for your family. A step-by-step guide to preparing advance directive documents.* Des Moines, IA: Drake Center for Health Issues.

Brown, D. R., & Gray, L. E. (1994). Religious involvement and health-status among African-American males. *Journal of the National Medical Association, 86*, 825-831.

Chang, B. H., Noonan, A. E., & Tennstedt, S. L. (1998). The role of religion/spirituality in coping with caregiver for disabled elders. *Gerontologist, 38*, 463-470.

Dosser, D., Smith, A. L., Markowski, M., & Cain, H. (in press). Including families' spiritual beliefs and their faith community in systems of care. *Journal of Family Social Work*.

Engel, G. L. (1980). The clinical application of the biopsychosocial model. *American Journal of Psychiatry, 137*, 535-544.

Family Caregivers Alliance (1990-1992). California's Caregiver Resource Centers, 425 Bush St., Suite 500, San Francisco, CA 94108.

Gallagher-Thompson, D., & DeVries, H. M. (1994). 'Coping with frustration' classes: Development and preliminary outcomes with women who care for relatives with dementia. *The Gerontologist, 34*, 548-552.

George, L. K., & Gwyther, L. P. (1986). Caregiver well-being: A multidimensional examination of family caregivers of demented adults. *The Gerontologist, 26*, 253-259.

Gwyther, L. P. (1985). *Care of Alzheimer's patients: A manual for nursing home staff* (pp. 25-27). American Health Care Association and ADRDA, Inc.

Harkness, J. L. (1997). Later-life marriage, chronic illness, and spouse-caregiver functioning. *Dissertation Abstracts International, 58*(6-B), 3339.

Helm, H. M., Hays, J. C., Flint, E. P., Koenig, H. G., & Blazer, D. G. (2000). Does private religious activity prolong survival? A six-year follow-up study of 3,851 older adults. *Journals of Gerontology Series A-Biological Sciences and Medical Sciences, 55*, 400-405.

Hooker, K., Monahan, D. J., Bowman, S. R., Frazier, L. D., & Shifren, K. (1998). Personality counts for a lot: Predictors of mental and physical health of spouse caregivers in two disease groups. *Journal of Gerontology: Series B: Psychological Sciences and Social Sciences, 53B*, 73-85.

Lofland, J., & Lofland, L. H. (1984). *Analyzing social settings*. Belmont, CA: Wadsworth.

Mace, N. L., & Rabins, P. V. (1991). *The 36-hour day* (revised ed.). Baltimore, MD: Johns Hopkins University Press.

Mace, N. L., & Rabins, P. V. (1981). *The 36-hour day*. Baltimore, MD: Johns Hopkins University Press.

Maltby, J., Lewis, C. A., & Day, L. (1999). Religious orientation and psychological well-being: The role of the frequency of personal prayer. *British Journal of Health Psychology, 4*, 363-378.

Max, W. (1993). The economic impact of Alzheimer's disease. *Neurology, 43*, 6-10.

McDaniel, S., Hepworth, J., & Doherty, W. (1992). Medical family therapy: A biopsychosocial approach to families with health problems. New York, NY: Basic Books.

Morycz, R. (1985). Caregiving strain and desire to institutionalize family members with Alzheimer's disease. *Research on Aging, 7*, 329-361.

Nadeau, J. W. (1998). *Families making sense of death*. Thousand Oaks, CA: Sage Publications.

Narrow, W., Regier, D. A., Rae, D., Manderscheid, R. N., & Locke, B. Z. (1993). Use of services by persons with mental and addictive disorders: Findings from the National Institute of Mental Health Epidemiologic Catchment Area Program. *Archives of General Psychiatry, 50*, 95-107.

Rabins, P.V., Mace, N.L., & Lucas, M.J. (1982). The impact of dementia on the family. *Journal of the American Medical Association, 248*, 333-335.

Ross, W., Petrovitch, H., & White, L. R. (1996-1997). Update on dementia. *Generations* (Winter), 22-27.

Schultz, R., Biegel, D., Morycz, R., & Visintainer, P. (1989). Current psychological paradigms for understanding caregiver well being and burden within the family context. In E. Light & B. Lebowitz (Eds.), *Alzheimer's disease treatment and family stress: Directions for research* (pp. 106-127). Washington, DC: U.S. Government Printing Office.

Schultz, R., & Williamson, G. M. (1991). A 2-year longitudinal study of depression among Alzheimer's caregivers. *Psychology and Aging*, *6*, 569-578.

Schurman, R. A., Kramer, P. D., & Mitchell, J. B. (1985). The hidden mental health network: Treatment of mental illness by nonpsychiatric physicians. *Archives of General Psychiatry*, *42*, 89-94.

Smith, A. L. (1999). The forgotten victim: An in-depth look and an overall assessment of Alzheimer's caregivers' needs, struggles, and satisfactions. *Dissertation Abstracts International*, *60*(4-A), 1272.

Straw, L. B., O'Bryant, S. L., & Meddaugh, D. L. (1991). Support system participation in spousal caregiving: Alzheimer's disease versus other illness. *Journal of Applied Gerontology*, *10*, 359-371.

Theesen, K. A., & Boyd, J. A. (1990). Dementia of the Alzheimer's type: An update. *The Consultant Pharmacist*, *5*, 535-540.

Tix, A. P., & Frazier, P. A. (1998). The use of religious coping during stressful life events: Main effects, moderation, and medication. *Journal of Consulting and Clinical Psychology*, *66*(2), 411-422.

Wright, L. M., Watson, W. L., & Bell, J. M. (1996). *Beliefs: The heart of healing in families and illness*. New York, NY: Basic Books.

Zarit, S. H., Reever, K. E., & Bach-Peterson, J. (1980). Relatives of impaired elderly: Correlates of feelings of burden. *The Gerontologist*, *20*, 649-655.

APPENDIX A

1. What has it been like to be the primary caregiver of an Alzheimer's patient?
2. What has it been like living with an Alzheimer's patient?
3. Which of your needs do you feel have not been met through your process as a primary caregiver?
4. Which of your needs do you feel have been met through your process as a primary caregiver?
5. Describe any changes in your style of living since becoming a primary caregiver.
6. Describe any changes in your occupation since becoming a primary caregiver.
7. What skills or assistance would help you most in your life as a primary caregiver?
8. Did you experience any differences after the diagnoses in
   1. finances,
   2. legal matters,
   3. medical assistance,
   4. housing situation,
   5. emotional support?
9. If you were to ask your mother how she would want to be remembered, what do you think her response would be?

Clients' Perceptions of Marriage and Family Therapists Addressing the Religious and Spiritual Aspects of Clients' Lives: A Pilot Study

Martin J. Erickson
Lorna Hecker
Dwight Kirkpatrick
Mark Killmer
Edassery James

SUMMARY. As marriage and family therapists are emphasizing the actual contexts of clients' lives, religion and spirituality are being addressed as important aspects of culture. This pilot study investigated whether clients felt their therapist adequately addressed the religious and

---

Martin J. Erickson is a PhD candidate in the Marriage and Family Therapy Program, Iowa State University, and is affiliated with Anasazi Foundation, Mesa, Arizona.

Lorna Hecker is Associate Professor, Marriage and Family Therapy Program, Department of Behavioral Sciences, Hammond, IN.

Dwight Kirkpatrick is Professor of Psychology, Behavioral Sciences Department, Purdue University Calumet, Hammond, IN.

Mark Killmer is Executive Director, Samaritan Counseling Center, Munster, IN.

Edassery James is Associate Professor of Psychology, Behavioral Sciences Department, Purdue University Calumet, Hammond, IN.

Address correspondence to: Marty Erickson, 1424 S. Stapley Dr., Mesa, AZ 85204 (E-mail: marty6@iastate.edu).

[Haworth co-indexing entry note]: "Clients' Perceptions of Marriage and Family Therapists Addressing the Religious and Spiritual Aspects of Clients' Lives: A Pilot Study." Erickson, Martin J. et al. Co-published simultaneously in *Journal of Family Psychotherapy* (The Haworth Press, Inc.) Vol. 13, No. 1/2, 2002, pp. 109-125; and: *Spirituality and Family Therapy* (ed: Thomas D. Carlson, and Martin J. Erickson) The Haworth Press, Inc., 2002, pp. 109-125. Single or multiple copies of this article are available for a fee from The Haworth Document Delivery Service [1-800-HAWORTH, 9:00 a.m. - 5:00 p.m. (EST). E-mail address: getinfo@haworthpressinc.com].

spiritual aspects of their lives according to their desires for such. Thirty-eight clients who attended therapy at university clinics were surveyed using a questionnaire about their own religiosity and spirituality, about their preferences to have religion and spirituality addressed, and whether they perceived their therapist addressed religion and spirituality in the therapy process according to their desires. Results show these family therapists did rather well at addressing the religious and spiritual aspects of their clients' lives. Demographic correlations showed that the gender of the client and whether the university clinic they attended was affiliated with a religious denomination were each positively correlated to whether the clients wanted religion and spirituality addressed and whether their therapist adequately addressed these issues. Detailed limitations are noted.

KEYWORDS. Spirituality, religion, research, family therapy

RELIGION AMONG THE GENERAL PUBLIC AND AMONG PSYCHOTHERAPISTS

Although the term "psychology" from the Greek literally means "knowledge of the soul," historically, mental health disciplines have either ignored or pathologized religion and spirituality, and this continues in subtle, and sometimes not so subtle, ways today. Even when religion and spirituality are not pathologized, therapists have often taken a neutral position on these issues. "The majority of therapists would not be hostile to spirituality. However, maintaining a neutral position generally means remaining silent on the issue and this may equate to rejection" (Adams, 1995, p. 202). In beginning this study, we wondered how this chasm between the two affects current practice of marriage and family therapy (MFT). Although the field of MFT has been addressing religion and spirituality, this is a more recent development. We wondered what clients themselves would report about whether their family therapist adequately addressed the religious and spiritual aspects of their lives in the manner they wanted these aspects addressed in their therapy. Unfortunately there is little empirical research that has addressed this important question.

Gallup surveys of the general population show that most Americans place a high value on religion and spirituality in their daily lives. A Gallup survey (Princeton Religion Research Center, 1985) found that 95% percent of people report believing in God or a Universal Spirit, 85% claim to pray, and 56% state that religion is very important in their lives. In a Gallup survey of 1987 (Gallup, 1987), 55% of Americans reported their religious beliefs to be very important in their lives, while 31% indicated their religious beliefs are somewhat important. A 1993 Gallup survey found that about four out of 10 Americans attend church or synagogue at least once a week, and about six out of 10 attend at least once a month. Additionally, almost nine in 10 American adults say that they pray to God at least occasionally (Gallup, 1993). A Gallup survey in 1990 showed that the rates of religious commitment and involvement have remained fairly constant in the United States over the past 60 years (Gallup, 1990). In a 1992 Gallup poll (Gallup, 1993) 66% of respondents stated that, if they were considering therapy, they would prefer to have a therapist who represented spiritual values and beliefs. These and other surveys show that clients most often prefer a counselor that would be sensitive and open to their religious beliefs and spirituality.

Generally, the religious population is under represented in the profession of psychology (Bergin & Jensen, 1990; Shafranske & Gorsuch, 1984; Shafranske & Malony, 1990). One study found that many graduate programs in psychology were less likely to accept overtly religious applicants during the 1980s (Gartner, 1986). In spite of the fact that therapists often serve a religious clientele, therapists (particularly psychologists) tend to be less religious than their clientele and indeed may evidence some bias against religion (Bergin & Jensen, 1990). The facts that the religious population is under represented among psychotherapists, and that a religion and spirituality bias remains among the psychotherapy disciplines, do not harmonize with the value placed on religion by the general public.

With regard to marriage and family therapists, Carlson (1996) found that 96% of his respondents (all marriage and family therapists) strongly agreed, or agreed with the statement that "there is a relationship between spiritual health and mental health." But in contrast, only 62% of those respondents strongly agreed or agreed that "the spiritual dimension should be considered in clinical practice." One may wonder what encourages family therapists to be reluctant toward views on religion and spirituality when it comes to actual therapy practice. Perhaps it is the simple adage that family therapists should allow the client to bring up what is appropriate to talk about. But, there may be an interesting dilemma taking place. Melissa Griffith (1996) discusses the feeling that many clients have that their private and meaningful conversations with a personal God are not welcome in therapy conversations. According to Griffith, this creates an unspoken censoring that family therapists can inadvertently participate in. From a narrative therapy perspective, she identifies "therapist certainty" as a major contributor to the oppression and constraint of the religious and spiritual stories of clients. Thus, both therapist and client alike may be waiting for cues from the other about the appropriateness of addressing religious and spiritual beliefs and issues. Perhaps the onus is on family therapists to take the first step to integrate religious and spiritual issues in therapy.

RELIGION AND SPIRITUALITY IN MARRIAGE AND FAMILY THERAPY LITERATURE

In 1990, the editor of the *Journal of Marital and Family Therapy* urged the field to explore the issue of religion, spirituality, and family therapy more closely (Sprenkle, 1990). Perhaps in response, spirituality and religion are being addressed more by family therapists as evidenced by a growing number of articles that directly or indirectly address these issues (see Anderson & Worthen, 1997; Bewley, 1995; Chubb, Gutsche, & Efron, 1994; Carlson & Erickson, 2000; Doherty, 1995; Griffith, 1986; Griffith, 1995; Harris, 1998; Kelly, 1992; Patterson, Hayworth, Turner, & Raskin, 2000; Prest & Keller, 1993; Prest, Russell, & D'Souza, 1999; Sperry & Giblin, 1996; Stander, Piercy, Mackinnon, & Helmke, 1994; Walsh, 1999; Watson, 1997; Weaver, Koenig, & Larson, 1997). In MFT, religion and spirituality are being included with all the other aspects of diversity including race, culture, socio-economic status, ethnicity, gender, generation, and so on (Stander, Piercy, McKinnon, & Helmeke, 1994; Ross, 1994).

Pinderhughes (1989) asserts that ethnicity typically refers to a person's nationality or country of origin but there are some peoples (i.e., Jewish and Latter-day Saint) whose identity and culture focuses more on their religion than their geographical location. Likewise, some have argued that religious beliefs may even have a more powerful impact in determining a person's identity than their culture (McGoldrick, Giordano, Pearce, & 1996; Prest & Keller, 1993).This review of literature indicates that the field of MFT is becoming more sensitive to the influence of religion and spirituality in the lives of clients.

As a whole, it appears that marriage and family therapists may be more religious than social workers, psychologists, and psychiatrists (Bergin & Jensen, 1990; Carlson, 1996). Perhaps higher religious involvement among marriage and family therapists is one reason for the growing interest in religion and spirituality. Since addressing religion and spirituality in therapy is a more recent trend, most of the articles in MFT are theoretically oriented-formulating and giving ideas and encouraging particular practices. Only one qualitative study to date directly addresses religion and spirituality in MFT (Kelly, 1992). Although, there have been a few significant quantitative studies (Carlson, 1996; Denton & Denton, 1992; DiBlasio, Fredrick, & Proctor, 1993; Hecker, Trepper, Wetchler, & Fontaine, 1995; Prest, Russell, & D'Souza,1999). Carlson (1996) found a high rate of religiousness among a sample of MFTs, 63% of respondents reported regular church attendance. When asked various questions about religion, spirituality and therapy, 62% percent agreed or strongly agreed with the statement "Every person has a spiritual dimension that should be considered in clinical practice." Perhaps most applicable to this current study, Carlson (1996) found that 68% of his sample agreed or strongly agreed that it is appropriate to ask a client about his/her spirituality.

DEFINING RELIGION AND SPIRITUALITY

One of the difficulties that has hampered research in religion and spirituality is the confusion of the two terms (Adams, 1995). Researchers in and out of MFT have called for a distinction between "religion" and "spirituality" (Adams, 1995; Carlson, 1996; Joanides, 1996; Miller, 1992; Prest & Keller, 1993; Prest, Russell, & D'Souza, 1999; Winston, 1990). Most of the literature that distinguishes between the two terms shows that therapists are more willing to address and incorporate spirituality than religion in therapy (Adams, 1995; Berenson, 1990; Carlson, 1996; Prest & Keller, 1993; Prest, Russell, & D'Souza, 1999). For this study, the operational definitions of Prest and Russell (1995; also see Prest, Russell, & D'Souza, 1999) were used in the theorizing and in the survey filled out by respondents. They define spirituality as ". . . the human experience of discovering meaning, purpose, and values, which may or may not include the concept of God or a supreme being." And they define religion as ". . . the formal, organized institutional contexts for spiritual beliefs and practices" (p. 62).

METHODS

Sample

We collected data from persons, couples, or families that were in therapy with a marriage and family therapist intern at various MFT university clinics around the United States. All of the MFT programs were accredited by the Commission on Accreditation for Marriage and Family Therapy Education (COAMFTE), or they were in candidacy for accreditation by COAMFTE. Some of these universities are public, some private; some of the private universities are affiliated with a religious denomination. Out of 43 MFT program directors and clinic directors we communicated with, only 11 agreed to participate in this project. Survey questionnaire packets were distributed to the clinic directors, and they were asked to acquire a list of clients that had terminated within the last 6 months, and address the packets to these clientele. In an effort to avoid methodology problems in the gathering of data, the surveys had instructions asking for one person (rather than couples or whole families) to respond to the questionnaire, although the instructions did encourage each member of a couple or family to have input in filling out the questionnaire. The former clients were asked to fill out the questionnaire, and then to return it in a postage-paid envelope included in the packet. A total of 235 surveys were sent out to the 11 participating university clinics; 38 surveys were returned filled out, a low response rate of 16%.

Questionnaire

The questionnaire consisted of 13 demographic questions, 38 questions concerning their personal religiosity and spirituality, their experiences from therapy with regard to religion and spirituality, and 2 open ended questions. The 38 core questions were answered on a 5 point Likert scale from strongly disagree (coded 1) to strongly agree (coded 5). Most of the questions in the questionnaire were developed and written for the purposes of this research. The questionnaire had an introductory paragraph that differentiated between the words "religion" and "spirituality" using the definitions given by Prest and Russell (1995; also see Prest, Russell, & D'Souza, 1999).

Demographics

Eighty-four percent of the respondents were female. The respondents ranged in age from 17 to 73 years with a mean age of 35 years (SD =

11.37). The race of the respondents included 86.8% Caucasian, 5.3% Hispanic, and 2.6% African-American (2 respondents, 5.3%, did not indicate their race). One half of the respondents were married, 21.8% were single, 18.4% were divorced, 7.9% were separated, and 2.6% were widowed.

The majority of the respondents indicated that they were Protestant (55.3%), 31.6% indicated they were members of The Church of Jesus Christ of Latter-day Saints (Mormon), 5.3% indicated they were Catholic, and 7.9% indicated "none." Therefore, this sample represented *only* Christian clients. Forty-two percent of these clients attended therapy at a public university clinic and 58% attended therapy at a private university clinic. The private universities were affiliated with Protestant denominations, or The Church of Jesus Christ of Latter-day Saints. The majority of the respondents (68.4%) had between 2 and 12 sessions. A large majority of respondents (81.6%) marked Strongly Agree or Agree that they liked the therapy experience, and almost the same majority (79%) marked Strongly Agree or Agree that they found the therapy experience helpful.

RESULTS

The main research question was "Do clients of MFT interns feel that the religious and/or spiritual aspects of their lives were adequately and/or appropriately addressed in the therapy process?" This research question was examined first by investigating the percentages of clients' responses on questions that collectively represented two sets of scales, first the Clients' Preferences for Therapist to Address Religion/Spirituality scales, and second the Therapist Addressed Religion/Spirituality scales. A reliability analysis using Chronbach's index of internal consistency was used to determine if the individual questions of each scale were reliable measures for that scale with regard to each other question in the scale. Questions that detracted from the reliability of the scales, and were thus not good predictors of the purpose of each scale, were excluded. The resultant questions for these scales included the following:

Clients' Preferences for Therapist to Address Religion [Spirituality] Scales (CPTAR and CPTAS)

- I wanted to talk about my religious [spiritual] beliefs.
- I felt it was necessary for my religious [spiritual] beliefs to be addressed in the therapy process.

Therapist Addressed Religion [Spirituality] Scales (TAR and TAS)

- I talked about my religious [spiritual] beliefs in therapy.
- My therapist encouraged me to discuss my religious [spiritual] beliefs in therapy.
- My therapist asked me about my religious [spiritual] beliefs.
- My therapist was sensitive to my religious [spiritual] beliefs.
- I felt comfortable talking about my religious [spiritual] beliefs with my therapist.

The means and standard deviations for the CPTAR, CPTAS, TAR, and TAS scales are given in Table 1. Table 2 shows the bivariate Pearson correlation coefficients for the four scales. As evident in Table 2, there was a significant (at the $p < .01$) positive correlation between each of the four scales with every other scale.

More than half of the respondents (57.9%) indicated that their religious and/or spiritual beliefs had some type of influence, either positive or negative, on the problems or difficulties they went to therapy for. Likewise, more than half of the respondents (59.5%) answered yes to the question "Was religion or spirituality necessary for healing?"

Some of the questionnaire asked respondents about their personal religiosity or spirituality. A religiosity scale and a spirituality scale were devised from these questions. Again a reliability analysis using Cronbach's index of internal consistency was used to determine if the individual questions of the religiosity and spirituality scales were reliable measures for their scale with regard to their fit with each other question of the scale. The resultant scales consisted of the following questions:

Religiosity [Spirituality] Scales

- I try hard to live my life according to my religious [spiritual] beliefs.
- My whole approach to life is based on my religion [spirituality].
- I consider myself to be a religious [spiritual] person.
- Religion [Spirituality] is relevant in my personal life.

Pearson bivariate correlations were conducted between the religiosity, spirituality, CPTAR, CPTAS, TAR, and TAS scales. Table 3 depicts the correlation matrix of coefficients for these scales. As evident in the Table, the correlation between the religiosity scale and the spirituality scale is not significant. The religiosity scale positively correlated with the scales concerning religion, and the spirituality scale positively correlated with the scales concerning spirituality. The only exception to this is the significant correlation between the religiosity scale and the CPTAS scale.

A paired samples *t* test showed that there was a significant difference between clients' responses to the religiosity scale versus the spirituality scale questions. The *t* statistic was significant ($t = -2.267$, $df = 36$, $p = 0.03$); therefore, the means of the respondents' answers to the questions in the two scales were significantly different. This shows that the respondents answered differently to the questions in the religiosity scale compared with the spirituality scale.

As mentioned previously, 84% of the respondents were female. An independent samples *t* test was run with the means of female and male respondents and the CPTAR, CPTAS, TAR, and TAS scales. The results are presented in Table 4. The *t* statistic was significant for the CPTAR and the CPTAS scales, but it was not significant for the TAR or TAS scales. The means for females and males and the *t* score results

TABLE 1. Means and Standard Deviations for the CPTAR, CPTAS, TAR, and TAS Scales

Scale	*M*	*SD*
Clients' preferences for therapist to address religion scale	3.000	1.389
Clients' preferences for therapist to address spirituality scale	3.189	1.304
Therapist addressed religion scale	3.438	0.986
Therapist addressed spirituality scale	3.454	1.061

TABLE 2. Bivariate Pearson Correlation Coefficients for Scales CPTAR, CPTAS, TAR, and TAS Scales

	CPTAR	CPTAS	TAR	TAS
Clients' preferences for therapist to address religion	-	0.774**	0.645**	0.418**
Clients' preferences for therapist to address spirituality		-	0.545**	0.645**
Therapist addressed religion			-	0.813**
Therapist addressed spirituality				-

**$p < .01$

TABLE 3. Bivariate Pearson Correlation Coefficients for the Religiosity, Spirituality, CPTAR, CPTAS, TAR, and TAS Scales

	Religiosity	Spirituality	CPTAR	CPTAS	TAR	TAS
Religiosity Scale	-	0.160	0.545**	0.378*	0.350*	0.227
Spirituality Scale		-	0.266	0.594**	0.192	0.534**

$^*p < .05$ $^{**}p < .01$

show that the response means for males on the CPTAR and CPTAS scales were significantly different than the response means for females on the same scales. Males tended to disagree more with the questions in the CPTAR and CPTAS scales than did females.

In order to determine if the university clinic at which the clients attended therapy had any effect on the clients' responses, a bivariate Pearson correlation test was run between the variable indicating if the clinic was at a religious affiliated university or not and the CPTAR, CPTAS, TAR, and TAS scales (Table 5). The questionnaire asked "Is the university, sponsoring the clinic you attended for therapy, associated with any particular religious denomination?" The response "No" was coded 1, "Yes" was coded as 2. The results show that clients who attended religious affiliated university clinics tended to prefer to have the therapist address religion, and tended to indicate that the therapist did address religion.

DISCUSSION

The results of this study should all be tempered by the fact that there was a low sample, which was a convenience sample which was not statistically representative of clients who have been to marriage and family therapists at university clinics. The results disconfirmed our hypothesis that clients would tend to perceive their therapist as having not done well at addressing the religious and spiritual aspects of their (the clients') lives. The correlations between the TAR and TAS scales and the clients' preferences as identified in the CPTAR and CPTAS scales were significant. Thus the clients' preferences to have religion or spirituality addressed (either to have it addressed or *not* have it addressed) were most often fulfilled by the therapist (according to the positive correlations). Our main finding is that these university clinic MFTs did rather

TABLE 4. Independent Samples *t* Test with Gender of Client and CPTAR, CPTAS, TAR, and TAS scales

Scale	Gender of Client	*N*	*M*	*SD*	*t*	*df*	*p* (2-tailed)
Clients' preferences for therapists to address religion	Female	31	3.194	1.412	−3.106	14.283	0.008**
	Male	6	2.000	0.707			
Clients' preferences for therapist to address spirituality	Female	31	3.387	1.308	−2.209	35	0.034*
	Male	6	2.167	0.683			
Therapist addressed religion	Female	31	3.523	1.030	−1.195	35	0.240
	Male	6	3.000	0.607			
Therapist addressed spirituality	Female	31	3.516	1.117	−0.085	35	0.426
	Male	6	3.133	0.689			

$^*p < .05$ $^{**}p < .01$

TABLE 5. Bivariate Pearson Correlation Coefficients Between the University Religious Affiliation and the CPTAR, CPTAS, TAR, and TAS Scales

	Religious Univ.	CPTAR	CPTAS	TAR	TAS
University religious affiliated?	-	0.338*	0.171	0.382*	0.274

$^*p < .05$

well at addressing the religious and spiritual aspects of clients' lives according to the clients' preferences for such. The literature review showed that religious and spiritual issues are being addressed more in the last 10 years than they ever have been in MFT. Perhaps this increased focus could be one of the reasons for the favorable results reported in this research. It may be that MFT interns at university clinics are in fact trying to address the religious and spiritual aspects of their clients lives more fully. If this is true, then this is an encouraging finding. Yet, because of the limitations of the research, and in light of the long history of a chasm between psychotherapy and the religious and spiritual worlds, we feel it best to recommend that marriage and family therapists make continued efforts to improve at addressing the religious and spiritual aspects of their clients' lives.

There was not complete agreement between the clients' preferences to have religion or spirituality addressed and their indications of whether their therapist did so. For example, the CPTAR and TAR scales were positively correlated, and the coefficient of determination indicates that just 41.6% of the variance in CPTAR is accounted for by the variance in TAR. The correlations are statistically significant, but because of the small sample size and the difficulties inherent with correlations and small samples, the results are not conclusive. Also, as with all Pearson correlation coefficients, one must consider the question of confounding variables which could easily be playing into the results obtained. For instance, more than half (55.3%) of the respondents attended a university clinic affiliated with a particular religious denomination. This is a higher than expected percentage since most MFT programs are not at religiously affiliated universities. This is also higher than expected because only 3 of the 11 university clinics that distributed surveys for this research are affiliated with a religious denomination. It may be that those who attended a religious affiliated university clinic were more likely to complete and return the survey.

The spirituality scale correlated with the two scales having to do with spirituality, CPTAS and TAS, but not with the same scales for religion. Likewise the religiosity scale correlated with the two scales having to do with religion, CPTAR and TAR, but did not correlate with the TAS scale. This shows that perhaps therapists did relatively well at being aware and addressing appropriately the differences between religiosity and spirituality for their clients. Clients that preferred religion be addressed also rated themselves high on the religiosity scale (or vice versa), and clients that preferred spirituality be addressed also rated themselves high on the spirituality scale (or vice versa). For the questions in the religiosity scale compared with those in the spirituality scale, the significant t statistics showed that clients differentiated between religiosity and spirituality; in fact the differentiation is quite clear. The only difference in the questions in the two scales is the words "religious" or "religion" being substituted with the words "spiritual" or "spirituality." Clients in this sample tended to differentiate between the words "religion"/"religious" and the terms "spiritual"/"spirituality" in responding to the questions about their personal religiosity and spirituality. For these respondents, their personal religiosity meant something distinct from their personal spirituality. This lends support to the differentiation of these items being called for in the research (Adams, 1995; Carlson, 1996; Joanides, 1996; Miller, 1992; Prest & Keller, 1993; Prest & Russell, 1995; Prest, Russell, & D'Souza, 1999; Winston,

1990). It was also interesting to see that the mean scores for the spirituality scale were quite a bit higher than the mean scores for the religiosity scale. It seems that religiosity is what most often gets negatively stigmatized in the psychotherapy literature, because it is religiosity and religious dogma that have often been questioned and pathologized in the historical chasm between religion and psychotherapy. Perhaps this thinking carries over in the clients' responses to these two scales; spirituality seems to be regarded more positively by them than religiosity.

The significant *t* statistics for the four scales and client gender disconfirmed our hypothesis that female and male clients would not differ on their responses to the four scales. According to the results, these male clients tended to score lower on the CPTAR and the CPTAS scales than did the female clients. This may coincide with the stereotypes in our culture concerning masculinity and femininity, with masculinity often being described as tough, macho, less-feeling oriented, independent, and so on, and therefore less spiritual or religious. If the male clients in this sample were influenced by this common stereotype, then this would explain their responses, although this is purely conjecture. The very low number of males ($N = 6$) is likely one of the main reasons for the differing results. Perhaps these six males are not representative of the population of male clients who have been to university clinics. For some reason, females were much more likely to complete and return the survey, which is fairly typical in questionnaire research.

Most of the clients in this sample responded that they liked the therapy experience (81.6%) and that they found it helpful (79%) (incidentally, the responses of "strongly agree" compared with "agree" were almost half and half for each question). This is a rather high percent of client satisfaction with therapy. In general, this could be interpreted as encouraging news for how MFT interns at university clinics are doing. Although, it may also be the case that those who were not satisfied were less likely to complete and return the survey. With regard to the correlations between these two questions and to the TAR and TAS scales, these correlations were also significant. This shows that clients who agreed to the two therapy satisfaction questions also tended to perceive that their therapist addressed religion and spirituality according to their preferences for such.

Respondents who attended a religiously affiliated university clinic tended to prefer that their therapist address religion, and also tended to indicate that their therapist did address religion, more so than those clients who did not attend a religious affiliated university clinic. Also, the results show that therapists at religiously affiliated university clinics tended to address religion more so than therapists at non-religious affiliated university clinics. One of the main confounding variables for this correlation is the simple availability of where they received services. Even if a client wanted to attend a clinic that was associated in some way with a religious denomination, such a clinic may have been unavailable. There was not a significant correlation between the CPTAS or TAS scales and whether the client attended a religious affiliated university clinic. This shows that clients who preferred to have the therapist address spirituality did not tend to go to a university clinic that was religious affiliated. Taken together, these results also lend support to the distinction these clients made between "religion" and "spirituality." Additionally, those clients who attended a religious affiliated university clinic may have expected religion to be addressed and this may have influenced the fact that it was by the therapist.

LIMITATIONS

The most glaring limitation of this pilot study was the low number of respondents in the sample. This may have affected the results if compared to a much larger, representative sample. Also, this sample was quite unique; it was drawn from a population of clients that attended therapy at a university clinic with an MFT intern. Therefore the results are not directly comparable to clients of MFTs in general. The sample also only consisted of six male respondents. Females do tend to seek therapy services more often than males, but the difference is not as great as it is in this research. More male respondents would have been helpful for the sample to be more representative of clients who see MFT interns at university clinics.

A couple of important questions could have been asked in the questionnaire but were not. Particularly two Likert scale questions to the effect of "My therapist did well at addressing the religious [spiritual] aspects of my life" could have been included in the TAR and TAS scales. It is questionable if the CPTAR, CPTAS, TAR, and TAS scales are sufficiently valid or reliable. For instance, the CPTAR and CPTAS scales each only consisted of two questions. More questions that would have inquired about their preferences to have religion and spirituality addressed may have been needed to make the scales more valid. More repeated testing and validating of the scales is needed to determine if they are reliable and valid.

It may be that clients who were more religiously inclined, or more interested in religion or spirituality, were more likely to complete and return the survey. The sample may be biased as consisting of persons who highly value religion and/or spirituality. This is an inherent problem with almost all survey research. These clients may also have felt pressured to answer positively to the questions about whether their therapist addressed religion and spirituality if they liked the therapy experience and found it helpful. It is hard to determine what all the many possible influences may have been on these clients to answer in the way they did.

Finally, the reliance on correlations for this research is problematic. Correlations show no cause and effect and there is always an infinite number of confounding variables that could be affecting the results. This is true of all survey and correlational research. Even if all of these limitations would have been addressed and removed, the results would still be problematic because of the reliance on statistics to infer personal opinions, feelings, experiences and responses. We encourage qualitative measures designed to adequately follow-up this study.

REFERENCES

Adams, N. (1995). Spirituality, science, and therapy. *Australian and New Zealand Journal of Family Therapy, 16* (4), 201-208.

Anderson, D. A., & Worthen, D. (1997). Exploring a fourth dimension: Spirituality as a resource for the couple therapist. *Journal of Marital and Family Therapy, 23* (1), 3-12.

Berenson, D. (1990). A systemic view of spirituality: God and twelve-step programs as resources in family therapy. *Journal of Strategic and Systemic Therapies, 9*, 50-70.

Bergin, A. E., & Jensen, S. P. (1990). Religiosity of psychotherapists: A national survey. *Psychotherapy, 27*, 2-7.

Bewley, A. R. (1995). Re-membering spirituality: Use of sacred ritual in psychotherapy. *Women & Therapy, 16* (2-3), 201-213.

Carlson, T. D. (1996). *Religion, Spirituality, and Marriage and Family Therapy*. Master Thesis, Purdue University Calumet.

Carlson, T. D., & Erickson, M. J. (2000). Re-authoring spiritual narratives: God in person's relational identity stories. *Journal of Systemic Therapies*.

Chubb, H., Gutsche, S., & Efron, D. (Eds.). (1994). Spirituality, religion, and world view. Introduction to the Special issue (editorial). *Journal of Systemic Therapies, 13* (3), 1-16.

Denton, R. T., & Denton, M. J. (1992). Therapists' ratings of fundamentalist and nonfundamentalist families in therapy: An empirical comparison. *Family Process, 31* (2), 175-185.

DiBlasio, F. A., & Proctor, J. H. (1993). Therapists and the clinical use of forgiveness. *American Journal of Family Therapy, 21* (2), 175-184.

Doherty, W. J. (1995). *Soul searching: Why psychotherapy must promote moral responsibility*. New York: Basic Books.
Gallup, G. H. (1987). *The Gallup poll: Public opinion 1986*. Wilmington, DE: Scholarly Resources.
Gallup, G. H. (1990). *Religion in America: 1990*. Princeton, NJ: The Gallup Organization.
Gallup, G. H. (1993). *Religion in America: 1992-1993*. Princeton, NJ: The Gallup Organization.
Gallup, G. H. (1994). *Religion in America: 1994, supplement*. Princeton, NJ: The Gallup Organization.
Gartner, J. D. (1986). Antireligious prejudice in admissions to doctoral programs in clinical psychology. *Professional Psychology: Research and Practice, 72*, 473-475.
Griffith, J. L. (1986). Employing the God-family relationship in therapy with religious families. *Family Process, 25*, 609-618.
Griffith, M. E. (1995). Opening therapy to conversations with a personal God. In K. Weingarten (Ed.), *Cultural resistance: Challenging beliefs about men, women, and therapy* (pp. 123-139). New York: Harrington Park Press/Haworth Press, Inc.
Harris, S. M. (1998). Finding a forest among trees: Spirituality hiding in family therapy theories. *Journal of Family Studies, 4* (1), 77-86.
Hecker, L. L., Trepper, T. S., Wetchler, J. L., & Fontaine, K. L. (1995). The influence of therapist values, religiosity and gender in the initial assessment of sexual addiction by family therapists. *American Journal of Family Therapy, 23* (3), 261-272.
Joanides, C. J. (1996). Collaborative family therapy with religious family systems. *Journal of Family Psychotherapy, 7* (4), 19-35.
Kelly, E. W. Jr. (1992). Religion in family therapy journals: A review and analysis. In L. A. Burton (Ed.), *Religion and the family: When God helps*. New York: The Haworth Pastoral Press.
McGoldrick, M., Giordano, J., & Pearce, J. (Eds.). (1996). *Ethnicity and family therapy* (2nd Ed.). NY: Guilford.
Patterson, J., Hayworth, M., Turner, C., & Raskin, M. (2000). Spiritual issues in family therapy: A graduate-level course. *Journal of Marital and Family Therapy, 26* (2), 199-210.
Pinderhughes, E. (1989). *Understanding race, ethnicity, and power*. NY: Free Press.
Prest, L. A., & Keller, J. F. (1993). Spirituality and family therapy: Spiritual beliefs, myths, and metaphors. *Journal of Marital and Family Therapy, 19* (2), 137-148.
Prest, L. A., & Russell, R. (1995). *Spirituality and religion in training, practice and person development*. Unpublished manuscript.
Prest, L. A., Russell, R., & D'Souza, H. (1999). Spirituality and religion in training, practice and person development. *Journal of Family Therapy, 21* (1), 60-77.
Princeton Religion Research Center. (1985). *Religion in America*. Princeton, NJ: Author.
Ross, J. L. (1994). Working with patients within their religious contexts: Religion, spirituality, and the secular therapist. *Journal of Systemic Therapies, 13* (3), 7-15.
Sperry, L., & Giblin, P. (1996). Marital and family therapy with religious persons. In E. P. Shafranske (Ed.), *Religion and the clinical practice of psychology* (pp. 511-532). Washington, DC: American Psychological Association.

Sprenkle, D. H. (1990). Continuity and change. *Journal of Marital and Family Therapy, 16*, 337-340.

Stander, V., Piercy, F. P., Mackinnon, D., & Helmke, K. (1994). Spirituality, religion and family therapy: Competing or complementary worlds? *The American Journal of Family Therapy, 22* (1), 27-41.

Walsh, F. (1999). *Spiritual resources in family therapy*. New York: Guilford.

Watson, W. H. (1997). Soul and system: The integrative possibilities of family therapy. *Journal of Psychology and Theology, 25* (1), 123-135.

Weaver, A. J., Koenig, H. G., & Larson, D. B. (1997). Marriage and family therapists and the clergy: A need for clinical collaboration, training, and research. *Journal of Marital and Family Therapy, 23* (1), 13-25.

Winston, A. (1990). *Family therapists, religiosity, and spirituality: A survey of personal and professional beliefs and practices*. Unpublished doctoral dissertation, The Union Institute.

The Effect of Spiritual Beliefs and Practices on Family Functioning: A Qualitative Study

C. Everett Bailey

SUMMARY. A paucity of research exists on thick descriptions of family functioning. Using in-depth semi-structured interviews, this paper presents the case study of a family that has close, positive relationships. The results reveal that the family's spiritual beliefs and practices are delicately interwoven into every aspect of the family's life. These results highlight the importance of professionals identifying and drawing on the spirituality of family members as a source of strength and support for the families they serve. *[Article copies available for a fee from The Haworth Document Delivery Service: 1-800-HAWORTH. E-mail address: <getinfo@haworthpressinc.com> Website: <http://www.HaworthPress.com> © 2002 by The Haworth Press, Inc. All rights reserved.]*

KEYWORDS. Spirituality, religion, family functioning

Religious beliefs and practices are deeply woven into the fabric of family life. According to surveys on the role of religion in their lives, 90% of all adults say religion is important, nearly 60% consider it very important and 30% state that it is the most important part of their lives

---

C. Everett Bailey is Assistant Professor, MFT Program Interim Director, North Dakota State University.

[Haworth co-indexing entry note]: "The Effect of Spiritual Beliefs and Practices on Family Functioning: A Qualitative Study." Bailey, C. Everett. Co-published simultaneously in *Journal of Family Psychotherapy* (The Haworth Press, Inc.) Vol. 13, No. 1/2, 2002, pp. 127-144; and: *Spirituality and Family Therapy* (ed: Thomas D. Carlson, and Martin J. Erickson) The Haworth Press, Inc., 2002, pp. 127-144. Single or multiple copies of this article are available for a fee from The Haworth Document Delivery Service [1-800-HAWORTH, 9:00 a.m. - 5:00 p.m. (EST). E-mail address: getinfo@haworthpressinc.com].

(Gallup, 1996). Research on family functioning reveals that spiritual beliefs and practices are "key ingredients in healthy family functioning" (Walsh, 1999b, p. 9). Gallup (1996) surveys report that over 82% of adults say that religion was very important or fairly important in their family growing up. In addition, almost 75% of respondents convey that religion in their homes has strengthened family relationships and that religion strengthens current family relationships a great deal. Furthermore, in a national survey of about 90,000 adolescents, the National Longitudinal Study of Adolescent Health reports that spirituality is a protective factor against adolescent risk behavior (e.g., suicide attempt, violence, pregnancy) (Blum, 1999). Finally, a survey of 153 clinical members of AAMFT, showed that 96% either agreed or strongly agreed that there was a relationship between spiritual health and mental health (Carlson, 1996).

Although survey research reports that issues of spirituality and religion are integral to most families, there has been very little, if any, research that describes *how* religious beliefs and practices are connected to family functioning (Thomas, 1988). As a result, the purpose of this article is not to identify ways that therapists can address religious and spirituality issue in therapy (see Walsh, 1999a for a good resource on that topic). Instead, the purpose of this article is to identify the need to address such issues because of its integral nature with the majority of American families. To accomplish this purpose, a case study of a family will be presented to illustrate the extent that religious beliefs and practices may be embedded in the lives of many families.

METHODOLOGY

The purpose of this study was to examine the meanings of quality family relationships as described by family members themselves. In order to gain the descriptive data necessary to reveal such meaning, a family case study was conducted using in-depth qualitative interviews of a family that had positive healthy relationships (Handel, 1991). By examining the context of family interaction in order to assess meanings, we offer richer possibilities in explanations than typically drawn from organizing constructs external to family meanings and operationally defining them independent of context, relationships, and history. For, when we create familial constructs detached from the family's context, relationships, and history, rather than increase understanding, we move one step away from the very experience we are trying to explain. But when we do not do that, and we go to a family itself, a new understanding or new possibility of how to make sense out of quality family living is given. Obtaining the meanings from family members themselves about the quality of their family relationships, we can better understand what beliefs and practices are related to healthy family relationships (Jarrett, 1992).

Sample. The data were gathered through in-depth interviews with one family, the Kendalls. I (and others in the community where the Kendalls lived) observed the parents and children to have close, healthy relationships. However, what was unique about the Kendalls was that they had a strict set of family practices, and yet their children showed no resentment toward their parents that may be typical of children in such circumstances. In contrast, the children had a great deal of respect for their parents. Some of the family practices that seemed noteworthy were that although the children attended the public schools, they did not participate in any extra-curricular activities like student government or sports. This was in spite of the fact that the children enjoyed such activities and also demonstrated in gym class that they were often the best athletes in the school. In addition, they did not attend any of the dances or observe any of the sporting events. They did not go out on the weekends with their friends, even though the children integrated quite well with the other students and had many friends at school. Another distinguishing element was that the girls always wore dresses, did not wear make-up, and had long hair. Also the family did not own a television, radio, or a compact disc player. They did not drink alcohol, use any tobacco products, or use drugs. They attended church every Sunday and one evening a week. The family was affiliated with a Christian religious group called the Plymouth Brethren or simply Brethren who take the Bible as its sole guide. The local congregation was about 150 to 200 in number in a rural community of about 1500. Although this group seems relatively unique and unknown, they do have congregations nationwide.

The family members included the parents, Ken, 44, a farmer, and Karen, 45, who was a stay at home mother, and their six children. The oldest child, Kathy, 23, was married and lived in another state. Their other five children lived at home: Karl, 21, Karina, 18, Kami, 16, Kelli, 14, and Kenneth, 12. Data collection took place during one interview with the entire family (including Kathy who was visiting), the father alone, the mother alone (over the phone), and written responses to questions from the children.

Analysis. Patterns themes and categories were identified in the data by the author. To avoid Type I (something is not significant when it is), and Type II errors (something is significant when it is not) (Patton, 1990), as much of the data as possible are reported in the findings to allow the reader to come to his/her own conclusions. In addition a colleague read the data and the write up of the results and concurred that the categories presented are consistent with the data. Finally, the family was given a copy of the study. They later reported that they thought the categories were accurate and that they were in the right order of importance.

RESULTS

In interpreting the data the following themes emerged as being conceptually significant in accounting for quality family relationships: religious belief, consistency of parental example, respect and trust, discipline and authority, and commitment to the family. Although each of these themes will be discussed separately, they overlap quite extensively and are best understood from within the context of their religious beliefs.

Religious Belief

Religious belief is generally interpreted as belief in a certain religious dogma. For this family, however, it is much more than that. The belief that the Lord directs and blesses their family permeates every aspect of their life. Their religion has no specific doctrine but believes in strict adherence to the teachings of the Bible. More fundamental than which church the family belongs to is their faith in Christ and a desire to live according to His word. In a letter, the father wrote, "It is this principle [faith in Christ] that our whole family is built on. We each one know the Lord as our Savior, and we seek to draw from His Word guidance. We know that God is righteous and holy, so if we get our direction from no other source than His Word, we will not go wrong." Their fourteen year old daughter, Kelli, reiterated this by saying that the "Lord is the leader of our family. He helps us through every trouble and trial."

Perspective. This belief in the Lord and His Word, the Bible, gives the family an eternal perspective in conducting their affairs. The father, Ken, believes it is important to have a sense of eternal things and the hereafter. Ken said, "Some raise their children with the perspective that this life is all there is. But if you see this life as only a time between eternities you raise your children differently. We are given this time to honor Him, and learn what is in the Lord's heart. Those who come to be like Him will have His life." So they raise their children with this in mind and prepare them for eternity and help them to get to know Him.

This spiritual perspective is also reflected in the parents' hopes and aspirations for their children. Karen, the mother, said that her only hope for her children is that they "will be happily married and continue in a path that is pleasing to the Lord." As a result, the parents have no desire that their children achieve success in the world's eyes by gaining some title or achieving some accomplishment. For them success is defined by the Apostle John who said there "is no greater joy than to hear that my children walk in truth" (3 John 1:4). The father said he hopes that his children are happy and have peace in their lives. He is thankful that his oldest child is happily married for that is more important than some other accomplishment.

The children have internalized this same perspective. When asked about their goals, most of the children said they would like to be happily married and to be an example for others. Karl, age 21, said, "Before I die I would like to encourage as many people to follow the Lord and try not to be a bad influence on anyone. If I can follow the Lord and accomplish this my years here will be well spent." Eighteen year old Karina said, "I hope to finish high school and be happily married." Kami, 16, said, "I plan to go on for the Lord, and be an example to others so they might come to know the Lord Jesus as their own personal Savior and enjoy Him as much as I do." Kelli, age 14, said, "I want to finish high school. Then, I want to be a teacher until I get married. When I get married I want to have two or four children. I want also to have a happy marriage until the Lord comes to take the saved ones home." Kathy, the oldest and married, responded, "I have no goals here on this earth. I have a home above which is far better, and where I long to spend eternity with my father, mother, brothers and sisters. I can be an example of testimony to those I am around, so that they may want what I have too."

Trust in the Lord. This eternal perspective is guided by a trust in the Lord and a deep desire to learn and do His will. The father, Ken, said, "I seek to do what I do on a spiritual level. Everything I try to do is in the light of God and His will, not of the world and what they think." This notion of doing things according to the Word and not the world is very important to the Kendalls. Their trust in the Lord and His Word seems to direct them in every aspect of their lives. This first became evident when the family often responded to questions by quoting scripture. For example, in explaining her relationship with Ken, Karen cited Ephesians 5:24 (Therefore as the church is subject to Christ, so let the wives be to their own husbands in every thing.), while Kathy quoted Ephesians 6:1 (Children, obey your parents in the Lord: for this is right.) to describe her relationship with her parents.

Furthermore, the father, Ken, stated that he has never read a book on parenting. Rather, as parents they use the scriptures as their guide. Ken said, "If it is not found in the scriptures then I don't do it." Likewise, Karen said that in her parenting she "seeks to be guided by the Word of God, and a desire to please the Lord." This desire to be taught from the scriptures has been passed on to their children. When he asks his parents questions, Karl, their oldest son, said, "I usually want the answer from the Bible. Ken added, "If you show it to them out of the Word, the Spirit of God can then show it to them in their own soul from the Word."

Another way the family learns the Lord's will is through prayer. For example, in deciding on whether to talk to a child about something that was bothering her, Karen said she prayed to know what she should say or if she should even say anything at all.

Confidence in the Lord. The trust the Kendalls have in the Lord is accompanied by a confidence that He will always work things for their good. Karl, 21, said, "[Even] trials are for our own good." For this reason the parents send their children to public school rather than teach them at home because they feel it is important that their children face challenges at school. However, they are not afraid of the influence that others, including peers and teachers, will have on their children because they have perfect confidence in allowing their children to go to school and "leaving them with the Lord." The father said, "If we are walking with the Lord and are alive to His Word, then we have that confidence that He will take care of them. I feel that you have to commit your children to the Lord in prayer." Moreover, they think it is important that their children go to the public schools because that is part of being "subject to the powers that be" and they believe that the Lord will watch over their children because they are following the laws of the land. However, after school they think the children should be home rather than with friends or involved in extra-curricular activities. Home is where they learn the things of the Lord.

Another example of their confidence in the Lord is how they feel about who their children will date and marry. The parents believe it is important to be "equally yoked" in marriage. Yet, they generally feel as parents they should not be involved in deciding who their children should marry. The father, Ken, feels that the Lord would not lead them wrong as long as they were going with someone who is "gathered to the Lord." Ken said, "If you really have confidence that the Lord will bring the right one in your life, you won't date other people. To do so would mean that you might lose confidence." A boy at school asked one of the girls if she would be allowed to date boys from school. She replied, "I can but I prefer not to." Karen, the mother, said, "What she wanted him to realize was it was *her* choice not to–not just because she knew we wouldn't want her to." Karen says she does not worry about who they will marry but she prays about it a lot. She says, "It gives me peace to know if they seek the Lord's mind He will make it clear to them."

Because of this confidence the family generally does not believe it would be any harder to live their beliefs outside of their rural community. For example, the oldest child, Kathy, who is married and lives in another state, said, "If you truly have a desire to go on and do the things that please the Lord, you will be able to do it wherever the Lord sends you." Her 14 year old sister agreed, "I don't think it would be any harder because the Lord is there at another state just as much as He is here."

Dependence on the Lord. This confidence is only found in the context of humility and dependence on the Lord. This humility was first evident in the father's hesitancy to do the interview at all. The mother, Karen, expressed that their family relationships were only possible because of the Lord in their lives. Similarly, Ken closed his letter by saying, "My family–by the grace of God–does not stand on any merits of its own. There is no good in us except what God has worked in our souls through His Son by His Spirit. To Him and Him alone belongs all praise because it is His work in our souls."

Consistency of Parental Example

In establishing good parent-child relationships and teaching their children the Lord's will, the importance of being a proper example was reiterated time and time again. The mother said, "We can't expect our children to be more than we are." Ken, the father, continued, "The most important thing is that your children must see you doing the things you are asking them to do. I myself should be doing the same thing I expect of them, the same thing I say to them."

Respect and Trust

The consistency of example in the parents' lives helps to develop respect and trust in the family's relationships. When asked what was the most important quality to have in a parent-child relationship, both the parents said "respect." Ken said, "If you lose your child's respect, you've lost everything." Karen said her father-in-law told her once and she has never forgotten, "If you don't have your child's respect, you don't have a chance." The children also said that the reason they felt they had such a good relationship with their parents was because they love and respect them.

Trust. Significantly, the respect the children have for their parents is nurtured by the trust the parents have in them. Kathy, said, "My parents have always trusted me. Never have they doubted what I said was true." Furthermore, accompanying the trust the parents have in the children is a trust the children have in the parents. The children seem to have a real confidence that their parents are only asking the children to do what is best for the children. When asked if there was anything they would change about their parents, Kami said, "I don't think I could really answer this question because everything my parents do is for my own good."

Blame and criticism. Even though the family members realize others' imperfections, what is more fundamental to them is that they accept them. Thus, despite their weaknesses, the family members do not blame and criticize each other. This fosters respect and trust in their relationships. A good example of how the family does not criticize each other is found in Kathy's response to the question 'What would you change about your parents?' She said, "In my eyes I never tried to find fault with my parents. I always respected what they did and said to me, because I knew as long as they had the Lord before them in how to raise their family, I should not question them at all. But I certainly don't mean that they never made mistakes."

When asked if he would do anything different as a parent, Ken responded, "I don't tend to view things that way. It is not realistic because there is no second chance. I believe the Lord led me that way for a reason to either benefit my soul or the soul of my children. Even mistakes are something you learn from." These statements also portray how the family's religious perspective undergird other aspects of their lives.

Discipline and Authority

Discipline plays a very important role in the family and is viewed as a very serious responsibility by the parents.

Conscience. One of the most important elements that the parents described in discipline was the role the conscience plays. The parents feel that it is very important to allow the conscience to work in the child. Both the parents and the children emphasized how primary the conscience is in an individual's life. Ken, the father, said, "The conscience is always on God's side. The difficulty comes in when we go against our conscience. Then after you do it a few times the conscience is seared or hardened and they are not sensitive. They don't care." When asked how the children learned what was right and wrong Karl, 21, responded, "As a child grows older, it's their conscience." This is another manifestation of their deep religious faith as the children are taught to obey the Lord (conscience), and not just the parents.

Teenagers. Because conscience develops as the children get older, the method of discipline changes. By the time the children are teenagers, the parents feel the child's conscience is developed and the children know right from wrong. At this point the children also know how their parents feel about issues, and as a result, the parents generally do not interfere with their children's decisions. Instead, the parents pray for the intervention of the Holy Spirit to guide their children in their decisions.

In describing how they were disciplined as teenagers the children supported the parents' responses. Karl, 21, said, "When I was a child I was spanked. Now there is no discipline by my parents, only by the Lord." He continued, "As you get older it's not 'What will Dad think?', but 'What will the Lord think?' and knowing I must bear the consequence of the wrong. When you are younger you obey out of respect for your parents but there comes a time when you do it for the Lord." Eighteen year old Karina explains, "As a child they spanked me, as a teenager they don't discipline me. I know when I have done wrong and I feel very ashamed. They don't need to discipline me because I feel bad enough and I ask the Lord to forgive me."

Reasoning. The parents said that generally they do not reason with their teenagers. However, there are times that the children, as adolescents, will ask their parents' thoughts on a subject. As these situations arise the parents will teach their children from the scriptures and counsel with them. They encourage the child to "see for yourself" in the Bible. They want their children to receive something because it is taught in the scriptures, not just because somebody says it.

Consistency. Another important ingredient in discipline is consistency. Karen says it is important to be consistent in order to gain the children's respect. She explained, "Consistency in our lives as parents, as well as consistent in how we deal with our children, is important."

Family rules. At first, it might seem that the family has a lot of rules that govern their behavior. However, rather than rules, the family members are guided by their conscience and a deep sense of love and respect for Christ and each other.

The father feels that rules are not conducive to family harmony. He said, "Nothing is ever mentioned as a 'rule' in the home. 'Rule' gives the sense of it being a 'law.' Law brings rebellion–respect brings love." His wife agreed, "It seems in our home things just seem to be 'understood' not laid out. If we are using the Word as our guide, then the rights and wrongs do not really change."

Although the family does not have explicit rules, there are some general characteristics that describe what they feel is right to do. The way the Kendalls govern their life are not done to make them different, nor are they rules set by "the church," but rather they are guidance given to them in the Word to help them live in accordance with the will of God. The way they conduct their life is drawn from the scriptures, not from society or man. Ken, the father, said, "There is no value in something if it comes from man, but if we can draw it from the Word, we know we have a divine source." So, they feel many activities should be avoided, according to the Word, because it brings too much of "the world" into the home. For instance, the family does not own a television, radio, nor a compact disc player. The children said this did not bother them because they feel it was "what you get used to" and they really did not know any different.

Another example is that the children do not participate in any extracurricular school activities. When asked why the oldest boy, Karl, responded that it is important to not be "unequally yoked" in marriage, business, or sports. He clarified by saying that to be "unequally yoked" is to be on a team with people "who are not of Christ" (2 Cor. 6: 14). Furthermore, the family does not believe in building on the principle of competition. They believe competition is the goal of the world, but not what Christ did. They also believe that they can not take worldly things with them. When asked if they would like to participate in some activities, some of the children indicated they had thought about it but knew their parents did not want them to.

Authority. Authority plays an important part in the way the parents discipline their children. The reason authority is mentioned towards the end is not because it is the least significant, but because its significance for the Kendalls can be understood best in the context of the above characteristics. As a natural outgrowth of the above characteristics, authority is established which guides the family and gives it stability. The father, Ken, said, "I don't reason with my children, but from the side of authority I say you're going to do this. Society frowns on taking up the side of authority, but to my way of thinking, it has to be that way." However, this statement can only be understood in the context of Ken's religious beliefs, the consistency of his example, his respect and trust for his children, his attitude in discipline, and his commitment to the family.

The roles in the family are very traditional and are conducted according to the Word. "The Word teaches that a man is responsible for his family and that the wife is subject to the husband. This is different in today's world where the husband is not the head of the home and the place of the woman is so belittled. Man has to act in such a way to take that place, as head of the home, not by force but in his practical way," relates Ken.

However, Ken does not feel this means the woman is inferior, even though that is often how the world interprets it. He says although the scriptures teach that the wife is subject to the husband, they do not teach that she is inferior. He said, "This in no way diminishes the importance of the woman. The woman has the most blessed place in scripture. She has the greatest influence on the family as she controls what comes into the home." When asked what it means for the wife to be subject to the husband, Ken said, "To be subject means to not speak against the husband's thoughts. The wife should not speak against the husband, especially in front of the children." At the same time he said that the husband must have the respect of the wife. "If the husband has a temper and flies off, he won't have the respect of his wife."

This is equally important to Karen, who respects Ken because he "is not controlled by a temper." As a result she feels she is one with him in their decisions and feelings. At the same time she says, "This isn't to indicate I think just like he does about everything–no I don't, but I feel my place is to submit to him as head (Ephesians 5:24). Not as my boss or me as his servant, but to give him his rightful place as *my* husband, in *our* home is important for *his* happiness, *my* happiness and our children's. This brings unity that will follow the children for years to come. My mom was a wonderful example to me of this. She never fought back or gave me to feel there were two sides in our home, but I knew Dad wasn't always right."

One example the mother gave was when she was dealing with a certain situation in the family and Ken felt differently than she did. She was talking with Ken about this over the phone while he was at work and some children were in the other room. So, she decided not to discuss it then but waited until later to talk it over with Ken in private. During that time she said she did not understand his thoughts on the subject. Ken then explained his reasoning, which was logical, and Karen agreed. Other times she says she does not agree. Ken also added that there are many times when he counsels with his wife and they end up choosing to do something because of something that she brought to his attention. Still, the most important thing is that they let the children know that they are one with each other. Karen says this is critical, even though she might have thought differently, because it shows respect. Karen said there are times when she has failed and asked Ken in front of the children, "Why are we going to do that?" But she tries not to do that. Likewise, Ken states that he must use his authority in the context of love. Ken stated that if affection is not involved, then in no way will his children or wife be motivated to heed his counsel and respect his authority.

Karen said they do not view authority as having power but as having a responsibility. She says, "It humbles you to realize you are responsible for all these people and that the decisions you make will affect all of their lives." She said, "It is important to be of one mind and do it out of real love, otherwise others' mistakes will overpower you."

Most importantly, both Karen and Ken feel that they need to submit to the Lord and teach their children to do the same. One of the reasons Karen feels they have good relationships with their children is because of the Lord in their lives. She said, "With the Lord as our center, it definitely makes a difference, for without the Lord in their lives, nothing is to be satisfactory." The father, Ken, said, "I don't want to take anything away though from the necessity of showing them a firm foundation to build their lives upon which is the Lord. He is 'the one who is the authority.' If they realize or rather bow to Him as Lord, they'll then be able to enjoy 'oneness' with the Lord and those who are His children."

Commitment to the Family

The parents feel that their children are a gift from God and thus feel a sacred responsibility for them. The mother said, "Children are a precious gift from the Lord, and it is most serious how we parent these gifts." She continues, "We are responsible to see that our children are disciplined, guided, respected, loved, and more." Ken explains, "In the scriptures the Lord stresses the importance of the family and does not divide the family. I feel uneasy about leaving my children home so I can go do something else. Our children are our responsibility and we want them to feel that we are glad they are."

Significantly, the parents have no outside interests that would distract them from their responsibility as parents. "I can't relate to the feeling that some people have that 'I've got to get away,' " expressed Ken. "That's not life. Life is not the high you might get from doing something. Life is everyday experiences."

Typical day. Their typical day consists of eating breakfast together, reading the family calendar, reading the scriptures, family prayer, and getting ready to go to school. With respect to reading scriptures in the morning Kathy, the oldest, said, "Sometimes it gives you something to think about, something that Dad said, during quiet moments during the day." At the same time the parents recognize that scripture reading can have negative effects if done with the wrong purpose or attitude. Ken, the father said, "There is a point where you can make scriptures obnoxious." When asked what happens if someone does not want to come to scripture reading, they said everybody just comes because it has always been that way. In fact when asked what they respect most about their parents, Karina, 18, said, "They read the Bible, they pray, they are consistent, they honor the Lord, and they are good testimonies." Similarly, 14 year old Kelli said, "Reading the Bible in the morning, praying before each meal, and going to meeting." In addition, Kenneth, age 12, said he respected his parents most for reading the Bible in the morning.

Vacations. The family particularly enjoys taking vacations together. When asked about their favorite things they did with their family all the children mentioned trips they had taken as a family. When asked if they enjoy spending time with their family, the children responded by saying, "I love spending time with my family. I like to play games. We all get along good together and we can talk about anything and just relax together."

Overall a deep sense of devotion and warmth exists between the family members. All of the children responded that they get along with each other. When asked about their relationship with their parents, most of the children said they had a good relationship and they were very close.

The parents hope that their commitment to the Lord and the family will be carried on by their children. Ken said he hopes his daughters will be subject to their husbands and have a healthy home. For his sons he hopes they will be good providers. Karen said, "To see them with a job that doesn't hinder a family relationship, or hinder their time with the Lord is important." She also wants both her sons and her daughters to be happily married and "equally yoked." She hopes her daughters will "continue on, being a wife and mother, and seeking to do it well, not in the eyes of the world perhaps, but to be 'keepers of the home,' to be subject to their husbands and fulfill their place in the home."

DISCUSSION

Religious Belief

The Kendall family's belief in God and doing His will is central to everything they do. This is consistent with Kim's (1988) review of the family strength literature from 1960 to 1985. Her review showed that faith/religion was the characteristic most often mentioned in research on strong families. She defined faith/religion as "a code for the guidance of living and a set of ideals toward which human life should be directed" (p. 10). Although religion is mentioned as being important in strong families, several studies have indicated it is not fundamental (Curran, 1983; Robinson & Blanton, 1993; Stinnett, Sanders, DeFrain, & Parkhurst, 1982). Schumm (1985) on the other hand, sees it differently. In his examination of the family strength literature, Schumm (1985) described a family's religious orientation as a "prime mover" that affected every other area of family life. Schumm's (1985) findings are supported and illuminated by this study which revealed that the family's religious beliefs as dictated by the Word guide *every* facet of their life. This includes their grooming standards, such as the girls wearing dresses and the length of their hair, the people they associate with, how they parent, how they conduct their marriage and parent-child relationships, their leisure activities, such as no television or extra-curricular school activities, etc. All of these beliefs are directly related to the teachings the Kendalls find in the Bible. The structure that the "Word" gives to their lives was evidenced by the fact that they often quoted scripture to explain their reasoning for doing something.

Family life satisfaction. Other research indicates that religion is a strong factor in promoting healthy family relationships and enhancing life satisfaction. Abbott, Berry, and Meredith (1990) say that religion may enhance family life five ways:

1. through social support,
2. by sponsoring family activities,
3. by supporting family teachings,
4. by providing family social and welfare services,
5. by encouraging members to seek divine intervention.

The Kendalls view the function of religion differently than these categories suggest. These categories portray religion as an organization that supports families in their goals. However, for the Kendalls, religion is not an organization or a support system, but a way of life. For the Kendalls, there is no distinction between their family life and their religion. Therefore, it is not their religion that supports their family teachings, but that their family teachings are their religious teachings. For instance, the parents said that they do not expect "the meeting" (church) to make their children what they are, but that it is the family that makes the meeting what it is.

In their study of 200 adults selected from the 20 major U.S. religious denominations in two midwestern cities, Abbott et al. (1990) found that one of the most important factors in life satisfaction is one's personal relationship with deity. This relationship with deity included the belief "that God is a reality and that his divine being is interested in the family well-being and is effective in facilitating it" (Abbott et al., 1990, p. 447). Although the Kendalls strongly believe that their family life satisfaction is due to divine intervention and that whatever goodness is in their lives is the Lord's doing, it is more than a means to enhance their family life. For them their personal relationship with deity is not just one of many important factors in establishing quality family relationships, it is the only factor. Thus, in contrast to Abbott et al.'s work, the Kendalls do not see religion as enhancing their family life but that their family life is what it is because of their personal faith in Christ. "Religion" seems to them to be an entity one step removed from spirituality. As the father said in one conversation, "We don't want religion, which is a body of people with a set of beliefs. Rather, we gather to seek the guidance of the will of God. There are a lot of religious people in the world, but there are very few who know the Lord." In any event, to explain the Kendalls' family through distinct "factors," turns us away from the wholistic contextual approach which guides this project. This study, then, gives insight into the nature of a family's relationship with deity as it is manifested in their recognition of their dependence on Him, their desire to be guided by His Word, and their willingness to do His will.

Consistency of Parental Example

Although the parents' example is important, this study suggests that there is something more fundamental than just the modeling that parents do. For the Kendalls, the fact that the parents' example takes place in the context of the parents' desire to do the Lord's will and also in the context of love and respect for their children is critical. In other words, the meaning of the parents' example would be transformed if it occurred in an atmosphere of self-righteousness and self-aggrandizement which would not foster love and respect in the parent-child relationship.

Respect and Trust

By examining the context in which respect takes place, this family reveals that respect is developed in an historical context of their religious beliefs and that they try to live by the teachings of the Word. So for them, to honor, love, and communicate respectfully despite one another's faults is what it means to be respectful.

There is a definite sense from the Kendall family that the parents respect and trust each other. Trust has also been developed as the children feel that their parents only ask them to do what is best for the child according to the teachings of the Bible. In other words, the parents are not acting on self-interest but on what they feel is right and is in accordance with the Lord's will. The trust the family members have for each other is generated by the trust they have in Christ. The children trust the parents because they know their parents trust the Lord. Likewise, the parents trust their children as they learn to trust in the Lord.

IMPLICATIONS

The social science and psychotherapy literature has not examined how religious belief and practices guide the day to day actions of families. Traditionally, psychotherapists have taken a pathological view towards the impact of religious beliefs on the problems of families in therapy rather than see such beliefs and practices as a resource to the family (Carlson, 1996). The initial purpose for conducting this research was to see how family members would explain the positive nature of their relationship, and not the impact of their religious beliefs on their family functioning. However, what emerged from the results was how the quality of their relationships and interactions are intertwined with their spiritual beliefs and practices. For the Kendalls, their spiritual beliefs provided the basis for every action, thought, and goal in their family. Such insight into the integral part of such beliefs in family and individual functioning illustrates the importance of addressing and drawing on such beliefs in our work with families. For many families their spiritual beliefs and practices are part and parcel of who they are. In order to understand such families and how they function it is critical to understand their behavior in the context of their spiritual beliefs and practices. To neglect doing so, is to risk misunderstanding the family at the least. A good example of this would be the importance of understanding the parent's marital relationship within the context of their religious beliefs. If a clinician were working with such a family, it would be easy to interpret the father's role as the authority figure in the home as domineering and superior, while the mother is submissive and inferior. This could be pathologized by the therapist and interpreted as being the source of any problem the family experiences. However, in the context of their religious beliefs and their interpretations of the Word, the parents feel that they are equal and can respectfully disagree in the decision making process. It would then be important for any clinician working with such a family to explore and understand the meanings of the parents' religious beliefs around the issues of power in their relationships to avoid pathologizing them.

Similarly, it would be important to understand the parents' religious beliefs regarding the children's extra-curricular activities. Again outside the context of their religious beliefs the family could be seen as rigid and enmeshed by a therapist. Rather, the parents are trying to impress on their children the importance and benefit of living by the teachings of the Word and that the place to learn about those teachings is in the home. The parents also want to communicate to their children that they are committed to them and that they use the Word as their guide on how to care for them. In addition, they want their children to know that they enjoy being with them, and that they perform their role as parents not just out of duty but out of love for them and the Lord.

Another important reason to incorporate the family's religious beliefs into therapy is the opportunity to draw on the great source of strength and support that such beliefs can be to a family in the midst of their struggles and problems. For example, a therapist could draw on a famiily's practice of scripture study by having the family find a scripture related to the problems that the family is experiencing. The family could then discuss how the scripture might be applied to the problem they are struggling with. Certainly, the family's emphasis on conscience could be a great resource in therapy. The therapist could explore family members' consciences related to their interacting, particularly around the problem. The therapist could ask, according to their conscience, how they felt about their own participation in the problem and what they felt they should do. Another possibility would be to ask them to search the Word and pray for guidance from the Lord on how to deal with the family's problem. One question a therapist could ask family members is "What guidance would the Word have on this matter?" Or "What would the Lord have you do in this situation?"

As therapists identify clients' spiritual resources, they can draw on them in many ways. Ultimately, clients can be better served as professionals utilize the family's spiritual beliefs and practices to support and strengthen them in their time of need.

REFERENCES

Abbott, D. A., Berry, M., & Meredith, W. H. (1990). Religious belief and practice: A potential asset in helping families. *Family Relations*, *39*, 443-448.

Blum, R. W. (1999). Protecting Adolescents from Risk. Washington, DC: The Institute for Youth Development:

Carlson, T. D. (1996). Religion, spirituality, and marriage and family therapy. Unpublished master's thesis, Purdue University, Calumet.

Curran, D. (1983). *Traits of a Healthy Family*. New York: Ballantine Books.

Gallup, G., Jr. (1996). *Religion in America: 1996 Report*. Princeton, NJ: Princeton Religion Research Center.

Handel, G. (1991). Case study in family research. In J. R. Feagin, A. M. Orum, & G. Sjoberg (Eds.), *A Case for the Case Study*. Chapel Hill, NC: The University of North Carolina Press.

Jarrett, R. L. (1992). A family case study: An examination of the underclass debate. In J. F. Gilgun, K. Daly, & G. Handel (Eds.), *Qualitative Methods in Family Research*. Newbury Park, CA: Sage Publications.

Kim, D. C. (1988). *A Review of Family Strength Literature: 1960-1985*. Unpublished master's thesis, Brigham Young University, Provo, UT.

Patton, M. Q. (1990). *Qualitative Evaluation and Research Methods* (2nd ed.). Newbury Park, CA: Sage Publications.

Robinson, L. C., & Blanton, P. W. (1993). Marital strengths in enduring marriages. *Family Relations*, *42*, 38-45.

Schumm, W. R. (1985). Beyond relationship characteristics of strong families: Constructing a model of family strengths. *Family Perspective*, *19(1)*, 1-9.

Stinnett, N., Sanders, G., DeFrain, J., & Parkhurst, A. (1982). A nationwide study of families who perceive themselves as strong. *Family Perspective*, *16(1)*, 15-22.

Thomas, D. L. (Ed.). (1998). *The Religion and Family Connection: Social science perspectives*. Provo, UT: Bookcraft.

Walsh, F. (Ed.) *(1999a). Spiritual Resources in Family Therapy*. New York: Guilford.

Walsh, F. (1999b). Religion and Spirituality: Wellspring for healing and resilience (pp. 3-27). In F. Walsh (ed.), *Spiritual Resources in Family Therapy*. New York: Guilford.

SPIRITUALITY AND ETHICS

A Cultural Trinity: Spirituality, Religion, and Gender in Clinical Practice

L. Scott Kimball
Carmen Knudson-Martin

SUMMARY. The authors present a framework for understanding the intersections of spirituality, religion, and gender in mental health and relationship problems, with special emphasis on gender equality. Clinicians are encouraged to distinguish religion and spirituality and to engage with clients at the spiritual level. Principles for practice that facilitate differentiation from cultural constructions that promote and reinforce gender inequality are proposed with case illustrations.

KEYWORDS. Spirituality, religion, gender, gender equality, differentiation

L. Scott Kimball is a doctoral student in Marriage and Family Therapy, Loma Linda University, Loma Linda, CA 92350 (E-mail: skimball@prodigy.net).

Carmen Knudson-Martin is Director of Doctoral Programs in Marriage and Family Therapy, Loma Linda University, Loma Linda, CA 92350 (E-mail: cknudsonmartin @mft.llu.edu).

[Haworth co-indexing entry note]: "A Cultural Trinity: Spirituality, Religion, and Gender in Clinical Practice." Kimball, L. Scott, and Carmen Knudson-Martin. Co-published simultaneously in *Journal of Family Psychotherapy* (The Haworth Press, Inc.) Vol. 13, No. 1/2, 2002, pp. 145-166; and: *Spirituality and Family Therapy* (ed: Thomas D. Carlson, and Martin J. Erickson) The Haworth Press, Inc., 2002, pp. 145-166. Single or multiple copies of this article are available for a fee from The Haworth Document Delivery Service [1-800-HAWORTH, 9:00 a.m. - 5:00 p.m. (EST). E-mail address: getinfo@haworthpressinc.com].

Spirituality, religion, and gender co-exist within a particular cultural context. In this paper we examine how they intersect in clinical practice, with special attention to issues of gender equality. We begin with three assumptions:

1. that spirituality is an inherent aspect of human experience,
2. that religion and gender are known through institutionalized social constructs,
3. that gender equality is central to the optimal development of intimate relationships.

We approach this paper as student and teacher in a doctoral program in Marital and Family Therapy that encourages a meaningful integration of spirituality into clinical practice. We are of different generations, genders, and faiths. We thus seek an approach inclusive of diverse perspectives and widely applicable. Because issues of gender, religion, and spirituality are value-laden, how to address them in therapy has not always been clear to us. Yet we see them as key to understanding clinical issues and how to address them, whether or not they are raised by the client or directly addressed in therapy. Believing that clinical neutrality is never fully possible, we hold ourselves accountable for the political and moral aspects of our work (e.g., Knudson-Martin, 1997; Doherty, 1995).

We first address spirituality, religion, and gender as separate dimensions of human experience relevant to therapy. Then, we draw on an expanded model of differentiation (Knudson-Martin, 1996; Knudson-Martin & Mahoney, 1999) to delineate a framework for practice that enables clinicians to use spirituality as a positive force for growth and change while attending to important gender equality issues and their relationship to religion. We conclude with three case examples that demonstrate how to use spirituality in therapy to help people differentiate from limited gender constructs and create new, more equal relationships.

THE "CULTURAL TRINITY" IN THERAPY

In Christian tradition "trinity" refers to three separate beings of the Godhead. Though bound together each has its own purpose and meaning. If the three are confused, understanding of the whole is incomplete. We use the trinity metaphor here as an important step in bringing spirituality, religion, and gender together in therapy. Though ignored for many years, it is now considered appropriate, even necessary, to address gender in therapy. Spirituality and religion, however, have been shunned from the clinical practice of family therapy (Walsh, 1999), a boundary drawn between issues of a spiritual nature and those things that are more easily addressed in therapy. According to Walsh, for most therapists opening up dialogues on spiritual issues "has been seen as more taboo than broaching such topics as sex, money, or death" (1999, p. 29). This has been changing, however, as more and more therapists have become interested in including these issues (Anderson, D. A. & Worthen, D., 1997; Prest, L. & Keller, J., 1993).

Figure 1 shows how we have put spirituality, religion, and gender together to form a cultural trinity that can serve as a guide for addressing these issues in therapy. Each reciprocally interacts with culture and is part of interpersonal and social change processes. Though distinct, each can overlap. How much they overlap depends on the degree to which they are differentiated within a particular person or group. As our Figure suggests, religion frequently overlaps both spirituality and gender, making the trinity hard to distinguish and placing religion as a mediating factor between the other two. Therapy and interpersonal change, also part of cultural processes, interact with all three.

FIGURE 1. A Model Integrating Spirituality, Religion, and Gender

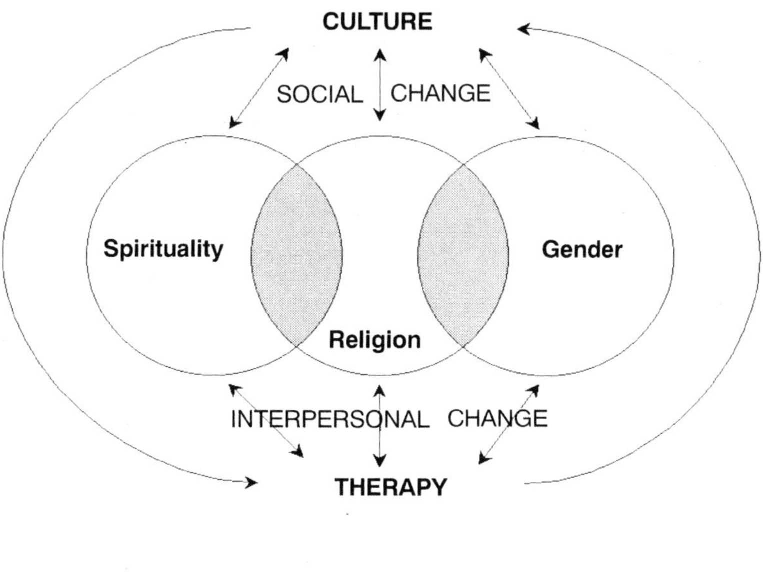

Spirituality

Systemic therapists interested in how the various aspects of clients' lives interact commonly have considered three domains, a bio-psycho-social approach. Anderson and Worthen (1997) refer to spirituality as the "fourth dimension" of family therapy. In our model spirituality refers to a vital essence within a person that "connects one to all there is" (Griffith & Griffith, 1999; Walsh 1999). Spirituality may or may not be experienced within established religious structures or institutions or include belief in a supreme being. Because it deals with the sacred and the transcendent, spirituality may be more easily understood intuitively than explained with language. It is expressed through beliefs and practices that frame the nature of a person's relation to God and/or the rest of the universe and provides a context for a personal meaning and purpose. Not all persons participate in spiritual practices, but arguably all persons are spiritual.

Spirituality is woven in some way or another into nearly all issues addressed in therapy. To leave spirituality out is to have an incomplete picture. Working in the spiritual dimension means to first identify how spirituality is related to the clinical issues. This includes how existential beliefs and experience function in a client's life and the extent to which meaning, purpose, and spiritual connection are resilient and accessible. It means asking how the issues around which the therapy is concerned impact the spiritual well-being of the clients, how developmental changes at the biological, psychological, and interpersonal levels touch the spiritual levels, and how culture and social institutions inform spirituality. It also means that we are interested in the kinds of practices, rituals, and beliefs that sustain the soul, recognizing that many clients enter therapy with damage to the soul, and that therapy can sometimes leave the soul depleted or even further damaged (Moore, 1994).

As we explore the spiritual aspect of our own lives and the lives of our clients, spirituality becomes a natural part of the therapeutic process. For some clients, therapy takes on a theme of spiritual healing or reconnection. A key to integrating spiritual work and understanding into practice is being in touch with our own spiritual nature and bringing that presence into the room. Throughout the development of this paper we have asked ourselves how our own spirituality influences our therapy and how we prepare ourselves spiritually for this work. Because spirituality is so personal, we each share here some of our own spiritual process and how we think of it in relation to therapy.

Scott. Spirituality has taken on different meanings at different times in my life. Throughout my childhood and youth, spirituality centered on knowing that there was a God with whom I could have a personal relationship. My spirituality revolved around my activity, along with my family, in an organized religion. There seemed to be unclear lines dividing my religiosity and spirituality. As I became a young adult, spirituality took on a new meaning for me as I started seeing God as a central influence in my life. I decided to serve as a missionary so as to share this part of my life with others. This process of sharing a spiritual message was similar to adding gasoline to a fire. It stimulated my spirituality with great force. Since this experience, I have placed more value on my spirituality, making a conscious effort to continue my exploration of my beliefs, my religious practices, God's role in my life, and also the manner in which I am striving for spiritual growth. As I entered the field of Marriage and Family Therapy, I brought with me a curiosity to discover the ways in which these issues could be used to promote change, growth and healing in the lives of my clients.

Whether or not the topic of spirituality will be discussed in a therapy session, I accept that my personal identity as a therapist includes my spiritual dimension. Clients come for therapy in search of answers to life's most difficult questions, often related to emotional scars, overwhelming trials, or interpersonal difficulties. Before each therapy session that I am a part of, I say a short prayer to my God that I might be effective in better understanding and assisting my clients with whom I am about to meet. This has served as a reminder to me of the spiritual aspect of my role as a therapist. It has encouraged me to broaden my visions, to strive to understand worldviews that differ from my own, and to be sensitive to my clients' personal needs.

As a therapist I espouse the notion of highlighting spirituality as a source of healing and growth (Walsh, 1999), and that spirituality can jump start therapy for some clients. For most, issues related to their own personal and unique spirituality become connected to their processes of personal growth and healing or improving their interpersonal relationships.

Carmen. Like Scott, religion was an integral part of my growing-up. Community and religion were virtually inseparable. Nearly everyone I knew shared similar beliefs about God. I learned to define myself as a "child of God" and that carried a responsibility to work toward "good." As my education and exposure to different cultures expanded, I began to distinguish between religion as a cultural institution and spirituality as a personal connection with the Divine. My early learning that "we are all God's children" has remained central, but taken on new meaning.

Spirituality connects me to "all." Spiritual practice helps me experience and maintain that connection. It expresses itself in a sense of personal and moral obligation to consider the implications of what I do on others and on the common good. I seek a faith community that supports this connection and helps me stay attuned to its meaning in my life.

As I became less fused with religion as it was handed to me, I was able (with trial and error) to distinguish my own spirituality in ways that allow me to maintain and expand upon my own religious practice while developing a more inclusive perspective. Core religious concepts from my childhood, though reconstructed, remain firmly embedded within me and impact how I define not only my spiritual life, but also my clinical roles. As a woman with a feminist consciousness, I am sensitive to the times when religion and gender bump against each other in the therapy room, as they inevitably do.

I cannot avoid bringing my spirituality, religion, and gender into the therapy room. But I have much choice about how I use them. When I bring my spiritual self to the therapy room, I am open and available to all, in touch with my common humanity and able to maintain emotional centeredness without becoming overwhelmed by the seriousness and complexity of client issues. Like Scott, I often take a moment prior to a clinical session to align myself spiritually. As I consider the spiritual aspects of my clients' lives, I want to be sure that what I do enhances spiritual growth and does not detract from it.

Religion

While spirituality is commonly associated with religious affiliation, there are some clear differences between the two. For example, a person might consider him/herself to be a spiritual person without being involved in an organized religion, and vice-versa. For many people, however, religious involvement provides a positive context within which they experience their spirituality. While spirituality and religion are deeply intertwined, when addressing gender we find it useful to distinguish the two.

We refer to religion in its institutional aspect and define spirituality as a personal construct. According to Berger and Luckman (1966), institutions are socially constructed through a series of habitualized routines and behavior that take on a reified structure that becomes separated from its original meaning. Even though the institution is socially constructed, the individual experiences it as a constant entity separate from themselves. Through socialization, institutions are legitimized within later generations. Like family processes, institutional constructs become part of the emotional substrata that influence people's behavior and help shape the personal meaning they attribute to religion. Thinking or behaving outside of these institutionalized constructs can make people feel anxious and uncomfortable, limiting the options available to them. Religion is so deeply embedded in culture that it can impact even those who do not participate in a religious body.

Religious involvement, or the degree to which a person's religion occupies his or her interests, beliefs, or activities offers a substantive type of social support, and as such has a direct effect on how one identifies him/herself (Ellison, 1994; Levin, 1994). Religion, as one aspect of context through which individuals perceive themselves and others, serves as a vehicle for socialization and identity formation for both men and women and for the definition of interpersonal roles. Relational aspects of religious activity, like friendships, are frequently a main source of social support for both men and women (Belle, 1987; Ellison & George, 1994; Ferraro & Koch, 1994; Thompson, 1991).

Religious constructs can punctuate and intensify the meaning through which moral issues are addressed. When norms or principles take on a religious or spiritual meaning, they are intensified and take on a deeper level of meaning. For example, when a person thinks that s/he needs to act in a certain way because that is "the way we do things in our society," s/he may or may not conform. However, when instructed that one must behave in a certain way because of religious beliefs, the negotiation is no longer between the individual and society, but rather between the individual and God.

As a social institution religion is not immune from cultural constructions of gender. Nor is gender sheltered from the teachings of religion. In fact, it has been part of religious teachings at least from the time of Adam and Eve. In Genesis 3:16 Eve was counseled by God, " . . . your desire shall be for your husband, and he shall rule over you." For some men, this type of doctrine may be literally interpreted and literally applied. This sense of being a "ruler" may be used to justify harmful acts such as violence, belittling acts, or "simply" not giving as much attention to the wife's opinions. Over the centuries many religions have endorsed the patriarchal role that placed the man before the woman and put women in a subordinate position to men. Men are often the leaders, directors, pastors, ministers, and preachers, making it likely that gender roles continue to be taught from a man's point of view. The repetitiveness of this pattern can make it difficult to attain a more egalitarian viewpoint.

While some religious institutions resist social change regarding gender equality, many have made great headway toward becoming more sensitive to the issue of gender in their teachings. More and more we see women fulfilling leadership positions, becoming ministers, preachers and teachers, having more voice in the religious domain. Religion need not be inherently biased against women. Many religions address teachings related to gender in a sensitive way. Some religious groups proclaim that we are all equally created and entitled, that husbands and wives are to love one another, lift each other up, support each other to be more spiritual, righteous and worthy. They attempt to use terms such as "help meet" that reflect equality rather than subordination, and emphasize doctrines suggesting equality, such as "let every one of you in particular so love his wife even as himself; and the wife see that she reverence her husband" (Ephesians 5:33).

Though religion is a social institution, one of its primary functions is to support personal spiritual growth. However, when religious beliefs are entrenched with institutionally based patriarchal dominance they can be fundamentally damaging to relationships and to the spirit. For this reason, religious beliefs can sometimes appear to contradict gender equality. Focusing on spirituality, because it is more personal, can allow individuals more freedom to move beyond institutional constructs.

Gender

We take a micro-structural view of gender; that is, what it means to be male or female is continually recreated during the life course by the opportunities available to each and through their interaction with each other (Risman & Schwartz, 1989). This view rejects essentialist ideas of inherent male and female roles and "natures." Instead, gender is seen as an institutional phenomenon, embedded in the organizations and institutions in which we interact daily (Kimmel, 2000). Family and religion constitute major venues through which male and female roles are defined and within which women and men know and create themselves. As ideas about gender change, so do these institutions.

Deeply embedded in the institutional constructions of gender is a power difference between women and men. To the extent that the old constructions remain, both women and men are encouraged to maintain these power differences. In traditional gender interaction couples conspire to hide female power and male dependencies. Women are expected to use less direct, less aggressive influence strategies than men. The legitimate sources of power are also different (Knudson-Martin &

Mahoney, 1999). Current research shows that these power differences persist despite widespread ideals of equality between women and men (Ball, Cowan, & Cowan, 1995; Knudson-Martin & Mahoney, 1998; Walker, 1996; Zvonkovic, Greaves, Schmeige, & Hall, 1996).

Many cultural images and meanings are organized around gender. These cultural constructions are not neutral, but reflect the historical legacy of a male dominant culture. Stereotypic gender differences are the result of this legacy and are perpetuated through on-going interpersonal interaction and social structures (Kimmel, 2000). They suggest that men's "traits" are more valuable and appropriate for the public sphere, that women "by nature" are more suited to the private sphere of the home, that male needs take priority, and that women are responsible for relationship quality (Zimmerman, Haddock, & McGeorge; 2001). While most clinicians are sensitive to instances of overt gender dominance, many power differences are so institutionally embedded that we do not even see them. In subtle and often invisible ways power differences shape a person's world view so that other options are not even imagined, certain issues are never raised, and accommodations to the powerful partner are automatically made (Komter, 1989; Knudson-Martin & Mahoney, 1999).

There is growing evidence that institutionally based, stereotypic gender differences are detrimental to mental health and to couple relationships. Prescriptions to be "in charge" and to function autonomously have encouraged men to deny their dependency needs and restricted the emotionality available to them, leading to neglect or denial of internal needs and behavior that can be self destructive and hurtful to others (Allen & Gordon, 1990; Meth, 1990). Many of women's symptoms such as depression, anxiety, addictions, and eating disorders have been related to prohibitions against expressing assertiveness and anger and to living in a societal context in which women are devalued (Anderson & Holder, 1989; Knudson-Martin, 2001; Lennon, 1996). While stereotypic gender differences are common among distressed couples, they virtually disappear among successful ones (Gottman, 1994; Gottman, Coan, Carrere, & Swanson, 1998). And, equality appears crucial to the establishment of intimacy (Steil, 1997).

Gender equality is therefore an important clinical concern. Yet gender inequality is so structured into social institutions that it often remains invisible and not directly raised by clients themselves. To avoid unintentionally advantaging one gender over the other, therapists need to recognize how gender inequalities may be contributing to symptoms/clinical issues and how some clinical approaches or strategies may inadvertently perpetuate gender inequality (see Knudson-Martin & Mahoney, 1996). Making the gender and power aspects of issues visible and externalizing them as part of social change processes can help free women and men from blaming themselves or each other for socially embedded problems and can open new personal and relational possibilities.

Most people fall into historical gender patterns with little or no conscious decision-making, negotiation, or recognition of how their problems are related to the social context. We advocate that therapists take a proactive role, creating space for people to consider how gender-related decisions were made and what other options might be available to them. Therapists can introduce equality-based models of health and relationship into the therapeutic conversation. Knudson-Martin and Mahoney (1996) suggest four relational criteria that can be used to address equality:

- *Equal status* (partner's hold and express equal entitlement to goals, wishes, and needs, share low status tasks, have equal power to define the relationship)
- *Mutual accommodation* (daily life is organized equally around each partner, no latent, invisible power to which one partner automatically accommodates)
- *Mutual attending* (attunement of each partner to the other's needs and interests, responsiveness to the other's state is equally demonstrated)
- *Mutual well-being* (the relationship equally supports each partner physically, psychologically, spiritually, and economically)

Few people, however, attain these goals. For example, a study of couples' "shared" decision-making found that the decisions nearly always favored the husbands' goals over the wives' (Zvonkovic et al., 1996). A study of couple's communication showed that while women initiated most topics for conversation, men determined which topics got addressed (Ball et al., 1996). In a study of newly-married "egalitarian" couples, partners created a "myth of equality" that allowed them to describe themselves as equal while behaving in unequal ways (Knudson-Martin & Mahoney, 1998). The common tendency for couples to avoid the conflicts that might arise if inequalities were addressed may maintain relationship stability in the short-term but, for reasons cited above, be destructive in the long-term.

We have found that spiritually devoted persons usually respond positively to invitations to consider each other in terms of equality. While they are often unaware of the ways institutionalized equalities seep into their lives, they typically aspire to hold "all of God's children" or "all of creation" in high regard. Men as well as women are expected to be sensitive and attentive to the needs of others and to also regard themselves as holy creations worthy of love. Spiritually attuned persons are likely to consider themselves stewards of their own well-being and that of others. As we will demonstrate in the case examples that follow, drawing upon the spiritual dimension in therapy can open the door to a more conscious consideration of equality issues.

As noted earlier, religious beliefs and practices may also form a solid basis for the development of gender equality. Many religious bodies now espouse gender equality and/or are seeking ways to address it institutionally. Religious leaders can be authoritative sources affirming equal worth and relational mutuality. On the other hand, some religious beliefs may encourage "pragmatic egalitarianism" that conceals inequalities and the existence of covert male power while professing equality (Fox & Murry, 2000; Gallagher & Smith, 1999; Kimball, 2000). Institutionalized gender and power differences oftentimes remain infused into religious tradition in ways that limit personal and relational options. The therapist's challenge is to remain respectful and open for the discussion of religious traditions without becoming stymied themselves by what may appear to be immutable beliefs supporting gender inequality.

DIFFERENTIATION AND THE CULTURAL TRINITY

Differentiation is a construct derived from Bowen's family systems theory (Bowen, 1978; Kerr & Bowen, 1988). We use it as previously expanded by Knudson-Martin (1994; 1996) to help clarify the interconnections between spirituality, religion, gender, and "self" at the emotional level and to suggest directions for practice. The expanded view explicitly includes attention to the development of togetherness as well as individuality. This is important because clinical approaches have historically valued individual autonomy over other-directedness. In so doing they not only devalue traits often associated with women, but overlook the importance of connection and experience outside or beyond the self to spiritual practice and growth.

Differentiation refers to processes within the *emotional substrata* that underlie human behavior. According to this way of thinking, culture and family generate an invisible emotional field that influences behavior. When persons remain fused within the emotional system, responses are automatic, with little choice or awareness. Movements to increase either individuality or connectedness can raise anxiety, impeding thinking and feeling. In these circumstances behavior is emotionally reactive and the repertoire of possible responses is limited. Internalized constructions of gender and religion constitute major components of the emotional system. When differentiation is low religious beliefs and practices may be rigidly and automatically adhered to or, in some cases, staunchly rejected, making spiritual connection more difficult and limiting how religious traditions, including the assignment of gender roles, can be understood and practiced.

At low levels of differentiation the ability to solve problems and accept differences is limited by the anxiety generated. Needs for individuality and togetherness become polarized, often along gender lines. Habitual ways of behaving feel like rules, making change difficult. As differentiation increases persons are able to respond independently of the emotional field, while remaining connected to the individuals and institutions that constitute it. A choice of response is possible. The ability to resolve conflicts and determine how to adapt to changing circumstances is improved.

What people experience internally is interwoven with the social context. Our approach focuses on creating emotional space for reflective response to the contextual aspects of gender and access to the more personal spiritual aspects. Like Bowen, we help people think reflectively about issues and situations to which they respond reactively. However, we depart from Bowen (or expand upon, depending on your point of view), in our respect for and attention to the subjective, intuitive, and affective dimensions, particularly in the spiritual domain. This approach is explained in more detail elsewhere (Knudson-Martin 1994, 1996; Knudson-Martin & Mahoney, 1999).

PRINCIPLES FOR PRACTICE

Our goal is to facilitate differentiation from cultural constructions that promote and reinforce gender inequality. The model outlined in Figure 1 shows a large overlap between religion and gender, but spirituality tends to be more free from institutionalized gender constructs. Thus, key to our approach is distinguishing the institutional aspect of religion from the spiritual. Working at the spiritual level allows more space for personal choice. The following principles guide our work.

1. *Recognize own emotional fusion with cultural constructions around gender and religion.* Identify ways that you automatically respond to or react against these prescriptions. What kind of behavior and thoughts seem so natural and/or God-given that you do not even consider them? This kind of response allows us to collude with or leave unchallenged hidden power differences that limit gender equality. Ask what issues raise our own anxiety or discomfort if we imagine raising them with clients? In what circumstances? For example, Carmen can feel stymied when people present religious or moral beliefs similar to those she was taught or when clients authoritatively justify unequal behavior with scripture.
2. *Join with clients around cultural constructions of gender and religion.* We often find many areas of agreement with clients on similar areas where we also struggle. In one of the case examples that follow, Scott says directly, "I share your belief (about God)." However, it is not necessary to agree with a perspective to respond in a way that validates the client's cultural experience. For example, you can honestly reflect that "being 'head of the household' carries a lot of responsibility" without agreeing that he *should* hold a hierarchical position. We agree with Doherty (1995), however, that it is important not to appear to agree with a position that carries moral consequences (such as gender inequality) without making room for the client to consider the implications of his or her position.
3. *Trust that accessing spirituality decreases anxiety associated with religion and gender.* When gender/religious issues are emotionally charged it is easy for the therapist to feel anxious too. He or she may be tempted to either avoid or "attack" the issue. In these instances we find that accessing our own spiritual awareness helps us remain engaged with clients and the difficult issues. It encourages us to look for ways to engage the spiritual dimension in the therapy and avoid defensiveness about religion. For example, Scott reports in one of the case examples that he felt confused. In this case his solution involved bringing an aspect of his own spirituality into the conversation. In other cases the therapist's own spirituality may "simply" help the therapist take a non-reactive position that keeps options open. Spiritual reflection, while oftentimes using similar words, comes from a different place than religious "talk" or dogma.

4. *Look for invitations by clients to engage in spiritual reflection.* When clients make passing reference to God or spiritual practice such as prayer, therapists often address the other content of the statement while by-passing the "private" spiritual/religious areas which may seem emotionally charged and not available for reflection. In contrast, we listen with an ear attuned to them. In the first case example, Carmen uses the client's spontaneous statement about God to engage in a reflective conversation that empowered the women.
5. *Contribute alternative visions of gender into the conversation.* While cultural constructions of gender are shifting toward egalitarian ideals, most of us are still so infused with constructions from a patriarchal context that we overlook many possibilities. The four criteria for equality listed in the previous section are very helpful. We can ask who accommodates and attends and how? We can help people examine how one person's welfare or decisions may end up taking priority. Though addressing interpersonal processes and structures, we find that this kind of conversation is facilitated in the spiritual dimension where the focus is more inherently open to mutual respect and where traditionally "male" characteristics are not automatically valued more than the "female" intuitive, expressive ones.
6. *Help clients identify ways to integrate spiritual practice and gender relationships.* When prayer is already a part (or former part) of people's lives, it can contribute to gender reconstruction processes. Daily or special rituals can also be developed. We encourage couples and families to find ways to make their spiritual connections real and visible to them. For example, one couple decided that when dealing with conflicts they would consciously invite Jesus to join them. Jesus, they said, would want them to listen to each other. Another couple decided to join hands and be aware of the love that flows through them.

The case examples that follow show how we applied these principles in three different types of cases. In each, spirituality was differentiated from reactive/automatic beliefs and behaviors to open new, more equal possibilities.

CASE EXAMPLES

"Like a Woman"

This example shows how fusion with patriarchal cultural constructs limited a female client's ability to feel entitled to equality. Differentiation was facilitated through a discussion of the "feminine" nature of God.

Unlike most clients, Jennifer identified relationship inequality as the issue for which she sought help. Though articulate and clear when seen individually, even the thought of disrupting her relationship by raising her concerns evoked extreme anxiety. She described fastidiously monitoring her husband William's needs, attending diligently to him, and carefully organizing their family schedule around his needs. As a religiously devoted couple she and William had formed what he described as a "team" based on a division of responsibility and separate spheres of authority. Jennifer appeared to accept these roles, but felt that she was in a one-down position, "like a dog on a leash." William described their relationship as "equals," but said there needed to be *a* leader. He thought Jennifer wanted to be the leader. Though concerned about her unhappiness, he could not conceive of a non-hierarchical partnership.

The hierarchy in their relationship was supported by a myriad of institutionalized constructions of family and religion. When she began to question one of these constructions in an individual session, I used the opportunity to expand the spiritual dialogue.

Jennifer: We listen to a program about family. They say God wants women to follow men. I don't think so. Why would He have given me a mind? Why not make me a robot?

Carmen: You think God wants you to use your mind?

As Jennifer connected with her personal spirituality, she began to expand her view of God and herself:

Jennifer: Yes . . . , I think God is more like a woman than a man!

Carmen: More caring?

Jennifer: And strong . . . in a good way.

Carmen: God is both caring and strong? Are you too?

Jennifer: Yes. I think I am.

Jennifer had always feared upsetting her husband. When she drew on her spiritual strength, the anxiety lessened, allowing her to address her concerns "without caving in" or feeling "guilty." Following the session, she found the courage to engage William, whom she believed was good and also like God (and whom she trusted would not physically hurt her), in an in-depth conversation about equality. Though William did not enjoy their conversation, both returned to couple's therapy more able to address conflicts that had been suppressed to maintain "harmony."

Becoming "Whole"

This is an example where fusion with social constructs of masculinity and femininity limited a couple's ability to experience emotions around grief and contributed to violent behavior. Encouraging them to reconnect with spiritual feelings and practices helped them differentiate from these old gender constructions and expand their emotional and relational options.

When Franco and Lucy were referred to me, their family was, in their words, "in complete shambles." Following several incidences of "spousal battery" involving both of them, Child Protective Services had declared them unfit parents and removed their children from the home. Though mandated to attend family therapy, both appeared to want to change their lives. But they did not know how. The more deeply entrenched their troubles, the more each responded according to stereotypic cultural constructions that limited the options available to each on the basis of their gender. Franco, reacting to strong prohibitions against showing weakness or vulnerability, was unable to express any emotion but anger. Lucy, trained to "hold her counsel," remained silent while her loneliness and resentments grew. Eventually violence would erupt. Their emotional volatility frightened them. Each felt powerless to impact the other or change their situation.

During the intake session, I asked the couple if they were members of a particular religion and if they practiced their faith. They reported that they had been baptized into a church several years ago but that they were not currently practicing members. I also discovered that in addition to the children removed from the home, the couple had a daughter named Jaycee, who had tragically passed away from cerebral meningitis at the age of 11, four years prior.

Therapy began traditionally. Goals were established around maintaining safety for the couple, integrating more positive interactions, parenting education, and assisting the couple in discovering new ways to resolve their conflicts. Periodically the couple would note that since the death of their daughter four years ago their life had deteriorated drastically. Apparently prior to Jaycee's death, they had functioned much better.

In the 5th session I created a spiritual opening by asking, "How is Jaycee involved in your lives today?" The couple did not understand the question. I attempted to clarify my question.

Scott: You have both shared with me that you believe that Jaycee is in Heaven. Is Jaycee able to see what you are doing on a day-to-day basis?

Franco began to cry:

Franco: I would be ashamed if Jaycee was able to see the way that I have treated her mother. I know she can see me because I feel her there. I just haven't wanted to admit that I know this.

Lucy added: I want to make her proud of us and let her know that we can be as good of parents as we were when she was alive.

Inviting the couple into the spiritual dimension through directed questioning changed the course of therapy. Almost immediately their relational options began to expand, with both of them expressing deep feelings and speaking openly from their hearts. As they reconnected spiritually through daily prayer, returning to church, acknowledging their continuing relationship with Jaycee, and showing respect for each other, they freed themselves to become whole, more able to be intimate, more able to address conflict.

"Man of the House"

This case shows how cultural constructs of masculinity were passed from father to son. As these constructs were challenged through spiritual conversation with the parents, the father became more able to differentiate from them, redefining his role in the family and modeling more egalitarian behavior for his son.

When 8-year-old Nick came in for therapy along with his mother, he was struggling to accept the recent separation and divorce of his parents. His parents, Layne and Lindsi, were very spiteful towards one another and had frequent vicious arguments in front of their two sons, Nick, age 8 and Josh, age 4. Lindsi was anxious to get him in for therapy to resolve his angry outbursts. Nick had recently started hitting his mother and would at times sneak up from behind and hit her with a baseball bat, a behavior not present prior to the parents' divorce.

At the initiation of therapy, it was made clear to Lindsi that success of therapy depended on the cooperation of both parents. Layne was invited and agreed to participate. In the second session, I met with the parents to discuss the situation. Lindsi shared her concern that Nick was possibly confused regarding his father's message that "now that he was out of the house, it was Nick's responsibility to become the man of the house." Lindsi also disclosed that the main reason for their divorce was a long history of domestic violence by Layne.

Layne appeared somewhat remorseful for his violence toward Lindsi and said that he was sorry for his behavior. He also shared his belief that as the patriarch of the home, he felt that it was his duty to "keep his home in order." His way of keeping his wife in order was to threaten or to actually use violence. He believed that God had organized families in a structured way that justified the violence as God's will:

Layne: . . . If a man couldn't control his house he would not be considered worthy of being at the head of the family.

I felt caught in a trap for a moment, not sure which way to turn. I wanted to present a respectful tone for their religious and spiritual beliefs without condoning the violence.

I asked Lindsi to share her personal beliefs in God, specifically about God's characteristics. She stated that God was "all loving, merciful, kind, powerful," and that she was able to pray to her God. Then I asked Layne if his beliefs in God were similar or different. He said that his beliefs were the same, that the two of them shared the same belief system. I joined with the couple around their spiritual beliefs by sharing, "I too believe in a God similar in characteristic to the God that you have described."

Then I challenged the discrepancy between Layne's vision of God and the violent behavior:

Scott: It is hard for me to believe that a God who is all loving, merciful, kind and powerful would want for a husband to hurt his wife in any way. (Directly to Layne) How could a God that is the way that you have both described to me want you to hurt your wife?

Layne seemed a little stunned by the question. I wondered if he had offended him, and possibly damaged the therapeutic relationship. Then Layne lowered his head and become silent for a moment. As tears rolled off of his cheeks, he looked at his ex-wife and said, "I'm sorry for what I did." He described how he had twisted the teachings of his religion in a way that endorsed the violent control.

Through further dialogue related to their religious beliefs, Layne was able to clarify the connection between his relationship with God, his religion's doctrine and his role as a father. When he shared his belief that he was a son of God, I encouraged him to consider how he could mirror the characteristics of God as a father. Through this process, Layne shifted his spiritual role in the family and his interpretation of his religious beliefs. The couple learned to co-parent effectively and Layne began to model a new way to be a man. Nick's aggressive behavior diminished.

CONCLUSION

Differentiating from cultural constructs of gender promotes options for growth and healing for both women and men. In some cases the institutional nature of a client's religion may have reified and endorsed gender constructs that promote inequality. Therefore, when addressing religious issues we have found that a move to a spiritual, more personal level opens up potential for change that might not be possible if the client remains emotionally fused with these constructs.

We have found that as we engage with conflicts between religion and gender equality, we are tapping into issues that can be very emotional both for clients and for us. We have needed to be well grounded in our own spirituality and be differentiated regarding these issues in our lives. Then we can show respect for clients' beliefs while encouraging new possibilities and addressing the moral and relational issues associated with gender inequality. Our experiences have increased our commitment to the value of encouraging clients to use their spiritual beliefs and relationships with God to promote healthy relationship change.

As we have worked with cases such as those previously shared, we have become aware that our willingness to engage at the spiritual level has been deeply important to our clients. Through this type of work we have been able to safely venture into emotionally charged terrain that may have otherwise been very difficult to access in a beneficial way. For example, Lindsi explained to Scott's supervisor how therapy helped her family develop spiritually and change destructive gender patterns. We conclude with her words stressing the importance of this work:

Lindsi: One session really stands out to me. It was like our beliefs were challenged, but not in a disrespectful way . . . he helped us clarify who we felt God really was. It was made clear to us that a loving God wouldn't support or encourage anybody to beat anybody else . . . After that session I went home and prayed for what seemed to be hours. I felt so hurt and angry that I didn't even care if I ever saw him again . . . the change that happened between my ex-husband and me would never have happened had we not included the Lord.

Supervisor: What if Scott hadn't been willing to include the spiritual sides of your lives in therapy?

Lindsi: Then I don't think I would have accepted him into our lives . . . we have rebuilt our family established on solid rock, without including this we wouldn't have had the foundation we needed to rebuild.

REFERENCES

Allen, J. & Gorden, S. (1990). Creating a framework for change (pp.131-151) In R. Meth & R. Pascik (eds.), *Men in therapy: The challenge of change*. New York: Guilford.

Anderson, C. & Holder, D. (1989). Women and serious mental disorders (pp. 381-405). In McGoldrick, M., Anderson, C., & Walsh, F. (eds.), *Women in families: A framework for family therapy*. New York: Norton.

Anderson, D. A., & Worthen, D. (1997). Exploring a fourth dimension: Spirituality as a resource for the couple therapist. *Journal of Marital and Family Therapy*, 23, 2-12.

Ball, J., Cowan, P., & Cowan, C. (1995). Who's got the power? Gender differences in partners' perceptions of influence during marital problem-solving discussions. *Family Process, 34*, 303-321.

Belle, D. (1987). Gender Differences. In The Social Moderators of Stress (pp. 257-277). In R. C., Barnett, L. Beaner, & G. K. Baruch (eds.), *Gender & Stress*. New York: Free Press.

Berger, P. & Luckmann, T. (1966). *The Social Construction of Reality: A Treatise in the Sociology of Knowledge.* New York: Anchor Books.

Bowen, M. (1978). *Family therapy in clinical practice*. New York: Jason Aronson.

Doherty, W. (1995). *Soul searching: Why psychotherapists must promote moral responsibility*. New York: Basic Books.

Ellison, C. (1994). Religion, the Life Stress Paradigm, & the Study of Depression. In J. Levin (pp. 78-121), *Religion in Aging and Health*. Thousand Oaks, CA: Sage.

Ellison, C., & George, L. (1994). Religious Involvement, Social Ties, & Social Support in a Southeastern Community. *Journal for the Scientific Study of Religion, 33,* 46-61.

Ferraro, K. F., & Koch, J. R. (1994). Religion and Health Among Black and White Adults. *Journal for the Scientific Study of Religion*, 33, 362-375.

Fox, G. R., & Murry, V. M., (2000). Gender and families: Feminist perspectives and family research. *Family Relations*, *62*, 1160-1172.

Gallaher, S. K., & Smith, C. (1999). Symbolic traditionalism and pragmatic egalitarianism: Contemporary evangelicals, families, and gender. *Gender and Society*, *13*, 211-233.

Gottman, J. (1994). *Why marriages succeed or fail*. New York: Simon & Schuster.

Gottman, J., Coan, J., Carrere, S., & Swanson, C. (1998). Predicting marital happiness and stability from newlywed interactions. *Journal of Marriage and the Family, 60,* 5-22.

Griffith, J. & Griffith, M. (1999). *Sacred encounters*. New York: Guilford.

Kerr, M. & Bowen, M. (1988). *Family Evaluation*. New York: Norton.

Kimball, L. S. (2000). *Couples' Communication Patterns: Avoidance of Addressing Power and Equality*. Unpublished research paper. Loma Linda University.

Kimmel, M. (2000). *The gendered society*. Oxford University Press.

Knudson-Martin, C. (1994). The female voice: Applications to Bowen's family systems theory. *Journal of Marital and Family Therapy,* 20, 35-46.

Knudson-Martin, C. (1996). Differentiation and self-development in the relationship context. *The Family Journal, 4*, 188-198.

Knudson-Martin, C. (1997). The politics of gender in family therapy. *Journal of Marital and Family Therapy*, 23, 421-437.

Knudson-Martin, C. (2001). Women and mental health: A feminist family systems approach (pp. 331-359). In M. MacFarlane (ed.), *Mental health and family therapy*. New York: The Haworth Press, Inc.

Knudson-Martin, C. & Mahoney, A. (1996). Gender dilemma and myth in the construction of marital bargains: Issues for marital therapy. *Family Process, 35,* 137-153.

Knudson-Martin, C. & Mahoney, A. (1998). Language and processes in the construction of equality in new marriages. *Family Relations*, *47*, 81-91.

Knudson-Martin, C. & Mahoney, A. (1999). Beyond different worlds: A "postgender" approach to relational development. *Family Process*, *38*, 325-340.

Komter, A. (1989). Hidden power in marriage. *Gender and Society*, *3*, 187-216.

Lennon, M. (1996). Depression and self-esteem among women (pp. 207-236). In M. Falik and K. Collins (eds.), *Women health: The commonwealth fund survey*. Baltimore: Johns Hopkins University Press.

Levin, J. (1994). Investigating the epidemiological effects of religious experience: Findings, explanations, and barriers. In J. Levin (pp. 78-121). *Religion in Aging and Health*. Thousand Oaks, CA: Sage.

Meth, R. (1990). The road to masculinity (pp. 3-34). In R. Meth & R. Pascik (eds.), *Men in therapy: The challenge of change*. New York: Guilford.

Moore, T. (1994). *Care of the soul: A guide for cultivating depth and sacredness in everyday life*. New York: Harper Perennial.

Risman, B. & Schwartz, P. (1989). Being gendered: A micro-structural view of intimate relationships (pp. 1-9). In B. Risman & P. Schwartz (eds.), *Gender in intimate relationships: A micro-structural approach*. Newbury Park, CA: Sage Publications.

Steil, J. (1997). *Marital equality: Its relationship to the well-being of husbands and wives*. Newbury Park, CA: Sage Publications.

Thompson, E. (1991). Beneath the Status Characteristic: Gender Variations in Religiousness. *Journal for the Scientific Study of Religion*, 30, 381-394.

Walker, A. (1996). Couples watching television: Gender, power, and the remote control. *Journal of Marriage and the Family*, *58*, 813-824.

Zimmerman, Haddock, & McGeorge. (2001). Mars and Venus: Unequal planets. *Journal of Marital and Family Therapy*, *27*, 55-67.

Zvonkovic, A., Greaves, K., Schmeige, C. & Hall, L. (1996). The marital construction of gender through work and family decisions. *Journal of Marriage and the Family*, *58*, 91-100.

Addressing Spirituality in Its Clinical Complexities: Its Potential for Healing, Its Potential for Harm

Melissa Elliott Griffith
James L. Griffith

SUMMARY. The decade of the 1990s brought increasing acknowledgment by mental health clinicians of the importance of spirituality in many clients' and patients' lives. This acknowledgment has opened therapy to healing resources that spirituality can offer. However, it also means that a clinician must address how spirituality can be expressed destructively. We illustrate a clinical approach towards elucidating this complexity, supporting healing roles for spirituality while countering harmful ones, through the telling of one mother and son's journey in search of treatment for a disabling psychiatric disorder. These clinical principles characterize a collaborative, dialogical approach for engaging a person's spiritual life in therapy, both its potential for healing and potential for harm. *[Article copies available for a fee from The Haworth Document Delivery Service: 1-800-HAWORTH. E-mail address: <getinfo@haworthpressinc.com> Website: <http://www.HaworthPress.com> © 2002 by The Haworth Press, Inc. All rights reserved.]*

Melissa Elliott Griffith is Clinical Assistant Professor of Psychiatry, The George Washington University Medical Center.

James L. Griffith is Professor of Psychiatry and Neurology, The George Washington University Medical Center.

Address correspondence to: James L. Griffith, MD, George Washington University Medical Center, Dept. of Psychiatry and Behavioral Sciences, 2150 Pennsylvania Avenue NW, Washington, DC 20037.

Some material in this article also appears in Griffith, J.L. & Griffith, M.E. (2001), *Encountering the Sacred in Psychotherapy: How to Talk with People About Their Spiritual Lives.* New York: Guilford Press.

[Haworth co-indexing entry note]: "Addressing Spirituality in Its Clinical Complexities: Its Potential for Healing, Its Potential for Harm." Griffith, Melissa Elliott, and James L. Griffith. Co-published simultaneously in *Journal of Family Psychotherapy* (The Haworth Press, Inc.) Vol. 13, No. 1/2, 2002, pp. 167-194; and: *Spirituality and Family Therapy* (ed: Thomas D. Carlson, and Martin J. Erickson) The Haworth Press, Inc., 2002, pp. 167-194. Single or multiple copies of this article are available for a fee from The Haworth Document Delivery Service [1-800-HAWORTH, 9:00 a.m. - 5:00 p.m. (EST). E-mail address: getinfo@haworthpressinc.com].

KEYWORDS. Spirituality, collaborative, family therapy

Often when we engage with people in therapy about their spiritual lives, it seems that we are dipping into a flowing, refreshing stream. We want it to flow through our therapy conversation both because it is vital to them and because it brings new stories and possibilities to the therapy. Sometimes, though, this stream seems to be polluted, and the pollutants almost toxic in their effect on people. Stepping out of the stream is not an option, certainly not one that we as therapists could promote when the person deems this water to be life giving. We are left, knee or neck deep, to work together with the person to see and strain out the pollutants from the refreshing water.

This paper will be about that process of dipping into the stream while straining the pollutants. We will illustrate the guiding principles and some of the methods we employ, both to open therapy to spirituality and religion and to counter those spiritual and religious elements that do harm. The central tenets are (Griffith & Griffith, 1994, 2001):

- Creating a sociobiological environment for dialogue
- Opening conversational space for both/and perspectives when participants disagree
- Engaging voices of the community of concern, including spiritual communities
- Structuring therapy as a participatory democracy, sufficiently egalitarian to enable each participant to speak freely, to be heard, and to be seriously considered
- Countering the destructive influence of a charismatic spiritual authority, respectfully but firmly
- Discerning collaboratively any adverse effects of personal spirituality–practices, beliefs, and community–on the individual and on others
- Supporting spiritual communities and honing counter-practices that oppose exploitation conducted under the guise of spirituality

We will illustrate these ideas and methods as we tell the story of our work with a Mozambican family, 18 year old Lutchi and his mother, Thelma, and their community. We have chosen this story for three reasons: First, it contains both the constructive and the destructive potentials of spirituality; second, Lutchi and Thelma actively helped us learn how to deal with the destructive elements; third, they want their story to be told so that others can learn.

We begin in the middle, taking this from a transcript of a particular family therapy session with Thelma and Lutchi that encapsulates both the healthful possibilities and the dangerous consequences of Lutchi's religious beliefs and spiritual community. This was one of many points of intersection between Lutchi's spirituality, the illness he bore and the treatment he needed.

It was the first time Lutchi, Thelma, and I (Melissa) had met since the horrible upheaval. After the confusing crisis of being put in jail, Lutchi had been psychiatrically hospitalized and had mood-stabilizing and anti-psychotic medications restarted. Now he was returning to his old self, the person we all knew, and he was reflecting on the episode. He was explaining to me and to Thelma what God had taught him through all this:

"You know, Melissa, I want to try to be like Jesus, but what I have to realize is that Jesus didn't have Bipolar Disorder," Lutchi said pensively. "I've been thinking about this and I am sure he didn't."

"Gosh, Lutchi, I've never thought about that. How do you know?" I was intrigued.

"Well, you know when Satan tempted Jesus in the desert?" Lutchi checked.

I nodded. Since my childhood, I had heard told repeatedly the Bible story about the temptations of Christ, in which Satan offered Jesus power over all the earth if he would simply obey him (Matthew 4:1-10).

Lutchi continued, "When Satan took Jesus to the side of the cliff and said to him, 'If you will follow me you can leap off this cliff and the angels will lift you so that you will not be hurt.' Well, you know, Jesus said, 'No!' Of course, he knew that was wrong. But if he had had Bipolar Disorder, and if he were not taking his medications, he would have thought that was a great idea! He would have said something like, 'Yeah, man, I can fly! Let me fly!' He would have jumped right off, not because he was proud, but because he would be tricked into thinking it was a great idea. That is what Bipolar Illness can do to you. It can let you get easily tricked and make you think wild things are possible. So if I am going to be like Jesus, I've got to take those medications."

Lutchi's reasoning seemed stunningly brilliant to me, a creative, coherent understanding that guided him to care for his body, his soul, and his relationships. Of these three, his first priority was his soul, his commitment to live in ways that honored his faith. While his faith was presently providing him safety and stability, only two weeks earlier it also had led him into chaos and danger.

Back then he had been convinced that the Christian response to his illness was to depend on God for healing. To take the medicines would show he doubted God's power. That was the belief held by Lutchi and many of his fellow church members. "It would be like a slap in the face to God, " he said, "if I ask God to work through the healer but on my own I still take the medicine." Despite our dire warnings and Thelma's pleas, Lutchi demonstrated his faith by ceasing his medications after the healing service. This was not a solo act, but one supported by Lutchi's like-minded friends. However, those friends were not there days later when mania and psychosis took over Lutchi's personality. He became irritable, loud and grandiose, misperceiving social cues, and approaching strangers too closely in public settings. In a restaurant the guests became frightened by his extreme behavior and wild talk. The police were called and Lutchi was taken away to jail. This jail was not a safe place for a confused, naïve Mozambican young man. Finally the authorities realized that he needed to be in a hospital instead of a jail and got him to the mental health emergency center. Diagnosed there as being in an acute state of mania, he was admitted to the inpatient unit. There, as it became possible for him to again think clearly, he began to reflect on his situation using the language, metaphors, and stories that were so well known to him, the stories of Jesus.

From these stories and in prayerful conversation with God, Lutchi made a commitment to take his medicine. He was drawing on meanings that were foundational to his life, meanings far more convincing than any that I, as his family therapist, or Griff as his psychiatrist, could provide. Nor could either of us have come up with an inventive question that could have prompted Lutchi's realization that if he were to be like Jesus, he would have to recognize that Jesus did not have Bipolar Illness, thus he would need to take his medication. This recognition came from Lutchi's own intimate knowledge of and relationship with Jesus. It was bolstered when the members of his church came to share his understanding of Bipolar Illness. Yet his earlier decision to stop the medication also came from his relationship with Jesus. So how did he get from there to here, from the either/or position that put him in danger to the both/and position that created safety and possibilities?

While we could not have convinced Lutchi to step into a both/and position, we do believe we can create an environment for a relaxed, fair, and just dialogue that will hold this space open. The potential obstacles to justice and openness in a dialogue with Lutchi and Thelma were not subtle. They were apparent from the moment we met. We, as settled white citizens, established in our professional communities, meeting them, non-citizens, people of color, having had to detach from that which created their honorable identity in their home community.

FROM MOZAMBIQUE TO THE UNITED STATES

Lutchi and Thelma were still quite new to the United States when we first made contact. They had not yet established a community that could stand with them together as mother and son to mitigate the effects of Lutchi's illness on their lives. They had left behind in Mozambique a rich network of family and friends who had been helping them during the illness. For Thelma, moving also meant forsaking meaningful and much needed work. Years earlier she had been in the United States to study how to establish small businesses. She had eagerly returned to Mozambique to apply her knowledge so that other women might gain a fairer economic chance in their newly independent country. To leave her homeland again had been a difficult departure, but not a difficult decision. The choice was clear: remain in a country where Lutchi's prognosis predicted deterioration and institutionalization, or to move to a country that held promise for his treatment and improvement.

Until this point, this was the course his suffering and search for help had taken:

As a seventeen year old, he began struggling with his school work for the first time, finding it hard to concentrate. The next year he affiliated with a local Christian church that became increasingly the central focus of his life as his school and social functioning declined. Dark, depressed moods appeared with days of weeping and isolation, alternating with other periods of intense activity when Lutchi would walk the streets at all hours of the night, aggressively proselytizing his religion upon strangers. Psychiatrists in Mozambique and in neighboring South Africa diagnosed schizophrenia and prescribed antipsychotic medications. They urged Thelma to accept that Lutchi had a chronic, disabling mental illness and predicted that he would need to be placed in an institution. "But the boy you are meeting in these quick consultations is not Lutchi!" she told them, "And you cannot make a judgment about him when you don't even know who he really is. He is still here," she insisted, for she could catch glimpses of the son she had known, the

Lutchi who had been a sensitive, friendly boy, a talented musician, an excellent student.

The symptoms fluctuated but wore on, eroding Lutchi's social connections and his future. Thelma determined that his best shot for good psychiatric treatment was in the United States and set about finding a way to get here. Some Catholic nuns she had known in college helped her and Lutchi to get set up in this country. They steered Thelma to contact Griff for psychiatric treatment. Griff's evaluation determined that Lutchi had symptoms of Bipolar I Disorder, with extreme mood swings and psychotic thought disturbances, a serious illness, but treatable. We then worked as a team with Griff serving as Lutchi's psychiatrist and me meeting with Thelma and Lutchi in family therapy.

Creating a Sociobiological Environment for Dialogue

"What are your concerns?" I (Griff) asked Thelma.

"I want Lutchi to listen when I need to discuss something with him," Thelma responded, "Not only when I talk with him about taking his medicines, but other times too, he loudly interrupts me and will not let me finish what I am saying,"

"But she will not listen!" Lutchi interjected. "I try to tell her that faith even the size of a mustard seed can move a mountain! But sin has bound her ears, and she will not hear the truth!"

"When you take your medicine," I asked, " is it easier or harder to have the kind of conversation and relationship with your mother that you believe God would want you to have?"

"I prayed that God would heal me of the Bipolar Disorder, and I believe that he already has. I don't believe that the medications are necessary, but I continue to take them because my mother is afraid. She does not have faith," Lutchi countered.

"I also want you to be healed," I responded. "But as a doctor, I don't have any authority to say whether God has provided that healing. I do want you to be able to listen in conversations, to have a respectful and kind relationship with your mother, and to be able to participate in the life of the family. These medicines have helped other people keep stable moods so they can accomplish these kinds of things. Who else in your life can help us judge whether the medicines are helping in that way or not?"

With Lutchi, I sought to create and to sustain a dialogue. That is, I tried to support a back-and-forth conversation of responding to Lutchi's concerns, listening to those from Thelma and family friends, while voicing as well the clinical perspective of psychiatry. I participated actively, encouraging a quiet, thoughtful consideration of ideas, while redirecting or reframing strong emotional expressions, particularly blaming or shaming comments. This was intended to keep the conversation at a low "emotional temperature," in which Lutchi could more fully participate without activating psychotic mental processes. If we could initiate and maintain this kind of multi-voiced dialogue long enough, I hoped that our conversation would generate a perspective inclusive enough for Lutchi to make use of the best that psychiatry could offer while still honoring his commitment to his religious beliefs and practices.

I hoped we could identify which medications would contribute most towards Lutchi residing in emotional postures of tranquillity. Emotional states of being of mammals, including humans, can be divided into two broad groups– those of tranquillity, which support nurturing, parenting, play, reflection, and other such life activities; and those of mobilization, which support attacking, defending, stalking, fleeing, and other such life activities (Griffith & Griffith, 1994). Lutchi could sustain a dialogue if he could reside mostly in emotional postures of tranquillity. As a psychiatrist, I could bring to the dialogue explanations for Lutchi's symptoms from clinical neuroscience, together with guidelines for psychopharmacological treatment. Other participants would evaluate the efficacy of the different medications in achieving these ends. In such a therapy, criteria for effectiveness of medications is the extent to which their influence opens possibilities for dialogue and relationship. Well-selected medications should make it easier for Lutchi to stay in dialogical, rather than monological, conversations and relationships.

Lutchi's illness highlighted the tension between two competing paradigms for treating mental illnesses. Most clinicians trained in the late twentieth century pursued a professional identity of an applied scientist who would value foremost a scientific understanding of illness. Such a clinician seeks what are the best-validated scientific facts about a problem and conveys this knowledge to the client or patient. Treatment is then organized by these scientific principles. Yet empirical research on clinical practice has emphasized that it is the therapeutic alliance that holds most sway in the success or failure of treatment. The relational rigor needed for a strong therapeutic alliance demands that a clinician begin by understanding the client's or patient's experience and organizing treatment within this framework. These stories of personal experience may have little to do with what science would say about a problem (Griffith & Griffith, 1994).

Our work with Lutchi has displayed this strain between science-oriented and person-oriented understandings of problems. On the one hand, Lutchi showed a spectrum of symptoms that would be diagnosed by psychiatric professionals as Bipolar Disorder–euphoria, irritability, irrational behavior, excessive energy, racing thoughts, rapid speech, impulsivity, loss of a capacity to self-critique one's behavior. Scientific research has suggested that this collection of symptoms is related to instability in brain systems that regulate biological rhythms involving energy, sleep, and mood. A voluminous body of psychiatric research has defined treatment principles for medications to control these symptoms.

On the other hand, Lutchi experienced his illness as a consequence of sin and a fallen world. The solidity of this belief was buttressed by the beliefs and practices of his church community. Guided by this sense of his illness, it followed for Lutchi that the appropriate solution for his distress lay in faith, prayer, and petitions to God for healing. A healer from within his religious tradition, not a mental health professional, would be the natural agent for invoking God's healing.

How can these divergent perspectives be integrated? As a psychiatrist, I must ask:

- How do I offer psychotropic medications in a manner that is collaborative?
- How can medications be prescribed in ways that would be responsive to Lutchi's relational world?

In seeking answers to these questions, I am aware that human life is always conducted under a dual set of enablements and constraints: those of discourse and those of physiology. Discourse refers to aspects of human life that are institutionalized by language and social practices. Physiology refers to aspects of human life that reflect interactions among the material elements of a person's body that give it a physical structure. Either changes in discourse, expressed through metaphors, stories, beliefs, customs, and traditions, or changes in physiology, expressed through states of neurotransmitter systems or neural networks, can open or close different possibilities for lived experiences. It follows from this notion that optimal clinical treatment will often draw from both discourse-based and physiology-based therapies. Thinking about deregulated brain systems or traumatic life events as enabling or constraining influences, instead of causes, helps avoid dead-end discussions that debate whether clinical problems are biological or psychological in essence. Concern then can focus upon what practical steps can make therapeutic changes easier to achieve (Griffith & Griffith, 2001).

Opening Conversational Space for Both/And Perspectives When Participants Disagree

We posed the question earlier of how Lutchi was able to move from his either/or position, faith/or medicine, to a both/and position. Our responsibility was not to move him, but to hold open an inviting space for him. Early on in our relationship, I (Melissa) recognized that this would be a challenge. I not only disagreed with Lutchi's beliefs, I was turned off by the way he espoused them. On one hand I knew that I respected him as a person, yet I could feel the therapeutic curiosity draining out of me as he proclaimed his truths. I could not discern whether the intensity of his proclamations was related to bipolar symptoms or to religious fervor, but this question did not provide me enough tentativeness to remain adequately engaged. Too automatically, I associated Lutchi's beliefs, tone and words with religious rigidity and sexism. Stereotyping was closing my mind and heart, pulling me to an either/or position. It had to be countered. Stereotypes do not just dissolve, or, I at least am unable dissolve them by force of will. For me, these stereotypes must be actively melted in a kiln of intellectual, emotional, and spiritual engagement. Inviting multiple stories, listening to what else might be contained in this canon of Lutchi's spirituality, desiring to be surprised rather than confirmed in my judgments, telling those stories to others–this is the work that fires that kiln. Here is a reconstruction of a session that took place after Lutchi had begun to take medicine, but before it had effected significant changes in his moods and thoughts. He was striving to be a good, cooperative son and house-mate. Rather than cleaning, however, he was preaching, and his intense preaching was exhausting Thelma's patience.

Only Thelma, Lutchi, and I were present for this session. Thelma had stated that she needed more help around the house and Lutchi agreed that he should be helping his mother more. In turn he wanted her to attend to his primary concern–her salvation. "What is the worth of a clean house without a pure and contrite heart?" he asked.

"Lutchi," Thelma responded, "I am interested in you and your thoughts and I like for you to read the Bible to me sometimes. Maybe we could share a daily devotional together, but I cannot take the preaching, preaching, preaching."

I asked more questions to make distinctions between Thelma's experience of being "preached at" and of "sharing with," hoping to find a middle ground for Lutchi to speak of what was important for him in a way that he could be heard. Thelma cast the distinctions along the lines one might expect: Preached at, she said, felt abrasive, intrusive. Sharing with felt inviting, respectful.

Lutchi said that he knew that his preaching, sometimes perhaps too harshly critical, was not a perfect reflection of Christ, but he felt in a bind. Though he was later to change to a more inclusive way of thinking, Lutchi did not, at that time, consider Thelma's Roman Catholicism to be sufficiently Christian. Besides, he added, he could see the ways his mother was not godly. He wanted his mother to be saved, and if not he, then who would tell her? He sometimes even feared his well intended efforts were pushing her away from God, but he could not cease. I understood this intellectually, but it was hard for me to empathically connect with Lutchi's bind.[1] Perhaps that is why the tone of my questions to him became increasingly more instructive than reflective. Predictably, this heightened the tension and Lutchi's speech became more and more pressured. I had privately wondered all along if the changes Thelma and Lutchi wanted were possible while the bipolar symptoms were not yet controlled. I felt I had pressed for a change too soon.

We had only ten minutes left when I acknowledged their desire for change and confessed that not only had I failed to help, but had made things worse. I said that I had no more ideas and asked if they had any ideas. Thelma did not, but Lutchi said, "Well, if you can't help us and we can't help ourselves, maybe we should ask God to help us. Let's be quiet and give God a chance to speak to us." Thelma and I agreed and we were quiet with our heads bowed. I was surprised that the long silence that followed was possible after such intense, pressured speech. This quiet alone seemed constructive.

Finally, Lutchi spoke, softly and at a much slower pace. "The Lord gave me a word," he said. "I have been hurting my mother when I need to honor her and help her. I have been hurting her feelings, but I've also been hurting her ears." Thelma nodded affirmatively. "You know the story, in the garden of Gesthemane, Jesus is praying, knowing he is going to die soon, and the Roman soldiers come to take him away. Well, Peter–you know, I am a lot like Peter–leaps up to defend Jesus. Peter takes his sword and slices the soldier's ear right off. But Jesus said, 'No, Peter, this is not what I ask of you.' Jesus puts his hand on the guard's head and heals him."

"And this is not what Jesus asks of me either. Hurting my mother cannot be of God," Lutchi said to me. I told him I was very moved and encouraged him to speak with Thelma about this ear hurting. "Have I hurt your ears, Mom?" he asked her.

"Yes, Lutchi, it's true, sometimes you have." Then Thelma smiled, "But you have not cut them off."

Lutchi laughed, "Well, that's good news."

Though his understanding of the effects of his actions and his desire to stop the abrasive preaching was obvious, I wanted to make a plan with Lutchi and Thelma to keep this healing story at the forefront of their exchanges. I wondered how they would know if the sword came out, if ear-hurting was about to begin to intrude into their relationship again. After all, I speculated, it sounded like Peter's hand went to his sword almost automatically. Maybe he didn't even know what he was doing till he did it. But since Lutchi and Thelma were in this together, they could make a signaling plan, so Lutchi would know and could stop in time.

They playfully constructed a signal. Thelma would cup her hand around her ear, and say, "Ouch! Your sword is nicking at my ear!" and Lutchi would "put down his sword" and stop.

I do not know how much change this session effected for Thelma and Lutchi, but the session changed me. With my own eyes I had seen escalating manic symptoms settle down. I was quieted by the power of Lutchi's spirituality, of his reflective reception of his word from the Lord, of this help that came with such therapeutic accuracy, that affected bodies, brains, and relationships when neither Thelma and Lutchi nor I could help.

In this session and in others to come, I was mystified by the shifts that so quickly occurred when Lutchi conversed with his God. I believed that his mind was more prepared to reflect on those conversations with his God, because the medicine had begun to stabilize his brain. This is the both/and perspective that Griff and I had adopted, and that we hoped would also be acceptable to Lutchi.

Engaging the Voices of the Community of Concern

With Lutchi, my (Griff's) agenda as a psychiatrist was first to gather those who should have input into treatment decisions. I wanted to engage his community whose members would own accountability for supporting him and staying engaged by observations, reflections, and conversation about the course of treatment. These participants were selected by asking Lutchi and Thelma: Who should be aware of your treatment with me? Whom do you want to be involved? Usually I met with Lutchi and Thelma together, at least for part of each session. When the conversation focused upon areas of Lutchi's life that needed privacy, I met with him alone. At other times, sessions included friends or church members whom Lutchi identified as his community. I did not want judgments about the need or effectiveness of medications to rest only with my professional assessment, but to include the assessments of other trusted people in Lutchi's life.

Likewise, our family meetings had an open format. Usually only Thelma, Lutchi, and I (Melissa) met, but sometimes they brought along other people, Mozambican visitors and American friends. Sometimes, we had agreed in advance to have a particular person join us for a specified purpose, but often the arrival of the guests was a surprise to me. Lutchi was happy to have other people in our sessions. Always an inclusive person, he seemed to enjoy introducing people he cared about to each other. This fit well with ideas I endorsed of gathering for therapy the problem-organized system (Anderson & Goolishian, 1988). Together we made the therapy a hospitable environment. Lutchi's illness easily became isolating for both Thelma and himself. It was difficult to explain to other people, and sometimes his symptoms could be misinterpreted as willful behavior, reflecting badly on both mother and son. Thelma wanted their friends to participate in the meetings, so that they could better understand the illness and could then become more supportive. This inclusion was consonant with the rest of their life. Thelma made her home open to Lutchi's friends, many of whom were from his church, an exuberant, warm African-American community who accepted him into their group, appreciating and encouraging his musical talents. When friends were down on their luck, Lutchi would bring them home offering shelter and Thelma's home cooking. Their apartment was sometimes crowded, but Thelma remained flexible and interested in getting to know Lutchi's friends.

Though she is a kind person, these were not simply acts of kindness. Thelma realized that in Lutchi's world of conservative charismatic Christianity along with the many who would nurture and support him, there were a few who could captivate and exploit him. This was not her world, but she literally opened her doors to it because she needed its doors to be open to her. She wanted to be able to enter when necessary to help Lutchi safely navigate it.

By the same token, though the therapy was hospitable, the inclusion of others was not simply an act of hospitality or of humility. To be effective, the meaning-making of this illness and the treatment offered needed to fit with the community which Lutchi chose. Otherwise, we posed dual risks of rejection: Either the treatment could be rejected or Lutchi could be marginalized or rejected.

Structuring Therapy as a Participatory Democracy

I was glad for their friends to join us for another reason: They helped to balance the power of the therapy relationship. The more community members involved, the more I shifted towards the position of a visitor, my learning their ways rather than vice versa.

Griff and I could not escape the reality that our roles positioned us as experts. Moreover, we knew that we might unwittingly perpetuate colonizing practices, by assuming to know too much what was best for them. We risked acting in culturally inappropriate or disrespectful ways. From her childhood experience in Mozambique, as well as in her later years, Thelma had experienced the effects of the lingering colonialist attitudes and racist habits of relating, even when these habits were unwittingly and inadvertently perpetuated by her friends. When our relationship felt solid enough, I shared with her my concerns and asked her to be on watch with me, to inform me if ever she sensed this. Should I inadvertently perpetuate these attitudes, I hoped we would have a means to address it. Thelma then informed me that from the first moment of our contact and all along, she had been watching both Griff and me. She explained that she watched, because it was her duty to watch, every health professional they met to see if they were treated with respect. She did not pursue treatment if they were not.

When Lutchi brought friends from his church to both our offices, we saw the respect and care they had for him. We were always listening for the meaning they made of his illness and of the role of medication in his treatment. Even within this relatively small religious community there were multiple positions. Some of the friends supported medical treatment for Lutchi while others did not. Among those who did not, some had witnessed miracles and hoped for such healing for Lutchi. Lutchi, emboldened by their support, could speak more freely of his desire to be totally healed, without the use of medicines. We could honestly join them in this wish. Who could argue that it would be wonderful for Lutchi to be healed? Who can really know what the future holds? On the other hand, we would consistently reinforce Thelma as she took the lead in explaining the medical understanding of the illness and treatment. Our intent was to have a therapy in which all positions could be heard and seriously considered, including those which, though benevolent in their intent, we definitely disagreed and even felt could be dangerous. In time, Lutchi's thoughts became more sequential and goal-directed. His irritability diminished with many fewer explosions of indignation directed towards Thelma. He could engage more easily in casual conversation, and was less pulled towards polemical preaching to others. His capacity for focused attention improved enough that he could read books again, restoring what had been a cherished leisure activity. He enrolled in school and restarted music lessons. At home, he accepted more household responsibilities and Thelma began to provide him with more autonomy. Thelma said she felt that the son she had known was coming back. While Lutchi recognized these changes as positive, he remained uncomfortable with the notion of being helped by medication and not solely by God.

Openly Presenting Our Own Dilemma When We Are at Odds with the Person Consulting Us

Within a few weeks it was obvious that our collaboration, always tenuous around the issue of medicine, was beginning to break down. Medication side-effects were partly to blame, but it was more that this kind of solution did not fit what Lutchi understood to be a spiritual problem. He felt an uncomfortable rigidity in his muscles that was a side-effect of the antipsychotic medication. More significantly, he said that the antipsychotic medication made it difficult "for me to hear God's voice."

In a family therapy session, Lutchi announced his decision to go to a religious meeting to seek healing by a faith-healer. He had seen this evangelist's upcoming visit advertised on television and heard good reports from other people. He believed that God had planned a healing for him and he wanted to receive it. He said he planned to discontinue the medicines the day before the meeting to show his faith in God.

Thelma had searched with Lutchi so long and so far for an effective treatment only to have it now abandoned for the faith healing. This prospect was distressing to Thelma and to us. Though none of us could have guessed that the psychosis would take him in such a disastrous direction, we all believed that he would be interrupting a well-functioning treatment and put himself at risk for a relapse.

The date of the faith-healer's meeting was weeks away, and Lutchi agreed to take his medicines until immediately prior to the healer's arrival. We continued to have family therapy meetings during this period. Looking back, I (Melissa) can see that it may have been just as difficult for Lutchi to stay in conversation with me as it was for me to stay in conversation with him. He was eagerly anticipating this glorious event, wanting the day to come soon, while Thelma and I were apprehensive and would have delayed it as long as possible. I think we all worked together during this period not to let our differences dominate our meetings.

Collaborating with Thelma and Lutchi, the meetings were expanded to include Lutchi's pastor and some of his church members, most often a man named Randy. Randy had a gentle sense of humor and regarded Lutchi as a younger brother, acting protectively yet holding him accountable. Lutchi's pastor, Randy, and the other, albeit selected, friends who came to our session endorsed both the medicines and meeting with the healer. These friends, Thelma, and I posed to Lutchi many questions: Could God's healing not work in concert with the medicine? Are there not many kinds of healing–physical, emotional, spiritual? To what community is this faith-healer accountable? If this person is not of God, how would you know? Does the belief by Thelma, your pastor, and your friends that you should take the medicine make you wonder if you are hearing God's direction clearly? Can you imagine anything that might be distorting how you hear the voice of God? Has that ever happened to you before? Or to other believers you have known?

The question I most frequently raised was, "Will you continue to talk with God about this? Can you hold open the possibility that God does not require of you that you stop the medicines?" I openly expressed my dilemma to Lutchi, "I know that I do not know what God has in store for you. I have seen with my own eyes the healing that comes through your listening to God, and I know you earnestly seek God's will. It is hard for me to see, though, how putting your newfound health at risk could serve God, and all that I have seen in this field indicates that stopping the medicines would do that. Will you continue to talk with God about this?" Lutchi always answered that he would do so, though he was nearly certain about this. He said that God would have to give him a very clear sign if he were not to stop the medicines. He often left the door open with, "God has been known to do that though. He just may. If so, I'll let you know."

Thelma, Griff and I were all concerned about what might happen if Lutchi discontinued his medicine. This would put much in danger: the stability of his nervous system, the predictability of his behavior, and the security of his relationship with God, if he were to perceive God as a breaker of promises. It also would pose a long term risk for exacerbation of the Bipolar Disorder. Mood-stabilizing medications when abruptly stopped often do not work as effectively when later restarted.

While both Thelma and I continued to hope Lutchi might reconsider, Griff accepted that Lutchi had chosen this course and worked towards holding open the possibility of future repair. He asked Lutchi to plan with him for the future. Did Lutchi have any ideas what he'd want to do if problems persisted after the healing, or if it was only partially successful? Lutchi told Griff that if the healing did not occur, "then perhaps this slower process [medicine] is better."

In the end, Lutchi was true to God's will as he understood it. He ceased his medications and went to the healing. In just a few days, the symptoms of mania began to escalate. This is when the earlier described episode of agitated behavior in the restaurant occurred. It led to jail, then to the psychiatric hospitalization, and, later, his reflections which we detailed in the beginning of this article. Not only did Lutchi realize that "Jesus was not bipolar," but friends who had encouraged him to go to the healer and stop taking the medicine realized that Bipolar Disorder is an illness that deserves medical treatment. They visited Thelma and Lutchi, apologized to Thelma for endangering Lutchi, and pledged their support for his treatment.

A New Illness Brings a New Challenge for Lutchi's Spirituality

This would seem to have been a good ending. Then several weeks later without warning a new illness intruded–a neurological movement disorder. In the space of a single day, Lutchi's head, arms, legs, and trunk began twitching and jerking, spontaneously and uncontrollably. Over ensuing days, the movements became exaggerated to the point where daily activities, such as walking, dressing, and eating were arduous tasks. Only during sleep did the movements cease.

Since the abnormal muscle movements of tardive dyskinesia are a well-known side-effect of antipsychotic medications, this was my (Griff's) first consideration. Yet the sudden onset and pattern of affected muscles was disturbingly different from tardive dyskinesia. I could only tell Lutchi that I did not know what was wrong, but would try to help him find someone who did. Over the ensuing weeks, however, the psychiatric and neurological consultants were also unable to establish a diagnosis or successfully control the movements. All treatment trials failed, except when medication doses were raised to such high levels that Lutchi could not stay awake. Indeed, the disorder intensified to tragic proportions. The writhing movements became so incapacitating that Lutchi was unable to attend to his basic needs and, as it progressed, could not sit in a chair or walk. He was so determined to keep going that he resorted to crawling. His knees became scraped and bloodied from crawling. His head became bald over the back from the unceasing twisting and rubbing against walls while bracing himself as he attempted to navigate.

One referral led to another and Lutchi was admitted to a prestigious psychiatric inpatient unit in another state. When the pharmacological treatments were again unsuccessful, the staff became convinced that his problem was psychological in origin and reinforced by the attention his illness received. They told Thelma that she was too emotionally involved with Lutchi and that she needed to let him be more independent. The treatment team pointedly asked her, did she really want to help Lutchi? "Of course! I would do anything to help Lutchi," she responded. Then she would need to join their team, they told her. They were certain they could help Lutchi, but only if she participated. In her company, they planned to confront Lutchi with their conclusions that he had been pretending illness to them and could stop the movements if he so chose. Their behavioral analysis had deemed the strongest motivator for Lutchi to be his mother's visits. Therefore, their behavioral modification protocol called for Thelma to tell Lutchi that she would return to visit him only when his doctors reported that he had improved himself. Additionally when Lutchi fell to the floor, she was not to help him up, and she was not to help him when he struggled with his food.

Very soon Thelma removed Lutchi from the hospital and brought him home. We had a family therapy meeting following these events. Together, mournfully, they told the story. Thelma, weeping, said she would never forget the betrayed expression on Lutchi's face when he saw her standing in line with the experts. The behavioral program had been briefly instigated but it had brought only pain and humiliation. Never again, Thelma said, would she follow an expert against her better judgment. In our session Lutchi's writhing body could not stay in the chair, but his mind was clear and focused. He had made meaning of his trial. He had not lost hope, but certainly had transferred it away from medicine. "Perhaps great difficulties are being manifest so that God's glory can be greater when he heals me," he reasoned.

He said the doctors' arrogance had made them "intellectual barbarians," and proclaimed he would see no other doctor save Griff from now on. "But Lutchi," I intoned, "Griff doesn't know what to do. He wants to help you by finding someone who does know."

He was adamant that he would see only Griff because he knew that Griff was "a man of God." Fairly certain that Griff had not discussed religion with Lutchi, I asked him why he said that. "Because he is not filled with the arrogance of men. None of them know what this disease is but only he will say, 'I don't know.'"

Before we concluded the meeting, Thelma turned to Lutchi and pleaded for him to forgive her for believing the experts instead of him and for participating in it all. Lutchi granted his forgiveness, acknowledging that he knew she was trying to do what was best for him. But, he said, it might take time to repair the trust that was broken. There was a gap now between Lutchi and the medical system, but more importantly, a rift between Thelma and Lutchi. Into this rift entered Sister Jane.

Countering the Destructive Influence of a Charismatic Spiritual Authority

Sister Jane was a semi-retired white evangelist with no particular denominational affiliation. She made her living by selling nutritional supplements. Though not a part of Lutchi's church, she had been peripherally involved in his life before the hospitalization. Following the failed behavioral approach, she became central. She persuaded Lutchi that God had appointed her to help him be miraculously healed. In our meetings, Thelma appeared tense and vigilant, as Lutchi exclaimed to me (Melissa) what an unbelievably wonderful woman Sister Jane was. She visited with him for hours every day, conducted prayer and Bible study with him, and even wanted to employ him in her business. Thelma and I raised serious questions with Lutchi about Sister Jane. Thelma went to others in Lutchi's community, ministers and friends, and asked them to help. Some did, but there was no convincing Lutchi that the intensity of his relationship with Sister Jane might not be in his best interest. He felt that she was a gift from God. Privately, Thelma told me she felt that her voicing further objections to Sister Jane would be counterproductive, so she chose to watch carefully and hold her tongue. This was hard, especially when Sister Jane would give Thelma tips on how to mother Lutchi.

The connection between Sister Jane and Lutchi posed an expensive dilemma for Thelma, emotionally and financially. Sister Jane insisted, and Lutchi believed, that dietary supplements, including the ones she sold, would help him, so Thelma purchased them. Thelma feared that Sister Jane was on the brink of directing Lutchi to cease contact with medical people. Thelma talked with me about how she should deal with Sister Jane. We had long conversations as she considered the possible actions she might like to take and the concerns that constrained her. She determined to continue her stance of cautious connection and I, in turn, asked her what role Griff and I should take in relation to Sister Jane. Thelma felt that, if it was acceptable to Lutchi, we should invite Sister Jane to visit one of our meetings that would include herself and Lutchi. She asked that we not confront Sister Jane but that we try to get acquainted and, if possible, to clarify what the requirements were for

Lutchi's health and safety. She felt that our meeting would diminish the likelihood of our being excluded from Lutchi's life.

Sister Jane initially declined invitations to our meetings, but Thelma urged us to invite her again. We did so, convening a meeting with both of us, Thelma and Lutchi, and Sister Jane. Sister Jane arrived armed with information about her dietary supplements, and told us how God had put Lutchi in her life as her "last great mission." Lutchi, usually lively and gregarious, was submissive and quiet in Sister Jane's presence, seemingly in awe of her. I also found myself silenced, not because I was in awe, but because I was in a bind. I knew that my task was to avoid polarization, yet the questions that came to my mind were in the service of debate, not dialogue (Becker et al., 1995). My goals became reduced to only "Do no harm." I quietly listened and asked if there was room for medicine or therapy within Sister Jane's plan. She said that since Lutchi was already seeing doctors, she would not stand in the way of medical treatment. She had not known Lutchi long, so Griff and I led a detailed recollection of what had happened previously when he had ceased all medications, and she nodded.

Thelma and I met a few days later. She reported that the day after the family session Sister Jane told Lutchi she had a new word from God that he should quit all medicines and other treatments. Also in this word, God had told Sister Jane to adopt Lutchi, that she was his true spiritual mother and that he should live with her to complete his healing. She would teach him music, manners, and Bible every day, so that when the healing was complete he would be ready to fulfill his special mission in life, for he could carry on the work she had begun. As a twenty year old, Lutchi was free to make his own decisions. He chose to stay connected with his earthly mother Thelma, but to live with his spiritual mother, Sister Jane. Because he wanted to honor his mother, Thelma, Lutchi said, he would continue to take the medicine. Lutchi still required assistance with physical mobility, eating, and other tasks of daily life. Thelma did not contest the move. As she and I talked this through, Thelma recognized her diplomatic success. She took heart in the knowledge that Lutchi was able maintain his tie to her in this potentially polarizing situation. Thelma decided to take this opportunity to get some needed rest, hoping that the work would soon wear Sister Jane out. It did, and within a few weeks Lutchi came back home, though Sister Jane continued to visit.

Several months had now passed since the onset of the movement disorder and, with the exception of Lutchi, we had all been coming to terms with the likelihood that he might never be able to control his movements again. Griff bore the burden that it was likely one of the medications he had prescribed, medication that Lutchi had not wanted, that had triggered the movement disorder. He was deeply saddened, but could not say what he would do differently if given the situation again, nor what he could do now except be faithful to the relationship and, as long as they wanted, to continue search for help. Thelma struggled with whether the time for acceptance had come, but felt in her heart that she had not exhausted all means. She persuaded Lutchi to see one more doctor, Dr. Jose Apud. He had been a researcher in the National Institutes of Health and was an expert in unusual movement disorders. He diagnosed Lutchi's problem as tardive dystonia, a rare complication of treatment with antipsychotic medications. Tardive dystonia has a poor prognosis with little known about effective treatments, unlike the more common tardive dyskinesia. Dr. Apud, however, had in mind an experimental regimen that had helped some other patients. With a combination of careful research, hope, and humility, Dr. Apud started Lutchi on the regimen.

Due to travel, I (Melissa) did not see Lutchi or Thelma for several weeks. Much changed during that time. Just as I was returning to the country, Thelma was returning to Mozambique, but before she departed, she left me a long phone message:

> After three months of treatment with Dr. Apud, there was some improvement. Lutchi could manage his basic physical needs now so she could take leave for this long needed trip. Randy had become a close and trusted friend to Thelma and to Lutchi, and he would be staying with Lutchi during her absence. She said she could feel better about leaving if an appointment was made for Lutchi to come and see me soon, as he was eager to do. She mentioned, too, that there was nothing more to worry about with Sister Jane.

When Lutchi arrived at my office, he walked in with a stunningly steady gait. He had asked Randy to hang back so he could independently show me how well he was. He sat in the chair, almost still, with only a few involuntary movements remaining. "These will get better too," he noted, "and if they don't, praise God anyway." While I had not dared to hope that such a recovery was possible, Lutchi had never considered that it would not occur. I cannot report much of the content of that meeting because the jumble of joy, surprise and relief overwhelmed my memory. I asked about Sister Jane, and Lutchi said that he had realized that she was "just a confused person," and that God had not intended her to be his guide. Lutchi had a solid friendship with Randy and had become wiser, he said, in knowing whom his true and safe spiritual friends were. I was eager to learn more about how he had become wiser, and he promised to explain it to me at a later meeting.

Discerning Collaboratively the Effects of Personal Spirituality Practices, Beliefs, and Community–on the Individual and on Others

The transcript below is taken verbatim from an audio recording that Lutchi and Randy made with me. In this meeting they were not in the role of clients, but as long distance co-teachers for a psychotherapy workshop. I had often told both Lutchi and Thelma how much I was learning from them, yet I was rarely able to fully articulate the lessons. As soon as I thought I knew something, another surprise would come along to challenge my thinking. Thelma, Lutchi and Randy knew that we relayed their story to other therapists, and they shared our desire that they be more directly involved in transmitting the lessons of their experience and of our work together. My initial focus for this teaching interview was the therapeutic dilemmas that arise when religion and spirituality threaten harm, the topic for a workshop that Griff and I were preparing. This focus widened, however, as soon as Lutchi began to speak:

Melissa: So I was planning to tell the workshop group about you and Thelma and Randy and your friends, but to especially focus on the story of your experience with Sister Jane. Would that be okay?

Lutchi: Wait. Don't just tell about her, but about my early immature faith. You should share that, too.

Melissa: What do you mean? What would you want me to say about that?

Lutchi: As a zealous, immature Christian–faith without knowledge. Not wanting to take the medicine. I don't mind, really, I would like for you to share that, too. There was a phase where I, like many religious people, was immature and a young believer. I would call spirituality, mature religion. Spirituality is the positive side of religion, and zeal without knowledge the negative side. Zeal without knowledge is religion with just rituals.

Melissa: Without spirit?

Lutchi: Without spirit. Like the Pharisees, the Zealots. Not zealots in the positive sense as people on fire for God, but people who are narrow-minded, stubborn and stiff-necked. We all go through that at some point in our lives. We meet God and God says come, and we run. We want to go ahead of God. We get overexcited. And there are so many doctrines out there, so many people saying so many things, and we don't know. It's normal that we don't. There is a foundation being built, a filter being built in our lives and not yet finished, and we don't know how to filter yet. When someone like Sister Jane comes on the scene, proclaiming that she is appointed by God to help heal you, with so much authority, well, the filter just doesn't always catch it.

Melissa: Is there a way that therapists can be of help with that?

Lutchi: I wasn't thinking so much of therapy. I was just thinking of myself, what I have to do.

Melissa: So, it's pretty much something you have to do alone?

Lutchi: Oh, no! [laughing] Not alone! You know the Holy Spirit is a pretty good therapist. And Randy is a pretty good therapist too sometimes. But real therapists, I think they just have to let it go, you know. You have to let me go through that trial. But it's okay, it's okay, because remember trials cause perseverance, and perseverance causes character, and character causes hope, and hope doesn't disappoint. I am wiser now. I know the signs, but the first time you see the signs you ignore them and then you shipwreck.

Melissa: The signs? You can look back and see signs?

Lutchi: Yes. Domination and intimidation. And I think I had something in me that was attracting this type of relationship.

Melissa: So you've done some serious thinking about that. But she was pretty convincing.

Lutchi: Yeah, very convincing. In fact, I sometimes miss her. It scares me. Not that I am afraid of her curses, but just afraid of being with an unstable person. I know that God will protect me, but still I will stay away from her. I've got to stay away from her. When she gets familiar with you, she starts treating you like trash.

Melissa: Lutchi, how did you get free of her influence? One time when I saw you she had so much power, then the next time, I saw you and Randy–no more Jane.

Lutchi: I didn't have to get shipwrecked, I got someone who could show me and wake me up to it.

Melissa: Who was that?

Lutchi: It was Randy, right here! He opened my eyes, showed me how she was using me.

Melissa: Randy, how did you do that?

Randy: We just talked.

Melissa: But, how did you know?

Randy: I just noticed several times where she kind of ran over us. I just told Lutchi. I'd been holding it in my gut a long time. So I told him, "Lutchi, she is hyper-religious and she is using you. She's intrusive."

Melissa: How did you spot the using thing?

Randy: Hey! Don't you know? I've had eleven years of experience working in a Christian bookstore. Lots of nice folks, but I met all types. I've been through it all.

Melissa: I bet you have, but still I don't know how you spot the users.

Randy: I just do. I don't know if it's their actions or what they say, or that they just have an air about them.

Melissa: An air?

Lutchi: I think Randy has a 'user-alarm.' [Much laughter all around] And it's a good one!

Melissa: A user-alarm! Wow, what a great thing to have. Do you really, Randy?

Randy: You know, I do keep my antennae up. And I knew Jane. She was so superior, like: 'I listen to God and you don't.' And I'm like–'Okay. Next!' I don't even entertain it. I walk circumspectly and can take care of myself, but when I found that Lutchi was involved with her, I said,

'Oh, yikes!' So I just started pointing out to Lutchi all of the day-to-day ways she was disrespecting him, and Thelma, and me.

Lutchi: And once he told me I started connecting things, and then, I just didn't believe her anymore.

Supporting Spiritual Communities and Honing Counter-Practices that Oppose Exploitation Conducted Under the Guise of Spirituality

As we continued the conversation, I tried to learn more from Lutchi and Randy about the role of a therapist. Lutchi commented on the fact that I was taking notes and explained to Randy that Griff and I often did that. He said that had been useful in the therapy, that with all the ups and downs, it was helpful for a therapist to make a record for a person. In supporting his movement towards accountability, I had written, as he dictated, what he had learned were signs to attend to, signs that he was on-track, warning signs, and his plan of what to do if he were about to get off-track. Most of our talking time was detailing and documenting what Lutchi, Randy and Thelma had done together. I learned and recorded in writing more from Randy about how people can develop good user-alarms, and from Lutchi about the both/and of believing the best about people even while assembling a user-alarm. I would later offer my notes back to Lutchi for revision and expansion, for continued honing of the counter practices he was developing along with Randy and others.

Following Lutchi's lead, we tried to respect the personhood of Sister Jane, even as we confronted her predatory practices. "Demonize ideas, not people. Fall in love with people, not ideas," was a dictum we wanted to follow. However strongly we objected to the dishonoring institutional practices of the behavioral psychiatry unit or to Sister Jane's exploitation, we could believe that both the psychiatrists and Sister Jane were complex people, likely doing some good in other contexts of their lives, even while doing harm in their interactions with Thelma and Lutchi.

Two years later Lutchi now continues to do well, and he and Thelma are quite willing to have their story shared with anyone who might benefit. As is obvious from the length of this vignette, it was impossible to isolate the thread of therapy or of spirituality from their story. To tug on one thread seemed to pull out another. Neither the problems nor the solutions were simple. Lutchi's movement disorder would not have occurred without the precedent of his psychiatric treatment. Sister Jane could not have bonded so powerfully with Lutchi, if the inpatient psychiatric treatment had not created the gap. If spirituality did not figure so prominently in Lutchi's life, he would not have been so vulnerable to the promises of either the faith healer or Sister Jane. One might speculate that he could have employed the medical system much more efficiently without those distractions. However, without the steadfast hope built on his foundation of faith, he may well have forsaken all systems of help much earlier. Were it not for the nuns who supported and assisted Thelma, she might not have gotten Lutchi to help. Were it not for his church friends who stood by him through it all, he might have caved in from loneliness. And, as Lutchi said, "The Holy Spirit is a pretty good therapist." Thus in all of the potentially isolating circumstances of illness and misguided treatments, he was never defeated and he never felt alone.

As for the solutions, there is no quick explanation of how therapy, including family therapy, helped Lutchi to escape Sister Jane's influence, because therapy alone could not have done so just as therapy alone could not have restored Lutchi's health. We believe that we have articulated some therapeutic principles worth considering, yet we know that this therapy was conducted with a wise mother, a resilient son, and a committed spiritual community. The tenets we have put forward are in the interest of avoiding the therapeutic errors that would fail to support and strengthen this wisdom, resilience, and commitment, or at the least having a relationship with sufficient checks so that if such errors are committed, a therapist can be informed and can change.

The principles we have highlighted in this story are not specific to working with spirituality. They are about maintaining dialogue, collaborating, respecting local knowledge and cultural wisdom. The ideas that helped us keep dialogue and avoid debate at points when we differed were drawn from therapists who have worked with warring groups to oppose destructive polarization (Becker et al., 1995). Notions from narrative approaches (Epston & White, 1990, 1992; Freedman & Combs, 1995; Weingarten, 1995; White, 1989, 1995) called us to curiosity about the other stories in Lutchi's cannon, to collaborative discernment with him and his community about the effects of ideas and influences, to design counter practices. They reminded us to attend to the power distribution in our culture and in our therapy. They helped us to listen intelligently by maintaining intentionally a not-knowing attitude. They kept us aware of and searching for multiple descriptions, and focused our work on the language, meanings, and values of the other.

DE-CENTERING THE THERAPY

Lutchi's response to the questions about therapy, "I wasn't thinking so much of therapy. I was just thinking of myself, what I have to do," reminded us of Michael White's (2000) message, "Be influential, but de-centered." It seems the best role for a therapist is to foster peoples' connection to those in their own community where knowledge, connectedness, credibility, and vigilance for exploitation are close at hand.

While we have focused primarily upon our clinical dilemmas involving Lutchi, the collaboration of Thelma in the therapy was more crucial to its success as any contributions we made as clinicians. We were tempted to regard Thelma with awe as "an amazing mother," but this would have reduced her to a uni-dimensional figure and granted her no space for doubts and failures, no room to be real. We wanted to meet her as a complex, multi-storied woman, to respect her power and wisdom by asking about their sources, her stories. She had told many stories of her heritage, the difficulties her father, mother, and grandparents had creatively met and much about her own political work and ideals. We inquired about these in a formal way when we were once again asking her and to help us teach the lessons of this story to other therapists. In preparation for a workshop in New Hampshire, I had typed a fax to send to Thelma in Mozambique. It contained several questions to elicit her reflections about their trials, the therapy, the medical treatments, the racism she had endured, the encounter with Sister Jane, and the community. As I was about to send it, I realized I had not asked the question that was most compelling to me, not just as a therapist and a teacher, but as a woman and a mother. At the bottom of the fax, I penned this longwinded query, "Just one more question, Thelma. *How did you do it?* Through it all, the mother-blaming, the vicissitudes of US culture, the separation from your family and your professional identity, and the worst, you said–the proddings of people to give up on your son and get on with your life. Even when you wondered what you should do, you seemed to remain clear about your identity. I realized that even with all our conversations I still don't know–How did you do that? How did you keep such clarity about who you were?"

Thelma faxed a typed response to almost all my questions. She said, however, that she wanted to give more thought to the last one and that she would send that answer later. Finally her second fax arrived.

17-9-99

Dear Melissa,

I was able to keep clear of who I am because I always felt proud of being a Mozambican. When I completed my studies at the American University in 1990, one of my professors offered to be my sponsor if I wanted to become an American citizen. I thanked him a lot and told him that I preferred to be a Mozambican. This was when according to The World Bank statistics Mozambique was considered the poorest country in the world. We are poor but confident that tomorrow will be better. We are a happy people with a rich culture. We have a great capacity to love, to share and to forgive. In 1975, after 10 years war for independence, we celebrated our achievement with the Portuguese. Many people of Portuguese origin choose to be Mozambicans. Mr. Andrew Young, an ex-ambassador of the USA to the United Nations, said that the only two multicultural societies in the world were the United States and Mozambique.

As an African woman I feel as a struggler. We are considered second-class citizens in our society, but we know we are the backbone of the family, the mothers, the breadwinners. Men are coming to understand and recognize our contribution. We will one day be part of the leadership of this country.

Melissa, it was a good question. This is how I did it. And remember what I told you–Never underestimate the power of a mother in pain.

Love,
Thelma

NOTE

1. Later that evening, at home, I heard myself lecturing our son, Van. Though Van was fairly tolerant, I knew as I spoke that I was diminishing my chances of being heard by him. Yet I could not stop "preaching" because I felt my message was so important to his well-being. All at once, I connected with Lutchi's bind, remembered the mangled ear, stopped and apologized. This was Lutchi's gift to me.

REFERENCES

Anderson, H., & Goolishian, H. (1988). Human systems as linguistic systems: Preliminary and evolving ideas about the implications for clinical theory. *Family Process*, 27, 371-393.

Becker, C., Chasin, L., Chasin, R., Herzig, M., & Roth, S. (1995). From stuck debate to new conversation on controversial issues: A report from the Public Conversations Project. *Journal of Feminist Family Therapy*, 7, 143-167; also in Weingarten, K. (Ed.) (1995), *Cultural Resistance: Challenging Beliefs about Men, Women, and Therapy*. New York: The Haworth Press, Inc.

Epston, D., & White, M. (1990). Consulting your consultants: The documentation of alternative knowledges. *Dulwich Centre Newsletter*, 4, 25-35.

Epston, D., & White, M. (Eds). (1992). *Experience, Contradiction, Narrative, and Imagination*, Adelaide, South Australia: Dulwich Centre Publications.

Freedman, J., & Combs, G. (1995). *Narrative Therapy: The Social Construction of Preferred Realities*. New York: W.W. Norton.

The Gospel of Matthew. *The Holy Bible, Revised Standard Version*. New York: Thomas Nelson & Sons, 1952.

Griffith, J.L., & Griffith, M.E. (1994) *The Body Speaks: Therapeutic Dialogues for Mind/Body Problems*, New York: Basic Books.

Griffith, J.L., & Griffith, M.E. (2001). *Encountering the Sacred in Psychotherapy: How to Talk with People about their Spiritual Lives*. New York: Guilford Press.

Weingarten, K. (1995). Radical listening: Challenging cultural beliefs for and about mothers. *Journal of Feminist Family Therapy*, 7, 7-22. Also in Weingarten, K. (Ed.) (1995), *Challenging Beliefs About Men, Women, and Therapy*, Binghamton, NY: The Haworth Press, Inc.

White, M. (1989). The externalizing of the problem and the re-authoring of lives and relationships. In M. White (Ed.), *Selected Papers*, Adelaide, South Australia: Dulwich Centre Publications.

White, M. (1995). *Re-Authoring Lives: Interviews and Essays*. Adelaide, South Australia: Dulwich Centre Publications.

White, M. (2000). Intensive workshop with Michael White, at Evanston Family Therapy Center, Evanston, IL, March 27-31, 2000.

Recognizing and Raising Spiritual and Religious Issues in Therapy: Guidelines for the Timid

Karen B. Helmeke
Gary H. Bischof

SUMMARY. Religious and spiritual experiences and practices comprise some of the most important aspects of many people's lives. Yet, for various reasons, mental health practitioners have been hesitant to bring these issues into overt discussions in therapy. This article proposes a four-part framework to assist therapists in addressing religion and spirituality in therapy. The four areas include spiritual issues raised by either the client or therapist, and religious issues raised by either the client or therapist. Guidelines for therapeutic conversation and clinical examples are offered for each of the four areas. *[Article copies available for a fee from The Haworth Document Delivery Service: 1-800-HAWORTH. E-mail address: <getinfo@haworthpressinc.com> Website: <http://www.HaworthPress.com> © 2002 by The Haworth Press, Inc. All rights reserved.]*

KEYWORDS. Psychotherapy, religion, spirituality, couple therapy, family therapy

---

Karen B. Helmeke is a faculty member with the Department of Counselor Education and Counseling Psychology, Western Michigan University, and has a private clinical practice in Kalamazoo, MI.

Gary H. Bischof is Assistant Professor of Counselor Education and Counseling Psychology, Western Michigan University.

The authors can be reached at Western Michigan University, 3102 Sangren Hall, Kalamazoo, MI 49008.

[Haworth co-indexing entry note]: "Recognizing and Raising Spiritual and Religious Issues in Therapy: Guidelines for the Timid." Helmeke, Karen B., and Gary H. Bischof. Co-published simultaneously in *Journal of Family Psychotherapy* (The Haworth Press, Inc.) Vol. 13, No. 1/2, 2002, pp. 195-214; and: *Spirituality and Family Therapy* (ed: Thomas D. Carlson, and Martin J. Erickson) The Haworth Press, Inc., 2002, pp. 195-214. Single or multiple copies of this article are available for a fee from The Haworth Document Delivery Service [1-800-HAWORTH, 9:00 a.m. - 5:00 p.m. (EST). E-mail address: getinfo@haworthpressinc.com].

Some topics are just more difficult than others for therapists to talk about with their clients. Discussions involving spirituality or religion seem to be one of those uncomfortable areas for many therapists. Some might even claim that talking about spirituality is more taboo than talking about sex. Many are not sure what to do when spirituality makes an appearance in therapy. "While some psychotherapists may speak metaphorically of the soul, with clients, many tend to follow one of three common pathways when spiritual or religious concerns arise: Duck, punt, or feint" (Goldberg, 1994, p. 9).

There are probably many reasons for this hesitancy, some of which are related to therapy and training issues and others that are more sociological and cultural in nature. Some of the reluctance stems from values held by therapists, such as respect for the client. Many therapists, as part of their training, have been taught to be cautious about imposing their values and beliefs on clients, out of respect for them. For others, the reluctance involves a lack of training, and therefore confidence, in knowing how religious and spiritual issues can be integrated appropriately into therapy. At times, therapists are not familiar with beliefs and practices of various denominations or religions, and perhaps are not aware of some of the practical implications of clients' theological beliefs. The lack of training in clinical programs also contributes to therapists viewing themselves as not being competent enough to address these issues in therapy (Haug, 1999; Stander, Piercy, Mackinnon, & Helmeke, 1994).

In a study of over 400 clinical psychologists, Shafranske and Malony (1990) report that only one-third of the survey respondents expressed personal competence in counseling clients regarding religious issues or matters of spirituality. Thus, a lack of training or confidence in addressing areas of religion or spirituality may leave even experienced therapists quite timid: "Spirituality scares me. As a therapist, I am constantly wrestling with powers I can't see, taste, hear, or smell. And the more mysterious these powers, the more they leave me feeling weak and helpless and vulnerable" (Pittman, 1990, p. 43).

Other therapists may be cautious about dealing with these issues in therapy because of their own personal religious or spiritual experiences. This tends to be true particularly if a therapist has had a negative religious experience, typically with organized religion and/or their family-of-origin. This can also occur if therapists do not consider themselves to be religious, or have difficulty relating to clients who are.

Sociocultural factors may also lead therapists to steer clear of discussions of religion or spirituality in therapy. Historically, one of the founding principles of the United States has been the separation of church and state and the right of the individual to hold and practice their own beliefs, without interference from government or family (Dunn & Dawes, 1999). Far be it for me, think some therapists, to violate this sacrosanct civil belief, by imposing my religious beliefs on a client.

Finally, in the field of psychology at least, the necessity of establishing itself as a legitimate science has probably served as a deterrent for considering the role of religion or spirituality in the healing process (Dunn & Dawes, 1999). In addition, the field of psychology has also been largely influenced by Freud's antagonism towards religion (Aponte, 1996).

Despite these well-founded concerns, it remains important to recognize spiritual and religious issues as they arise in therapy, especially since these issues are significant for many clients. The number of Americans who profess a belief in God has remained stable, around 95%, ever since the question was first asked in 1944 (Hoge, 1996). Recent surveys have shown that 93% of Americans identify with a religious group (Shafranske, 1996). Further, Hoge (1996) reports that several studies reveal that 87% of Americans said that religion is either "very" or "fairly" important in their lives. Addressing issues of spirituality or religion may be especially indicated with certain ethnic or racial groups. For example, for many African-Americans, spirituality and church involvement are integral aspects of their lives and are significant parts of their identification with the African-American community (Dunn & Dawes, 1999; Hines & Boyd-Franklin, 1996).

Even more revealing are the results of a recent study in which only half of the clients surveyed who wanted to discuss their religious and spiritual beliefs in the context of therapy felt free to do so (Lindgren & Coursey, 1995). So not only the therapists, but the clients themselves, felt constrained about bringing spirituality or religion into the therapy room.

So how does a therapist know if, when, and how to broach religious and spiritual issues in therapy? Recently, issues addressing the need for integration of spiritual issues in therapy have appeared in professional literature, and several articles suggest various techniques for doing so (Anderson, 1994; Butler & Harper, 1994; Nakhaima & Dicks, 1995; Prest & Keller, 1993; Rotz, Russell, & Wright,1993; Stander et al., 1994; Walsh, 1999). A few publications do provide guidance about bringing religion and spirituality into the realm of therapy. Haug (1998) offers several guidelines intended to address the ethical complexities of raising spiritual issues in therapy, based upon the model of medical ethics: respect for clients' autonomy, safeguarding clients' welfare, protecting clients from harm, and treating clients justly and honestly.

Doherty (1999) presents a model for integrating spirituality into therapy based upon three domains of language and meaning: spirituality, morality, and clinical care, and each domain has its own language, epistemology, and standards of evidence. Therapists can use both the differences and the connections between the three domains. For instance, "God's will," "miracle," "reborn" are examples from the spiritual domain, while "personality," "family dysfunction," and "boundaries" are examples from the clinical domain. Moral-only terms include "right and wrong," "obligation," and "justice." Words such as "serenity," "centeredness," and "wholeness" cut across both the clinical and spiritual domains, while "commitment" and "responsibility" are examples of words contained in the overlap between the clinical and moral domains (p. 185). Doherty gives examples of various clinical situations in which it is appropriate to use language from one, two, or all three domains.

Tan (1996) makes the distinction between two models for integrating religion and psychotherapy, one of them an "implicit integration" and the other an "extrinsic integration." Implicit integration is an approach in which discussions of religion are not initiated by the therapist and spiritual resources such as prayer and the use of scripture are not openly utilized in therapy. In these cases the therapist may pray for clients outside of sessions or utilize scripture to guide one's clinical work, but these issues do not enter therapy sessions directly. Extrinsic integration, on the other hand, involves overtly utilizing spiritual resources such as prayer, scripture or other sacred texts, and making referrals to church or other religious groups or counselors, and other religious practices within sessions. In this approach, the therapist initiates discussions of religion or spirituality, pertaining to both the therapist and client. Tan cautions, however, that when using extrinsic integration, the therapist needs to be sensitive to and respectful of clients' religious issues and resources, but he does not offer any specific guidelines.

In summary, there has been a growing encouragement in the mental health literature to recognize the importance of religion and spirituality in clients' lives and to include these issues more openly in the therapeutic process. Little has been written that provides practical guidelines for addressing these issues, especially for those clinicians who may be timid around such matters or who may view themselves as lacking adequate experience with religious or spiritual realms. This article addresses these practical concerns and offers guidelines for various scenarios, depending upon whether the therapist or client raises the issue, and whether it involves spirituality or religion. Thus, a four-part framework is suggested that discusses spiritual issues raised by either the therapist or client, and religious issues raised by either the therapist or client. Practical considerations, case examples, and possible therapeutic questions and interventions are discussed for each of the four areas.

EXPLANATION OF THE FRAMEWORK

This paper provides guidance on recognizing and raising issues with spiritual or religious significance for clients through the use of a conceptual framework. This framework consists of a two-by-two grid, made up of four quadrants. The vertical axis addresses who actually raises the issue:

1. the Client,
2. the Therapist.

The horizontal axis specifies whether the issue is:

1. Religious,
2. Spiritual in nature.

This framework, or grid, makes two very important distinctions (see Table 1). The first is who initiates the discussion, the therapist or the client(s). The second is whether the issue being discussed is more of a religious issue or a spiritual one. See Table 2 in Appendix A for examples of topics that fit each quadrant.

Clearly, there are times when religious and spiritual categories overlap, but usually this distinction can be made. While we recognize that making a clear distinction between religion and spirituality is somewhat artificial and is a matter of some debate, we retain this distinction in this framework to highlight some of the special considerations for addressing each of these areas in therapy. Typically, therapists can identify an issue as a religious one if the issue is related to a specific religious orga-

TABLE 1. Conceptual Framework for Responding to Religious and Spiritual Issues in Therapy

	Spiritual Issue	**Religious Issue**
Raised by Client	Quadrant I: Spiritual Issue Raised by Client	Quadrant II: Religious Issue Raised by Client
Raised by Therapist	Quadrant III: Spiritual Issue Raised by Therapist	Quadrant IV: Religious Issue Raised by Therapist

nization, if specific religious affiliations or denominations are named by the client, if the issue pertains to certain church policies, doctrines, stances, etc., or if a specific name is used by the client for a deity, for example, "according to the teaching of Buddha," "I received Jesus into my life when I was twelve." Spiritual matters, on the other hand, usually involve more personal experiences, a sense of purpose, or a way of life that provides a worldview or guide for living (Aponte, 1996), and may include qualities such as wholeness, faith, love, interconnectedness, mystery, meaning, value, and purpose (Giblin, 1996).

Stander et al. (1994) make the following distinction between religion and spirituality: "Religion includes shared and generally institutionalized values and beliefs about God. It implies involvement in a religious community. Spirituality is a more personal belief in and experience of a supreme being or the ultimate human condition. It includes an internal set of values and active involvement in those values. Spirituality is also a sense of connection, a sense of meaning, and a sense of inner wholeness" (p. 39).

This framework can be useful to therapists because slightly different guidelines for clinical work are associated with each quadrant. For instance, when it is the client who raises the issue, it is safer to make the assumption that the client is willing to discuss religious and/or spiritual issues, and the therapist can be less concerned about imposing his/her own agenda. When clients are the ones to raise issues, perhaps even as the presenting problem, therapists can proceed with more confidence.

QUADRANT I: SPIRITUAL ISSUES RAISED BY CLIENT

In this quadrant, clients may not explicitly refer to God or the name of some other religious figure or authority or be associated with an organized religion, but still consider themselves to be spiritual. They may subscribe to New Age beliefs, humanism, Native American religion or some other spiritual practice. Another example might be clients who consider themselves as moral, who follow their own ethical code, but do not adhere to any specific organized religion. Even those clients who are non-religious may be dealing with issues in therapy with spiritually explicit or implicit overtones.

Examples of how clients might raise spiritual issues in therapy range from a client mentioning a book on some type of spirituality, to offering a description of a spiritual practice, or raising philosophical and existential questions such as "I believe that I am meant to have some purpose in this life, but I think I have lost my way somehow." In whatever way spirituality is raised in therapy, there are some guidelines to follow for therapists uneasy broaching such topics.

One of the first, most basic guidelines is for the therapist to acknowledge that the client has just made some comment regarding spirituality (Doherty, 1999). When uncertain how to respond when a client brings his or her spirituality into the therapy room, therapists often respond with silence, which may be perceived by the client as communicating the therapist's discomfort, disapproval, or disbelief. Instead, therapists can make a simple response that in some way acknowledges their openness to what the client just said. For instance, the therapist might say something like, "It seems that spirituality is important to you. Would you like to say more about that?"

Next, the therapist can assess the current impact of the client's spiritual beliefs and practices on the presenting problem. Examples of questions to consider in such an assessment are "Has the client's spirituality contributed to the problem in any way?" "Has it been a positive influence, providing some relief, peace of mind, or healthier functioning to the client?" "Have the beliefs/practices of the client affected other areas of the client's life?"

In a similar way, the therapist can assess the potential for the client's spirituality to be part of the solution for the presenting problem. Spirituality may be an untapped well of strength for the client that the therapist may be able to help him or her utilize (Walsh, 1996). What is called for here is not merely taking a neutral stance towards clients' religious expressions, but finding a way to respect and utilize the client's beliefs as potential strengths and resources. For instance, one client happened to mention that she had spent the weekend on a spirituality retreat. The client was a non-churched individual who had previously disavowed any interest in religion. The therapist, curious about how she had decided to go on the retreat and how it had been helpful, asked the client about her experience. She discovered that the client went on the retreat primarily because she heard it was supposed to help her learn how to lose weight. At the retreat, she had a spiritual experience in which she had a positive image of her body for the first time in her life. The therapist utilized this transforming experience of the client to further her own acceptance of her body and her self.

Another guideline in this first quadrant of spiritual issues raised by the client is to assess what role the therapist might take vis-a-vis the client's spirituality. A therapist might simply inquire as to how she can respond to the client's expression of spirituality. Options could include reading a book with a client, sharing the therapist's own religious or spiritual experiences with the client, challenging certain beliefs, offering to pray or meditate with the client and so forth.

Next, it might be helpful to find out, when a client raises spirituality, how the client came to their spirituality, perhaps exploring what life experiences contributed to their spirituality or what impact one's spirituality has had on their life. Therapists might also be especially attentive to whether the spirituality emerged from a background of no religion, from a negative experience with organized religion, from a dissatisfaction or boredom with a certain religious denomination, as an expression of a cut-off from family-of-origin, or through some other means. Knowing this may provide cues to the therapist to follow up on other spiritual or religious issues. For instance, the client referred to above who had attended a spirituality retreat had cut herself off from her parents' religion, which she felt "had been forced down my throat" the whole time she was growing up. Ever since she was on her own, she wanted nothing to do with religion of any kind.

When a client raises an issue that is spiritual in nature, but not religious, it may provide an indication of what kind of language the therapist should use in response. A middle-aged woman disavowed any contact with a religious institution, but described how she had come around to the need for some kind of spirituality in her life. Some of the spiritual disciplines she was practicing had helped her to find peace and acceptance in her life, as she had been able to release the bitterness she had felt towards her ex-husband. It would not have been useful with this client to use religious terms such as "forgiveness," "sin," or "confession," but to use her own terminology that included words such as "release," "serenity," and "moving on."

QUADRANT II: RELIGIOUS ISSUES RAISED BY CLIENT

In contrast to the first quadrant, in which a client's comment might be more of a veiled reference to spirituality, in the second quadrant, a client makes some explicit reference to a belief in God, to another religious figure or religion, or to a religious belief, practice, or organization. An example of a client raising a religious issue would be a client who came to therapy feeling very depressed, and during the course of therapy brought up her struggles with her church's stance against abortion and the fact that she aborted a baby 15 years before. She feared that the marital problems she and her husband were experiencing might be God's punishment for the abortion, and was afraid that someone at her church might find out about the abortion. For this client, the presenting problem was depression, but she did not make any progress in therapy until the underlying religious issues were addressed.

One common guideline associated with this quadrant is for the therapist to do some homework about the particular religious denomination the client is discussing, in order to understand some of the ramifications of that affiliation. A good resource for therapists wanting to have at least some brief background information on several religious traditions is Lovinger (1996). For instance, the therapist in the case just mentioned made himself familiar with Roman Catholic beliefs and practices regarding abortion, confession, penance, and reconciliation. Another example is a therapist working with a couple in which the wife is contemplating divorce, who discovers that the couple's religious tradition not only forbids divorce, but does not allow women in the church a voice or a vote, and expects the wife to be submissive to her husband.

When clients who have raised religious issues also indicate a strong religious affiliation, the therapist may consider whether to use a collaborative approach, in which the minister, rabbi, or religious leader is consulted or perhaps even included in a session (Haug, 1999). One advantage of this collaborative approach is the prevention of inadvertent loyalty conflicts for clients, whereby clients might feel that steps taken in therapy might conflict with the practices and beliefs spelled out by their church or synagogue.

As with spiritual issues in Quadrant I, therapists whose clients raise religious issues need to listen carefully to the specific religious language used by clients (Haug, 1999). This provides a way of joining, being respectful, and becoming educated about a client's particular theological beliefs, as well as being aware of one's own reaction to the use of particular language. For instance, a mainstream Protestant couple who may be discussing family conflicts that arose during their infant's baptism might feel confused or even offended by a therapist from a different background who keeps referring to the event of baptism as a "sprinkling" or a "christening." Or a therapist who hears a client's discussion of the changes he experienced since he was "born again" could know from the client's phraseology some of the theological orientation of the client, be respectful of the power of such a religious experience to transform an individual, and work in tandem with such an experience.

Butler and Harper (1994) and Griffith (1986) suggest that therapists need to be alert for those times when couples may use religious issues as a way to work out power conflicts in their relationship. When the religious problem presented is a smokescreen, other underlying issues need to be carefully examined also. For instance, one couple who presented initially with communication problems was also having severe conflict around their decision whether to attend a church from the wife's religious background or one from the husband's background. This was a concrete issue that needed to be resolved, but it was also indicative of larger patterns concerning power issues between the two of them. In another couple therapy case, one of the primary complaints by a wife was that her husband had been attempting to convert her to the Jehovah's Witness religion, which was reflective of a wider pattern of his attempts to dominate in their relationship.

Another way this four-part framework can be useful when clients raise religious issues is to recognize that one important task for therapists is their own self-of-the-therapist work, to explore their own reactivity based on family-of-origin or "church-of-origin" influences. Perhaps therapists realize that they are especially reactive to particular denominational (or non-denominational) affiliations, and recognize when their reactivity may interfere with therapy.

For example, one beginning therapist wrote for a class assignment the following about her experience of interviewing a couple who talked about the importance of their religious faith to their marriage:

> I was acutely aware of a personal 'hot button.' I felt uncomfortable each time the subject of religion was broached. I was raised in a Christian Reformed home and have since almost wholly rejected what I was taught. Thus I now have what might be called an aversion to any remotely Christian faith. Despite my strong negative reaction, I feel I was able to keep my opinion separate.

While it may be argued that it would be practically impossible for her to keep her opinion completely separate or neutral, this trainee recognized how important and central this couple's faith was to them, and was able to increase her self-awareness of her own reactivity. She became aware of the possibility that her own personal baggage could get in the way of being helpful to them, or prevent her from allowing their religious faith to function as a strength in their relationship. She decided to do a follow-up assignment, in which she explored the narratives about religion in her own family-of-origin. This was a crucial task in her development as a therapist, because as Shafranske and Malony (1990) found, "the more negatively the subject viewed the religious experience in their past, the less likely they were of utilizing interventions of a religious nature" (p. 76).

QUADRANT III: SPIRITUAL ISSUE RAISED BY THERAPIST

The preceding have involved suggestions for how to proceed in therapy when a client is the one to raise a religious or spiritual issue. What about when the client does not bring up anything of a religious or spiritual nature? Might there be times or situations when it is appropriate for the therapist to initiate such conversation? Should the therapist proceed any differently than when a client opened up the topic for discussion?

When the therapist initiates the topic, some of the same guidelines apply, regardless of whether it is a religious or spiritual topic being raised. In general, Quadrants III and IV call for the same general tentative and cautious approach. A useful metaphor for this situation might be to think of the work of the therapist in this situation as being more in a spirit of expedition. Together, the therapist and clients set forth on a journey to probe and explore, looking for buried treasure while being aware of minefields that might contain old explosives yet to go off. The therapist certainly would not expect clients to go on the expedition unless the clients were willing to go. And the therapist would not be certain ahead of time what they might find, if anything. Yet the therapist can at least encourage the exploration and accompany the client on the journey. Haug (1999) discusses how spiritually sensitive therapists can open space for conversations which reflect clients' religious or spiritual beliefs, and the ways that those beliefs might constrain or empower them (p. 187). Therapists may feel more freedom to be the one to raise these issues if they recognize how a person's theological beliefs and practices can function in ways that contribute either to healthier functioning or in ways that impede a client's growth.

Two of the most important guidelines when inviting clients to go on this discovery journey are being respectful when the client declines to go on the trip, and recognizing that the buried treasure that is found may be gold to the therapist but merely dross to the client. Those religiously committed therapists may hope, and even pray, that their clients be transformed by a certain religious experience, but that event may not have the same meaning for the client.

The following case is an example of the former, in which the therapist was the one to initiate the topic of religion and spirituality. During the second session, while gathering data with a gay male client, the therapist was assessing possible strengths and resources available to the client:

Therapist: Is your spirituality a possible resource for you?

Client: No. Not really. I used to go to church when I was young, but then I got turned off.

Therapist: Do you mind sharing with me what happened that turned you off?

Client: I liked church okay when I was younger. But then we got a different minister, and I didn't like the way he treated me.

Therapist: How did he treat you?

Client: I think he knew that I was gay, and I felt like he was looking down on me all the time. I don't think he was comfortable with me being gay.

Therapist: So ever since that negative experience, church or your personal faith hasn't been all that important to you?

Client: No, not really. I've really gotten away from all of that.

Therapist: The reason I'm asking you is not to tell you that I think it should be important to you, but I'm asking just to find out whether these are possible areas of support for you.

Client: No, not really.

Therapist: Okay.

Clearly, for this client, religion or spirituality was not viewed as a positive source in his life, and so the subject was dropped and not brought up again, at least by the therapist. Just as a number of different areas are broached during the first early sessions with a client, spirituality was mentioned, so that the client knew at least that that was an area he could feel free to discuss later. In this case the client never brought it up again. But the invitation to make the journey was at least extended, and the refusal was graciously accepted.

However, it can be very challenging to exercise such restraint. As Haug (1999, p. 187) states, "clinicians who themselves have a strong religious/spiritual commitment may find it difficult to respect clients' disinterest, or strongly held divergent views, without judging, proselytizing, or claiming religious authority." Thus, when the therapist holds strong views about religion or spirituality, one must be especially sensitive to feedback from clients that indicate a different point of view.

In another case, the therapist's "sin" was one of omission, rather than commission, to use a common Christian theological expression. Partially because of the therapist's own revulsion to organized religion, she failed to explore the spiritual dimensions implicated in a client's presenting problem of loss and grief, although it would have been entirely appropriate to do so. A 16-year-old came to therapy to deal with the sudden, traumatic death of her best friend who was killed in a car accident. Even though the client did not use any specific spiritual or religious language, there were spiritual implications in her struggle to make sense of her loss, and it might have been very beneficial to the client to have included this kind of discussion.

In general, it is important for the therapist to look for the possibility of spiritual issues being involved when the presenting problem relates to a loss or trauma experienced by the client. The death of a loved one will almost inevitably raise questions of spiritual significance. "Why do such bad things have to happen? What was the point of this tragedy, and what does this mean for my life? Did I, or the person who died, do something horrible to deserve this? How can I trust again in a world where such terrible things happen?" (Of course, more religious questions are often asked in situations of loss and grief, such as "Where was God for me? Why didn't God prevent this?")

Presenting issues of loss and grief, and other issues such as serious illness for oneself or a loved one, often can be opportunities for the therapist to initiate an assessment of client's spiritual resources or potential resources. For instance, in the preceding example, the therapist might want to ask the client if there is a spiritual or religious community that has already or might be able to provide support during the crisis, when assessing for other resources such as friends, books, support groups, hospice, etc., that might be available to the client. A therapist might also inquire as to whether and how spiritual beliefs or practices have been resources for the client or perhaps if these may have been challenged by one's difficult life circumstances.

Another clinical problem that often involves spiritual matters is recovery from addictions. Clients who have been involved with 12-step self-help groups such as Alcoholics Anonymous or Al-Anon may have embraced spiritual emphasis of these programs, perhaps reflected in references to a "Higher Power" or "Let go and let God." Such clients might be hesitant to talk about spiritual issues in psychotherapy, especially if they sense the therapist might be uncomfortable discussing these matters. Thus, if the therapist can create space to address the role of spirituality in the person's recovery, this may indeed be quite helpful. Ignoring the role of spirituality in the recovery process might lead some clients to view the therapist as less credible. Conversely, some clients who have been exposed to 12-step self-help programs might be turned off by the emphasis upon spirituality, and may be seeking a more secular treatment approach through therapy.

In cases when the client has not brought up anything related to spirituality, the therapist may want to listen to the client in a different way, and be open to the possibility that some of the "secular" issues being discussed might have spiritual overtones. Perhaps clients are waiting for some kind of cue from their therapist that spirituality is a topic acceptable in therapy. As mentioned previously, Lindgren and Coursey (1995) conducted a study in which 34% of the clients in the study reported wanting to discuss spirituality with the therapist "very much" or "occasionally," but had never done so. There may be many reasons for clients to be hesitant to bring up spiritual issues directly. Lindgren and Coursey found that some felt the therapist would not understand their beliefs, others knew the therapist had a different religious background than their own, and still others felt some general discomfort in therapy around these issues. Other possible reasons might be that clients fear their therapist might judge them, laugh at them, be offended by their beliefs or be scornful of them, or they might be concerned that their therapist would think some of their spiritual experiences were strange.

QUADRANT IV: RELIGIOUS ISSUES RAISED BY THERAPIST

Although the suggestions for how to proceed are similar to those for spiritual issues, situations when the therapist is the one raising a religious issue call for the greatest exercise of caution and restraint. This is the quadrant that dredges up the most trepidation both for those therapists unsure as to what to do with religion in therapy and for those who have experienced less-than-life-giving efforts of the religiously zealous. Before therapists initiate a religious discussion, there are several questions they can ask themselves. "Are there clear reasons for raising a religious issue? What does the therapist hope to achieve? Does the client have a similar religious background as the therapist? If so, what assumptions are being made about being a participant in that particular denomination or religion that might need to be challenged? If not, does the therapist sense any desire on his or her part to sway the client to the therapist's own persuasion, or believe that the client would be better off if he or she held the same beliefs as the therapist? Has the client made some indication that he or she would be open to the religious issue brought up by the therapist?"

One of the dangers that can be present in this quadrant is when the therapist and client share a similar religious background, and therapists assume too much knowledge of the meaning of religious beliefs, practices, scripture, etc., for clients. Griffith (1999) asserts that therapists are more likely to intrude into, oppress, and constrain the possibilities for conversations including God in therapy when they hold "stories of certainty" in their work. Some of these stories are:

1. I know what God is like for you because I know your religious denomination,
2. I know what God is like for you because I know what your language about God means,
3. I know what God is like for you because your image of God is a reflection of your early attachment figures,
4. I know what God is like, and you need to know God as I do (pp. 212 - 218).

Griffith suggests that therapists challenge their stories of certainty by looking at them more from a perspective of tentativeness, curiosity, and wonder.

As with therapists raising spiritual issues, one legitimate reason for clinicians to initiate discussions of religion in therapy is for the purpose of assessing strengths and resources in the client. One way to assess the importance of religion and spirituality for a client is to ask for this information prior to therapy. An intake form could ask questions about the role of religion or spirituality in the client's life. One might ask about religious preference, affiliation, attendance, or practices. Therapists can also add an open-ended question about the role that religion and/or spirituality plays in the lives of the client. This itself may be enough to indicate to clients that they have implicit permission to explore these areas of their life with the therapist. Even if the client indicates that religion plays no part in their life, it still may be worthy of a follow-up question, as long as the therapist inquires with curiosity and tentativeness, because such a response may indicate a cut-off that still needs to be processed. For instance, the therapist can find out whether there were any particular circumstances that contributed to religion not being important in their lives. Another question that could be included on an intake form is whether the client is satisfied with his or her spiritual/religious life, and if not, how they would hope it could be different.

If, on the other hand, the client has indicated on an intake form that religion does play a central role in his or her life, the therapist can follow up in a session with a statement such as, "I see you marked down that your religious faith is very important to you. Can you tell me more about that, and what might be important for me to know about your religious or spiritual life in order for us to work together?"

Similarly, some therapists may include a brief explanation in their disclosure forms of the importance of their own spirituality or religion, and a description of how they tend to include or not include these issues in therapy. Of course, the freedom to do this clearly depends on the therapist's setting; some governmental or school settings may prohibit direct discussion of specific religions or religious practices. The decision to disclose this information involves criteria not unlike other decisions about therapist self-disclosure: why disclose, when to disclose, and what the therapist hopes to accomplish by the disclosure.

Another time it is legitimate for therapists to raise questions about a client's religion is while collecting information for a genogram. A therapist can routinely include brief questions about religious affiliation, preferences, and experiences, and determine whether these issues need to be probed in more depth. For one client, a woman in her late twenties, it was clear that a punitive view of religion had become woven into the family narrative. When her mother was growing up, two of her brothers died in a drowning accident. Three years later, her father died when she was 13. In high school she questioned God, wondering what God's reasons could be for destroying her family. The nuns at her Catholic high school were less than responsive to her questions, and she was punished for her doubts by having a ruler smacked across her knuckles and by being forced to kneel on pencils. When she was a senior, she became pregnant, and the church instructed the client's grandmother not to have a baby shower or to celebrate the arrival of the baby in any way. Then, three months before the birth, the father of the baby died. This young woman, while doing her genogram, realized that she had inherited a negative legacy about religion from her mother (with good reason, it might be added), and wanted to explore whether it was possible for religion to play a more central, positive role in her life. The therapist also designed a ritual with her and her mother, to acknowledge and celebrate the client's birth.

One cue for the therapist to raise a religious issue is when a client has already raised a related yet separate spiritual issue. One client had never attended any kind of religious organization throughout his childhood. After some time, however, coinciding with the personal work he was doing as part of marital therapy, he realized that his discontent with his wife had less to do with her, and more to do with something that he felt he was missing in his life. He began raising spiritual questions, such as wondering whether and how he could have God be more a part of his life, and he was feeling a need to go to a church. The therapist, knowing that he did not have a religious background of any kind, encouraged the client to do some exploring of some different faith traditions and denominations, to see if there was something that could enhance the growth the client was already experiencing. The client openly accepted this suggestion.

Another therapist had a depressed Jewish client whose daughter died from leukemia. They were discussing her concerns and fears about whether there was an afterlife, when the therapist asked what her rabbi would tell her. She responded by saying that she had not attended synagogue since her daughter's death, which opened the door for further discussion about her need and readiness to reclaim her faith.

Another situation in which it is helpful for the therapist to initiate discussion of religion is when the therapist is aware of religious issues that may be impacting the client's presenting problem. For instance, knowing the stress placed on the lives of the individual and the family from an interfaith marriage (Sousa, 1995), a therapist may want to ask about whether and how their religious differences have created any conflict in their marriage or in their families, as well as look for ways these differences had enriched their marriage. A therapist seeing a couple with presenting problems of infertility may want to inquire about their religious background, knowing that certain religions do not approve of specific reproductive medical procedures, and find out how the couple has balanced their faith commitments with their strong desire for a child.

A final example is when the therapist has knowledge of a family's strong commitment and involvement in their church/synagogue. For such families, it is not unusual for their own functioning to be impacted by the events taking place in their religious "family." Thus, the loss or addition of a minister or rabbi, especially sudden ones, scandals involving one of the church leaders or staff, or conflicted triangles revolving around issues or people, all are examples of situations going on in a religious community that might influence dynamics within a client family, even to the point of similar patterns being created in the family. For instance, one family came to therapy with concerns about their adolescent daughter. The therapist was aware that this family was actively involved in their church in which the pastor and his wife had been brutally murdered by a youth in the church. The therapist assessed the impact of those events on the issues that brought the family to therapy.

CONCLUSION

Obviously, therapists will exhibit a range of comfort and expertise in dealing with spiritual and religious issues in therapy, yet hopefully more therapists will be willing to undertake this endeavor with the assistance of some of the basic guidelines offered here. By listening closely to the client's responses, both verbal and non-verbal, therapists are likely to be aware of when they are treading on ground that is sacred for a client, as well as whether they are trespassing or are being invited to journey further.

REFERENCES

Aponte, H. J. (1996). Political bias, moral values, and spirituality in the training of psychotherapists. *Bulletin of the Menninger Clinic*, *60*, pp. 488-502.

Anderson, D. A. (1994). Transcendence and relinquishment in couple therapy. *Journal of Systemic Therapies*, *13*, pp. 36-41.

Butler, M. H., & Harper, J. M. (1994). The divine triangle: God in the marital system of religious couples. *Family Process*, *33*, 277-286.

Doherty, W. J. (1999). Morality and spirituality in therapy. In F. Walsh (Ed.), *Spiritual resources in family therapy* (pp. 179-192). New York: Guilford.

Dunn, A. D., & Dawes, S. J. (1999). Spirituality-focused genograms: Keys to uncovering spiritual resources in African American families. *Journal of Multicultural Counseling and Development*, *27*, 240-254.

Giblin, P. (1996). Spirituality, marriage, and family. *The Family Journal: Counseling and Therapy for Couples and Families*, *4*, 46-52.

Goldberg, J. R. (1994, June). Spirituality, religion, and secular values: What role in psychotherapy? *Family Therapy News*, p. 9.

Griffith, J. L. (1986). Employing the God-family relationship in therapy with religious families. *Family Process*, *25*, 609-618.

Griffith, M. E. (1999). Opening therapy to conversations with a personal God. In F. Walsh (Ed.), *Spiritual resources in family therapy* (pp. 209-222). New York: Guilford.

Haug, I. E. (1998). Including a spiritual dimension in family therapy: Ethical considerations. *Contemporary Family Therapy*, *20*, 181-194.

Hines, P. M., & Boyd-Franklin, N. (1996). African American families. In M. McGoldrick, J. Giordano, & J. K. Pearce (Eds.), *Ethnicity and family therapy* (2nd ed., pp. 66-84). New York: Guilford.

Hoge, D. (1996). Religion in America: The demographics of belief and affiliation. In E. P. Shafranske (Ed.), *Religion and the clinical practice of psychology* (pp. 365-387). Washington, DC: American Psychological Association.

Lindgren, K. N., & Coursey, R. D. (1995). Spirituality and serious mental illness: A two-part study. *Psychosocial Rehabilitation Journal, 18*, 93-111.

Lovinger, R. J. (1996). Considering the religious dimension in assessment and treatment. In E. P. Shafranske (Ed.), *Religion and the clinical practice of psychology* (pp. 327-363). Washington, DC: American Psychological Association.

Nakhaima, J. M. & Dicks, B. H. (1995). Social work practice with religious families. *Families in Society, 76*, 360-368.

Pittman, F. (1990, September/October). The rattle of God. *Family Therapy Networker*, p. 43.

Prest, L., & Keller, J. (1993). Spirituality and family therapy: Spiritual beliefs, myths, and metaphors. *Journal of Marital and Family Therapy, 19*, 137-148.

Rotz, E., Russell, C., & Wright, D. (1993). The therapist who is perceived as "spiritually correct": Strategies for avoiding collusion with the "spiritually one-up" spouse. *Journal of Marital and Family Therapy, 19*, 369-375.

Shafranske, E. P., & Malony, H. N. (1990). Clinical psychologists' religious and spiritual orientations and their practice of psychotherapy. *Psychotherapy, 27*, 72-78.

Sousa, L. A. (1995). Interfaith marriage and the individual and family life cycle. *Family Therapy, 22*, 97-104.

Stander, V., Piercy, F., Mackinnon, D., & Helmeke, K. (1994). Spirituality, religion, and family therapy: Competing or complementary worlds? *American Journal of Family Therapy, 22*, 27-41.

Tan, S. (1996). Religion in clinical practice: Implicit and explicit integration. In E. P. Shafranske (Ed.), *Religion and the clinical practice of psychology* (pp. 365-387). Washington, DC: American Psychological Association.

Walsh, F. (1999). Opening family therapy to spirituality. In F. Walsh (Ed.), *Spiritual resources in family therapy* (pp. 28-58). New York: Guilford.

Walsh, F. (Ed.). (1999). *Spiritual resources in family therapy*. New York: Guilford.

APPENDIX A

TABLE 2. Examples of Possible Issues for Each Quadrant

Quadrant I: Spiritual Issue Raised by Client	**Quadrant II: Religious Issue Raised by Client**
General discontent or malaise with life. Seeking larger questions of the meaning of life, and/or the purpose of client's life. Experience of loss or trauma. Concern and regard for the environment. Questions about basic human nature, good or bad, in self or others. Struggles between one's actions and one's values and morality. Needing to take responsibility for one's own actions. Difficulty in responding when one has been wronged or harmed. Client expresses interest in knowing about therapist's spirituality. Client mentions spiritual practices or disciplines or books read on spirituality. Client asks therapist to pray or meditate with him or her.	Spouse's discontent with spouse's failure to attend church/synagogue or adherence to specific religious practices. Couple's conflict due to different religious backgrounds. Client who was abused by a member of the clergy. Client's childhood experiences of a punitive religious system. Client's childhood experiences of family-of-origin's punitive religion. Client's adult negative experiences with a religious institution. Clients' distress/struggle regarding their own behavior/experiences relative to their church's stance (e.g., divorce, abortion, marital affairs, homosexuality). Feelings of guilt, shame, doubt relative to religious beliefs. Client expresses interest/curiosity in therapist's religious affiliation/practices. Client's statements regarding the positive role their faith and religious practices have played in their life and in coping with presenting problem.
Quadrant III: Spiritual Issue Raised by Therapist	**Quadrant IV: Religious Issue Raised by Therapist**
Conducting a life review with aging clients. Recovery from addictions. The need to be accountable for one's actions and making retribution where possible. Facing mortality. Assigning rituals. Assessing for resources and strengths. Client dealing with loss and trauma.	Assessment of client resources. Genogram exploration. Assessment of impact of larger systems on functioning of client family. Premarital work with couples. Explore spiritual/religious cut-offs with God, with church/synagogue. Follow-up questions to responses on an intake form.

SPIRITUALITY AND MFT TRAINING

The Spiritualities of Therapists' Lives: Using Therapists' Spiritual Beliefs as a Resource for Relational Ethics

Thomas D. Carlson
Martin J. Erickson
Angela Seewald-Marquardt

SUMMARY. We situate how the personal spiritual quests of our own lives have influenced our work as family therapists, particularly influencing our chosen theories of change. We provide a definition of and ap-

---

Thomas D. Carlson is Associate Professor of Marriage and Family Therapy, North Dakota State University.

Martin J. Erickson is a doctoral candidate in the Marriage and Family Therapy Program at Iowa State University, and is affiliated with Anasazi Foundation, Mesa, AZ.

Angela Seewald-Marquardt is a master's student in Marriage and Family Therapy, North Dakota State University.

Address correspondence to Thomas D. Carlson, Marriage and Family Therapy Program, Child Development and Family Science Department, North Dakota State University, P.O. Box 5057, Fargo, ND 58105-5057 (E-mail: tom_carlson@ndsu.nodak.edu or marty6@iastate.edu).

[Haworth co-indexing entry note]: "The Spiritualities of Therapists' Lives: Using Therapists' Spiritual Beliefs as a Resource for Relational Ethics." Carlson, Thomas D., Martin J. Erickson, and Angela Seewald-Marquardt. Co-published simultaneously in *Journal of Family Psychotherapy* (The Haworth Press, Inc.) Vol. 13, No. 3/4, 2002, pp. 215-236; and: *Spirituality and Family Therapy* (ed: Thomas D. Carlson, and Martin J. Erickson) The Haworth Press, Inc., 2002, pp. 215-236. Single or multiple copies of this article are available for a fee from The Haworth Document Delivery Service [1-800-HAWORTH, 9:00 a.m. - 5:00 p.m. (EST). E-mail address: getinfo@haworthpressinc.com].

proach to spirituality that centers its ethical, moral, and deeply relational nature, and propose that therapists' own spirituality can be a beneficial resource in the relationships they build and foster with those who consult them. Careful attention is given to how God calls us into relationships with others. Narrative therapy and spirituality are both defined as inherently relationalist practices and ways of being. Drawing on narrative therapy ideas, we describe a four step process we have used to explore therapists' spirituality in supervisory contexts specifically focusing on the relational nature of their work, and illustrate this process by giving supervision dialogues from some of our experiences.

KEYWORDS. Spirituality, family therapy training, narrative therapy

Thankfully there is a growing trend in the field of Marriage and Family Therapy (MFT) and in the psychotherapy professions at large toward the inclusion of client's religion and spirituality in therapy as an important aspect of culture. We seem to be in the beginnings of this trend in MFT and notice that there is yet much to be said, theorized, explained, researched, and reviewed in this important integration in order that we may serve our clients with the greatest care, help, and compassion possible. While we as a field have identified the need to address our clients' spirituality as an important aspect of culture, and while we have been encouraged to be careful about the potential influence of our own religious and spiritual beliefs in the therapy encounter, we have not been encouraged to draw on the unique relational experiences of our personal spiritualities in order to enhance and promote communal connection in the relationships we enter into and foster with our clients. The purpose of this article is to offer some suggestions for doing this. We suggest that all spiritualities center in *relational* experiences with the divine, and/or with humanity, and/or with all of creation. The sacred nature of these relational experiences have the potential to offer us a wealth of hope and understanding as we seek to be genuinely connected with those who seek our help. We will offer some unique ideas which we have found very helpful in supervisory contexts with one another and with other therapists. But in order to adequately share the thoughts and ideas of this article, we first must begin by situating our perspective, and sharing our own theoretical conceptualizations of spirituality and relationalism.

OUR THEORIES OF CHANGE AND OUR SPIRITUAL LIVES

Because it colors all that we say it is necessary for us to situate the role of spirituality in our (TC and ME) own personal lives and how this influences both our chosen theoretical orientations and the work we do as family therapists. Together we have been working in the ideas of Narrative Therapy since 1995. Through this time we have very often been struck by the experiential "feeling" associated with working with others using these ideas and developing these types of relationships. Narrative therapy is an intrinsically *relational* endeavor–the ideas continually invite us to be reflexive, thoughtful, and critically careful about the relationships we invite, support, encourage, foster, and develop, not only in therapy but in our personal lives as well. Narrative therapy is not just another theoretical approach to therapy; rather it represents both a critical lens of understanding and a way of being with others. Narrative therapy centers a relational ethics of practice which is much less about specified techniques, and much more about the moral and ethical imperatives involved in the relationships we are each a part of. In fact, the positive influence of narrative therapy ideas in our (TC and ME) personal lives is what has most encouraged us to continue to use and explore these ideas together and with those who consult us.

Both of us (TC and ME) have embraced religion and spirituality in our lives. Religious worship and church service, along with personal, relational, and community spirituality have been the centers of our lives and relationships. Like many persons who value religion and spirituality, we feel our religious and spiritual selves are absolutely foundational to our lives. Our spirituality has always been a lens of intelligibility from which we have interpreted and made sense of our journeys as family therapists–from training to practice to teaching–particularly in the relationships these experiences have brought us into. Because of this we have been interested in theories, ideas, and practices that we feel resonate with the spiritual centers of our lives, and this has been our experience with narrative therapy ideas especially. There has also been a recursive effect between our religious and spiritual lives and our interests in narrative therapy ideas and practices–each having the effect of influencing and shaping the other in positive ways. Narrative ideas have offered us a unique scaffolding from which to both view and enter into our religious beliefs and spirituality. Narrative therapy as a growing expanding body of work has been either influenced by or shares the same spirit with a wide variety of theories, ideas, and practices including feminism, postmodernism, poststructuralism, social constructionism, cultural anthropology, narrative theory, critical theory, post-colonialism, relationalist philosophies (i.e., Emmanuel Levinas, 1981; 1985, and C. Terry Warner, 1985; 1997; see also Jordan, 1997; Noddings, 1984; Palmer, 1983; Richardson, 1997), and recent movements in qualitative research (see Lincoln & Denzin, 2001). Within each of these perspectives there is a call to some type of relationalism. We have most enjoyed the ideas from these various traditions that encourage relationalism and resonate with the spiritual centers of personal lives.

DEFINING SPIRITUALITY

To describe our ideas for helping therapists draw on their spirituality as a relational resource in therapy requires a definition of spirituality. We believe spirituality is an ethic or a way of being, and such a way of being that is a lived, day by day, endeavor. It is a way of being which requires continual practice, and daily mindfulness, rather than some place or state to which one arrives, or some trait or ability one gains. Spirituality is a profoundly relational and moral way of being, as the primary purpose centers on our intimate relationship with the Divine (which we take the liberty to call God), and how that relationship invites us into communal relations of respect, mutuality, accountability, compassion, and love with all humanity, and with all creation. Descriptions of spirituality as either objective (as is often found in extreme fundamentalist approaches to religion) or completely subjective (the idea that spirituality is wholly merely a matter of individual preference and individual belief) ultimately are inadequate because spirituality is a *relational* way of being (see Palmer, 1983, chapter 4). Defining it as either objective or subjective forces an individualism which is incommensurate with spirituality as a relational way of being.

In our own personal experiences, religion or religiosity is an intricate part of our spirituality. When it comes to our personal lives, it is hard for us to separate the two as is often done in definitions given in MFT and psychotherapy literature (i.e., defining religion as the formal, institutionalized belief system and structure, and spirituality as the personal relationship with a higher power). We believe this type of separation can dichotomize significant areas of person's lives which are often inseparably intertwined; and we suggest many others may feel this is true for them as well. Conversely, we do not define religion and spirituality as simply the same either, they are different concepts, and again for us religion is *a part* of our spirituality. We like David Dollahite's definition of religion: "a covenant faith community with teachings and narratives that enhance spirituality and encourage morality" (1998, p. 5). Throughout this paper, we discuss therapists' spirituality as a resource in their work, and in this discussion we are focusing primarily on spirituality. We have chosen to use the term "spirituality" whether it includes the therapists' religiosity in some way or not we hope that our ideas and examples are sufficiently inclusive. The process we articulate, and the dialogue examples we give focus more generally on the therapist's own personal relationship with God, and not specifically on membership in a covenant faith community.

For us (TC and ME), our lives involve a continual search for the spiritual, a quest to embody and to live that which uplifts and enlightens, that which flows from God–the source of *all* good. This is not simplistic or easy, in fact it is often a very difficult and trying journey where we have at times felt the darkness and despair that is such a common part of life–when our spiritual eyes are clouded and the spiritual clarity we once had seems elusive. We have found this struggle often characterizes spiritual quests. All else tends to be colored by the central spiritual quests of our lives. We have tried to bring our journeys as family therapists *into* the spiritual quests of our lives, and we suppose this is likely true for many therapists. Sometimes this integration has been clear and unencumbered, sometimes not so. We believe more than ever before that our spiritual lives and our professional lives are inextricably interconnected. We feel called by our spirituality and by our work as family therapists to connect with others in a spirit of mutuality, compassion, love, and community. We do not doubt that many therapists feel very much the same, and we hope the ideas we share here can adequately articulate ways for bringing our spiritual lives more fully into our professional relationships.

SPIRITUALITY AND FAMILY THERAPY

An integration of our personal spiritual lives into our professional work and relationships regrettably often runs counter to the professional culture of therapy and counseling; we are saddened that this is the case. Unfortunately, the longstanding separation, chasm, or rift between religion (and by association spirituality) and psychology still manages to persist in subtle and sometimes not so subtle ways even in MFT. In our own life experiences (TC and ME) we have found it not an easy task to somehow bring together our spiritual quests and our work as family therapists. There has been little formal training and few resources that have even encouraged such a coming together. For us, our friendship has allowed us to explore this in many ways and also given us the encouragement to have made this central to our "becoming" as family therapists. We have participated in informal supervision with one another as an addendum to the formal supervision we've received. This has allowed us to openly explore the relationship between our own spiritualities and our journeys as family therapists. This has proved to be a very enriching experience, which in turn has encouraged us to work with colleagues, conference participants, and students in informal and formal supervision contexts in an effort to help them explore their own spirituality, how it relates to their work as family therapists, and how this all impacts their personal lives and relationships.

The consequences of maintaining the separation between therapists' spiritual and professional lives are grave. Spirituality is often a tremendous source of help, strength, comfort, peace, security, serenity, and hope in the lives of most persons, including most therapists. Why would such a powerful resource need to be excluded from our professional work as therapists? Persons, couples, and families seeking therapeutic help are often suffering, discouraged, and feeling a loss of hope–all problems for which spirituality can be a powerful help. Despite the movement in our field toward addressing and incorporating the spiritual dimensions of clients' lives, there has been little written encouraging therapists themselves to develop *their own* spiritual lives and draw on such as a resource in their work. Could this neglect support a subtle "us/them" dichotomy in our relationships with those who consult us, suggesting that their spirituality is important in the therapeutic endeavor (assuming we are addressing it and seeing it as such), while our own spirituality must not be addressed, or is somehow unimportant in these professional relationships?

SPIRITUALITY AND ETHICS

Perhaps the most significant and persuasive argument for ethics in our field will address the inherent and intimately relational nature of our work with those who consult us, and the moral imperatives we are brought into by virtue of being called to help others. To be ethical requires more than an appeal to current regulations, rules, and standards, and invites us to be ever mindful of the moral quality of the relationships we are inviting, encouraging, fostering, responding to, and a part of in our work. This relationalist stance calls for a definition of ethics as a way of being that we seek to embody and live *in relationship with others*. Opening our therapeutic conversations to our clients' spiritualities *and* to the relational calls of our own spiritualities can allow us to meaningfully partner with the Divine in the complexities of our clients' difficulties and struggles, opening space to communal relationships of mutuality that are beyond our or the clients' capacity to engender alone. We are interested in passionately exploring with other therapists and ourselves *how* our spiritualities call us to be *in relation* to others.

THE VALUE OF A REFLEXIVELY CRITICAL APPROACH

Topics of incorporating religion or spirituality in our work probably give rise to some uneasiness among MFTs. Although this is an unfortunate state of affairs, we realize it is necessary due to the often violent disagreements that have occurred and do occur throughout the world in the name of religious and/or spiritual beliefs. Throughout this article we assume that as therapists connect to their own spirituality this will provide them connection to that which is moral and ethical. But we acknowledge that *in the name of spirituality* therapists could possibly be connecting to feelings, thoughts, or beliefs that come from an immoral or unethical way of being. The work of philosopher Terry Warner suggests that most behaviors, practices, or techniques can be enacted immorally and unethically as well as morally and ethically (Warner, 1985; 1997; see also Williams, 1992; 1994). Therefore, in order to embrace our own spiritualities and the attendant calls to relational connection in our work, we need to be in a stance of critical reflexivity about the moral nature of our way of being. This stance is required so that we can be mindful, moment by moment, of the real moral and relational effects of our way of being and our words and actions that accompany that way of being. This critical stance is a central component of narrative therapy ideas and practices. Our hope is to help guide therapists to connect to the moral and ethical places in their hearts, those places that speak of love, connection, compassion, togetherness, and community, those deep feelings of their hearts that invite respect for all creation and that open to the spiritual wonders of their lives and relationships. We hope that by entering into this sacred space in their hearts, therapists can approach their relationships with those who consult them with a careful spiritual sensitivity and an awareness of the sacred nature of those relationships.

DEVELOPING A PERSONAL ETHICS

During the last few years our work has been centered around helping therapists establish a personal ethics in their work (Carlson & Erickson, 1999; 2000b; Bair & Erickson, 2000). In this work we have developed ideas and practices to explore with therapists their moral preferences in regard to their preferred relationships with those they help, as well as with all relationships in their lives. Moral preferences are the personal desires and hopes that therapists have for how they want others to experience themselves when they are in their presence, in *relationship* with them. These preferences are centered first and foremost in a concern for the other. Embracing a personal ethic requires the therapist to critically reflect on how their interactions potentially shape the identities of others (a shaping that occurs through the ways in which we invite or incite others to construct their relational identities according to particular cultural discourses), and to actively commit to embracing an ethics that fits with their moral preferences. While we believe that most therapists have positive desires for their relationships with clients, we have found that these desires and hopes are too often not meaningfully integrated into their work. The purpose of the following explorations are to help therapists place these moral preferences at the center of their work. In order to facilitate this process we might ask therapists any one of the following questions:

- What is your desire or hope for how you hope others will experience themselves when they are in your presence?
- How do you hope others will feel about themselves when you are with them?
- What kinds of feelings would you hope your clients receive from you?

Almost invariably therapists have shared with us their desires for others to feel loved, cared for, and/or understood. What is interesting about these expressions is that therapists also become quite aware that the desires to love and care for clients are feelings that were often discouraged in their training. Despite this discouragement, however, they have also shared how they have somehow kept these desires present in their work to some extent.

As therapists are able to identify the desires they have for their relationships, we encourage them to name these desires. In naming their desires, we invite therapists to choose a quality, feeling, or an ethic that they would like to guide their relationships with others. One question we have asked in this situation is: "Can you name a quality or feeling that you would like to guide your relationships with others?" The most common qualities that therapists have shared with us are love, compassion, and understanding. Once their preferences have been named we invite them to carry questions such as these into their work:

- What would love have you do?
- How would compassion have you see and understand the people you are working with?
- What would understanding have you say in this moment? In this situation?
- What are some of the ways that love would want you to interact with others?

The purpose of these questions is to help therapists embrace these qualities in their lives and relationships. We first began asking each other these questions, and we found it a wonderful help in our work and relationships with those who consult us. This way of thinking about our work seems to carry with it so much wonder, a unique way of considering what is at the center of what we do as therapists. In our conversations with other therapists we have found that embracing these moral preferences in their work has brought more meaning and purpose to their work. They have noticed that as they have attended to the ethics of their relationships with others and made a purposeful effort to live these ethics, they have experienced a qualitative difference in the impact of their work in the lives of their clients and in their own lives.

Another important aspect of developing a personal ethics involves guiding therapists through re-membering exercises (Myerhoff, 1982; White, 1997, 2000). Re-membering exercises involve helping therapists to connect their desires and preferences to the significant relationships of their lives. As therapists desires and preferences are tied to the people in their lives with whom those desires were experienced and nurtured, those relationships can serve as a sustaining influence in the therapists' lives. For example, we might ask therapists to consider the following questions:

- Is there a person that seemed to champion this desire you have to love others?
- What was it like for you to be with this person?
- How did you feel about yourself when you were with this person?
- How did this person share love with you?

These questions help therapists to make a meaningful connection between their lives and the lives of others. Their ability to love and care for others no longer rests merely in their own minds, but belongs to a rich history of relationships with others. These re-membering conversations are almost always emotional experiences as therapists experience a return to membership with loved ones. In fact, it has been our experience that re-membering conversations are quite often a spiritual experience for those involved. Perhaps it is that spirituality is often tied to our relationships with family and ancestors those who taught us about God or spirituality or religion, or who nurtured such feelings in our hearts by the way they lived their lives and cared for us. Or perhaps it is that recollecting the most significant relationships in our lives carries with it the "spirit" of what spirituality is about–feeling connected to something loving, profound, beautiful, and greater than ourselves.

While we initially did not purposefully bring spirituality into these conversations, it was quite common for therapists to share how their preferences and desires were connected to their spiritual beliefs and relationship with God. For example, it was a common experience for therapists to identify God, Jesus Christ, persons from scriptures, church leaders, or spiritual leaders as the person who they felt best champions their most heartfelt desires. These common experiences of therapists situating their preferences and desires in their spiritual beliefs led us to consider the implications of more explicitly drawing upon the spiritual beliefs of therapists as the foundation of their moral preferences.

SPIRITUALLY INFORMED MORAL PREFERENCES

Spirituality is often a meaningful part of therapists' lives; however, many therapists have not considered bringing their spiritual lives into their work. This may be related to the popular idea that therapists need to create a clear distinction between their professional and personal lives. While the very possibility and value of such a distinction has been highly criticized by feminist and postmodern authors to mention just some of the main critics–this notion of separation of work and self is powerful in our field. The tragedy of this belief is that those very things that bring beauty and meaning to the personal lives of therapists are somehow discouraged or not allowed to be brought into their work. Spirituality is something that brings meaning and purpose to many therapists' lives. Much of that meaning and purpose has to do with what their spiritualities offer them in terms of caring for and relating to others. When therapists are encouraged to make this unfortunate distinction between their personal and professional lives, something important is lost.

Due to the influence that narrative ideas have had on our own experiences of spirituality, we began to draw upon Michael White's idea of "spiritualities of the surface" (Hoyt & Combs, 1996) to inform our work with therapists. In this conversation piece, White explains that spirituality is often considered mystical and something that is beyond the grasp of humans. This mystical explanation of spirituality may lead persons to remain somewhat distant from their spirituality in the sense that the immediate daily effects of their spiritual beliefs are left obscured. Therefore, rather than a spirituality of depth, White describes a spirituality of the surface where persons critically and purposefully reflect on the sacredness of their daily thoughts and actions. Discussing spiritualities of the surface in this way has helped us more clearly see the sacredness of daily life, and the way that our own spirituality was central and significant in almost every aspect of our lives, especially if we would stop and take the time to notice it. While White sought to bring out the sacredness of daily life in a way not necessarily connected to spiritualities of the deep, we find this understanding of spiritualities of the surface an additional invitation to consider how our deepest spiritual beliefs are connected to the sacredness of daily life and the influence of this all on our lives and relationships.

While we initially left spiritual conversations up to chance, we have recently made a specific exploration of therapists' spiritualities (both of the surface and of the depth) a part of our training experiences. While some may be concerned with the idea of therapists purposefully drawing upon and using their spiritual beliefs in therapy we want to be clear that we are referring to therapists using their spiritual beliefs as the foundation of their personal ethics. Here we are not referring to atemporal or acontextual beliefs, but rather the very sincere and personal desires that therapists have for how to care for others which will always be contextually sensitive. What we are interested in then is to explore what the spiritualities of therapists have to say about their relationships with others and how those beliefs might contribute to the embracing of a personal ethics. In the following section we will share some thoughts about how this might be accomplished.

Step One–Spiritual Preferences

The purpose of this first step is to help therapists to identify the spiritual preferences they have for their relationships with others. Initially this exploration is similar to the process we identified earlier for establishing moral preferences. Therapists are asked to reflect upon their personal desires and hopes for their relationships with others in a way that is centered in a relational concern for the other. Once therapists have begun to identify these desires we invite them to situate these desires within their spiritualities. For example, a therapist who shared that she wanted her clients to feel loved might be asked the following questions:

- Is this desire for others to feel loved connected to any spiritual beliefs you might have? What do these beliefs say about loving others?
- How might these beliefs be a resource to you in your preference to help others feel loved?
- Can you share an experience where your spiritual beliefs helped you follow your preference to love others?
- If you were to bring these spiritual beliefs about loving others more fully into your work, how would this change your experience of others? How would this change how you experience therapy?
- What would it mean to you if you were able to bring these spiritual desires more fully into your work? To those who consult you? What possibilities might this bring to your work and relationships with others?

Of course, these questions open up possibilities for many conversations about the role therapists' spiritual beliefs might play in their work with clients. As the moral preferences of therapists' lives become centered in their spiritual beliefs, it helps them to bridge the gap between the personal and the professional. Their own spiritual beliefs that have been a strength and resource to them in their personal lives and relationships can now be a living resource in their professional lives, and all in a way that will turn to further enrich their personal lives.

Step Two–Critical Reflection of Therapists' Spiritual Preferences

The next step in this process is to help therapists begin to critically reflect on the daily implications of their spiritual preferences in their lives and in the lives of their clients. The purpose of this step is to help therapists begin a meaningful exploration of the real moral effects that the embracing of these spiritual preferences will have on the lives of their clients and on their own lives. Accountability is an important aspect of this critical reflection. Narrative therapy ideas support a constitutionalist (White & Epston, 1990) or social constructionist conviction that our identity stories are always relational–literally shaped by our interactions with one another, thus "relational identity stories" (Carlson & Erickson, 2000a). Therefore, it is important for therapists to seriously reflect on the shaping invitations their spiritual preferences will have on the lives and stories of their clients. This reflection needs to include the potential positive shaping invitations as well as the potentially negative invitations this preference might have. Another important aspect of accountability involves our accountability as supervisors. Not only will the spiritual preferences of therapists potentially shape the lives of clients, but the very naming and embracing of spiritual preferences will have a significant shaping influence in the therapists' lives as well. Therefore in this process we also involve therapists in a critical reflection of the potential influence their spiritual preferences might have on their professional and personal lives.

In order to help therapists to explore the shaping invitations their spiritual preferences might have on both their lives and the lives of clients, initially we invite them to consider a number of questions. For example, a therapist who has named compassion as a spiritual preference might be asked to consider the following questions:

- As you embrace this ethic of compassion in your work how do you think compassion would have you thinking about those with whom you work?
- As you follow how compassion would want you to think about others, what effect do you think this will have on how others experience themselves when you are working with them?
- How might your experience of thinking about others in this way effect your life as a therapist?
- How would compassion want you to see them?
- What effect may it have on those with whom you work when you are seeing them in these ways? How do you think it might effect how they are seeing themselves?
- What effect would seeing others through the eyes of compassion have on your life?
- How would compassion have you listening to them?
- What effect would listening to others in these ways have on their lives? What effect would it have on how they may experience themselves?

- How might your experience of listening to others in these ways change your professional life? Your personal life?
- How would compassion have you understanding their experience?
- What effect would it have on their lives as you are understanding them in this way?
- What would this way of understanding others mean to your work as a therapist? How might it contribute to your views about what is important in therapy?

As readers may notice, we use externalizing conversations in our questioning. However, we are using externalizing conversations with a different purpose. Usually externalizing conversations are used to help persons separate from problems. Here we use externalizing conversations as a means of deconstructing or unpacking therapists' spiritual preferences in order to make those preferences become *more* available to them. As therapists practice these preferences in their lives, we invite them to participate in a continual reflection of the real moral effects these practices have in their lives and the lives of clients. It is often in this reflective process that the real meaning of their spiritual preferences and the real effects become visible to them.

Step Three–Re-Membering Spiritual Relationships

In this final step we again turn to re-membering conversations, this time focused on spiritual relationships. Re-membering is a practice in narrative therapy that seeks to help persons experience a return to membership with those persons who have shaped their lives in enriching and meaningful ways. From a narrative perspective, this process of re-membering is important because as people enter into new stories and experiences of self those new stories need to be maintained and nurtured through the relationships of their lives. As therapists are involved in naming and embracing the spiritual preferences of their lives, it is important that these preferences be tied or connected to those relationships where these were nurtured. As therapists' spiritual preferences are re-membered to the significant relationships of their lives, those relationships provide a sustaining influence in their lives, they provide a place where those preferences can continue to be nurtured. It is in these re-membering experiences with therapists that we began to see the importance of creating space for spiritual conversations.

Before we made spirituality a more conscious focus of our supervision, we noticed that therapists often described their remembering experience as a spiritual one. As they experienced a renewed membership with the significant persons of their lives, they would often share with us that they felt a spiritual connection with these persons. As we reflected on these spiritual connections we noticed that therapists would often begin to refer to their relationship with God as a sustaining influence in their lives. As we opened ourselves up to being more specific about the spirituality of therapists' lives, we noticed that one of the most common figures that therapists would remember was God. For example, if a therapist had named love as her spiritual preference, we might ask her to consider the following questions:

- Can you think of someone that has shared love with you?
- What was this experience like?
- What has this person meant for your life?
- As you have experienced love from this person, how has it changed you? How has it changed how you feel about yourself and others?
- If you were to carry this person with you into your work, what would it bring to your relationships with others?

When therapists name God as the person they want to remember in these questions we invite them to reflect upon that relationship with God. We invite them to retell experiences where they have felt love, compassion, or mercy from God and what those experiences have taught them about caring for others. Many therapists have not considered or have not been allowed to consider how their relationship with God might be a similar resource in their professional lives. The therapists we have worked with have shared with us how remembering God in their professional lives has allowed them to bring their spirituality more directly into their work. For example, after inviting therapists to consider what it might mean for them if they were to have their relationship with God more present in their work, many therapists have shared with us how they have begun to pray to God before or during each session inviting God to join them in the session to help them stay connected with their desires to love and care for those consulting them.

Example

The following is an excerpt from a conversation I (TC) had with Angela, one of the therapists I was working with in supervision. In this re-membering conversation, Angela shared how God had touched her life through others and how those relationships have helped her feel a desire to do the same for others.

Tom: Can you think of an experience where you felt particularly cared for by God?

Therapist: After college I took a job two hours away from home and two hours away from my boyfriend (now husband) Brent. It was a tough year. I felt very lonely and cried a lot. One morning around 2:00 a.m. I couldn't sleep and I was feeling particularly lonely. I was thinking about quitting my job and moving home. I was startled when the phone rang. It was Brent. He said he was sleeping, but something told him to wake up and call me. I felt and still feel that that something was God. He [God] did not want me to feel alone anymore. He knew that I needed to feel loved and comforted right that night. This experience was so meaningful to me. Not only did it bring me closer to Brent, but more importantly, I felt God working through Brent. God knew exactly how I felt and I had been praying earlier. He knew what I needed and how to give it to me. God worked through Brent to comfort me. Just knowing that I wasn't alone, that there was someone who knew me and still accepted me helped me gain perspective that night. I felt stronger and knew I could continue living here. If I could do that for a client, I would consider the therapy successful.

Tom: What would it mean to you to have Brent's presence with you in your work?

Therapist: On a few occasions I have felt Brent's connection in the therapy room. It has brought me comfort because I can imagine Brent cheering me on, telling me I'm doing a good job, and letting me know that he thinks I'm helping the other person. He is so supportive when I have been down on myself, that I can actually hear his words of encouragement when I feel down or frustrated even when he's not around. This is most helpful when I feel stuck in a case or I'm second-guessing my effectiveness as a therapist. Having his connection with me always gives me confidence. It also means to me that I always have someone to lean on, someone that accepts me even if my therapy stinks that day. Brent is also an incredibly open and accepting person. He seems to connect with everyone he meets and he is respectful to everyone. He inspires me to be the same. He helps point out when I am not being respectful or when I'm being judgmental when I tell him stories about my day or about the people I've met. I need that kind of person in my life to remind me of God's wish for us to love one another. When I'm with Brent or even think of our connection, I believe I am a kinder person. This definitely helps me stay connected with my desire to bring God's love into the therapy room as a way to comfort others. When I feel confident of my abilities, when I feel that I am a kind and respectful person, and when I remember the love that God has allowed Brent to give me, I am much more ready to use God's love for others.

Tom: Besides Brent is there anyone else in your life who has championed these qualities that you desire?

Therapist: Other life experiences have shown me that someone, even a stranger, can comfort through caring. One example is Sister Clara. She was a Sister at the school I attended in Belgium when I was an exchange student. Zuster Clara did not know me at all and we met in an unusual way. She disciplined me in the hallway for having my uniform strings untied. I had had a bad day and was feeling very isolated, unaccepted, unwanted and not understood. I cried because I didn't even understand what she was disciplining me for (my language skills were still new). Once Zuster Clara saw my tears and understood that I was not a typical student, she brought me into the private library and listened to my bad day (in English). I told her how lonely I was, how I was tired of not understanding conversations around me, how I missed my family, and the many things that were troubling me that day. She comforted me by listening and she knew just what to say to give me hope that tomorrow would be better. Most importantly, she introduced me to the only other exchange student in the school. Diana was having many of the same feelings I was. Diana and I became best friends and we had a terrific year together. We met many other friends. Who knows what kind of year I would have had had it not been for Zuster Clara taking the time to listen and care. Zuster Clara even took time out of her day to give me additional Dutch and French lessons. Without even knowing me Zuster Clara showed me that she accepted and cared for me.

The purpose of these conversation were to help Angela connect her desires with the significant people and relationships in her life. The relationships she re-membered are relationships that help her to feel God's love and compassion in her own life. These very real and personal connections allow her own desires to be compassionate and loving to express themselves more in her work with others. A few weeks after this conversation, I invited her to reflect upon the influence that this desire to invite God into the therapy has had on her work with others.

Tom: Last time we met, we talked about your desire to invite God into the therapy room with you. I am wondering if you have had any experiences with this over the past few months?

Therapist: I feel fortunate to be in a position to know people when they are vulnerable and hurting because God has given me an opportunity to comfort. This is a gift, but one that I need God to help me use well. When I allow myself to bring my spiritual beliefs and experiences into the therapy room, I feel like I have a purpose. I feel like God can help guide me to make the right decisions and to say the right things. I feel like I'm serving God by bringing comfort to others. I think I am more committed to my clients when I allow my spiritual beliefs to come out. I'm not just in the therapy room to complete my internship or to get a paycheck, but to spread God's love. That sounds corny as I read it. But, that's how I feel. God says to "love thy neighbor." I want to do that with everyone in my life, but especially clients, because they seem to need love and comfort and often don't seem to get it elsewhere. By showing them that I care, accepting them for who they are, and helping them work through their problems, I think I am loving them the way God wants us to all love our neighbors. That's fulfilling to me and it makes me more dedicated to doing my job well.

In this conversation, it is clear that Angela's spiritual beliefs and relationship with God form a powerful foundation for the relational nature of her clinical work. Bringing these beliefs into her professional life allows them to be a sustaining influence in her work. Not only is she working as a therapist because of her personal desire to care for others, but she feels that by being a therapist she can share God's love with others by comforting them in ways that she has been comforted by God and by others. This example speaks to the type of spirituality we hope to invite therapists to bring into their work. Our point is not to encourage therapists to share their spiritual beliefs or doctrines with clients (although this could be helpful at appropriate times), but rather to invite therapists to consider the relational implications of their spiritual beliefs and their spiritual selves their relationships with those who consult them.

Step Four–Ongoing Reflection

Embracing a personal ethics is never a neutral activity. It has real effects in our lives and the lives of those with whom we work. Therefore, as therapists begin to embrace a new ethics based on their spiritual beliefs about being in relationship with others, it is vital that they be invited to participate in an ongoing reflection about the shaping influence these beliefs have in their lives and the lives of the persons with whom they meet. In our work with therapists, after our initial conversations, we meet together for follow up visits with the purpose of specifically exploring the real effects that our conversations have had on their lives and the lives of others. The following is an excerpt from one of these reflective conversations with Angela.

Tom: It has been a little while since we last met. I am curious to know if you have found any opportunities to invite God into the therapy room with you as you had hoped?

Therapist: I think that bringing God into the therapy room helps me in numerous ways. A recent experience I had in which God helped me was with a developmentally disabled client. I met him for the first time, and he was very unpleasant to look at. He was bleeding from a bicycle accident, so I had to help perform first aid. I felt myself being disgusted by the blood and did not like being in a position of nurse. I thought that I would feel better once he was cleaned up and we started talking. I was wrong. He had terrible hygiene and stared blankly at me. I felt myself judging him. I did not like how he looked, and I was having a difficult time looking past his appearance. I realized what I was doing and my first thought was that I was being terribly unfair. I didn't know him, yet I judged him based on looks. God accepts everyone. This man is God's child as much as I am and I should accept him as God's child. There must be good in this person, and I would need to look beyond his appearance to discover it. Once I began thinking about what God would do if he were the therapist, I began accepting this client and pushed away my judgments long enough for me to really listen to him. I discovered that he hurts just like I do. He is concerned with what others think, he is lonely, he feels belittled, he doubts himself and he is sometimes controlled by anger. I have felt all of those things before, and I was reminded of how similar we were instead of how different he was. Once I was able to do this, I could provide some amount of comfort and help to him. By thinking about God and his love for all of his children, I was able to overcome my superficial bias. Sometimes, when I have worked with clients who I just don't understand or who I don't particularly like, I try to imagine what God's plan is for them. I believe that all of God's creations have incredible potential and good in them. So, when I'm having trouble seeing good, I try to imagine looking through God's eyes. This has helped me become more empathetic and less judgmental. I think the caring comes through much more. When I feel that I'm keeping God close to me in therapy, I feel like I have additional guidance. I feel like the therapy I provide is meaningful. Sometimes, when I haven't known what to say or do, I mentally ask God for guidance. This makes me feel stronger. I think it's healthy to realize that I won't be able to "fix" everything for clients, and that I need help too. Keeping God close also helps me feel like I'm OK even if I don't really think my therapy was first rate that day. It helps me realize I'm more than a therapist. Keeping him close helps me deal with my own problems so they don't interfere with the therapeutic process. Finally, when I keep God close to me, I feel accepted even when my clients seem to push me away.

Tom: What has it meant to your work to bring your spiritual beliefs, especially about how you hope to be in relationship with others, into your work? How has it changed how you experience yourself and others?

Therapist: When I bring my spiritual beliefs into the therapy room, I am much more likely to ask the client what their spiritual beliefs are. I am also more likely to incorporate their spiritual beliefs into helpful aspects of therapy. I think this is respectful and takes into account all things that are important to the client. When I bring my spiritual beliefs in, I also feel that I relate on a more human level with clients. I am not so much a "therapist" as a person who wants to help. I think this helps reduce power differentials that exist. An example of this came from working with the mentally retarded adult I told you about before. I didn't feel as if I had anything in common with him and felt very distant from him. When he shared that reading the Bible and copying scriptures onto paper were enjoyable pastimes for him, I was reminded that we are the same in God's eyes. My spiritual belief is that God loves all His children, and this affected my connection with this man because I now saw him as a brother through Christ. I was not just a therapist, but another child of God who wanted to bring comfort. I feel more loving and accepting towards others. I also experience myself as weak, and needing the strength of God. I know that all of my talents and skills are blessings of God. I am humbled by this belief. My spiritual beliefs make me think of the therapist role as a gift. I am in the position to facilitate healing in people. This gives me pleasure and satisfaction. I feel good about myself when I help others. I also know that God helps me in my role. Sometimes I think of God as my co-therapist because he gives me strength and encourages me to do my best.

Angela's responses to these questions give life to what we hope our conversations with therapists will offer. As she reflects on inviting her relationship with God into her work, it is important to note that she is drawing upon her personal experience of God as loving and compassionate and purposefully inviting her own experience of that compassion and love into her relationships with those who consult her. Angela also expresses how inviting God's love and compassion into her relationships with clients has helped her to enter into the relational and ethical preferences, the personal ethics, she is developing.

CONCLUSION

As therapists attend to the relational calls of their own spiritual lives and allow these sacred experiences and personal knowledges to be a sustaining resource in their work, this can allow them to enter into relationships which will invite a connection centered in mutuality, accountability, ethics, morality, compassion, and love. In addition we have found that such a spiritual and relational focus in our work, whether with clients or with therapists, offers us many entrances into conversations and relationships that can serve to foster community, to promote social justice, and to stand with and walk with others in ways that deeply honor them as persons and treat as sacred the relational connection we have made. Therapists, as exemplified in Angela's comments above, have shared with us that drawing on their own spiritualities in this way has brought a significant reauthoring to their work and to their personal lives. We have experienced similar reauthorings of our own professional and personal lives and relationships. We hope these ideas offer therapists some unique ways to consider their place of their spirituality in their professional lives, particularly in their relationships with those who seek their consultation.

REFERENCES

Bair, S., & Erickson, M. J. (2000). *Ethical practices in Marriage and Family Therapy: From modernist individual traditions to postmodern relational possibilities*. Unpublished manuscript in preparation for submission.

Carlson, T. D., & Erickson, M. J. (1999). Re-capturing the person *in* the therapist: An exploration of personal values, commitments, and beliefs. *Contemporary Journal of Family Therapy, 21* (1), 57-76.

Carlson, T. D., & Erickson, M. J. (2000a). Re-authoring spiritual narratives: God in person's relational identity stories. *Journal of Systemic Therapies,19*(2), 65-83.

Carlson, T. D. & Erickson, M. J. (2000b). Honoring and privileging therapists' personal experience and knowledges: Ideas for a narrative approach to the training and supervision of new therapists. *Contemporary Journal of Family Therapy, 23*(2), 199-220.

Dollahite, D. C. (1998). Fathering, faith, and spirituality. *The Journal of Men's Studies, 7* (1), 3-15.

Hoyt, M. F., & Combs, G. (1996). On ethics and the spiritualities of the surface: A conversation with Michael White. In M. F. Hoyt (Ed.), *Constructive Therapies 2*. New York: Guilford Press.

Jordan, J. V. (Ed.). (1997). *Women's growth in diversity: More writings from the Stone Center*. New York: Guilford Press.

Levinas, E. (1981). *Otherwise than being, or beyond essence* (Lingis trans.) The Hague: Martinus Nijhoff.

Levinas, E. (1985). *Ethics and infinity* (Cohen trans.) Pittsburgh, PA: Duquesne University Press. (French 1982).

Myerhoff, B. (1982). "Life history among the elderly: Performance, visibility and remembering." In J. Ruby (Ed.), *A crack in the mirror: Reflexive perspectives in anthropology*. Philadelphia: University of Pennsylvania Press.

Noddings, N. (1984). *Caring: A feminine approach to ethics and moral education*. Berkeley: University of California Press.

Palmer, P. (1983, 1993). *To know as we are known: Education as a spiritual journey*. San Francisco: Harper & Row.

Richardson, L. (1997). *Fields of Play: Constructing an Academic Life*. New Brunswick, NJ: University of Rutgers Press.

Warner, C. T. (1985). Anger and similar delusions. In R. Harré (Ed.), *The Social Construction of Emotion* (pp. 135-166). Oxford, England: Basil Blackwell.

Warner, C. T. (1997). *Oxford papers*. Salt Lake City, UT: Arbinger.

White, M. (1995). *Re-authoring lives: Interviews and essays*. Adelaide, South Australia: Dulwich Centre Publications.

White, M. (1997). *Narratives of therapists' lives*. Adelaide, South Australia: Dulwich Centre Publications.

White, M. (2000). *Reflections on narrative practice: Essays and interviews*. Adelaide, South Australia: Dulwich Centre Publications.

White, M. & Epston, D. (1990). *Narrative means to therapeutic ends*. New York: W. W. Norton.

Williams, R. N. (1992). The Human Context of Agency. *American Psychologist, 47* (6), 752-760.

Williams, R. N. (1994). The modern, the post-modern, and the question of truth: Perspectives on the problem of agency. *Journal of Theoretical and Philosophical Psychology, 14* (1), 25-39.

Conversing and Constructing Spirituality in a Postmodern Training Context

Saliha Bava
Chuck Burchard
Kayo Ichihashi
Avan Irani
Christina Zunker

KEYWORDS. Spirituality, training, postmodernism

COMING TOGETHER

I (Saliha) was honored when Tom Carlson invited me to write an article for this special edition. I approached the learners at Houston Galveston Institute who expressed interest and enthusiasm in collaborating together in writing the article. We decided to take notes for a few months on what each one of us may consider "spirituality" or "spiritual moments" in the course of the training experience. The learners who decided to participate in this project were from a diverse background as each describes her/himself.

Our intent for this conversational style paper was to create dialogical space for multiple meanings and to honor each of our unique voices and to invite you, the reader, to reflect on and juxtapose your own experience. After explicating the writing style and a brief positioning of ourselves, we introduce our notions of spirituality, followed by our tales of training within the postmodern context of the Houston Galveston Insti-

[Haworth co-indexing entry note]: "Conversing and Constructing Spirituality in a Postmodern Training Context." Bava, Saliha et al. Co-published simultaneously in *Journal of Family Psychotherapy* (The Haworth Press, Inc.) Vol. 13, No. 3/4, 2002, pp. 237-258; and: *Spirituality and Family Therapy* (ed: Thomas D. Carlson, and Martin J. Erickson) The Haworth Press, Inc., 2002, pp. 237-258. Single or multiple copies of this article are available for a fee from The Haworth Document Delivery Service [1-800-HAWORTH, 9:00 a.m. - 5:00 p.m. (EST). E-mail address: getinfo@haworthpressinc.com].

tute. We will conclude our conversation with reflective and analytical comments. The paper is praxis of selected postmodern practices, such as constructing local knowledge, critical questioning of self and other, and reflexivity in conversation (Anderson, 1997; Agger, 1998; Gergen, 1999; Hertz, 1997; Holzman & Morss, 2000).

The purpose of the conversational style paper is to focus on the generative nature of conversations within a training context that brought us together rather than to create a consensual community of thought about spirituality. Though, ironically, we form a consensual knowledge community (Bruffee, 1999) that privileges the plurality of ideas. Our intent is to create spatial pockets for reflection and critical questioning of the notion of spirituality.

WRITING STYLE

Plurality, polyphony, dialogue, reflexivity and deconstruction have evolved as a critique and response to positivism, objectivism, and crises of representation. Writing genres, embodying the former ideas and identified as *new literary forms* (Woolgar, 1988) have been a growing trend, over the past 10-15 years, in the fields of sociology, anthropology, Women studies, and Critical Cultural schools, thus closing the gap between scientific and literary genres that has existed since the seventeenth century (Richardson, 1997). The new writing genres in social sciences, such as performance scripts (McCall, Becker & Meshejian, 1990), second voice device, decentering original texts (Schneider, 1991; Pinch & Pinch, 1988), poetry (Richardson, 1993, 1997), drama (Ellis & Bochner, 1996; Richardson, 1993, 1997; Richardson & Lockridge, 1991), polyvocal texts (Schneider, 1991), and webtext (Pockley, 1999, 2000) are forms of postmodern praxis. However, such genres are relatively new to the discipline of marriage and family therapy. Though, therapist-client or supervisor-supervisee conversation transcripts are legitimized academic writing styles but there is a sparseness of theoretical conversational style scripts in professional or academic journals within our discipline.

We utilize the performance script and invite you to imagine that you are attending a script reading, listening or sitting in with members of the Institute's conversational cluster who are talking about spirituality and its local meanings, as well as the relevance of spirituality in training, therapy and personal life. Due to the conversational style of the script, one may experience abrupt shifts in the ideas and conversational frames

(Chenail, 1993; Keeney, 1991). This style was intentionally maintained to illustrate the reflexive and generative nature of the dialogical process which is fragmented and connected depending on the recursive analysis frames (Chenail, 1993) one brings to the conversation. References to each other's ideas are in *italics* while ideas from secondary sources are in quotes.

WHO ARE WE?

Saliha Bava: I was born and raised as a middle-class, Muslim urbanite in New Delhi, India. I came of age as a career woman in Bombay, as a "Training Officer" with indigenous people in rural areas in India after completing my Masters in Social Work. Today, as a transient border-crosser doctoral candidate (Virginia Tech), I am on the staff of the Houston Galveston Institute, interacting with clients, interns, faculty, and staff, with primary intent to promote a collaborative learning community. I am also a learner, researcher, supervisor, and an adjunct faculty member in the MS Psychology, Our Lady of the Lake University, Houston Program.

Chuck Burchard: I was raised and am in the United Methodist Church. I have attended seminary at Perkins School of Theology at SMU and worked for the church in a variety of capacities. I graduated from Stephen F. Austin State University earning my Masters degree in the Counseling Arts.

Kayo Ichihashi: I was born and brought up in a rural area of Japan. My family has Shin (Buddhism) and Shinto background. After I graduated from medical school, I was trained as a pediatrician. Four years later, I changed my specialty to psychiatry. When I was a pediatrician, I started to learn psychotherapy and work with children and their families who have some trouble in their lives. From May 2000 through January 2001 I paused my work in Japan to learn at the Institute as a Visiting Scholar.

Avan Irani: I am a Zoroastrian, born in Bombay, a wife and a mother who decided to go to college after she had raised her two daughters. I have an undergraduate degree, BSc (Hons) in Psychology from the UK. Presently I am a post graduate student with Our Lady of the Lake University, working toward a Masters of Science in Psychology, with an emphasis on Marriage and Family Therapy. At this time, I am an intern at the Institute, involved in postmodern training, with emphasis on Collaborative Language Systems.

Christina Zunker: I am a thirty-two year old Masters student in the Marriage and Family Therapy program at the University of Houston at Clear Lake. As part of my curriculum, I am currently an intern at the Houston Galveston Institute. Prior to entering the Masters program, I trained and practiced as an attorney, first with a large national law firm and then as corporate counsel for a telecommunications company. My religious affiliations and interests have changed numerous times throughout my life; however, I am presently a member of an Episcopal church.

SPIRITUALITY: A CONVERSATIONAL LOG

The ensuing text is a re-constructed conversation on the unique meaning of spirituality for each of us. In one of our meetings, we decided to explore the meaning of spirituality by responding to the following questions via e-mail and then reflect on each other's responses. We subsequently continued to meet, reflect and discuss more about our evolving ideas in face-to-face conversations and via e-mails. Three questions sparked our initial conversation: *How do we define spirituality? What does spirituality mean to us? Why do we think about it?*

Avan: Spirituality is a set of practices that guide me in both my personal and professional life (Simon, 1996). Gutshe (1994) differentiates between religiosity, religious experience, and spirituality. The first is a "rigid adherence to externally imposed rules," more or less blindly followed with little or no thought. Religious experience is an active participation in creating meaning; a personal interpretation that is meaningful because of a personal interpretation of the experience (Ross, 1994). Spirituality, on the other hand, is a search for universal connections that "may or may not involve a deity" (Ross, 1994). For me it is an ongoing process of personal growth, thinking about life and its meaning, and attempting to understand what is most important for me within my own frameworks of values and beliefs. What I would be willing to do and what I would not. How I conduct myself in my everyday life, in my family and my relationships. It is tied up with a sense of self that allows me to live comfortably with myself, that allows me to acknowledge errors and mistakes and makes me question the intentionality behind those events. It also makes me question the things I do–why, for whom, toward what purpose. It is always a quest to find meaning within my own life and within myself.

Kayo: Spirituality is such an uncertain word for me. I may think of it as something which connects with my comfortable sensations. If I can explain it "rationally," it might not be spirituality. Maybe my definition of spirituality is something I feel but I can not explain well or put in words. It means I "feel" both emotionally and physically, undifferentiated. But I have to be cautious in using the term "spirituality" lest I save myself explaining my experience by using the word of "spirituality." Thus, instead of using "spirituality," I want to explain what happened to me as much as I can.

Why do people use the notion of spirituality? There might be a creation of experiences that they thought of as spiritual. It is important for the person even if I don't experience it as such. However, it's difficult for me to understand the person's experience. I want to know what happened to the person at that moment that they identify as spiritual.

Christina: I appreciate your comment regarding the importance of spirituality for the person, even though you might not feel like that. I like this because, in this process of our discussing spirituality, I sense that each of us is tied to our own experience and definition of spirituality, yet we are debating with each other somewhat about the meaning and/or usefulness of spirituality. I attended Harlene Anderson's intensive seminar (2000) where she cautioned about "bumping up the level of blame." She mentioned that originally it was commonplace to "blame" the client, then it was in vogue to "blame" the client's family, next is society, etc., expanding to ever larger circles. This got me thinking about how, at this point, I would never question a client's experience of "spirituality"; however, I am likely to question another therapist's view of spirituality and its usefulness–is this analogous to "bumping up the level of blame?" I don't know. Should each therapist's view of spirituality be left intact and unquestioned, just as I would leave each client's views intact?

Saliha: In attempting to understand your client's view, I would imagine that you might be implicitly questioning their beliefs. It is in the nature of conversations. Just as I am doing right now in response to your views. It's a language game (Wittgenstein, 1965).

Chuck: Spirituality to me is a language generated by action. I describe spirituality as the praxis of forming new possibilities through human storytelling. I have created this definition through reflecting on my personal spiritual formation, which occurs in relation to some extraordinary tales. Some of these stories are found in the Judeo-Christian tradition and are so durable that they have been told for thousands of years and have served as the inspiration for most of the theology, ethics, and moral law that Jews and Christians have written. Others are new stories generated as I witness client narratives and participate in storytelling with my own family and community. Through the telling and hearing of these stories, I give life meaning, and I generate a spiritual language. Among Jews and Christians, it has been a fundamental praxis to tell and retell, to interpret and reinterpret stories. The stories of our patriarchs and matriarchs like Abraham and Sarah, the parables and life of Jesus, as well as many others, lay the foundation of our spiritual life. Jewish rabbis have told more tales to interpret the basic core of the biblical narrative. Christian clergy, standing in the same tradition, use stories to illustrate sermons, and it is usually the picture language of the story that listeners of all ages remember long after the particular ethical, moral, or theological abstraction is forgotten. In my faith tradition when questions are asked with curiosity, possibilities emerge from a telling of stories. As a therapist, I witness client stories, and I ask questions that create an atmosphere for storytelling.

Avan: Language orders and evaluates knowledge and experience in relation to deeply held beliefs and values that tend to become dominant discourses in specific social contexts (this is more akin to narrative therapy). For instance, my guess is that for Chuck the Judeo-Christian discourses might dominate his values and beliefs, thus creating languaged realities and practices. Thus, when we use any of the postmodern theories, we deconstruct subverted "taken for granted realities and practices" (White, 1991). So through conversation, the therapist and the client engage in a shared inquiry and intentionality that opens up mutual exploration and development of ideas, beliefs and values (Anderson, 1997). Thus, the question is *how do we socially construct spirituality*?

Chuck: The client generates characters, plots, and story lines as they share. I try not to be overwhelmed by plot developments or character surprises, but try to be curious about where the client is taking the story line. As I witness the story, the client continually adds to, retells, or reinterprets his story and new possibilities emerge. As I participate in these relationships, new possibilities emerge for the client (I assume) and me. It is my experience that the act of human storytelling is linked to spirituality. Through storytelling the meaning of life is defined and a spiritual language is generated.

Christina: I believe spirituality is a very subjective concept. For me, spirituality is an experience made up of many elements. It is a feeling of connectedness to myself or to another person or group of people. At times of spirituality, I am very focused on the moment, and my thoughts aren't invaded by worries about today's tasks, the past or the future. I also feel calm, safe and joyful. When all of these things occur simultaneously, I experience my "spirituality."

Spirituality is a feeling I prefer over others; therefore, spirituality is meaningful to me. Spirituality is also meaningful to me because it has a tendency to give me courage to take risks. I'm not sure why I think about spirituality in the context of therapy. Perhaps I would like others to experience what is meaningful to me and have it be equally rewarding for them (not a very client-centered approach). Perhaps I will be a better therapist, better able to focus on my clients, if I experience my "spirituality" in session.

Kayo: You mainly mentioned the connection between people. For me, it's unique. I feel my connection with everything, rather than only with people. I don't think our talking about spirituality is bad. But somehow this word reminds me of the cult. It might be a Japanese misunderstanding of English. At the same time, I'm very careful to believe "therapists help clients." I rather think clients might help us so that we can believe that we (therapists) do something or help someone. We, as professionals, have to be skeptical about our usefulness/helpfulness to our clients, I believe. My stance and comments toward therapists may sound severe but by writing, I noticed that my thinking about therapists is very black and white.

Saliha: I'm curious, how do you make sense of spirituality as a *cult* and why do you think it might be a Japanese misunderstanding of English?

Kayo: When some people talk about "spirituality," it sounds to me like they believe something fantastic that only some privileged people can access the experience to feel that is labeled as "spirituality." We have no single word to express "spirituality" in Japanese. I understand "spirituality" as something among soul and mind and natural power and our feeling and so on. It's ambiguous, in a sense. Some healers utilize the notion of spirituality and sometimes their method works well. We don't know how it happens. They might explain it as spirituality. But we don't understand, and the healer never explains more. Sometimes they say only the people who can believe that spirituality can receive benefit from it. For me, *cult* means a group who believes something which the other people outside the group never understand and the group doesn't make enough effort to be understood (they repeat stereotypical explanation again and again). Sometimes I feel it's dangerous for me to believe that explanation without doubt. If each of us has our own "spirituality" and we acknowledge each other, I don't feel that fear. When I feel excluded from some specific group and I think they don't acknowledge the difference, I feel it's like a cult. So, maybe *cult* means a 'closed group' for me.

Avan: I would imagine that like everything else there are multiple individual meanings and experiences that make us wonder about spirituality and *cult* and how it relates to each of us. Perhaps there only can be moments of connectedness because otherwise our lives would be too full of sensory experiences and I am not sure that this could be handled on a daily basis. For me, there are very definite moments that stand out and that I will never forget–the feeling, the wonder, and the sadness too. These moments are incorporated into what I am, what I have become and what, perhaps, I will be. Special, unforgettable, and in the end, I think, giving meaning to the life we live.

Saliha: Spirituality is ephemeral–it's a way of being and it's momentary; it's a moment of wonderment, a moment of awe, a moment of connection, a moment of serenity, a moment of calmness, a moment of sense making and enlightenment. A moment when I wonder how my body coordinates my walking, talking, eating, listening, thinking, looking, smelling and all the non-conscious activity at any given time. It's a moment of awe to know that I–a human being–am a miracle. It's a moment when I am speaking to a person (client) and sense an invisible thread or a laser from my eyes to his/her eyes. It is a moment when the mist lifts up to reveal a gently shimmering lake. It's a moment when I finally understood my 3-year-old niece's want when she was frustrated because I did not understand her obvious and explicit gesticulations! It's a wonderment at how the amaryllis blooms to reveal four gorgeous red flowers, each blooming a day later.

Spirituality is a metaphor more than a tangible, concrete notion for me. As individuals-in-relationships (Anderson, 1997), we are in relationship with ideas and notions which are fluid and evolving. Thus, the context of training provides for social meaning-making processes such as the one we all are involved in currently.

Christina: In response to the question regarding the meaning of training, when I think of *training,* I think of anything I've learned through the Institute (through conversations with staff, faculty, client or other learners) that will be useful in my career as a therapist.

Chuck: I am amazed at how the process of studying to be a therapist at the Institute has affected me. While I have learned a lot as a therapist, I am particularly amazed at how I have changed in my relationships with my family and friends. I have become more able to stay present with my friends, especially in times where they have something unpleasant to share with me about me. I have begun to see these situations not as a personal attack during which I must either flee or counterattack, but an opportunity for our relationship to change. Through learning to relate to others in therapeutic relationships, I have become increasingly able to ask how I am creating problems for others and how we might change this together.

Saliha: What do you mean by *stay*?

Chuck: For me *staying* means that I keep the conversation going. I try to hear the concerns and hopes of my friends and family and attempt to respond. I try to keep the important parts of their conversation my main focus of response instead of avoiding their communication as I interpret it.

Christina: What else, Chuck? [As Chuck looks thoughtful.]

Chuck: Additionally, I have decided to say what I think when I am discouraged or confused by others as well. When I have done this, it seems that while there might be initial sadness, they are pleased that I have approached the subject with them. Generally, in the end we have been able to discuss our relationship and create new plans for the future. I am certainly still learning this process, but I do find it surprising that I have begun to have these sorts of conversations as a result of my training. I do see this change as a spiritual one for me. It has changed the way I talk to others, and has created new possibilities for they way I relate that were not previously possible. I am developing a sense of not being overwhelmed by the controversy in life but staying with the story to see how it will work out. In these places of relational change, I find a moment of spiritual action.

Christina: It sounds like your experiences at the Institute with training have been personally very rewarding. I wonder if there is a way to give these same benefits to clients, should they desire them?

Avan: Within the Institute I would like to believe that there is reciprocity of respect and openness in the way we interrelate with each other. We are mindful of each other. I would hope that this comes from the heart and not the mind, that the spirit of appreciation and respect is for each other as well as our clients. That we honor existence and understand that one's existence is related to others in and around different contexts. There is little room for ego gratification at the Institute. I have no illusions of power or control. I like the idea of relinquishment–a letting go stance that dissolves a want to 'fix it' mode. It is of value to recognize that one can 'sit with' another's pain or despair and acknowledge our own helplessness and anxiety about failing to help. (Too often, though I fail to do this!) Part of my own personal growth is in this area of realizing that one's response can become one of relinquishment–of one's own anxieties, as well as stopping assigning responsibility to others for having caused those anxieties. If I feel my cup is empty, I should fill it myself with what I consider to be of worth and valuable. (Is that too individualistic an idea?) There has been a shift–an understanding that solutions lie not in the hands of the therapist, or others in one's life, but only in one's own. Being human, of course, there is, at times, a sliding back into prescribed roles that are part and parcel of one's cultural heritage, but it is as essential to keep the awareness of those 'other' prescribed ways of being in the forefront. How we think, behave, and relate to people will influence our behavior in all areas of our lives because we live in what Simon (1996) calls a "witnessed universe."

Kayo: I don't understand the difference between "heart" and "mind." Could you explain more? I like your ideas about relinquishment. I totally agree with you.

Avan: Yes, it comes from the heart and has nothing to do with cognitive thinking. It is a way of being, a mindfulness that has a certain respect and reverence for other people, no matter who or what they are. But, of course, I qualify this because I do not accept all things about all people. I also believe very strongly in responsibility and doing what is right, in thoughts, words, and deeds. It is part of my creed.

Saliha: If words create a reality, then when we use terms like "mindfulness" are we cutting off our body? How does the "mind" in "mindfulness" act on/with the body?

Avan: I sense it, I feel it. I sometimes think that being intellectual about it in fact takes away from the experience. I could explain in language, and if I were a writer or poet, I would probably do a great job. But to describe moments that to me seem spiritual would almost be taking away from the experience. I define spirituality in relations, but I also define it as something very deep within myself–perhaps the core of who I am. Toward that end I hope that it never stops and that it is a process of growth.

Kayo: It is difficult for me to think of my experiences at the Institute as *training*. What is the meaning of *training* for me? In my definition, training is a certain skill gaining experience, which I can use as a professional. In this meaning, I don't think I was *trained* at the Institute. As a personal experience, I think I had good experiences at the Institute. I hope I carry these experiences back to my work in Japan. But I don't know whether they might be beneficial for my patients in the future or not. Hopefully, I want to listen to the words of my patients slowly and mention how to open up dialogical conversation.

Saliha: You apparently differentiate between personal and professional experiences. And I do agree that we tend to label various experiences as "personal" or "professional." However, can the personal and professional be teased apart without stripping the context and texts within which we locate our own expectations of *training*? In my experience of training and practicing in India and America, I have encountered the separation of personal and professional, and I have also experienced the non-universality of the potential distinctions.

Christina: One of my supervisors suggested I read T. Byram Karasu's article "Spiritual Psychotherapy." On reading the article I was excited by the lofty position it gave the therapist, describing therapy "not so much as a profession [but] as a way of being in harmonious relationship to man [sic] and infinite nature" (1999, p. 161). The article seems to call therapists to become supremely loving, centered, and connected human beings, in order that they may help their clients achieve a similar state. Always inspired by a challenge, and in keeping with my life-long desire to evolve into an exemplary human being who could be a beacon of light to others (I wanted to be a nun at the age of five), I immediately began my mental to-do list to achieve the exalted state (i.e., "1. daily meditation, 2. decrease focus on the material, 3. eat only vegetarian fare . . . "). Nevertheless, as the days passed, and as I engaged in different conversations at the Institute, specifically those relating to the Collaborative Language Systems ideas of "not knowing" and "the client is the expert" (Anderson, 1997, Anderson & Goolishian, 1992), I began to wonder whether my transmogrification into the next great prophet was just an attempt to make me feel more important in a profession where, it seems to me, a client's "success" in therapy is most frequently supported by very basic interactions (i.e., being listened to and being respected).

Saliha: I think you beautifully illustrate the coming together of the *personal* and *professional* as (con)textualized by the socially co-created meaning frames of becoming a therapist.

Christina: Speaking of social, Karasu (1999) states that "the quality of spirituality, religious or not . . . depends . . . on the social relations it advances" (p. 149). I agree with this statement and am afraid that mixing spirituality with psychotherapy will simply create another, novel circumstance where the therapist is the "expert" on a concept, this time spirituality. Any type of spirituality which creates such a relationship between the client and the therapist is not of a quality I believe should be used in therapy.

Avan: I agree with you. If the therapeutic encounter is one of alliance and connectedness, it can only benefit both the client and therapist but an 'expert' position that I am not comfortable with.

The conversation shifts into reflective posturing. The focus of the conversation is a conversation about the purpose of our conversation.

Christina: What is the purpose of this talk? Will this help train someone else? What is the purpose of addressing this issue?

Avan: When we talk about it in training, I can see how it is useful but don't see how it is useful with a client unless they want to talk about it. On second thought, if spirituality is a set of practices that encompasses respect, gratitude, and reverence then surely it might be useful to the client. I can see the idea of spirituality can help us to be better therapists; you can connect better if you have that kind of feeling.

Christina: What is *that kind of feeling?*

Avan: That I'm not separate from others. This training has surprised me, much like Chuck, in that I have a greater awareness and tolerance of all aspects of diversity. I have met clients with whom I would never have encounters outside the therapy session and I found them to be much like me, that is, their worries, their love for their children, but, even more, their amazing strengths that make them cope with their adversity in situations when I think I would have been devastated. So my respect increases and I am grateful that they can trust or have faith in me to talk about their travails. I'm very surprised that I can be so non-judgmental and feel the relatedness and not want to marginalize anybody. Something I learned about myself that I did not know about myself.

Chuck: I'm thinking about Christina's question. Maybe, to talk about the *training piece*, we can describe the kinds of conversations in training that have been helpful in defining the meaning of spirituality within a postmodern context.

Avan: Very clearly, the approach, that I don't think of myself as an expert in the client's life and hope I will never be. I think that people who are attracted to this approach are primarily those who have the feeling that they don't want to put others down. I don't want to be thought of as "superior" or the "expert" in the client's life, rather I attempt to "understand" the events that have unfolded in the person's (client) life. The training allows me to explore that element much more than would otherwise be possible.

Kayo: Talking about spirituality is like talking about another of our personal experiences and may be related to training and help us as professionals, but I don't understand how we can separate spirituality from our personal experiences. I think spirituality is part of the personal. To separate spirituality from the personal is to probably risk making it special.

Avan: Spirituality is not a verb or a noun but a moment, a feeling, a way of being and living.

Chuck: When I'm talking about spirituality, I talk about it in much different kinds of ways. For me spirituality happens in a different way. Places we meet would be moments of spirituality and where we do not meet is not a spiritual moment.

Saliha: We are talking about spirituality in terms of what it means to each of us. And for you [to Chuck] there are aspects of your religion interwoven with spirituality.

Avan: What it means to me as a person? It's postmodern because it's not broadly defined by religion. I'm not as religious as you [to Chuck], that is, as far as religion playing a large part in my life. In postmodernism we can tie some of those concepts with spirituality. I mean if you ask Chuck, he was talking a bit about what religion means to him. In my life it's a presence that's greater than the self. That's what I associate with what religion means to me with spirituality. I have no idea about the training bit.

Another thing is that, I would like to feel that I'm living it in my every day life, rather than talking about it in an abstract way. If I can conduct myself in a way that is true to myself I would feel that there is some sort of connection I have. In my religion the tenet of spirituality is: good words, good thoughts, good deeds. I think you need to be aware of it everyday in how you are doing good and where are you doing it.

Saliha: Can you please say more about your tenets?

Avan: In my religion we try to live by three basis tenets: good words, good thoughts, and good deeds. Good words are connected to the ways in which we speak to our clients without putting labels on them, without demeaning them, and without making ourselves out to be the experts of our clients' lives. We strive not to transform the identified person from responsible subject to an object of medical psychological practice that is deficit in some way and that marginalizes them. We strive not to create a 'non-ideal' identity for a person, undermining local or personal knowledge. We believe that statements that subjugate and take away power become internalized statements that, in turn, become life experiences. "Reverence" Simon (1996) says, is about honoring existence and understanding that one's existence is related to others in and around different contexts. In therapy and the training we have received at the Institute it relates to respecting the client, and respecting the client means believing in the client's resourcefulness that he/she has the inner resources to solve the problem. It means believing that the client knows what is best for him or her, from the stage of problem defining to what is making it better. When we ask a client "How did you manage to do that?" we express our appreciation for the small steps, the small changes, that the client is making. We acknowledge and appreciate the client's ideas, resources, experiences, and solutions in the face of sometimes great difficulties, trials, and pain. "Receptivity" reflects the therapist's position of curiosity and openness. It also gives up the illusion of power and control. It acknowledges that we do not know it all, do not have all the answers. We stay nonjudgmental, inviting, open to all possibilities and ways of being. This is akin to what I had said earlier about the principle of letting go or relinquishment acknowledging we do not have all the answers, are not the expert, and therefore hopefully we can let go of the 'fix it' mode. Simon (1996) calls for "surrendering the security of dichotomies as a way of parsing reality and choosing instead the uncertain terrain of unpredictable, chaotic life." It makes for a more equal playing field and does away with traditional hierarchical positions of therapist/client. It requires humility to understand that each person's story is the same as your own, with the same aspirations, struggles, and pain. This ties into the concept of connectedness, that we are all part of the same universe, and that "there is no individual mind apart from the whole." How we behave, think, and relate to people is similar both in and out of sessions; it influences our behavior in all areas of our life. This is what I think Simon meant when he says we live in a "witnessed universe."

Kayo: What about *good thoughts and good deeds*?

Avan: Good thoughts are representative of the meaning people attribute to their lives. It is a way of thinking that gives strength and self-agency back to the person. They become the authors of their own stories and move forward to greater self-reliance. Perhaps what is most thought provoking to me is "good deeds" for in this particular domain I see the stance of the therapist as a way in which the most positive, respectful, genuine, and honest relationship can develop between the client and the therapist. Do no harm, to my mind, is equivalent of keeping this tenet in mind. Putting the client's needs before one's own, always being mindful of the words we use; the nature of power and how it can be constructed and deconstructed; how we communicate and how we influence–all these practices are representative of good deeds on the part of the therapist. I believe that in many ways these practices have been part of our *training* at the Institute, but I also believe that these practices exist within each one of us at the Institute, otherwise we would not choose to be here.

Saliha: We have been referring to *training* as a given, but now I am starting to wonder *how do you each define training?* Kayo and Christina defined it earlier.

Chuck: Training at the Institute is dialogical. It's the actual act of dialogue that is training here. In the moment of participating in the dialogue, something occurs and we take something away from it.

Christina: What do you mean by dialogue?

Chuck: People being interested in each other, verbally and nonverbally.

Avan: Would that be curiosity?

Chuck: When we are trying to understand each other's language, then we are interested in each other. Training at the Institute is dialogue. Through these conversations I continually develop and redevelop a practical view of the everyday world of a therapist and therapist activities. I do not believe that this dialogue has enabled me to completely understand my colleagues and clients or that I have found a way to send them clear messages about what I have to say. I do not believe that we have discovered the true nature of what it means for each of us to work or participate in therapy at the Institute or how we impact each other in particular circumstances. We do, however, generate possibilities through our conversations that seem to allow us to make sense of one another enough that we continue our relationships with interest. Training at the Institute is primarily beneficial for me in that it is an ongoing experience of dialoging with others where I try to create ways to be with them in a way that makes sense in our relationship. Reflections on theory or the true nature of human beings occur at the Institute but are always secondary to me to the moment by moment relationship we share. Through them we find ways to value one another at least enough to continue being interested in each other. Through my training I am learning each day how to put my truth claims aside and listen and be listened to. At times I struggle with this, as I would rather rely on a previously constructed truth claim than truly participate in the moment. I have experienced the subtle and not so subtle ways my colleagues and clients remind me that I am there to participate in that moment.

Saliha: So how have these dialogues affected your notions of spirituality?

Chuck: Have these dialogues affected me at any time as far as my spirituality is concerned? Yes. For instance in these dialogues about spirituality, I have taken what each of you has said and integrated it into my view of spirituality and so changes in my *notions* of spirituality continue.

Avan: What has happened is the way we have learned to relate to other people and understand better that, words we use can have very different meanings. I have encountered words like respect, reverence, and reciprocity in my training, and I am appreciative to a larger degree that they can influence one's life and change one's life. The thing that really bugs me is that they don't understand that in what ways are they showing respect or reverence and to me that is the meaning of what I have taken from my training.

Christina: Are you saying spirituality is relational?

Avan: Both. That it can be experienced relationally and can be purely an "alone" experience and the meaning I take from that. By *alone* I mean something that has affected or touched you in a way that is your own unique experience.

Chuck: Is that *unique experience* you describe created by your self, is it given to you, or is it created for you?

Avan: It can't be created if we are not in relationship to something or someone else. So even a *unique* experience has to involve someone or something else. I think that when we talk about "we live in a witnessed universe" every thought that we think, every deed we do is witnessed by others and witnessed by myself.

Chuck: We are also struggling to find a place for what each other is saying and its usefulness.

Christina: For me, I would not call it a struggle as much as learning to tolerate.

Chuck: For me this is an exercise in tolerance. The Institute is a really good environment for dialogue and for tolerating difference if we want to.

And so the conversation goes on among us, with our clients, friends and family.

AN AFTERWORD: REFLECTIVE AND ANALYTICAL MOMENTS

Saliha: The conversation of spirituality continued with implicit and explicit references to *spirituality* and references to this project that brought us together in a unique manner. Over the course of the various meetings, each of us would have some process reflections which are presented below as after thoughts. These thoughts cover the gamut of *conversational process, struggles and conflict arising in the course of our conversations, theoretical notions and reflections on the writing process.*

Kayo: Initially in the process of talking about spirituality, I think we tended to talk about ourselves rather than listen to others in the discussion. In spite of this verbal monological process (overlabeled?), I feel I could connect with others in the group.

In counseling settings, I seldom make a statement which sounds like opposition to the client. But in the process of our discussion, I didn't hold back. If we need some agreement, it might be a conflict. When we define "our spiritual moment," do we refer to same moment? Do we (all of us) have a common spiritual moment? Do we feel spirituality simultaneously?

If we feel our spirituality in the same situation, it might be easier to discuss. But it does not happen a lot actually. At least I feel like that. No one can force us to feel spirituality.

I don't know about spirituality, but could we find a moment we felt something simultaneously? If we perceive/feel/recognize the same moment as a struggle/conflict/confrontation, how is it different from a spiritual moment?

In the first place in my bias we, mental health professionals, focus on others rather than on ourselves in our practice. If we don't do this, I think it's complacent. Complacency is okay in some situations, but I would hate if this happened to the therapist in the session.

I think this leads to the discussion about "scary." If something excluded someone and he/she became complacent within particular individual/group, I might feel it's scary. It's violent/dangerous. Do you feel/perceive/think our spirituality conversation worked to exclude someone? Is the struggle/conflict/confrontation scary? How did you feel? Or what do you think of as a scare? I'm not happy in the group if we did not appreciate each other. But I didn't feel it as scary. I'm very curious where the word of scary came from?

At the beginning I said, spirituality sounds like a cult in Japanese. I believe what we discussed as *spirituality* is different from Japanese connotation. I think we appreciate each other in this process. At least I felt like that when others referred to my statement. Did you feel something (even not spiritual in your definition) in you was appreciated by others?

Christina: The only time I felt a real struggle during the process of working on this spirituality paper was during the first discussion (not performed in this script) when I felt like Chuck was trying to summarize and combine all of our ideas to come up with a common theme for our "spiritualities." I felt like his description did not fit with my experience of spirituality, and I felt like I needed to protect my own definition, which I think I did. I felt tension after this experience and a concern about whether we could continue in our discussions without polarizing or escalating into an argument. Nevertheless, my fears were allayed when we met the next time and, although we never came to agreement about various aspects of spirituality, the discussion seemed less tense. From that point forward, I felt like it was okay to agree to disagree, knowing that our relationships would still continue. Kayo's directness (e.g., her comments regarding our not listening to each other) also gave me guidance on how to "confront with kindness."

During our last discussion, I do feel like we dichotomized our ideas regarding the danger of individual versus group spirituality (which is not described in this paper). However, since I have begun to feel closer to the group as our discussions have continued, the last discussion did not feel tense at all. Disagreeing seemed more like a sport than a struggle. Kayo's (or Saliha's?) direct comments regarding dichotomizing brought the discussion one step further for me, past the sport of disagreeing and on to a willingness to accept the validity of both my points and Chuck's points, and the weaknesses of both.

Avan: Our struggles and conflicts were collaborative because we never presumed that one definition was better than the other was. There was no either/or but lots of both(s)/and. During the discussions we had and in the actual writing of the paper, we really defined Collaborative Language Systems (CLS) (Anderson, 1997). For each of us the word spirituality held a different definition, and yet we were able to hold these different views and at the same time give equal importance to each one of our voices. In a way, through the dialogues we had, we co-explored and co-created this paper which is really what CLS is about. The meaning(s) that we derived did not have to be the "absolute truth" nor did any one of us claim to be experts or claim that our individual way of thinking was the right one. I also think that what came out of this was our 'being in relationship,' that is, an alliance or a trust was formed that allowed us to express our thoughts without thinking that we would be judged in any way.

Chuck: Also my training at the Institute has helped me to have faith that it is possible to form relationships through paying attention to how we attempt to make sense of our surroundings together and that as we do so we create new ways of being for our relationship and ourselves as persons, therapists, clients, etc. And this current instance of generating this paper was another example of training that occurs in dialogue.

Saliha: Our conversations are illustrative of the unexpected learning–new knowledge–that occurs through collaborative conversations (Anderson, 2001, personal communication). What started out as conversations about spirituality and postmodernism generated conversations about differences, feeling of connections, cultural connotations of language, personal transformations of how to relate to another colleague without the fear of polarizing discussions, and introduced new ways for each of us to interact with the other.

I wonder about how the reader might be influenced by such conversations. Such conversations have the undertones of the "autobiographical voice" in human science. Gergen (1997) asserts that autobiographical voice is an alternate genre of scholarship in human science, which has the potential to "bring the reader even closer to the author. The author's experience (soul) is rendered transparent and accessible." Even though we did not relate specific personal lived experiences, we have spoken very (inter)subjectively about spirituality and training at the Institute that makes us public and vulnerable to each other and the reader. So, not unlike the autobiographical voice, my expectation is that the reader may be drawn into self-reflection about his/her own position, either to assert his/her voice and/or to identify with one of the speakers (writers) of the current script.

Dan Friedman, member of the Castillo theatre of New York, says, "unlike a plot, a conversation need have no point. It is an open-ended social activity with the potential to go somewhere or to dissipate or fracture or spin or transform in any number of ways." And we have retained certain aspects of conversation in our paper as we re-perform our dialogues. As you (the reader) perform with us in these dialogues via the medium of paper reading, you might experience the open-ended and informal style. Our intent to recreate the postmodern context of training in the deconstruction and reconstruction of spirituality may leave you with more questions and loose ends than answers. However, these experiences are learnable moments, and we invite you to join the dialogues with others and us, thus extending the possibilities of and for conversation.

Similar to the experience of the members of the Castillo improvisational theatre group, our conversations go beyond the formal nature of this paper to informal settings, such as conversations with each other, colleagues, friends, and family and onto other formal settings like the conversations with our clients and colleagues. Thus, the possibility of conversation extends beyond organized forums. My intent is that some of this will extend informally into your (the reader's) life, thus blurring the lines between professional and personal lives.

We invite you to share your experience of reading this paper with us by e-mailing or writing to us.

REFERENCES

Agger, B. (1998). *Critical social theories: An introduction*. Boulder, CO: Westview Press.

Anderson, D. A. (1994). Transcendence and relinquishment in couple therapy. *Journal of Systemic Therapies*, *13*, 36-41.

Anderson, H. (1997). *Conversation, language, and possibilities: A postmodern approach to therapy*. NY: Basic Books.

Bruffee, K. (1999). *Collaborative learning: Higher education, interdependence, and the authority of knowledge* (Second ed.). Baltimore: The Johns Hopkins University Press.

Chenail, R. J. (1990/1991). Bradford Keeney's Cybernetic Project and the Creation of Recursive Frame Analysis. *The Qualitative Report*, *1* (Numbers 2 and 3, Winter/Spring).

Chenail, R. (1993). Creating frames and constructing galleries. In A. H. Rambo, A. Heath, & R. J. Chenail (Eds.), *Practicing therapy: Exercises for growing therapists* (pp. 155-168). New York: W. W. Norton & Company.

Ellis, C., & Bochner, A. (1996). *Composing Ethnography: Alternative forms of qualitative writing.*

Friedman, D. (2001). Available: http://www.california.com/~rathbone/friedman.htm [2001].

Gergen, K. (1997). *Who speaks and who replies in human science scholarship?* Available: http://www.swarthmore.edu/SocSci/kgergen1/whospeak.html [2000, March 21].

Gergen, K. (1999). *An invitation to social construction.* Thousand Oaks, CA: Sage Publications Inc.

Gutsche, S. (1994). Voices of healing: Therapists and clients journey towards spirituality. *Journal of Systemic Therapies, 13*, 3-5.

Hertz, R. (Ed.). (1997). *Reflexivity and voice.* Thousand Oaks, CA: Sage Publications.

Holzman, L., & Morss, J. (Eds.). (2000). *Postmodern psychologies, societal practices and political life.* New York: Routledge.

Karasu, B. (1999). Spiritual psychotherapy. *American Journal of Psychotherapy, Vol. 53*, 143-161.

Keeney, B. (1991). *Improvisational therapy: A practical guide for creative clinical strategies.* New York: Guilford Press.

McCall, M. M., & Becker, H. S. (1990). Performance science. *Social Problems, 37*(1), 117-132.

Pinch, T., & Pinch, T. (1988). Reservations about reflexivity and new literary forms or why let the devil have all the good times? In S. Woolgar (Ed.), *Knowledge and reflexivity: New frontiers in the sociology of knowledge* (pp. 178-197). Newbury Park, CA: Sage Publication, Inc.

Pockley, S. (1995). *The Flight of Ducks: Duck Song*, [WWW]. Available: http://www.cinemedia.net/FOD/FOD0259.html [1999].

Richardson, L. (1993). Poetics, dramatics, and transgressive validity: The case of the skipped line. *Sociological Quarterly, 35*, 695-710.

Richardson, L. (1997). *Fields of play: Constructing an academic life.* New Brunswick, New Jersey: Rutgers University Press.

Richardson, L., & Lockridge, E. (1991). The sea monster: An ethnographic drama and comment on ethnographic fiction. *Symbolic Interaction*, 335-341.

Ross, J. L. (1994). Working with patients within their religious contexts: Religion, spirituality, and the secular therapist. *Journal of Systemic Therapies, 13*, 7-15.

Schneider, J. W. (1991). Troubles with textual authority in sociology. *Symbolic Interaction, 14*(3), 295-319.

Simon, D. (1996). Crafting consciousness through form: Solution-focused therapy as a spiritual path. In S. Miller, M. Hubble, & B. Duncan (Eds.), *Handbook of solution focused brief therapy* (pp. 44-62). San Francisco: Jossey-Bass.

White, M. (1993). Deconstruction and therapy. In S. Gilligan & R. Price (Eds.), *Therapeutic Conversations* (pp. 22-61). New York: W.W. Norton.

Wittgenstein, L. (1965). *Philosophical Investigations* (G. E. M. Anscombe, Trans.). New York: The Macmillan Company.

Woolgar, S. (1988). *Knowledge and reflexivity: New frontiers in the sociology of knowledge.* Newbury Park, CA: Sage Publications.

SPIRITUAL APPROACHES TO WORKING WITH SPECIFIC POPULATIONS

Fathering, Faith, and Family Therapy: Generative Narrative Therapy with Religious Fathers

David C. Dollahite
Loren D. Marks
Michael M. Olson

David C. Dollahite is Professor, Department of Marriage, Family, and Human Development, Brigham Young University.

Loren D. Marks is Assistant Professor, Division of Family, Child, and Consumer Sciences, Louisiana State University.

Michael M. Olson is Assistant Professor, Department of Family Medicine, University of Texas Medical Branch at Galveston.

The authors would like to thank the Family Studies Center and the Religious Studies Center at Brigham Young University for research support for this paper. They also express appreciation to Karen Hahne, Director of the Kids on the Move early intervention program, for giving them access to fathers in that program. The authors are especially grateful to the fathers who opened their homes and lives to them.

Address corresondence to: David C. Dollahite, Department of Marriage, Family, and Human Development, School of Family Life, Brigham Young University, 1044 Kimball Tower, Provo, UT 84602 (E-mail: dave_dollahite@byu.edu).

[Haworth co-indexing entry note]: "Fathering, Faith, and Family Therapy: Generative Narrative Therapy with Religious Fathers." Dollahite, David C., Loren D. Marks, and Michael M. Olson. Co-published simultaneously in *Journal of Family Psychotherapy* (The Haworth Press, Inc.) Vol. 13, No. 3/4, 2002, pp. 259-290; and: *Spirituality and Family Therapy* (ed: Thomas D. Carlson, and Martin J. Erickson) The Haworth Press, Inc., 2002, pp. 259-290. Single or multiple copies of this article are available for a fee from The Haworth Document Delivery Service [1-800-HAWORTH, 9:00 a.m. - 5:00 p.m. (EST). E-mail address: getinfo@haworthpressinc.com].

SUMMARY. This article presents the major conceptual and clinical ideas on fathering, religion, and counseling developed by David C. Dollahite and his colleagues. The concepts of *generative fathering* and *generative narrative therapy* are presented and illustrated with narratives of religious fathers. These ideas address a number of issues believed important to consider in family therapy with fathers–particularly religious fathers. Concepts are illustrated with personal narratives from two samples of Latter-day Saint (Mormon) fathers of children with special needs. Although the narratives are non-clinical, implications for family therapy from these and related theories and stories are suggested. The article emphasizes father strengths, the power of religion to assist fathers in challenging circumstances, and the importance of therapists' sensitivity to spiritual and religious matters.

KEYWORDS. Spirituality, religion, fathering

There has been intense and contested scholarly focus on fathers and fathering in the past decade. Evidence indicates that forces such as individualization, materialism, secularization, increasing occupational demands, work-oriented technological intrusions into family life, pervasive media influence, along with increasing out-of-wedlock births and divorce have adversely impacted connections between fathers and children. A now substantial body of research summarized by Doherty, Kouneski, and Erickson (1998) and Popenoe (1996) show that when fathers are present and meaningfully involved, children fare better in almost every way. With few exceptions (e.g., Silverstein & Auerbach, 1999), contemporary family scholars acknowledge the overwhelming scientific evidence that fathers matter greatly to children's well-being.

This article presents the concepts of *generative fathering* and *generative narrative therapy* and illustrates them with narrative accounts of religious fathers. These ideas address a number of issues we believe are important to consider in family therapy with fathers–particularly religious fathers. These concepts are illustrated with personal narratives from two non-clinical samples of Latter-day Saint (Mormon) fathers of children with special needs. The article emphasizes the strengths that fathers bring to their work, the power that religious belief has in assisting fathers in challenging circumstances, and the importance of therapists being sensitive to spiritual experience and religious involvement. Our use of both theoretical constructs and narrative accounts furthers the connection between theory, story, and intervention begun in earlier work (Dienhart & Dollahite, 1997; Dollahite, Hawkins, & Brotherson, 1996; Dollahite & Hawkins, 1998).

GENERATIVE FATHERING

Dollahite et al. (1997) and Dollahite and Hawkins (1998) proposed a "conceptual ethic of fathering as generative work" that draws from the developmental conceptual work of Erik Erikson (1950, 1982) and John Snarey (1993). Erikson (1950, 1982) coined the term *generativity* to refer to adults caring for and contributing to the next generation (see Christiansen & Palkovitz, 1998). Generative fathering is *fathering that meets the needs of children by working to create and maintain a developing ethical relationship with them.*

Needs of the Next Generation

The generative approach is grounded both in fathers' personal desires to meet their children's needs and their moral responsibility to strive to meet those needs. Dollahite and Hawkins (1998) offered a systematic framework of children's needs that emerge from fundamental and universal challenges of the human condition–challenges such as dependency, scarcity, change, stress, perplexity, isolation, and obligation. Emphasizing fathers' working to meet children's needs "places fathering on the firm foundation of the needs of the next generation rather than on the shifting sands of societal role expectations, the fragile fault line of adult gender relations, or the engulfing quagmire of expressive individualism" (Dollahite et al., 1997, p. 34). Thus, while the generative framework explicitly affirms that fathering is complex, demanding, and dynamic, and that most fathers are faced with challenges that make good fathering a challenging labor, it also suggests that most fathers have the desire and ability to meet these needs and that all fathers have the obligation to try to do so.

Fatherwork: Fathering as Generative Work

The generative perspective uses the concept of *work* to understand and encourage responsible, involved fathering. Indeed, the terms *fatherwork* and generative fathering are used interchangeably in the model. The framework proposes that fathers' work is best viewed as a "calling" in which "work constitutes a practical ideal of activity and character that makes a person's work morally inseparable from his or her life" (Bellah, Madsen, Sullivan, Swindler, & Tipton, 1985, p. 66).

The framework proposes seven areas of fatherwork made necessary by children's needs: *ethical work* (continuing commitment), *stewardship work* (providing resources), *development work* (growth and change), *spiritual work* (helping children make meaning), *recreation work* (play), *relational work* (maintaining connection), and *mentoring work* (teaching skills).

The metaphor of work for fathering

a. reconnects the concepts of family life and meaningful labor,
b. makes fathering familiar for men since most men work hard and try to improve their work,
c. evokes transformative images and ideals (e.g., perseverance, problem solving, decision making, creativity, choice, skills training, education, competence, improvement).

The concept of fathering as generative work (rather than mere social role enactment) can help practitioners move beyond educational programs and clinical interventions that may not be respectful of most fathers' actual motivations, capabilities, and experiences.

Beyond Deficit Perspectives

Doherty (1991) and Hawkins and Dollahite (1997) argue that a deficit perspective on men and fathering pervades the clinical literature. Among others, the following concepts, labels, and terms referring to men and fathers are part and parcel of the scholarly and popular clinical literature: incompetent, unaware, underdeveloped femininity, fear of intimacy, distant, infantile, emotional children, emotionally constricted, emotionally constipated, toxic masculinity, hypermasculine, mascupathology, narcissistic, abusive, oppressive, and the scientifically sounding term alexithymic (inability to express emotion). In fact, given the way men are sometimes viewed and treated in clinical settings, it should not be surprising that many men avoid family therapy.

The generative fathering framework moves beyond deficit ideologies including what Hawkins and Dollahite (1997) referred to as the "role-inadequacy perspective" (RIP) of fathering. The RIP emphasizes fathers' seeming unwillingness to adapt to recent sociohistorical change, their relative lack of involvement with children (compared to mothers), and their alleged resistance to greater paternal involvement. While acknowledging that too much fathering is deficient or harmful, Hawkins and Dollahite (1997) critiqued the role-inadequacy perspective because it

a. tends to overemphasize fathers' inadequacies and ignore their strengths,
b. is primarily intended to rescript social roles rather than facilitate personal transformation,
c. does not adequately acknowledge the motivations most fathers have to be good fathers,
d. creates barriers to change by maintaining low expectations for fathers,
e. does not challenge the explicit or implicit assumption that the parenting practices typically associated with mothering fully meet the needs of children.

Of course, we recognize that in many cases when a family is in therapy the father is either not present or not functioning well. Since clinicians often deal with people whose fathers were or are harmful or with dysfunctional fathers themselves, we think it is difficult for therapists to avoid developing a deficit perspective on men and fathers. Additionally, some therapists have deficit perspectives of religion and religious parents. When a deficit perspective of religion is combined with a deficit perspective of men this leads some therapists to approach religious men with negative stereotypes. However, there are a great many highly functioning fathers and the literature suggests that many of these are religious men. Thus, we believe it is imperative for clinicians not to adopt an a priori negative view of religious fathers who come to them for counseling.

A Summary of the Generative Framework

The generative framework integrates two important concepts in the fathering literature: father involvement and father responsibility, puts them into a broader context, and provides additional important issues to attend to in relation to good fathering (e.g., development, change). In summary, the major assumptions of the generative perspective include the following:

1. Fathering takes place in a context of constraints, barriers, and challenges for father and child.
2. Good fathering involves meeting children's changing needs more than responding to societal expectations or changing social roles.
3. Children's needs are grounded in the challenges and opportunities of the human and family conditions.
4. Fathering is inherently a moral and ethical response to the needs of children.
5. Good fathering is one of the most challenging and important kinds of work that men who are fathers do.
6. Fathers have the ability and the responsibility to choose to be involved and responsible fathers.
7. Most fathers have strong desires to be responsible and involved.
8. Men bring varied abilities, interests, and strengths to their fathering.
9. Responsible, involved fathering is consistent with healthy mens' development since father's and children's developmental needs are often complementary.
10. Fathers develop through their fathering and grow into their fathering. (Adapted from Dollahite & Hawkins, 1998.)

The clinical implications of the narratives to be presented below are undergirded by these concepts and we believe that interventions that are not consistent with these basic ideas will not be as likely to encourage responsible, involved fathering as interventions that are consistent with them.

Support for Empirical and Practical Applications of the Generative Framework

Empirical Support for a Generative Framework. Several studies have supported the major conceptual and applied ideas of the generative framework (Borrows, 1996; Brotherson, 1995; Brotherson and Dollahite, 1997; Dollahite, in press; Dollahite, Marks, & Olson, 1998; Grant, Hawkins, & Dollahite, 2001; Marks & Dollahite, 2001; Marks, 1999; Morris, 1998; Morris, Dollahite, & Hawkins, 1999; Olson, 1999). This research, which has involved qualitative research with fathers of children with special needs along with some Ojibway fathers (Borrows, 1996), has found that most fathers take their paternal responsibilities seriously, are committed to meeting their children's needs, strive to understand their children's needs, and work to meet their children's needs.

Educational and Clinical Applications of the Generative Framework. Fagan and Hawkins (2001) edited a volume of clinical and educational interventions for fathers using the generative framework as the overarching conceptual model. Palm (1997, 2001) incorporated the concepts of generative fathering into a framework of goals for parent and family education with fathers. Dollahite, Hawkins, and Brotherson (1996) demonstrated how the framework could be used in family life education using a narrative approach to illustrate concepts. Dollahite, Morris, and Hawkins (1997) proposed various activities and questions for college and university educators to use to incorporate concepts of generative fathering into courses. Dollahite, Hawkins, and Associates (1997) used the framework as the basis for a narrative-oriented family life education web site. Evaluative feedback from users of the site and some initial quantitative findings from module evaluation surveys suggest that users find the ideas and stories helpful (Grant, Hawkins, & Dollahite, 2001; Morris et al., 1999). Dienhart and Dollahite (1997) suggested that the conceptual ethic of fathering as generative work has important implications for therapeutic work with fathers and they presented an approach to therapy that combines the ideas of generative fathering with narrative therapy (White & Epston, 1990) to form what they called "Generative Narrative Therapy." Dollahite, Slife, and Hawkins (1998) used the major concepts of a generative approach to develop the concepts of *family generativity* and an approach to intergenerational clinical work with families called *generative counseling*. Finally, the fatherwork perspective is currently being used to design fathering workshops for corporate fathers, new fathers, fathers of children with special needs, and incarcerated fathers (see http://fatherwork.com).

Religion and Responsible Fathering

Scholars, including us, have recently begun to conceptualize and measure the concept of *responsible fathering* (Doherty et al., 1998; Dollahite, in press; Dollahite et al., 1997; Marks & Dollahite, 2001). This "value-based" approach (Marsiglio, Amato, Day, & Lamb, 2000) to the scholarship of fathering focuses on the personal, relational, and cultural factors that facilitate responsible father involvement. Research has shown that the quantity and quality of responsible father involvement more so than mother involvement is strongly influenced by institutional practices, employment opportunities, cultural expectations, and social support (Dienhart & Daly, 1997; Doherty et al., 1998; Gerson, 1997).

From a generative perspective, responsible fathering has been defined as *active, responsive involvement with one's child, working to meet her/his varied needs* (Dollahite, in press; Marks & Dollahite, 2001). This definition emphasizes a father's moral obligation to work to meet the needs of his child

a. by actively responding to the "call" for care and connection exerted by his child
b. by responding to own his deepest feelings for and commitments to that child.

This definition centers on a father's *responsiveness* to the needs of his child and *responsiveness* to his own deeply held beliefs, rather than on his enacting a role obligation imposed by external cultural or societal ideologies.

Although the potential for religious belief and practice to foster responsible fathering is beginning to receive some attention (Dollahite, 1998; Dollahite et al., 1998; Latshaw, 1998; Palkovitz & Palm, 1998; Marks & Dollahite, 2001), religion is seldom mentioned as a possible influence in responsible father involvement (Dollahite, 1998; Marciano, 1991). However, empirical evidence scattered throughout the literature supports the idea that religion is positively related to better health (Koenig, McCullough, & Larson, 2001) and mental health (Judd, 1999; Koenig, 1998) as well as to familial factors such as stronger marital and family relationships (Dollahite, 2000; Mahoney et al., 1999), egalitarian parenting (Mahoney, Pargament, Tarakeshwar, & Swank, in press), and responsible fathering (Dollahite, 1998; Dollahite et al., 1998; Marks & Dollahite, 2001).

Family and religion are linked in complex and important ways (Houseknecht & Pankhurst, 2000) and matters of marriage and parenting are central to virtually all the world's faiths (Madsen, Lawrence, & Christiansen, 2000). Religious belief may bring adherents a sense of meaning and stability that promotes responsible family involvement. Practices such as participation in prayer, sacred rituals, pilgrimage, scriptural study, and the retelling of sacred stories may give transcendent meaning to everyday family life and relationships (Browing et al., 1997; Dollahite, 1998). Religious communities may provide motivation and resources to encourage responsible fathering (Ellison & George, 1994). For example, Snarey (1993) found that father-child church attendance provided significant "social-emotional child-rearing support" for fathers (p. 315). And Nock (1998) found that religious communities strengthen the father child bond by encouraging men to be committed to their families and encouraging them to be responsible to their children.

Marks and Dollahite's (2001) research with LDS fathers found that their religious beliefs and practices served as the center of meaning for their family relationships. They found that it was the *personal* and *relational* dimensions of religion that seemed to serve as the fathers' center of meaning. Fathers' religious beliefs were meaningful, in large measure, because they encouraged the fathers to frame their family relationships in personally meaningful ways.

Additionally, in connection with the dimension of religious practices, Marks and Dollahite (2001) found that certain *sacred, binding practices* (e.g., prayer, father's blessings) served to profoundly connect a father to his child through encouraging him to reflect on

a. his relationship to God,
b. his relationships to his child and wife,
c. the sacred and timeless nature of these relationships.

These findings are consistent with Wright et al.'s (1996) theoretical work on the organizing power of beliefs, with research on the importance of religious beliefs for fathers specifically (Latshaw, 1998; Palkovitz & Palm, 1998), and with research on the salience of religious beliefs for LDS families of children with special needs (Dollahite et al., 1998). They also are consistent with the generative fathering perspective on responsiveness to personal values and the needs of one's child.

Of course, we are not suggesting that non-religious men cannot be responsible, involved fathers, only that fathers with strong religious commitment may have additional resources to assist them. When discussing the narratives below, we will refer briefly to this research on faithful fathering as part of the conceptual context within which to think about clinical implications for working with strongly religious fathers in family therapy.

GENERATIVE NARRATIVE THERAPY

Generative Narrative Therapy (GNT) is based on concepts from Dollahite, Slife et al. (1998), Dollahite et al. (1997), Dienhart and

Dollahite (1997), Dollahite (1991), and Olson's (1999) adaptation of these ideas.

Dienhart and Dollahite (1997) used concepts from White and Epston's (1990) narrative therapy and the concepts of generative fathering to formulate what they called generative narrative therapy. Their model focused on using narrative clinical methods to assist men in their fatherwork. In a master's thesis, Olson (1999) integrated ideas from GNT and concepts from the Resource Management Model of change (Dollahite, 1991) along with findings from his research.

This model suggested the following:

1. Potentially challenging circumstances elicit or "call forth" some type of response by the father.
2. Fathers make meaning of their condition or situation by comparing their available resources with the demands facing them.
3. Fathers actively construct narratives and interpretations of their work as a father.
4. Fathers' decisions about their fathering are influenced by how they see themselves and their situation.
5. Fathers' ability to be generative is related to their ability to make meaning through storying their experience in generative ways.
6. Fathers choosing to be generatively involved in meeting their children's needs will likely experience the positive effects of that work.
7. The clinical process should involve a father's construction and reconstruction of meaning, adapting and readapting of behavior and thinking, and continually changing outcomes.

Dollahite, Slife et al. (1998) proposed six integrated "core concepts" of generative counseling (holism, temporality, agency, capability, spirituality, and morality). The generative counseling model suggests that

a. connection with a community of care helps the next generation (holism),
b. generative transformation is possible and clinical understanding is contextual (temporality),
c. human beings can choose to grow and change in generative ways (agency),
d. people and families can, with support, develop their inherent potential for care (capability),
e. spiritual reality exists and is relevant to caring for the next generation (spirituality),

f. there are ethics and morals that can guide parents in caring for their children (morality).

The generative counseling approach combines these core concepts into an integrated framework to guide clinical decision-making and action. The conceptual and clinical implications of the narratives to be presented below are all undergirded by these clinical concepts and we believe that interventions that are not consistent with these basic ideas will not be as likely to encourage responsible, involved fathering as interventions that are consistent with them.

LINKING STORY, THEORY, AND THERAPY: NARRATIVES AND FRAMEWORKS

This section presents several narratives along with interpretive commentary that will include "conceptual context" from the generative framework and the faithful fathering framework and clinical implications from the generative narrative framework (as well as from other clinical models). Given the nature of this special volume, most (but not all) of the narratives address spiritual or religious issues.

The narratives are drawn from interviews from two sets of fathers (described in detail in Dollahite, in press). The samples included 35 Latter-day Saint fathers of children with special needs. The modal father was in his early 30s, white, married, well educated, and had 3 children. Most were involved in a support program for families with children with special needs. The types of special needs in the children included a variety of moderate to severe physical and cognitive delays, serious chronic and terminal conditions and illnesses, autism, Tourette Syndrome, Down Syndrome, heart disease, severe scoliosis, deafness, and blindness.

These narratives, while not clinical in nature (i.e., not gathered from fathers that were or necessarily should be in therapy), describe struggles with meaning and poignant challenges. The narratives are used as a springboard to a discussion of theoretical and clinical concepts that have implication for therapy with fathers. However, rather than recommending specific clinical interventions, we suggest general clinical implications. Thus, we focus on the process of understanding the stories a father tells about his challenges and his faith rather than on case specific recommendations. We hope the narratives and corresponding clinical implications provide clinicians with helpful ideas for working with religious fathers. The narratives are presented first, followed by the interpretive commentary. Names have been changed.

Lucas

I think the best thing that the church has done for me and indirectly for Caleb [born at 5 ½ months gestation] is [that] it's allowed me to give him [priesthood] blessings . . . I was there by myself [by his] incubator, and he was really having a hard time. They had a couple of nurses around him and they had his respirator in. He had some kind of infection that was filling up his lungs with secretions and he was having a really hard time breathing. [The respirator] was as high as the machine would go and he was still, I could just see in his eyes . . . there was that deer in the headlight panic look in his eyes. It was really hard for me because what can you do? They had the oxygen turned all the way up . . . [it was] a humbling thing for me, and anything I could do to help him I'll do . . . I gave him a blessing. [It made] me want to be a better person so that if there is something that I can do for him, even if it is just giving a blessing, I can be worthy to do that. In that way it [the church] makes me a better person.

Conceptual Context. Lucas' narrative illustrates a father's desire to meet his child's needs ("anything I could do to help him I'll do"). The desire and effort of a father to answer moral "calls" from his child are central to generative fathering, along with the assumption that most fathers want to meet the needs of their children. Lucas' decision to give his son a priesthood blessing (a special prayer accompanied by the laying on of hands) is significant in this narrative not only because it allowed the father to try to meet a need his child had, but also because of the effect it had on Lucas as a father. Notice how Lucas emphasized that one effect that giving this "blessing" had on him as a father was that it made him "want to be a better person." The opportunity and ability to give blessings to family members in challenging times has also been documented as deeply meaningful for fathers in previous research (Dollahite et al.,1998), although meaning can be found in a variety of sacred, binding practices such as family prayer, scripture study, and singing hymns (Lee, Rice, & Gillespie, 1997; Marks & Dollahite, 2001).

Generative Narrative Therapy. The medical model and its ideology of materialism are not sensitive to the influence of spirituality on fathers and families (Dollahite, Slife et al., 1998). GNT acknowledges that spirituality is influential for many fathers and that spirituality can be both a temporal and transcendental resource for fathers and their families. In Lucas' narrative, medicine was doing all it could for his child but Caleb was still failing. Lucas' spiritual beliefs and practices were deeply meaningful to him at this time and helped him to cope with an extreme challenge and to discourage hopelessness.

Lucas related how the church, or priesthood blessings specifically, became a resource that helped him behave in a generative way toward his child. Meth (1990), in a discussion of what he terms the "power-paradox," outlines how men are often constrained by the tools they have been socialized to use as a means of expressing themselves to others. Religious practices, such as priesthood blessings, can provide additional "tools" or resources for fathers to care for and connect with their children. In application, a goal of therapy might not only be to challenge a father's constraining or problem-saturated beliefs (Wright et al., 1996; White & Epston, 1990) that may discourage generative fathering; but to also investigate and language current or alternative beliefs and practices that may provide a resource in the construction of a more facilitative or solution-focused narrative. Lucas' statement " . . . it made me want to be a better person" shows how generative actions toward others can reinforce and strengthen the generative narrative.

Ethan

The (doctrines) of persuasion, longsuffering, gentleness, all those kind of characteristics are not just Sunday practices. I have an interesting relationship with my children in that I invite them to help correct me when I demonstrate that I'm not being patient or longsuffering or kind or those kind of things. My oldest daughter is really quite good at it and (Bryce) is becoming good at it. They'll be very candid with me, saying, "Dad, I feel uncomfortable with the way you're handling this." So the doctrine, the theology, to me, defines fatherhood and it's just me learning how to apply those principles . . . My children can help me do that.

Conceptual Context. A central feature of generative fathering is the concept that good fathering is not defined by successfully filling an externally prescribed social "role" but by meeting the specific changing needs of one's own children (Dollahite et al., 1997). The ability to meet the needs of one's children requires an awareness of those needs, including physical, emotional, spiritual, and relational needs. Ethan's humility and willingness to listen to his children's needs, even when those needs include a constructive change in his own behavior, illustrate sensitive, child-focused fathering.

The faith and fathering connection is a troubling one for some, with one root of protest drawing heavily on the Freudian notion of the stereotypical oppressive, religious father. Contrary to this stereotype, research indicates that religious fathers may be more warm and less punitive than non-religious fathers (Bartowski & Xu, 2000) and that religion may promote responsible, generative fathering in a number of ways (Marks & Dollahite, 2001). Additionally, it has been found that shared religious meaning can offer a core ideology that helps fathers with their children (Latshaw, 1998). In Ethan's narrative, we see the potential benefits of the families' religion for everyone when a father avoids hypocrisy, while trying to do his best. A shared meaning of the importance of honesty and willingness to change, based on religious beliefs, allows this resource to be part of his family experience.

Generative Narrative Therapy. Ethan's narrative exemplifies GNT's concept of *holism*, the idea that family life "resides in the relationships between generations, rather than only within individuals" (Dollahite et al., 1998, p. 456). GNT's concept of *morality* is illustrated as the younger generation promotes responsible, generative fathering by telling their father what they need from him relationally, while the father encourages such openness and feedback by trying to adapt, adjust, and improve as a father as opposed to being stagnant, inflexible, and nongenerative.

Ethan's commentary on how the doctrines of his faith and his relationship with his children intertwine with his definition of fatherhood exemplifies of the interplay between multiple systems and subsequent meaning construction. Ethan's family and faith have become important resources for him. They have helped him to examine his behavior and its congruence with the meanings or stories that Ethan tells about himself as a father.

Wright et al. (1996) state that all families have often unrealized strengths and conclude that "as clinicians abandon the lens that pathologizes families, they adopt a view of families as resourceful. All families possess the strengths and abilities necessary to solve their own problems" (p. 50). Therapists can help families see their own strengths and resourcefulness, especially as those strengths contribute to a collective family narrative or story that emphasizes a father's capabilities in meeting the needs of the next generation. Families often come to therapy after their efforts for solving problems have been exhausted or they are feeling stuck. White and Epston (1990) propose that therapy helps people locate, generate, or resurrect alternative stories that offer a different sense of self and a different relationship with problems. Ethan clearly sees his family and his faith as resources in helping him to be a generative father.

Tom

I have just about spent my life caring for and nurturing Megan [young daughter who died of leukemia], when I wasn't at work. Maybe the hospital is the part we like to forget but can't. When her pain got to the point that she couldn't go to the bathroom, I was the one that got to do her bedpans for her. She would only let me do it; I was the one that did that. It wasn't a thing for Mom, and she didn't want anybody else in the room. She kicked everybody out of the room; nurses, Mom (Mom had to be outside the door)–and I would get the bedpan as best as I could under her bottom without hurting her. Moving the sheets hurt her. It was not a good thing. But she let me do that for her, and I was able to take care of her needs, and it helped me that I was the only one she'd let do it . . . You wouldn't expect bedpan shuffling to be a wonderful memory, but it was. She trusted me to do my best job not to hurt her, and that was special to me that she let me do that.

Conceptual Context. A critical element of generative fathering is "choosing to care" (Dollahite et al., 1997). The difficulties, pain, and challenges associated with having a child with special needs discourage some fathers and have led to father abandonment rates that are above the national average (Fewell & Vadasy, 1986; Olson, 1999). However, although Tom's daughter, Megan, was dying of leukemia, he "chose to care" and be responsibly involved in spite of the obvious challenges. In his interview, Tom referred repeatedly to the support he and his family felt from certain members of their religious community. He also discussed experiences with priesthood blessings and other sacred practices that profoundly influenced and encouraged their family. However, and perhaps most importantly, he expressed the comfort he and his family drew from their belief that they would be reunited with Megan again and that the reunion would be especially sweet due to the fact that Megan would no longer be suffering from the horrible effects of advanced leukemia. This belief in an eternal family perspective has emerged as significant and central in at least three different studies on LDS families with special needs children (Dollahite et al., 1998; Marks & Dollahite, 2001; Marshall et al., 1998).

Generative Narrative Therapy. A concept of GNT is *capability*, or the importance of focusing on strengths or what *can* be done instead of what cannot. While Tom could not heal Megan or make the pain go away, he *could* be there for her. In this case, "being there" included doing a job ("shuffling bedpans") that would be distasteful to many. However, notice how Tom describes this experience as "wonderful" and how he adds that it "was special to me that she let me do that." Tom's efforts and his choice to "frame" his story of Megan's struggle for life in this way are examples of *making generative choices* (Dollahite, Slife et al., 1998) and constructing a *generative narrative* (Olson, Dollahite, & White, 2001).

Michael

Michael's son Alan was born with shortened forearms, no fingers, and with extreme scoliosis that has required multiple surgeries. He expresses how "extraordinary" Alan is:

> [Thinking about Alan] I thought, "Well, what is the purpose of life?" And you know, to say it in a succinct way, life is not a beauty contest. Christ never said, "Blessed are the physically most beautiful, for they shall inherit the kingdom of God." You know, if you read the beatitudes, they're pretty non-physical, instead they have everything to do with the quality of our heart and our spirit. And Alan is an exceptionally extraordinary individual. Alan has this natural ability to elicit love from people. He elicits Godly, goodwill from people. In a real natural way. We've flown all over the country talking to physicians and everywhere he goes, people like him. They act in Godly, kindly, unselfish, genuine ways around him. He brings this out of people. And when you look on a hierarchal scale, or if you could imagine what talents would be nice to have, from an eternal perspective . . . if you could shoot three pointers endlessly from half-court or you could bring Godliness out of other people . . . what do you think matters most? It's an easy question. Godliness, obviously, is more important. And Alan has an innate gift about that, and a real sensitivity about spiritual things . . . One time Alan and I were alone in the kitchen and he just looked up at me and said, "You know Dad, if I were born again, I would like to have hands like Kathleen, and like Benjamin." . . . And I didn't say anything for just a moment, just a short pause, and then he said, "But this is just the challenge that Heavenly Father has given me for this life." And he paused again, and he goes, "So it's okay." But it wasn't a mournful okay, it was kind of a "this is alright" almost like a little bit of a spunk, and possibly even enthusiasm in the tone, "This is alright, this is just my challenge."

Michael later explained:

> Thanks to my religion, thanks to my faith, I see fatherhood as an eternal position and relationship. I see my family relationships as eternal. And, so fatherhood is really, perhaps the greatest thing that I could attain to. If I'm president of the United States, if I'm a C.E.O. of a major corporation, or if I receive recognition in any particular endeavor, no matter what it may be, that will end. The time would come and I would be voted out of office, or I would resign or retire, or I would lose my faculty position or whatever it may be, and yet I will always be the father of my children. There's a natural intimacy there . . . a connection to your children. I think this eternal perspective makes it supremely important.

Conceptual Context. Generative fathering includes trying to meet the needs of one's child in creative ways (what Brotherson & Dollahite, 1997, called *generative ingenuity*). Such efforts often extend beyond "typical" fathering; unusual challenges may require unusual effort to overcome them. Michael interviewed several families with children who were similar to his son in order to gain information regarding the best approaches to take medically, educationally, socially, and familially. He also traveled extensively, both with and without Alan, to speak with specialists, and stayed on the cutting edge of relevant medical research by reading medical conference reports online. Through his efforts to meet Alan's needs, Michael became an able advocate for Alan in addition to being a supportive father.

Michael, like Tom earlier, and consistent with other studies of LDS fathers and families (Dollahite et al., 1998; Marshall et al., 1998; Marks & Dollahite, 2001) refers to a belief in "an eternal perspective" that helped him to see Alan in a different and more positive light. This belief also appears to influence the way Michael "frames" his generative narrative. Additionally, and perhaps just as importantly, this "eternal perspective" appears to influence the way Alan assesses and copes with his "challenge"; a challenge that only exists "for this life."

Generative Narrative Therapy. Michael's detailed description of Alan tells us a great deal about the father as well as the son. Michael's emphasis on the "non-physical" abilities of his son instead of his physical limitations provides an illustration of at least two of the GNT's concepts. First, Michael articulates (Alan's) strengths instead of weaknesses, consistent with the GNT's emphasis on capability (Dollahite, Slife et al., 1998). Second, while Alan had staggering physical challenges, Michael's delighted focus on the "quality of [Alan's] heart and spirit" are indicative of positive benefits associated with a sensitivity to spirituality, as proposed by GNT (Dollahite, Slife et al., 1998).

GNT proposes a process of fathers' repeated construction and reconstruction of meaning, adapting and readapting of behavior and thinking, and continually changing outcomes. Michael's experience and narrative description provide some insight into the dynamic nature of this process over time. Michael has constructed meaning around Alan's disability; so has Alan, largely influenced by his father's beliefs and practices over the course of his young life. A father's generative narrative can have a profound ripple effect on the family, especially the child with the special need. So much so, that the child actually internalizes the narrative to the extent it provides a sense of meaning and coherence to him/her.

Along these lines, Michael expressed the following when asked about his initial reaction upon finding out about Alan's disabilities:

> When Alan was born we were videotaping the birth in a discreet way. As soon as he started to come out the doctor said, "Ooh, " he paused and fumbled a bit and said, "Well, there's something going on with his hands, we have something here." I think Kristy was a little nervous, I was. When the doctor brought him up we could see that he had shortened forearms and was missing some fingers. They wrapped him and set him on Kristy's tummy. I was concerned about how Alan might interpret that someday. It was very important that he know how much he is loved. I don't remember exactly what I said but I made sure that we kept video taping, expressing our love and acceptance of this neat little soul.

While some fathers describe the process of creating meaning in response to having a child with special needs to take an extended period of time, this particular narrative illustrates how immediate the process of constructing meaning around a stressor or challenge can be. Michael had the tools for a "generative narrative" in place; a sort of "capabilities" oriented frame. The resources for constructing generative meaning seemed immediate in this case as evidenced by the unhesitating expression of love and acceptance for this special child. This narrative also reveals how the narrative process "feeds-back" or reciprocates as each new challenge can potentially elicit further generative meaning construction and responses. From a narrative oriented approach, one of the things that becomes especially important in therapy is the identification of the various voices (i.e., people, traditions, beliefs, cultures) that have led to either a "problem saturated" (White & Epston, 1990) or a more strength or solution saturated account of their lives.

Based on both the Marks and Dollahite (2001) and the Olson et al. (2001) studies of fathers of children with special needs, religious beliefs and practices can emerge as powerful and shaping "voices" in helping fathers to construct generative meaning in response to the challenge of having a child with special needs. These ideas have been applied elsewhere by Dienhart and Dollahite (1997), who have integrated concepts from generative fathering and narrative therapy to suggest that through the identification or creation of generative accounts, fathers may create new meanings, bringing desirable possibilities that are more helpful, satisfying, and open ended in their attempts to generatively father a special needs child. These authors also suggest that listening to fathers' stories provides an opportunity to draw out their contributions to the children's lives and point out their resourcefulness in meeting the challenges of parenting.

Kenny

In the process of dying my father was ill and would frequently call us over to be with him. I can't think of a specific moment, but it was just those times that he called us over to talk about religious things with us. He always called for a blessing. That was basically our relationship, either arguing over a gospel topic or discussing it, one way or the other . . . He always wanted [his] immediate children to finish music lessons and none of us took more than a year or two. But his grand kids have excelled in music and so as he was dying, within a month of his death, they took a flute and violin over there and two of [my] girls played for him. That was somehow a connection between him and me and them, and so it was . . . an emotional time because I knew that it meant something deep to him. For me it was reconciliation, because we didn't have an open relationship as an adolescent and a parent. I was able to kiss him and hug him while he was dying. Everything just melted away and there were no more bad feelings . . .

Conceptual Context. An important feature of generative fathering ethic is that the father child relationship requires sustained work across the life span (Dollahite et al., 1997). Additionally, throughout the life span, connection is essential. Kenny's relationship with his father was not always a close one but they were able to find a "reconciliation" that finally allowed Kenny to feel what he described as "a connection between him and me." Kenny's narrative is one of *hope* (a core of Eriksonian generativity) in that it shows that new (or renewed) healing and connection are possible, even in late adulthood, thus providing hope to both fathers and children who did not establish a relational connection earlier in life.

In Kenny's narrative, he indicated that religion served as the impetus for both discussions and arguments. However, at the time of crisis, father and son shared a common bond of faith through priesthood blessings the son was able to give to the father. As addressed in previous research and mentioned in connection with Lucas' narrative in this paper, the opportunity to give these sacred blessings tends to strengthen the sense of relationship not only between the giver and receiver, but between the giver and his God, whom Latter-day Saints consider their literal "Father in Heaven" (Dollahite et al., 1998; Marks & Dollahite, 2001). The fact that Kenny's reconciliation with his father occurred so late in life was unfortunate but Kenny's eternal perspective (as discussed in connection with previous narratives) provides a hope that family relationships will endure beyond the grave, offering them a chance to continue the connection they established in life.

Generative Narrative Therapy. Kenny's narrative closely relates to several concepts within the GNT framework, including *holism* and *temporality*. As previously discussed in connection with Ethan's narrative, the GNT's concept of holism includes the idea that family generativity exists in the relationships between generations. Kenny's narrative portrays three generations generatively "caring" for each other:

1. Kenny's dying father reaches out to his son by asking for priesthood blessings from him.
2. Although this brief segment fails to fully capture the depth of Kenny's sensitivity to his father's needs, we also see his generative, other-focused orientation through his efforts to meet his father's present needs and in his efforts to meet a desire his father had to see his children share his love for music and develop skill in that area. While Kenny did not personally fill his father's desire, he creatively met this perceived need by asking his daughters to play for their grandfather.
3. Finally, the youngest generation (Kenny's daughters) are involved in the "generating" (not just reception) of care for two previous generations.

GNT's concept of temporality includes a sensitivity to the possibility, in fact the likelihood, of change across time. The ability of Kenny and his father to move beyond the arguments and closed relationship of the past, and their refusal to give up on each other in the present, finally provided a moment when time, context, sensitivity, and support from a younger generation all came together in a culminating moment of "reconciliation" and "connection."

Ethan

Bryce [son with severe heart problems] jerks me back to reality, to what's really important. Early on [in my career] I got involved in a big research study with IBM. I was working with their Chief Information Officer, one of the most senior I.T. people in the world and it was one of the most exciting research projects, because it was right in my research domain. So I was this thirty-year-old kid leading this team of 500 people at IBM in this huge project, actually it was several hundred million dollars IBM was investing in this thing. We had the executive sponsor come out and meet with a couple of the professors who were involved with me in this thing. We spent the day going through the project and it was kind of a critical moment because [the sponsor] had to determine whether we were going to continue the project or not. At the end of the day he said, "This is great. You're making good progress. This goes on." We were planning on going to dinner that evening. For some reason I thought I'd drop by my office and I noticed the voice mail light was flashing, so I just checked my voice mail. The first message was from my wife; she said, "Bryce has run away from home." My heart just sank. He was on this medication that he *had* to have two times a day. He couldn't go out roughing it for a few days. So all of the sudden, that was all that was important. I told all of them, "Sorry, I can't go to dinner." I just rushed home and my wife showed me this little note he had left on his bed: "I'm gonna go visit Grandma and Grandpa in California." So here's this, I think he was eight years old with a pacemaker, he'd taken his bike, he'd taken $20 from my wife's wallet and he's headed to California. So I just started thinking, OK, how [would] I start toward California if I was Bryce? So I just started driving around the area kind of making circles and for some reason I just happened to turn into [a store] and there was Bryce's bike sitting out front. So I parked the car, I ran, I literally ran, up and down those aisles until I found him. And he had a bottle of Sprite and a bag of Doritos, he was headed for California and stocked up on food. [When] he saw me you could see this moment of panic in his face and I just knelt down and hugged him and we [went] out to the car and drove around for a little bit. I was just trying to think

[of] what to say. I'd never dealt with something like this. Physical, medical problems (I found) were a lot easier all of a sudden. We ended up parking over by [the park]. I just sat there thinking and I said, "Bryce, what's going on?" And he said, "Dad, I don't know you. You're never home." You know, at that moment, I was a bishop [pastor of a Latter-day Saint congregation]. I had a wonderful wife. I had wonderful children, I was getting research awards, I mean by every measure I was on top of the world: And in one instant he put it all into focus.

Conceptual Context. In the conceptual ethic of generative fathering, successful fathering is not defined by meeting external role prescriptions but by meeting the specific, individual needs of one's child (Dollahite et al., 1997). In Ethan's narrative, he emphasizes that by "every measure I was on top of the world." He was doing outstanding work as a professional and even as a lay clergyman for his church; however, he had forgotten what was "really important." Eight-year old Bryce issued a jolting reminder.

Although Ethan described his religious faith as beneficial in his interview, it is interesting to note that his positive involvement with his church did not displace the necessity of personal involvement with his child. In spite of the potential benefits religion has to offer fathers and families, some fathers have reported the challenge of balancing involvement in a religious community with being an involved father (Marks & Dollahite, 2001).

Generative Narrative Therapy. GNT's concept of *holism* is framed in Ethan's narrative. While Ethan had achieved a high level of success as an individual with his career, this success did not fulfill his son's need for a personal relationship with his father. A generative connection between generations can be vital not only for optimal child development but also because of the enrichment these connections give back to the father.

Steven

When I first got this diagnosis of Autism, the hope, the high expectations, the assumed success that your child is going to have in life, just sort of all drained out of me. I mean the blood probably left my head, I probably turned white as a ghost or something when the realization hit me that here's this diagnosis–AUTISM. And it just sort of hits you like someone just swung a bat at you and knocked the wind right out of you. And so the first thing I would say [to a father in a similar situation] is this is not a death sentence. There is hope here. And it is not just false hope and "stay positive" for your child. Our child has made enormous gains by getting some very specific treatment. There was a poem [that] talks about a person who wants to go on a vacation to Hawaii [and] the plane ends up going to Sweden. And their whole world was turned upside down because their expectations of where they were going to end up, what types of things they were going to experience and what joys they were going to experience in life, have all of a sudden been turned up side down, because they walk off the plane and they are in a totally different country where they don't speak the language, and they are stuck there. I mean they have to make do with what they have. You thought you were going to Hawaii but you end up in Sweden. So, take your vacation in Sweden. Find out what there is to love about that country. In terms of Autism, find your fulfillment in your autistic child, or your disabled child, the same way that you would with any of your other children, but understand that this is not Hawaii. It is another country and another language. So there is always hope. You don't know what you are going to run into. You don't know what great insights and blessings are going to come to you because you are devoting your life and your resources in a different direction than the one you anticipated. Your child may not go to college. They may never get married . . . but I am convinced that there is a plan for Melissa and we are a part of that plan and I don't want to thwart the purposes of God by denying her ability to achieve all that she can achieve, and being all that I can be. Quite frankly, as her father, I do whatever I can all the way around, making the best of the situation.

Conceptual Context. Generative fathering's central ethic, that a good father tries to meet his child's needs, can take on additional weight when one has a child with special needs. In Steven's case, his daughter's autism brought a number of unique needs to the forefront. Although Steven has traveled "in a different direction than the one [he] anticipated" with his two children with special needs, he has actively sought to meet these needs through self-education and by first participating in, and then taking leadership roles in the state's society for autism. He credited much of his involvement to his wife's encouragement and positive example.

Steven's desire to fulfill "the purposes of God" by helping Melissa "achieve all that she can achieve" is an example of a facilitative, motivational religious belief. The importance of beliefs (religious or otherwise) has served as the foundation for theoretical work in marriage and family therapy (e.g., Wright et al., 1996) and has recently been identified as an often overlooked but salient feature of religion for fathers (Marks & Dollahite, 2001).

In addition to the narratives the fathers shared in their interviews, some fathers discussed their wrestle with the deeper existential questions their child's condition invoked. The following two segments illustrate the challenges two fathers and their families faced in connection with the question of "Why did this happen to us?"

Generative Narrative Therapy. Steven's emphasis that "there is hope here" is an explicit effort to *discourage hopelessness*, a component of the GNT's concept of *spirituality*. While Steven is painfully aware that his daughter may not fulfill the hopes he would have had for a "normal"child, he has found meaning trying to help her "to achieve all that she can achieve." This effort to focus on strengths, potential, and "making the best of the situation" also serves as an additional illustration of the GNT's core concept of *capability*.

Jesse

There are always two sides and two views to everything. There is always a good and there is always a bad, and there is a happy and a sad. We could have been one of those that when this [our child born with disability] happened asked, "Why? It's not fair. Why did this happen to us?" The problem with that is there isn't an answer to the "Why?" You never know why it happens. As hard as it might be to look at the positive, at least then there is something finite to the situation that you're in. There is something firm and something that you can grasp a hold of, something that can end your thought process at that time. I think that is important. I think that is why positive people have such an advantage over other people, because then they can take the next step. If you look at it the other way [and ask "Why?" instead of "What now?"] you can't take the next step because you are still trying to get the answer to the first question.

Tom

We did our best to make sure that we got through it [Megan's leukemia] well. We weren't going to say, "Why me?" and that is something I spent very little time on. I still wondered from time to time why she had to go through this, but I didn't spend any time being mad at God. I decided early on that we were going to tackle this with faith and determination, and we were going to make it. We were going to come out being in love with God and not hating Him.

Conceptual Context. Confusion and change are challenges that are inherent in life. A critical feature of generative fathering is that fathers need to "adapt to varying situations [and] maintain supportive conditions" in the face of these challenges (Dollahite et al., 1997, p. 24). Jesse's description of how "positive" people move on and "take the next step" is a prime example of trying to adapt and progress, even in the most challenging of contexts.

Tom's discussion of the "Why me?" question indicates that not even his religious beliefs could offer a comforting satisfactory answer to his question of why his daughter had to suffer with, and eventually die from, leukemia. However, his conviction (and a combination of "faith and determination") helped to transform the harrowing experience of losing Megan into one that, as he later explained, brought insight, meaning, and the attitude of "being in love with God" he described (see Dollahite, Marks et al., 1998).

Generative Narrative Therapy. Jesse and Tom discuss moving past the "Why me?" dilemma as a "next step," a choice, a decision. Both fathers juxtapose their generative decisions to take the next step with the alternative choice. Jesse explains that if he hadn't stopped asking "Why?" then he would not have been able "to look at the positive" and "take the next step." Tom concluded that his family had the option to hate God or love God, and "decided to tackle [their challenge] with faith" so that they would "come out being in love with God and not hating him." Jesse's and Tom's explanations offer models of making generative choices, a component of the GNT's concept of *agency*.

Devan

Interviewer: Can you tell me about a time when you felt especially close to Adrienne? Devan: That would be when I blessed her as a baby. That's one of the times that I felt extremely close to Adrienne . . . I learned that I would die for this person. I learned that from this moment on we will be linked forever. This child is my responsibility forever, to guide, to direct, and to nurture.

Monty

(whose two-year-old son has experienced severe stomach problems and moderate developmental delays since birth)

> When my little boy was blessed in church [given a name and a blessing], it was really neat . . . just being in that circle, holding him, being near him, it was great. After he was blessed I took and just held him . . . The spirit in that circle, just after, was very strong. It was marvelous; it was great. It was wonderful. It was indescribable.

Literature on fathers of children with special needs has emphasized the importance of establishing an early paternal bond (e.g., Fewell & Vadasy, 1986). However, recommendations regarding how to facilitate this connection are limited. Dollahite et al. (1998) found that, for an LDS father, the sacred practice of giving his infant child a "name and a blessing" often strengthens the father-child bond and carries significant meaning. Several fathers recalled this experience with their child with special needs and the effect it had on them as fathers.

Conceptual Context. An emphasis of generative fathering, in connection with *relationship work* (one of the seven areas in the framework), is the importance of facilitating attachments between fathers and their children. The above narratives indicate a connection that is often felt and strengthened when an LDS father gives his child a name and a blessing.

The expressions of the above fathers regarding the personal and relational significance of giving their child a name and a blessing is consistent with Marks and Dollahite's (2001) finding that *sacred binding practices* can be influential both in terms of the *responsibility* a father feels toward his child (e.g., "This child is my responsibility forever, to guide, to direct, and to nurture") and his sense of *relationship* with his child (e.g., "That's one of the times that I felt extremely close to Adrienne . . . I learned that I would die for [her]").

Generative Narrative Therapy. The practice of a father giving his child a name and a blessing can be helpful in promoting responsibility and in helping him to keep generative commitments (components of the GNT's concept of *morality*). This practice is also related to GNT emphasis on *fostering relationships* between fathers and their children, and encouraging fathers to sustain these connections with their children (Dollahite, Slife et al., 1998).

CONCLUSION

In summary, Generative Narrative Therapy conceptualizes generative fathering as an unfolding process of meaning-making (i.e., the construction of beliefs, truths, and story) in the context of family and larger systems. This process is clearly amenable to clinical intervention with distinct clinical implications. Therapists, aware of the dynamic nature in which meaning is created and unfolds, can facilitate the process by intervening in ways that will lead fathers to story from a capabilities perspective and to connect with and care for their children and families often under extreme challenges and conditions.

The final section discusses how religious communities can support generative fathering and the goals of Generative Narrative Therapy and how and why counselors can and should be open to supporting religious involvement with their clients.

Religious Communities Can Promote Generative Fathering and Generative Therapy

The article illustrates "father strengths" and the power that religious belief has in assisting fathers in challenging circumstances. Religion may be of value in connection with efforts to support and encourage responsible fathering for at least three reasons. First, religious communities can have tremendous reach since, as Horn (2001) argued, there is no secular organizational network that has the degree of contact with as many men as do churches and synagogues. Second, while most interventions and programs have rigid time constraints, religious communities often have ongoing contact with men for extended periods of time, sometimes throughout a lifetime. Third, religious approaches can be highly motivational since they emphasize sacred and spiritual beliefs about being a father and husband that resonate more with many fathers than the motivation available from secular intervention efforts.

Dollahite et al. (1998) argue that religious communities can be sources of support for generative counseling approaches since religious communities encourage and support people in generative commitments and actions. This is because religious communities help bind members together through a "coherent and meaningful set of beliefs, practices, and supportive connections to others that give purpose and aid to a family's efforts to care for the next generation" (p. 477).

Dollahite, Slife et al. (1998) proposed that generative counselors can encourage their clients to benefit from and contribute to generative faith communities by:

a. helping clients to make holistic generative *connections* through meaningful and joyful participation in a religious community,

b. helping clients to initiate generative *changes* by drawing upon religious beliefs and images that involve the possibility of transformation,
c. helping clients to maintain generative spiritual *convictions* through reference to religious beliefs and stories that focus on transcendent realities,
d. helping clients to develop generative *capabilities* by drawing upon religious stories that illustrate people in difficult circumstances discovering strengths,
e. helping clients to keep generative *commitments* by encouraging adherence to religious covenants that emphasize faith with God and one's community through sacrifice and service,
f. helping clients to exercise their agency to make generative *choices* by referring to religious beliefs that emphasize choosing goodness in times of struggle and trial (pp. 447-448).

There is much room for growth in the clinical community in the ways we work with religious individuals, families, and communities, and growth in this direction is crucial. Clinicians can and should draw upon communities of faith, to assist the fathers and families they work with better meet the needs of the next generation. Then, clinicians working with fathers would be helping fathers draw upon all resources at their disposal, including religious resources, to help them in their fatherwork.

REFERENCES

Bartowski, J. P. & Xu, X. (2000). Distant patriarchs or expressive dads? The discourse and practice of fathering in Conservative Protestant families. *The Sociological Quarterly*, *41*, 465-485.

Bellah, R. N., Madsen, R., Sullivan, W. M., Swindler, A., & Tipton, S. M. (1985). *Habits of the heart: Individualism and commitment in American life*. Berkeley: University of California Press.

Brotherson, S. E. (1995). *Using fathers' narrative accounts to refine a conceptual model of generative fathering*. Unpublished masters thesis, Brigham Young University, Provo, Utah.

Brotherson, S. E. & Dollahite, D. C. (1997). Generative ingenuity in fatherwork with young children with special needs. In A. J. Hawkins & D. C. Dollahite (Eds.), *Generative fathering: Beyond deficit perspectives* (pp. 89-104). Thousand Oaks, CA: Sage.

Browning, D. S., Miller-McLemore, B. J., Couture, P. D., Brynolf Lyon, K., & Franklin, R. M. (1997). *From culture wars to common ground: Religion and the American family debate*. Louisville, KY: Westminster John Knox Press.

Christiansen, S. L., & Palkovitz, R. (1998). Exploring Erikson's psychosocial theory of development: Generativity and its relationship to paternal identity, intimacy, and involvement in child care. *The Journal of Men's Studies*, *7*, 133-156.

Dienhart, A., & Daly, K. (1997). Men and women cocreating father involvement in a nongenerative culture. In A. J. Hawkins & D. C. Dollahite (Eds.), *Generative fathering: Beyond deficit perspectives* (pp. 147-164). Thousand Oaks, CA: Sage.

Dienhart, A., & Dollahite, D. C. (1997). A generative narrative approach to clinical work with fathers. In A. J. Hawkins & D. C. Dollahite (Eds.), *Generative fathering: Beyond deficit perspectives* (pp. 183-199). Thousand Oaks, CA: Sage.

Doherty, W. J. (1991). Beyond reactivity and the deficit model of manhood: A commentary on articles by Napier, Pittman, and Gottman. *Journal of Marital and Family Therapy*, *17*, 29-32.

Doherty, W. J., Kouneski, E. F., & Erickson, M. F. (1998). Responsible fathering: An overview and conceptual framework. *Journal of Marriage and the Family*, *60*, 277-292.

Dollahite, D. C. (in press). A narrative approach to exploring responsible father involvement of fathers with their special needs children. In R. D. Day & M. E. Lamb (Eds.), *Measuring father involvement*. Mahwah, NJ: Lawrence Erlbaum.

Dollahite, D. C. (Ed.). (2000). *Strengthening our families: An in-depth look at the proclamation on the family*. Salt Lake City: Bookcraft.

Dollahite, D. C. (1991). Family resource management and family stress theories: Toward a conceptual integration. *Journal of Family and Economic Issues*, *12*, 361-377.

Dollahite, D. C. (1998). Fathering, faith, and spirituality. *The Journal of Men's Studies*, *7*, 3-16.

Dollahite, D. C., & Hawkins, A. J. (1998). A conceptual ethic of generative fathering. *The Journal of Men's Studies*, *7*, 109-132.

Dollahite, D. C., Hawkins, A. J., & Associates (1997). *Fatherwork: Stories, ideas, and activities to encourage generative fathering*. [Online]. Available: http://fatherwork.byu.edu.

Dollahite, D. C., Hawkins, A. J., & Brotherson, S. E. (1997). A conceptual ethic of fathering as generative work. In A. J. Hawkins & D. C. Dollahite (Eds.), *Generative fathering: Beyond deficit perspectives* (pp. 17-35). Thousand Oaks, CA: Sage.

Dollahite, D. C., Hawkins, A. J., & Brotherson, S. E. (1996). Narrative accounts, generative fathering, and family life education. *Marriage & Family Review*, *24*, 333-352.

Dollahite, D. C., Marks, L. D., & Olson, M. M. (1998). Faithful fathering in trying times: Religious beliefs and practices of Latter-day Saint fathers of children with special needs. *The Journal of Men's Studies*, 7, 71-94.

Dollahite, D. C., Morris, S. N., & Hawkins, A. J. (1997). Questions and activities for teaching about generative fathering in university courses. In A. J. Hawkins & D. C. Dollahite (Eds.), *Generative fathering: Beyond deficit perspectives* (pp. 228-240). Thousand Oaks, CA: Sage.

Dollahite, D. C., Slife, B. D., & Hawkins, A. J. (1998). Family generativity and generative counseling: Helping families keep faith with the next generation. In D. P. McAdams & E. de St. Aubin (Eds.), *Generativity and adult development: How and why we care for the next generation* (pp. 449-481). Washington, DC: American Psychological Association.

Ellison, C. G. & George, L. K. (1994). Religious involvement, social ties, and social support in a southeastern community. *Journal for the Scientific Study of Religion, 33*, 46-61.

Erikson, E. H. (1950). *Childhood and society*. New York: Norton.

Erikson, E. H. (1982). *The life cycle completed*. New York: Norton.

Fagan, J., & Hawkins, A. J. (Eds.). (2001). *Clinical and educational interventions with fathers*. New York: The Haworth Press, Inc.

Fewell, R., & Vadasy, P. (1986). *Families of handicapped children*. Austin: Pro-Ed.

Gerson, K. (1997). An institutional perspective on generative fathering: Creating social supports for parenting equality. In A. J. Hawkins & D. C. Dollahite (Eds.), *Generative fathering: Beyond deficit perspectives* (pp. 36-51). Thousand Oaks, CA: Sage.

Grant, T. R., Hawkins, A. J., & Dollahite, D. C. (2001). Web-based education and support for fathers: Remote but promising. In J. Fagan & A. J. Hawkins (Eds.), *Clinical and educational interventions with fathers* (pp. 143-167). New York: The Haworth Press, Inc.

Hawkins, A. J., & Dollahite, D. C. (1997). Beyond the role-inadequacy perspective of fathering. In A. J. Hawkins & D. C. Dollahite (Eds.), *Generative fathering: Beyond deficit perspectives* (pp. 3-17). Thousand Oaks, CA: Sage.

Houseknecht, S. K. & Pankhurst, J. G. (Eds.). (2000). *Family, religion, and social change in diverse societies*. New York: Oxford University Press.

Horn, W. F. (2001). Turning the hearts of the fathers: Faith-based approaches to promoting responsible fatherhood. In J. Fagan & A. J. Hawkins (Eds.), *Clinical and educational interventions with fathers* (pp. 191-214). New York: The Haworth Press, Inc.

Judd, D. K. (Ed.). (1999). *Religion, mental health, and the Latter-day Saints*. Salt Lake City: Bookcraft.

Koenig, H. G. (1998). *Handbook of religion and mental health*. San Diego: Academic Press.

Koenig, H. G., McCullough, M. E., & Larson, D. B. (Eds.). (2001). *Handbook of religion and health*. New York: Oxford University Press.

Latshaw, J. S. (1998). The centrality of faith in father's role construction: The faithful father and the axis mundi paradigm. *The Journal of Men's Studies, 7*, 53-70.

Lee, J. W., Rice, G. T., & Gillespie, V. B. (1997). Family worship patterns and their correlation with adolescent behavior and beliefs. *Journal for the Scientific Study of Religion, 36*, 372-381.

Madsen, T. G., Lawrence, K., & Christiansen, S. (2000). The centrality of family across world faiths. In D. C. Dollahite (Ed.), *Strengthening our families: An in-depth look at the proclamation on the family* (pp. 370-381). Salt Lake City: Bookcraft.

Mahoney, A., Pargament, K. I., Tarakeshwar, N., & Swank, A. B. (in press). Religion in the home in the 1980s and 1990s: Meta-analyses and conceptual analyses of links between religion, marriage and parenting. *Journal of Family Psychology*.

Mahoney, A., Pargament, K. I., Jewell, T., Swank, A. B., Scott, E., Emery, E., & Rye, M. (1999). Marriage and the spiritual realm: The role of proximal and distal religious constructs in marital functioning. *Journal of Family Psychology, 13*, 321-338.

Marciano, T. D. (1991). Families and religion. In M. B. Sussman & S. K. Steinmetz (Eds.), *Handbook of marriage and the family* (pp. 285-315). New York: Plenum.

Marks, L. D. (1999). *The meaning of religious belief, practice, and community for Latter-day Saint fathers of children with special needs.* Unpublished master's thesis, Brigham Young University, Provo, Utah.

Marks, L. D., & Dollahite, D. C. (2001). Religion, relationships, and responsible fathering in Latter-day Saint families of children with special needs. *Journal of Social and Personal Relationships, 18*(5), 625-650.

Marshall, E. S., Olsen, S. F., Allred, K. W., Mandleco, B. L., & Dyches, T. T. (1998, November). *Themes of religious support among Latter-day Saint (Mormon) families with a child with disability.* Paper presented at National Council on Family Relations: Milwaukee, WI.

Marsiglio, W., Amato, P., Day, R. D., & Lamb, M. E. (2001). Scholarship on fatherhood in the 1990s and beyond. *Journal of Marriage and the Family, 62*, 1173-1191.

Meth, R. L. (1990). *Men in therapy: The challenge of change.* New York: Guilford Press.

Morris, S. N., Dollahite, D. C., & Hawkins, A. J. (1999). Virtual family life education: A qualitative study of father education on the World Wide Web. *Family Relations, 48*, 23-30.

Olson, M. M. (1999). *Latter-day Saint fathers of children with special needs: A phenomonological study.* Unpublished masters thesis, Brigham Young University, Provo, Utah.

Olson, M. M., Dollahite, D. C., & White, M. B. (2001). *Involved fathering of children with special needs: Relationships and religion as resources.* Manuscript submitted for publication.

Nock, S. J. (1998). *Marriage in men's lives.* New York: Oxford University Press.

Palkovitz, R., & Palm, G. F. (1998). Fatherhood and faith in formation: The developmental effects of fathering on religiosity, morals, and values. *The Journal of Men's Studies, 7*, 33-52.

Palm, G. F. (1997). Promoting generative fathering through parent and family education. In A. J. Hawkins & D. C. Dollahite (Eds.), *Generative fathering: Beyond deficit perspectives* (pp. 167-182). Thousand Oaks, CA: Sage.

Palm, G. F. (2001). Parent education for incarcerated fathers. In J. Fagan & A. J. Hawkins (Eds.), *Clinical and educational interventions with fathers* (pp. 117-141). New York: The Haworth Press, Inc.

Pargament, K. I. (1997). *The psychology of religion and coping: Theory, research, and practice.* New York: Guilford Press.

Popenoe, D. (1996). *Life without father.* New York: Free Press.

Silverstein, L. B., & Auerbach, C. F. (1999). Deconstructing the essential father. *American Psychologist, 54*(6), 397-407.

Snarey, J. (1993). *How fathers care for the next generation: A four decade study*. Cambridge, MA: Harvard University Press.

White, M., & Epston, D. (1990). *Narrative means to therapeutic ends*. New York: W. W. Norton.

Wright, L. M., Watson, W. L., & Bell, J. M. (1996). *Beliefs: The heart of healing in families and illness*. New York: Basic.

The Use of Christian Meditation with Religious Couples: A Collaborative Language Systems Perspective

P. Gregg Blanton

SUMMARY. Even though Eastern forms of meditation have received the most attention in clinical practice, Christian meditation may be a better fit for some Christian couples. Couples may benefit from treatment when this intervention is used within the context of Anderson's collaborative theoretical perspective. In this paper, key concepts of Anderson's approach are described and their compatibility with Christian meditation is examined. Clinical applications of this integrated approach are discussed and transcripts from a session are presented to illustrate its use. *[Article copies available for a fee from The Haworth Document Delivery Service: 1-800-HAWORTH. E-mail address: <getinfo@haworthpressinc.com> Website: <http://www.HaworthPress.com> © 2002 by The Haworth Press, Inc. All rights reserved.]*

KEYWORDS. Christian meditation, Harlene Anderson, collaborative therapy, couples therapy

---

P. Gregg Blanton is Associate Professor of Human Services, Montreat College, Montreat, NC. He is affiliated with the Pastoral Counseling and Growth Center, Asheville, NC, and is an Approved Supervisor and Clinical Member of AAMFT and a Member of AAPC.

[Haworth co-indexing entry note]: "The Use of Christian Meditation with Religious Couples: A Collaborative Language Systems Perspective." Blanton, P. Gregg. Co-published simultaneously in *Journal of Family Psychotherapy* (The Haworth Press, Inc.) Vol. 13, No. 3/4, 2002, pp. 291-307; and: *Spirituality and Family Therapy* (ed: Thomas D. Carlson, and Martin J. Erickson) The Haworth Press, Inc., 2002, pp. 291-307. Single or multiple copies of this article are available for a fee from The Haworth Document Delivery Service [1-800-HAWORTH, 9:00 a.m. - 5:00 p.m. (EST). E-mail address: getinfo@haworthpressinc.com].

Increasingly, family therapists are embracing spirituality as an important dimension of and a powerful resource for family therapy (Walsh, 1999). Clients, who themselves are generally religious, are clearly supportive of this trend among family therapists. A survey by Bergin and Jensen (1990) found that 75% of the respondents wanted therapists to address spiritual practices and beliefs in therapy. Spirituality is defined for the purpose of this paper as a search for the sacred (Pargament, 1999).

How can family therapists access this spiritual dimension and integrate it into their practices? In response to this question, family therapists are turning to a variety of spiritual interventions: eliciting fundamental beliefs, engaging in personal prayer, using religious texts, and encouraging church attendance (Haug, 1998; Prest & Keller, 1993; Stander, Piercy, Mackinnon, & Helmeke, 1994). One such intervention that has received increased attention during the past decade is meditation.

CURRENT USE OF MEDITATION IN THERAPY

Clinical application of meditation has draw considerable attention during the past two decades. During this time, Hindu- and Buddhist-based meditation has gained the most attention in the United States (Larson, Swyers, & McCollough, 1998; Marlatt & Kristeller, 1999). According to Goleman (1988), there are two types of meditation: concentration and mindfulness. In mindfulness, a Buddhist-based form of meditation, the meditator focuses alertly but nonjudgmentally on all processes passing through the mind. This type of meditation has been used for the treatment of addiction (Groves & Farmer, 1994), anxiety disorders (Kabat-Zinn, Massion, Kristeller, Peterson, Fletcher, Pbert, Lenderking, & Santorelli, 1992), and borderline personality disorder (Linehan, 1993). In the field of marriage and family therapy, a review of the literature reveals that Buddhist meditation is the most common form of meditation recommended (Anderson & Worthen, 1997; Becvar, 1997; Butler, 1990; Rosenthal, 1990; Walter, 1994).

The second typed of meditation, concentration, has been popularized by Transcendental Mediation (TM). In TM, a Hindu-based intervention, the meditator focuses on a Sanskrit term, minimizes distractions, and brings the wandering mind back to the term as needed (Larson et al., 1998). TM has been used extensively in the treatment of chemical substance abuse (Gelderloos, Walton, Orme-Johnson, & Alexander, 1991).

Various attempts have been made to secularize meditation for its use in clinical practice. Some writers suggest that disengaging meditation from Buddhist and Hindu roots would make it more appealing to clients who react negatively to Eastern forms of meditation (Carrington, 1998; McLemore, 1982). They argue that relaxation is the major benefit of meditation, so the spiritual aspects can be omitted (Benson & Proctor, 1984). However, other writers argue that leaving out the spiritual aspects of meditation may limit its usefulness within the psychotherapeutic context (Goldstein & Kornfield, 1987).

How is meditation integrated into theories of psychotherapy? In Bogart's (1991) review of the literature, he found that meditation has been integrated with various theories of individual counseling: cognitive, behavioral, and psychoanalytic. In Walsh's (1999) review of family therapy literature, she discovered that various family therapists advocate the use of meditation by themselves and their clients. However, she did not find a model that integrated meditation with a family therapy approach.

PURPOSE OF MY RESEARCH

In response to the literature on the use of meditation in psychotherapy, I created a model that integrates Christian meditation with the collaborative theory of Harlene Anderson. There are several reasons why I advocate for a Christian form of meditation. First, in addition to the religions of Hinduism and Buddhism, meditation is deeply rooted and extensively used in Christianity (Larson et al., 1998). Second, Christian meditation is not limited to either concentration or mindfulness. It includes both types of meditation and engenders the benefits of both. Third, various forms of meditation have been implemented and researched within clinical practice. However, Christian meditation has been largely ignored. It is time to examine its usefulness as a therapeutic intervention. Finally, those clients who react negatively to Eastern forms of meditation may respond positively to a Christian form of meditation. Since 85% of the people in the United States describe themselves as Christians (Gallup, 1996), Christian meditation, with its religious associations, may be a better fit for many clients.

There are several reasons why I think Christian meditation may be a good fit for some Christian clients. First, Christian meditation elicits the fundamental Christian beliefs of Christian clients, and this is an important strategy when working with Christian clients (Prest & Keller,

1993). Second, it uses Scripture with which Christian clients are familiar, and this Scripture may suggest directions for change (Prest & Keller, 1993). Third, Christian meditation opens up therapeutic conversations between clients and God. Marriage and family therapists are recognizing that many couples view God as part of the marital system, and as such, they talk with him on a regular basis (Butler, Gardner, & Bird, 1998; Butler & Harper, 1994; Stewart & Gale, 1994). Since they see God as a member of the marital system, God should be included in the conversation of therapy (Griffith, 1986; Griffith, 1999; Kudlac, 1991). Meditation is one way of making God part of the therapeutic conversation.

I believe that Christian meditation, as an intervention, should be clearly integrated into a sound theoretical model. The literature reveals that meditation has been used within the context of leading individual theories of counseling. We know that meditation is useful with some individual problems. However, no attempts have been made to locate meditation, theoretically and practically, within a family therapy approach. Such an integrated approach is necessary in order to examine the systemic effects of spiritual interventions, such as Christian meditation (Butler et al., 1998).

Why have I chosen to locate Christian meditation within Anderson's collaborative language systems theory? In the next section, I will answer this question.

THEORETICAL COMPONENTS OF COLLABORATIVE APPROACH

Several authors have identified Harlene Anderson's collaborative approach as particularly well-suited for the general task of integrating spirituality and family therapy (Kudlac, 1991; Prest & Keller, 1993; Stander et al., 1994; Wright, Watson, & Bell, 1996). In addition to this general task, I believe that Anderson's theoretical orientation provides a useful framework for the particular task of using Christian meditation with Christian couples. I find the five following concepts particularly compatible with the use of Christian meditation: problem organized system, collaborative conversations, not knowing, possibility conversations, and dissolving.

The first concept, *problem organized system*, addresses the question of who is involved in the therapy system. According to Anderson (1997), individuals who are communicating with each other about the problem should be included as members of treatment. Anderson recognizes that the client has conversations with many others about the problem. They may or may not be family members. They may be friends. Whoever is trying to solve the problem is invited to be part of the therapy session.

According to Anderson, not all conversations bring about change. Only *collaborative conversations* bring about change. In this type of conversation, both the therapist and client are committed to learning about and trying to understand what the other means. Both the therapist and client join in a "shared inquiry" into the concerns being addressed. They are both trying to create a shared understanding of the client's story as it is told and retold.

The concept of *not knowing* addresses the question of how the therapist positions himself or herself in the conversation. Not knowing, according to Anderson, removes the therapist from the expert position and puts him or her in the learner position: "I am here to learn from you." In this position of being informed by the client, the therapist approaches the client's story with interest and respect. Allowing the client to lead the conversation, the therapist asks questions that allow him or her to learn more about the client's story. Each question grows out of an effort to understand the just said and the unsaid. What the client has just said leads to the next question by the therapist. Through this collaborative effort, the story becomes different than it would have been if the question had not been asked. Through this collaborative, give-and-take process, the therapist and client attempt to come to a mutual understanding of something.

The concept of *possibility conversations* also addresses the issue of how to accomplish the purpose of therapy: change. For Anderson, "change is inherent in dialogue." "Therapeutic conversations are the medium of change" (Wright et al., 1996). However, all conversations do not bring about change. Instead, change occurs within a conversation when new meanings, new understandings, and new possibilities emerge. As the therapist and clients join in a collaborative conversation, they begin to discover new possibilities in the said and unsaid. They begin to grasp a deeper sense of significance to the client's story.

The final concept, *dissolving*, addresses the purpose of therapy. According to Anderson, problems are not solved or fixed. Instead, through collaborative conversations, new possibilities begin to emerge and unworkable problems are changed into workable ones. Through this process, the client achieves a sense of "self-agency." The client who entered therapy with a sense of his or her inability to address the problem now has a sense of competency. The changed client says: "Now I know what to do, think, or feel in order to be liberated from my problem." At this point in therapy, the problem is dissolved. "The person who was saying there was a problem, no longer says there is a problem" (Wright et al., 1996, p. 93).

Anderson's concept of dissolving is similar to a concept being used by other postmodern thinkers: healing. According to Walsh (1998), the concepts of treatment and healing are quite different. Unlike treatment, which refers to solving problems, healing can occur even when problems cannot be solved. And unlike treatment, which is externally administered by the therapist, healing comes from within. Therapy that promotes healing accesses resources within the individual. This type of therapy encourages beliefs that increase healing. According to Becvar (1997), a healing perspective looks for the "meaning of an experience in terms of what it can teach us" (p. 42).

CHRISTIAN MEDITATION

This section is designed for the therapist who is unfamiliar with core beliefs of the Christian tradition in general and Christian meditation in particular. As Haug (1998) recommends, it is desirable for therapists to be knowledgeable about the practices and language used by Christian clients. I will examine how these key concepts are similar to the terms used by Anderson. Being aware of these key beliefs will help the therapist offer Christian meditation for couples desiring such an intervention.

First, Christian meditation embraces ideas similar to Anderson's concept of problem-organized system. Christian meditation assumes that God wants to communicate with people in a personal way about their cares and concerns (Hebrews 4:15-16). How does God communicate with people? According to Christian theology, God converses with people in three main ways: through Jesus, through the Holy Spirit, and through Scripture. (Christian meditation makes use of each of these vehicles of communication.) The Christian faith teaches that God was so eager to communicate with man that He became incarnate in the form of Jesus. Referring to how God communicates with man through Jesus, Hall (1988) states: "Jesus is the revelation of God, in a language I can understand" (pp. 38-39).

According to Christian tradition, God also speaks to people through the Holy Spirit and Scripture, and the Holy Spirit often speaks to people through Scripture. As St. John of the Cross states clearly in *The Ascent of Mount Carmel*: "My help will be sacred Scripture. Taking Scripture as our guide we do not err, since the Holy Spirit speaks to us through it." How does the Holy Spirit speak to man? The Christian faith teaches that the Holy Spirit speaks as an inner voice.

The second premise of Christian meditation is that man has the ability to hear God's voice. However, since God speaks in an inner voice, people must become quiet in order to hear His voice. As people become still and quiet through the process of meditation, they can then hear the "Divine Whisper."

Even though man has the ability to hear God, conversations with God through meditation may be somewhat unclear. To help people understand their meditations, the Christian faith has for centuries employed "spiritual directors" who take a collaborative approach with their directees. Spiritual direction can be defined as "help given by one Christian to another which enables that person to pay attention to God's personal communication to him or her" (Barry & Connolly, 1982, p. 8). Notice that the spiritual director shares responsibility, but does not take responsibility, for helping another Christian hear the voice of God.

The Christian faith in general describes a collaborative relationship between God and man (Pargament, Kennell, Hathaway, Grevengoed, Newman, & Jones, 1988). God and man are often depicted in Christian Scripture as partners. The individual and God jointly hold responsibility for solving problems. Various biblical passages (I Corinthians 3:7-9; Matthew 11:28-30) describe God as coming alongside people to help them complete their tasks and carry their burdens.

Not knowing is not a new concept for the Christian tradition in general or Christian meditation in particular. Centuries before Anderson introduced the concept of not knowing, Christian spiritual directors were employing this approach while helping directees understand their meditations. According to Hardy (2000), Christian spiritual direction literature emphasizes the directee-God relationship; therefore, the director has historically taken a "self-negating" position. May (1982), drawing on the same Christian literature, states that "insights come more from not-knowing than knowing" (p. 28). He says that responding to questions in a way that "keep them nourished, alive, and increasing friendly" is more desirable than answering someone's questions. The Christian writer, Kierkegaard (1859/1939), said it well when he stated that "the helper must first humble himself under him he would help, and therewith must understand that to help does not mean to be a sovereign but to be a servant" (pp. 27-28). Within the Christian practice of spiritual direction, it is evident that the effective change agent is not the spiritual director. Instead, the relationship between the directee and God is the vehicle of change.

Like Anderson, who believes in the power of new possibilities, the Christian message is one of possibilities. Lester (1995) says: "The Christian sacred story has as one of its core narratives the Easter story, the proclamation of resurrection" (p. 92). He posits that the resurrection story illustrates that there is always another possibility. The Christian Scriptures contain numerous accounts of people who had given up hope. Their stories contained no escape, and they felt imprisoned by the future they imagined. However, after a conversation with Jesus, their eyes were opened to new possibilities. Christian meditation assumes that new possibilities can emerge out of conversations with God. As people sit in silence and listen to that small, inner voice, they become open to new understandings. According to Kelsey (1976), the key to Christian meditation is the imagination. By using their imaginations, clients can step into the stories told by Jesus. Through this process of meditation, the images begin to speak to the person meditating. "Images are more like living beings with a life and purpose of their own" (p. 179), states Kelsey. Through this process of meditation, one may be surprised by new possibilities. Speaking of meditation, Foster (1988) observes that God often gives people "images of what can be" (p. 26), and he shows them "exciting new alternatives for the future" (p. 108).

Do problems begin to "dissolve" as Christian couples meditate? Many times they do. By accessing the inner voice, clients see new possibilities. As a result of their conversations with God, clients sometimes identify new approaches to old problems. Most importantly, clients begin to see themselves differently. After participating in healing conversations with God and the therapist, they see themselves as competent to handle their difficulties. In a statement of self-agency, they verbalize something similar to the following biblical passage: "I can do all things through him who gives me strength" (Philippians 4:13).

COLLABORATIVE THERAPY AND CHRISTIAN MEDITATION

Just as Anderson desires to include in therapy other people with whom the client is talking, I believe in including God in the therapy session. Just as Anderson invites clients' friends to therapy, I employ the practice of inviting clients' "Divine friend" (John 15:15) into the session. As Christian clients discuss their problems with God through meditation, they often discover new ideas and possibilities. These new ideas that emerge through meditation need to be part of the therapeutic conversation. As Kudlac (1991) says: "If God is part of the problem-organized system, then God must be part of the solution" (p. 284).

Anderson believes that understanding the client's story is a collaborative, or shared, process. The therapist and client are both trying to achieve a mutual understanding of the client's experience. Helping people hear what God is saying during meditation is also a shared experience. What is God saying to you? What does it mean? Through a dialogue between the therapist and client, the therapist and client create a shared understanding of what the client has heard from God.

Like Anderson, I do not see the therapist as the person in charge of change. Instead of taking a one-up position, I believe the therapist needs to take the position of a learner. A Divine-human encounter, through meditation, is the real change agent. When the Christian couple comes to the therapy session, after they have each meditated, the therapist asks humble and respectful questions. What did God say to you? What does it mean to you in your situation? Taking this not-knowing stance puts the therapist in the position of respectfully dialoguing with clients about their conversations with God. To use Anderson's (1997) words:

> I consider myself a guest, albeit a temporary one, who visits clients for a brief moment, who participates with them in a small slice of their life, and who floats in and out of the continuous and changing conversations they are having with others. (p. 99)

In the case of Christian meditation, the other is God.

Anderson (1997) states that possibility conversations open up new meaning, understanding, and interpretation. She defines this interpretative process as "grasping the deeper sense or significance" (p. 115). Anderson believes that clients can grasp the deeper sense or significance through conversations. I believe Christian clients may often gain this deeper sense through communicating with God in meditation. Christian meditation literature teaches that meditation involves the deeper level of one's being. These writers often speak of descending to the level of the heart. At this deeper level, one begins to respond to the images of meditation. This deeper level referred to in Christian meditation literature may be similar to what Anderson means by "deeper sense."

CLINICAL GUIDELINES

Early in my work with couples, I conduct an assessment to determine if Christian meditation should be used in therapy. I am particularly interested in the couple's problem-solving style (Pargament et al., 1988).

I am looking for couples with a collaborative style. These couples believe that:

> responsibility for the problem-solving process is held jointly by the individual and God . . . Both . . . are viewed as active contributors working together to solve problems. (Pargament et al., 1988, p. 92)

In addition, I am assessing whether they are intrinsically or extrinsically religiously motivated (Allport & Ross, 1967). Couples who are intrinsically motivated view their religious beliefs as a source of meaning, support, and strength. They believe that their religious beliefs can help them grow and change (Richards & Bergin, 1997).

In helping clients learn to meditate, I take the approach of a coach. As such, I provide them with written instructions in the form of a manual (Blanton, 2001). This manual describes a step-by-step approach for practicing Christian meditation, and it explains how between session meditations are integrated into the therapy conversation. In addition, I provide encouragement, identify difficulties with meditating, brainstorm new approaches to meditation, model how to meditate, and even join in meditating during the session if necessary.

During the session, I draw boundaries between the meditations of each spouse. There are several ways I do this. One way is by taking turns. In no particular order, I talk with one spouse about his or her meditations, and then I converse with the other spouse. I try to spend equal time exploring each spouse's meditations. While one spouse is talking, I encourage the other one to listen attentively and respectfully. I do not ask or allow one spouse to evaluate the other spouse's meditation.

In my position as a learner, I ask many questions. I am very curious about the spouse's conversation with God. What did God say to you? What did it mean? I also ask application questions. How does that message apply to your marital situation? What difference will that new idea make in your marriage? Finally, I ask observation questions. Have you observed yourself changing as a result of your meditation? I ask spouses questions concerning the other person. Have you seen any changes in how your husband relates to you since God told him that?

I think it is vitally important for me to encourage clients. I encourage them in several ways. I share their excitement when meditations open up conversations with God. I applaud their effort when their meditations seem unproductive. I communicate to them that I value their times of meditation. I let them know that I view their conversations with God through meditation as the real change agent. Finally, many times I encourage clients to take their questions to God during their next time of meditation. Again, this removes me from the position of expert and situates their conversation with God as the real agent of change.

A CONVERSATION

In this section, I will illustrate the compatibility of Anderson's theoretical concepts and Christian meditation. I will do this with a partial transcript of a conversation I had with a Christian couple. The wife and husband are both in the session, but in these excerpts I am talking with the wife about her meditations. I can tell that the husband is listening attentively to our conversation, because at one point he interjects an observation. I will include personal comments as well.

JILL: I have been meditating on a passage of Scripture in John. In this passage, a woman was talking with Jesus at a well. Jesus told her that she would be thirsty again if she drank water from the well. But, if she drank the water he gave her, then she would never thirst.

GREGG: What did God say to you as you meditated on this passage?

JILL: God told me that I look to my husband to meet my needs just as that woman looked to the well to meet her need for water.

(*REFLECTIONS*: I am thinking that Jill's conversations with God come so easily and naturally for her. Her conversations with God are such an important part of her life. I feel honored that she is discussing these conversations with me. I want to respect her conversations with God and explore what they mean to her.)

GREGG: So, in your meditation, you identified with the woman at the well.

JILL: Yes, I saw that Jesus is my water and life. I can't get life from my husband. When I try to, I become disappointed. Richard tells me that I have unrealistic expectations of him. I had never realized that before. It was a real eye-opener for me.

(*REFLECTIONS:* I hear that Jill is coming to some new understanding about how she relates to her husband. I wonder if these new ideas about herself and her marriage will open up new possibilities for her.)

GREGG: How do you think you will be different in the future as a result of seeing how much you depend on your husband and how you need to depend more on God?

JILL: If I depend less on him and more on God, I think I will be less disappointed.

(REFLECTIONS: I notice that Jill can imagine herself as being different in the future. I wonder if she has already made some changes.)

GREGG: Have you noticed being less dependent on Richard since your meditation?

JILL: Well, it is hard to say because my meditation was only yesterday.

RICHARD: Yesterday, we communicated pretty well.

(REFLECTIONS: I feel a little anxious about Richard entering the conversation. However, since he is making a positive observation about Jill's behavior, and he is not commenting on her meditation or conversation with God, I welcome him into the conversation.)

GREGG: (To Richard) What do you think was different?

RICHARD: I could tell a load had lifted from her. She had a kind of lightness, inner joy, and contentment.

JILL: Yes, you mentioned that.

(REFLECTIONS: I am amazed that such an immediate change has occurred since Jill's time of meditation. Even her husband has noticed the difference. I am awed that Jill's conversation with God has made such a difference. Once again, I realize that her conversations with God are making a profound difference in her life. I feel honored that I can dialogue with Jill about these conversations, and I am enthused about the impact that these conversations are having in her life.)

GREGG: Isn't it amazing that just a few words from God can be so energizing and renewing?!

JILL: Yeah. Toward the end of the meditation, God said: "I want to give you life." Now, I see God differently.

(*REFLECTIONS*: I notice that Jill discloses even more content from her conversation with God after I showed excitement about that conversation. I realize that our dialogue has helped her not only see herself differently. It has also led her to a different view of God.)

OTHER APPLICATIONS

Even though the strength of this intervention is its application with Christian couples, I believe it can be adapted to clients who desire some other form of meditation. If the couple practices another monotheistic religion (e.g., Judaism, Islam, Zoroastrianism, Sikhism), the therapist may want to ask them about their conversations with God. The therapist can also use the same theoretical approach and clinical techniques I have described in this paper. If the couple follows an Eastern spiritual tradition (e.g., Hinduism, Buddhism, Jainism, Shintoism, Confucianism, Taoism), the therapist can ask them about new ideas or information they received during their times of meditation. Again, the approach described in this paper could be implemented. If the couple uses a non-religious form of meditation, such as Benson's (1996) relaxation response, the therapist could inquire about new thoughts and possibilities that emerged during their times of meditation. The benefits of non-religious meditation are described by Benson (1996):

> The brain seems to use the quiet time to wipe the slate clean so that new ideas and beliefs can present themselves. Thoughts are redirected to interpret life events in a more positive, more realistic fashion. (p. 138)

Obviously, clients can benefit from various forms of meditation. It is the therapist's responsibility to explore the new possibilities that emerge as couples make use of this intervention within the context of marital therapy.

FINAL REFLECTIONS

As I reflect on the use of this integrated approach with religious couples, several thoughts come to mind. To begin with, I am very selective in the use of this intervention with couples. I only use this approach with Christian couples that read Scripture, pray, and want to meditate. In addition, it must be clear to me that God is part of the marital system. In other words, it is important that the couple has been talking with God about their problems, and they must view God as someone who can help them with their concerns.

This approach rests on the assumption that clients will have conversations with God as they meditate. I know that my clients will be engaged in important conversations with their Divine friend between sessions, and I know that these conversations will unearth new ideas and thoughts for them. I anticipate them coming to our sessions to explore the meanings of these conversations and to examine the application of these ideas to their lives.

How am I affected by the knowledge that these Christian couples are talking with God about their marriages? I am confident that my clients will come to our sessions prepared to talk about their conversations with God. It is not up to me to generate or lead the conversation, because I know my clients will take responsibility for leading the session. In addition, I realize that I am not the primary change agent in my clients' lives. Yes, I am having an important conversation with my clients during our session, and I can play a role in dissolving their problems. However, they have typically had several conversations with God between our sessions, and these conversations with God are the ones that make the real difference in couples' lives. I also feel that it is a privilege to talk with religious couples about their conversations with God. Because of this feeling, I explore my clients' conversations with God with a sense of respect and as a learner.

This integrated approach is an invitation to God to be part of the therapeutic conversation. What is that like? First, it affords me a sense of connection to my clients. We are all relying on the same source to help us identify new possibilities. Second, it helps me relax, because I do not feel responsible for the outcome of therapy. Ultimately, my clients and I are relying on God to reveal new understandings to them regarding the problems that bring them to therapy. Third, it brings a sense of awe and excitement to our sessions. What is God going to say to my clients this week and what does it mean? I feel as if I am participating in a wonderful treasure hunt with my clients.

Finally, I reflect on all the questions that linger with me about the use of this integrated approach. How much time should I spend during a session helping people learn how to meditate? Should I worry if a partner is not experiencing productive times of meditation? Would this approach be effective with multi-couple groups? Would it be effective with parents and children? Even though Anderson's collaborative approach works well with Christian meditation, will it work as well with other forms of meditation? These questions and others remain unanswered. Hopefully, others will join with me in the study of the use of meditation within the context of spirituality and family therapy.

REFERENCES

Allport, G.W. & Ross, J.M. (1967). Personal religious orientation and prejudice. *Journal of Personality and Social Psychology*, *5*, 432-443.

Anderson, D.A. & Worthen, D. (1997). Exploring a fourth dimension: Spirituality as a resource for the couple therapist. *Journal of Marital and Family Therapy*, *23*, 3-12.

Anderson, H. (1997). *Conversation, language, and possibilities*. New York: Basic Books.

Barry, W.A., & Connolly, W.J. (1982). *The practice of spiritual direction*. San Francisco: Harper & Row.

Becvar, D.S. (1997). *Soul healing: A spiritual orientation in counseling and therapy*. New York: Basic Books.

Bergin, A.E., & Jensen, J.P. (1990). Religiosity of psychotherapists: A national survey. *Psychotherapy*, *27*, 3-7.

Benson, H. & Proctor, W. (1984). *Beyond the relaxation response*. New York: Putnam/Berkeley.

Benson, H. (1996). *Timeless healing: The power and biology of belief*. New York: Fireside.

Blanton, P. G. (2001). Christian meditation in marital therapy: A manual for clients. In L. Vandecreek, & T. Jackson (Eds.), *Innovations in Clinical Practice: A Source Book: Vol. 19* (pp. 451-458). Sarasota, FL: Professional Resource Press.

Bogart, G. (1991). The use of meditation in psychotherapy: A review of the literature. *American Journal of Psychotherapy*, *45*, 383-413.

Butler, K. (1990). Spirituality reconsidered. *Family Therapy Networker*, *14*, 26-37.

Butler, M.H., Gardner, B.C., & Bird, M.H. (1998). Not just a time-out: Change dynamics of prayer for religious couples in conflict situations. *Family Process*, *37*, 451-475.

Butler, M.H., & Harper, J.M. (1994). The divine triangle: God in the marital system of religious couples. *Family Process*, *33*, 277-286.

Carrington, P. (1998). *The book of meditation*. Boston: Element Books.

Foster, R.J. (1988). *Celebration of discipline: The path to spiritual growth*. New York: Harper & Row.

Gallup, G., Jr. (1996). *Religion in America: 1996 report*. Princeton, NJ: Princeton Religion Research Center.

Gelderloos, P., Walton, K.G., Orme-Johnson, D.W., & Alexander, C.N. (1991). Effectiveness of the Transcendental Meditation program in preventing and treating substance misuse: A review. *International Journal of Addiction*, *26*, 293-325.

Goldstein, J., & Kornfield, J. (1987). *Seeking the heart of wisdom: The path of insight meditation*. Boston: Shambhala.

Goleman, D. (1988). *The meditative mind.* Los Angeles, CA: Thatcher.
Griffith, J. L. (1986). Employing the God-family relationship in therapy with religious families. *Family Process, 25,* 609-618.
Griffith, M.E. (1999). Opening therapy to conversations with a personal God. In F. Walsh (Ed.), *Spiritual resources in family therapy* (pp. 209-222). New York: The Guilford Press.
Groves, P., & Farmer, R. (1994). Buddhism and addiction. *Addiction Research, 2,* 183-194.
Hall, T. (1988). *Too deep for words.* New York: Paulist Press.
Hardy, D.S. (2000). A Winnicottian redescription of Christian spiritual direction relationships: Illustrating the potential contribution of psychology of religion to Christian spiritual practice. *Journal of Psychology and Theology, 28,* 263-275.
Haug, I.E. (1998). Including a spiritual dimension in family therapy: Ethical considerations. *Contemporary Family Therapy, 20,* 181-193.
Kabat-Zinn, J., Massion, A., Kristeller, J., Peterson, L.G., Fletcher, K.E., Pbert, L., Lenderking, W.R., & Santorelli, S.F. (1992). Effectiveness of a meditation-based stress reduction intervention in the treatment of anxiety disorders. *American Journal of Psychiatry, 149,* 936-943.
Kelsey, M.T. (1976). *The other side of silence: A guide to Christian meditation.* Mahwah, NJ: Paulist Press.
Kierkegaard, S. (1939). *The point of view for my work as an author.* (W. Lowrie, Trans.). London: Oxford University Press. (Original work published 1859).
Kudlac, K.E. (1991). Including God in the conversation: The influence of religious beliefs in the problem-organized system. *Family Therapy, 18,* 277-286.
Larson, D.B., Swyers, J.P., & McCullough. (1998). *Scientific research on spirituality and health.* National Institute for Healthcare Research.
Lester, A.D. (1995). *Hope in pastoral care and counseling.* Louisville, KY: Westminster John Knox Press.
Linehan, M.M. (1993). *Cognitive-behavioral treatment of borderline personality disorder.* New York: Guilford Press.
Marlatt, G.A. & Kristeller, J.L. (1999). *Integrating spirituality into therapy.* In W.R. Miller (pp. 67-84). Washington, DC: American Psychological Association.
May, G.G. (1982). *Will and spirit: A contemplative psychology.* New York: Harper Collins.
McLemore, C. (1982). *The scandal of psychotherapy.* Wheaton, IL: Tyndale House.
Pargament, K.I. (1999). The psychology of religion and spirituality? Yes and no. *The International Journal for the Psychology of Religion, 9,* 3-16.
Pargament, K.I., Kennell, J., Hathaway, W., Grevengoed, N., Newman, J., & Jones, W. (1988). Religion and the problem-solving process: Three styles of coping. *Journal for the Scientific Study of Religion, 27,* 90-104.
Prest, L.A., & Keller, J.F. (1993). Spirituality and family therapy: Spiritual beliefs, myths, and metaphors. *Journal of Marital and Family Therapy, 19,* 137-148.
Richards, P.S. & Bergin, A.E. (1997). *A spiritual strategy for counseling and psychotherapy.* Washington, DC: American Psychological Association.
Rosenthal, J. (1990). The meditative therapist. *Family Therapy Networker, 14,* 38-41, 70.

Stander, V., Piercy, F.P., MacKinnon, D., & Helmeke, K. (1994). Spirituality, religion and family therapy: Competing or complementary worlds? *The American Journal of Family Therapy*, *22*, 27-41.

Stewart, S.P., & Gale, J.E. (1994). On hallowed ground: Marital therapy with couples on the religious right. *Journal of Systemic Therapies*, *13*, 16-25.

Walsh, F. (1998). Beliefs, spirituality, and transcendence: Keys to family resilience. In M. McGoldrick (Ed.), *Re-visioning family therapy: Race, culture, and gender in clinical practice* (pp. 62-77). New York: The Guilford Press.

Walsh, F. (1999). Opening family therapy to spirituality. In F. Walsh (Ed.), *Spiritual resources in family therapy* (pp. 28-58). New York: The Guilford Press.

Walter, S. (1994). Does a systemic therapist have a Buddha nature? *Journal of Systemic Therapies*, *13*, 42-49.

Wright, L.M., Watson, W.L., & Bell, J.M. (1996). *Beliefs: The heart of healing in families and illness*. New York: Basic Books.

The Treatment of Anxiety Disorders in Devout Christian Clients

J. Mark Killmer

SUMMARY. Anxiety raises key spiritual concerns, such as control, letting go, fear, trust, and priorities for devout Christian clients. This article strives to increase the sensitivity of therapists to these spiritual concerns. While clinical interventions emphasize the management of anxiety, Christian spirituality points beyond mere coping with this disorder to a freedom from it. A review of biblical insights draws the conclusion that the spiritual antidote to anxiety is a radical trust rooted in an intimate relationship with God. A model for intervention is presented for helping devout Christian clients develop radical trust and intimate relationships through spiritual resources and spiritual dialogue. *[Article copies available for a fee from The Haworth Document Delivery Service: 1-800-HAWORTH. E-mail address: <getinfo@haworthpressinc.com> Website: <http://www.HaworthPress.com> © 2002 by The Haworth Press, Inc. All rights reserved.]*

KEYWORDS. Anxiety, therapy, spirituality, Christian counseling, coping

Anxiety is one of the most common mental health disorders in our society. From a Christian perspective, it is a significant spiritual problem

---

J. Mark Killmer is Executive Director, Samaritan Counseling Center, 8955 Columbia Avenue, Munster, IN 46321 (E-mail: jmk62653@aol.com).

[Haworth co-indexing entry note]: "The Treatment of Anxiety Disorders in Devout Christian Clients." Killmer, J. Mark. Co-published simultaneously in *Journal of Family Psychotherapy* (The Haworth Press, Inc.) Vol. 13, No. 3/4, 2002, pp. 309-327; and: *Spirituality and Family Therapy* (ed: Thomas D. Carlson, and Martin J. Erickson) The Haworth Press, Inc., 2002, pp. 309-327. Single or multiple copies of this article are available for a fee from The Haworth Document Delivery Service [1-800-HAWORTH, 9:00 a.m. - 5:00 p.m. (EST). E-mail address: getinfo@haworthpressinc.com].

that challenges core beliefs and raises important issues of faith. While clinical interventions emphasize the management of anxiety, Christian spirituality points beyond mere coping with this disorder to a freedom from its effects.

The primary goal of this article is to increase the sensitivity of Christian and non-Christian therapists to the spiritual dimension of anxiety for devout Christian clients. This heightened sensitivity can prevent harmful behaviors such as ignoring, minimizing, belittling or undermining the spiritual concerns of these clients. An in-depth understanding of this spiritual perspective can equip spiritually sensitive therapists to work effectively with devout Christians.

A devout client is defined as a Christian from any denominational background who perceives faith as essential to their life. Devout Christians often enter therapy hoping to discern God's perspective about their situation and wanting to respond in a faithful manner. From a Christian perspective, human beings benefit both individually and collectively when their faith is lived out in an authentic manner by discerning, developing and acting out cherished beliefs.

The Christian perspective on anxiety presented in this article is the product of an in-depth study of relevant passages from scripture. The Bible has a special authority in guiding the spiritual path of most devout Christians who are often interested in discovering how it speaks to their situation. Over the years, I have worked with colleagues and clients from the rich diversity of Christian traditions. It seems that serious distress often bridges rather than accentuates our doctrinal differences. As a result, I have found Christian clients of varied faith backgrounds usually receptive to the spiritual perspective of anxiety presented in this article. We seem joined by the challenge of facing anxiety in a faithful manner.

This spiritual perspective on anxiety was guided by the work of biblical scholars, Christian theologians and spiritual mentors drawn from a broad spectrum of Christian viewpoints. It represents a sincere attempt to discern and communicate faithfully the biblical message. It is not my intention to present my conclusions as THE Christian position on anxiety. Thus, some Christian readers and clients may have a divergent faith stance regarding anxiety.

A HOLISTIC VIEW OF HEALTH

Throughout the 20th Century, a compartmentalized perspective of human beings often created sharp distinctions in the physical and psychological treatment of persons. From this perspective, spirituality generally was perceived as irrelevant or even harmful to the treatment process. In contrast, the current trend to view human beings from a holistic perspective asserts that spirituality can be related to health and well-being. This belief provides the rationale for the integration of spirituality into the healing process of therapy.

In general, the Bible appears to promote a holistic perspective of human beings by offering spiritual insights into an array of human experience ranging from medical conditions to community hygiene to thoughts, feelings and behavior to all types of personal relationships. Support for a holistic perspective is important to devout Christians who seek therapy grounded in biblical principles. Other Christians, heavily influenced by the compartmentalized perspective, enter therapy with a hunger to integrate their faith into their current distress.

RELEVANT RESEARCH

Religion and spirituality often emerges from recent research into a myriad of physical and psychological health issues as a vital factor in health and well-being. Research on anxiety has found that spiritually active persons have significantly lower levels of anxiety and less frequency of anxiety disorders (Kaczorowski, 1989; Thorson and Powell, 1990; Koenig, Ford, George, Blazer, and Meador, 1993). Other research on the relation of religion to physical illness and aging has led to the conclusion that religion and strong social support form a potent team in reducing anxiety *and* increasing behaviors that improve physical health (Koenig, 1997). This growing body of research lends strong support for a holistic approach to health care.

Religion or spirituality is often found to be a valuable coping mechanism in research of trauma victims. Pargament has identified four particularly effective religious coping devices. *Spiritual support* is "the perception of support and guidance by God in times of trouble." *Collaborative religious coping* is a perspective that "the individual and divine work together to solve problems." Belief in a loving God who is "in control" is termed *benevolent religious reframing*. Finally, the activation of a faith community is called *congregational support* (Pargament, 1997, pp. 288-89). These specific aspects of religion and spirituality can be used to guide the spiritual treatment of persons in serious distress.

SPIRITUAL DIALOGUES

In-depth intervention with the spiritual dimension of therapeutic issues requires a willingness and ability to enter into dialogue with clients. My understanding of dialogue is grounded in the I Thou relationship of Martin Buber where a healing interaction can occur between two people willing to disclose honestly and open to considering the truths of another (Buber, 1958). Contextual family therapy uses Buber's relational notions in a clinical intervention called *direct address* defined as a willingness to risk speaking honestly in order to build trust and promote healing (Krasner and Joyce, 1997). In spiritual dialogues, therapist and client engage serious concerns such as meaning, moral responsibility and ultimate values.

In my view, therapists are qualified for spiritual dialogues of depth only when actively pursuing a personal spiritual path that may or may not be related to a formal religion. Since a rigorous lifelong process of education, reflection and supervision is needed for effective therapy, it follows that a parallel spiritual process with the same level of effort and commitment is needed for spiritual competence. Doherty argues persuasively that therapists must "soul search" before engaging in moral conversations with clients. Without this reflection, a therapist is vulnerable to an uncritical acceptance of shifting cultural values (Doherty, 1995). In this article, soul searching is re-expanded from the specific context of moral responsibility to all spiritual facets.

The clinical training and spiritual path of the therapist each present a vision of health. These visions can have a complex relationship. Many times, the two perspectives may be complementary serving to reinforce an understanding of health. Other times, they can inform one another creating a more in-depth perception of what is healthy for human beings.

At times, the two perspectives can present conflicting visions of health that may raise serious concerns about the other. Wrestling with this tension involves a willingness to risk examining our spiritual perspective while assessing the clinical viewpoint for its underlying values. From my viewpoint, this initiates a spiritual dialogue with colleagues and mentors that weigh the merits of each perspective. This dialogue may lead to strong reaffirmation, significant expansion or serious revision of one's spiritual and/or clinical perspective.

The potential tension between clinical and spiritual perspectives is important to note since the Christian message can be counter-cultural. Jesus contrasted the "broad way" of a culture's conventional wisdom of a culture with the "narrow way" of transformation (Borg, 1987). The reader may experience the spiritual perspective on anxiety presented below as counter-cultural. This quality may represent a challenge for the therapist in working with devout Christian clients.

The next four sections provide an overview of biblical insights that moves from spiritual resources for coping to understanding its message of freedom. These sections strive to prepare the therapist to work conceptually with Christian clients. It also models a soul searching process as the therapist "dialogues" with its spiritual insights. These insights easily could be dismissed as unrealistic or utopian. They are also vulnerable to becoming shallow platitudes offered by the presently well to the currently distressed. Their context, however, is one of great pain and suffering. The authors are spiritually resilient people who have weathered anxiety unexpectedly strengthened by the experience and armed spiritually to face the stresses of the future.

Most of the following quotes come from the widely recognized Revised Standard Version of the Bible. To help readers experience the full impact of a passage, some quotes are from *The Message* (marked M) that renders biblical idioms into understandable modern expressions.

BIBLICAL RESOURCES FOR COPING

> My insides are turned inside out: specters of death have me down. I shake with fear. I shudder from head to foot. Who will give me wings–wings like a dove? Psalm 55:4-6 (M)

This graphic description of the overwhelming impact of fear is one of many biblical passages that address anxiety. The psalmist wonders if and how he is going to escape from its powerful grip. The passages reviewed in this section present a variety of recommendations for coping with anxiety that clinicians may find comparable to clinical interventions for anxiety. Again, this compatibility with biblical insights can be comforting for many devout Christians.

> Anxiety in a person's heart weighs them down but a good word (from a friend) makes them glad. Proverbs 12:25

> Cast your burden (anxieties) on the Lord and God will sustain you. Psalm 55:22

These passages advocate mustering social and spiritual support through relationships with friends and with God to cope with anxiety. In response to his question "who will give me wings," the author of Psalm 55 finds relief by "casting" his anxieties "on the Lord." This experience of shedding a heavy burden by not carrying them alone can be particularly pertinent to anxious persons who tend to isolate themselves during stressful times.

> Don't fret or worry. Instead of worrying, pray. Let petition and praise shape your worries into prayers so a sense of God's wholeness will come to settle you down. Philippians 4:5-7 (M)

Throughout scripture, prayer is emphasized as a critical spiritual resource for coping with anxiety. Prayer is envisioned as the source of communication that fosters an intimate relationship with God. The author of this passage found that this intimate relationship produced a "sense of God's wholeness" that was a profound source of spiritual support.

> Do not be anxious about tomorrow . . . Let each day's trouble be sufficient. Matthew 6:34

Recognizing that anxiety often entails excessive rumination about the past and trepidation about the future, Jesus recommends the adoption of a "one day at a time" attitude. Excessive focus on the past and/or future can accentuate our inability to exert much control over life. Paralyzing or disabling anxiety often seems to be rooted in an overwhelming sense of a lack of control. A present-oriented attitude strives to narrow the focus to the "here and now." This may empower a person to meet the more "manageable" challenges of the day.

> Friend, guard clear thinking and common sense with your life. Proverbs 3:21 (M)

For the wisdom tradition of Proverbs, clear thinking is a gift that is produced through a close relationship with God. This clear thinking is perceived as an anchor for the faithful person as he/she navigates the stressful times in their lives. In this sense, clear thinking appears to function as a counterbalance to anxiety that is rooted in unreasonable fears or irrational beliefs.

> I will remember the deeds of the Lord. I will remember your miracles of long ago. I will meditate on all of your works and consider all of your mighty deeds. Psalm 77:11-12

In anxious times, biblical writers often recommend remembering the past. In these memories, the faithful person may see with clarity the presence of "God's hand" in the successful negotiation of past trials. This recognition can instill a confidence that God is working in the midst of the current distress even when the individual feels alone. Such confidence can become a very valuable spiritual resource in coping with anxiety.

The psalmist's plea to remember the past evoked Israel's dominant narrative the Exodus. Armed only with the divine promise that "I will be with you," Moses led Israel on a dangerous journey out of oppressive slavery in Egypt toward freedom in a Promised Land. Most of the journey is spent in the harsh wilderness between slavery and freedom where the people face numerous serious crises. Each crisis creates great anxiety that engenders a desire to return to slavery. The triumph over each crisis decisively demonstrates the trustworthiness of God. As the arduous journey ends, the people made the fascinating choice *not* to enter the Promised Land because they were afraid. Thus, the potential of being derailed by anxiety and fear seems to exist at every juncture of the journey from slavery to freedom.

The dominant narrative, with its key themes of fear, trust, presence, slavery and freedom, is often perceived not only as history but also as a metaphor for human existence. Shackled by cognition, emotional, behavioral or relational problems, God calls each individual to find freedom from this slavery. The journey is filled with fearsome trials that call for a deep sense of trust that God will provide what is needed to make significant changes. In the context of this metaphor, therapy might be seen as a journey from slavery to freedom.

SPIRITUAL ASSESSMENT

These words from Jesus' Sermon on the Mount are at the heart of the Bible's teaching on anxiety:

> Therefore, I tell you, do not be anxious about your life, what you will eat or drink; or about your body, what you will wear. Is not life more important than food, and the body more important than clothes? Look at the birds of the air; they do not sow or reap or store away in barns and yet your heavenly Father feeds them. Are you not much more valuable than they? Who of you by being anxious can add a single hour to his life? And why do you worry about

> clothes? See how the lilies of the field grow. They do not labor or spin. Yet I tell you that not even Solomon in all his splendor was dressed like one of these. If that is how God clothes the grass of the field will he not clothe you, *O you of little faith?* So do not worry saying, "what shall we eat?" or what shall we wear? For the pagans run after all these things and your heavenly Father knows that you need them. But seek first his kingdom and his righteousness, and all these things will be given to you as well. Therefore do not be anxious about tomorrow, for tomorrow will be anxious about itself. Each day has enough trouble of its own. (Matthew 6:25-34)

The challenging quality of this message can provoke strong emotional responses when Christians equate worrying about basic needs with a lack of faith. It seems to create impossibly high expectations. In actuality, Jesus is issuing a call to freedom from the enslavement of anxiety. An antidote is being offered in these troubling words. To grasp this recommended cure, it is crucial to understand that the statement "you of little faith" functions as a spiritual diagnosis. In therapy, clinical diagnoses are not made to create anguish for clients but rather to make sense of their distress. This assessment guides the planning of treatment. There are times when this assessment is painful to hear or when the level of denial calls for a confrontational intervention. Therapists intervene out of a belief that the client needs to see clearly in order to become healthy. This new vision is the motivation of Jesus in these words.

In contemporary culture, faith is often understood in a cognitive manner as a person's beliefs. The biblical words for faith, however, convey a relational understanding of trust the faithful person places his/her trust in God. The understanding of faith as trust is critical to the interpretation of this passage. In the assessment of Jesus, people lacked both the knowledge of and a trust in God. These spiritual deficiencies can lead to problematic beliefs and actions that ultimately bear bitter fruit including the experience of anxiety.

Anxiety is seen as inexorably intertwined with a need to control. Inordinate energy is invested in seeking security. New Testament scholar Marcus Borg describes this process:

> we often are preoccupied with our own concerns, anxious about our well-being, limited in our vision, grasping in our attempts to make ourselves secure. The world of concerns created by conventional wisdom–the broad way–was dominated by the quest for security. (Borg, 1987, p. 106-07)

Seeking security functions as an anxiety prevention plan that creates an illusion of control. Still, anxiety often occurs when the realization hits that it is impossible to exert this control over life.

The attempt to control not only affects the individual but also has serious systemic implications. Again, Marcus Borg expresses the impact of seeking security:

> Anxious about securing their own well-being, people experience a narrowing of vision, become insensitive to others and blind to God's glory all around us. (Borg, 1987, p. 107-08)

Seeking security can create a competitive atmosphere that may be "insensitive to others" and can reduce openness, cooperation and mutual concern, the very qualities necessary for an effective *systemic response* to anxiety. In sum, the desire to control through seeking security ironically can have adverse effects on physical, psychological, relational and spiritual health.

SPIRITUAL PRESCRIPTION

If enslavement to anxiety is assessed as a lack of trust, it follows that radical trust is the cornerstone of freedom from anxiety. Jesus suggests the possibility of living with a confidence that our needs will be met. This confidence is deemed *radical* trust because it appears unrealistic or even dangerous in contrast to a seemingly more prudent faith in control and security. Instead, radical trust is lived out not through the denial of needs and danger but in spite of their reality.

Since trust is a relational concept, it seems reasonable that this radical trust in God is rooted in intimate relationship. Many devout Christians describe this intimacy as "having a personal relationship with Jesus Christ." In his spiritual assessment, Jesus maintains that radical trust requires intimate relationship in order to know that God is trustworthy. This connection between intimate relationship and radical trust makes sense if God is experienced as benevolent. It is not surprising, then, that the compassionate nature of God is a central theme in the message of Jesus. Interestingly, his word for compassion is the plural of "womb" conveying a notion that compassion is nourishing and life-giving (Borg, 1987). In effect, the assessment of "little faith" extends an invitation to intimacy with a compassionate God that is the source of dealing with anxiety. It is not possible to control all circumstances *but* it is possible to trust the relationship.

A second key quality of intimate relationship is the *promise of presence.* "God with us" is a recurrent theme in scripture from the divine promise to Moses that "I will be with you" to the final words of the risen Jesus that "I am with you always to the end of the age" (Matthew 25:15). Many devout Christian clients will describe their experience of divine presence as the work of the Holy Spirit. Jesus promised the sustaining, empowering presence of the Spirit to his disciples in the panic-stricken context of his imminent death. The promise of divine presence is intended to bolster courage and create confidence. These are critical qualities when facing the frightening prospect of risky new behaviors such as letting go of control, reducing security seeking behaviors and/or making bold new decisions.

THE FRUITS OF RADICAL TRUST

An intimate relationship rooted in radical trust in a compassionate God can lead to significant personal change or *transformation.* This transformation produces "spiritual fruit" defined here as the growth of inner spiritual resources and personality characteristics that result in new spiritually based behaviors. Key spiritual fruits related to anxiety are described below.

The Peace that Passes Understanding

In Philippians 4:4-7, the apostle Paul maintains that the process of bringing anxieties to the intimate relationship with God through prayer can result in a spiritual fruit he calls "the peace that passes understanding" (v. 7). In Greek, this peace is conveyed through the image of a royal guard zealously protecting its king pointing to an inner serenity embedded in a sense of God's protective presence in the midst of distress. This inner peace is perceived as empowering the devout Christian to handle whatever life might dish out.

Spiritual Vision

Another fruit of intimate relationship can be spiritual vision, a reevaluation of life from the viewpoint of spiritual values. This process can have the effect of turning an individual's values and priorities upside down. The biblical word for anxiety means roughly "weighed down by the world's cares" and appears to ground the experience of anxiety in cultural priorities and values. In contrast, words that express a concern for others such as righteousness, kindness, humility and sacrificial love are found in passages on anxiety. They seem curiously out of place in the midst of the writer's distress. Interestingly, the biblical word for a genuine concern for others is from the same root as the word for anxiety. Taken together, they point to a relationship between focusing outside of self and the reduction of anxiety. In the Sermon on the Mount, the alternative that Jesus presented to seeking security was to "seek first God's Kingdom and his righteousness" (v. 33). This conveys a belief that shifting priority from self-focus to other focus has a paradoxical effect on anxiety. Thus, the surprising contention is made that living out the new priority of being other focused is a long-term buffer against anxiety.

Christian Community

A third product of an intimate relationship with God can be the desire to create community based on relational values such as generosity, kindness and sacrificial love. Living out these values in community can have the systemic impact of reducing anxiety. Radical trust in God can lead to radical trust in one another in the context of this community. Such a community offers not only an alternative to the "every person for themselves" mentality created by the quest for security but also creates a "wombish" context for spiritual transformation.

CHOOSING TO INTERVENE

This conceptual background can guide a therapist in working with devout Christian clients. To intervene spiritually with clients, the therapist must assess his/her own readiness to engage in spiritual dialogues. The key factors in making this decision include openness, comfort, experience and expertise with spiritual issues. Therapists who do not meet this criterion should refer devout Christian clients either to a pastor that will work in conjunction with the therapy or to a pastoral therapist. Clinicians who are emotionally reactive to and/or cut-off from religion are particularly vulnerable to harmful interactions with devoutly religious clients.

Therapists often express concern about imposing religion on clients. Like other abuse of power issues, this can be a legitimate concern. In my assessment, however, this concern often reflects a lack of differentiation for the therapist about spirituality. Traditionally, therapy has dealt with this tension by ignoring the client's spirituality. Other times, the dilemma is managed through a passive stance waiting for clients to raise their spiritual concerns. These solutions can be a disservice to clients who wish to integrate their spirituality in therapy. Clients often interpret silence about spirituality as disinterest in or a taboo against addressing these concerns.

Clinicians do not regard the introduction of new ideas or interventions as imposing their clinical theory on clients. Since clients are seeking help, these recommendations are offered respectfully in the context of being helpful. This respect exists even in confrontational interventions. Clients always retain the right to implement or reject these recommendations. This respectful, differentiated approach is used in spiritual dialogues. Working within the client's faith framework, a therapist wrestles honestly with the spiritual dimension of their distress. Like clinical interventions, the client always has the right to accept or reject spiritual insights.

Before presenting a model for spiritual intervention with anxious Christian clients, it is necessary to describe spiritual resources that can be helpful throughout the course of treatment. These resources are drawn from across the spectrum of Christian viewpoints. Since many Christians may be unfamiliar with many of these resources, this section strives to increase awareness of the rich array of spiritual resources that can facilitate the growth of intimate relationship and radical trust.

SPIRITUAL RESOURCES

The following spiritual resources seem especially amenable to the treatment of anxiety. These descriptions are introductory rather than in-depth in nature. Thus, the therapist wishing to integrate spiritual resources in therapy is encouraged to expand their knowledge of them.

Personal Prayer

The daily practice of personal prayer is a primary resource in building an intimate relationship with God. Prayer can counteract the sense of loneliness often felt in the midst of distress, produce the experience of a compassionate God and build a strong trusting relationship. It may activate the spiritual support, benevolent reframing and collaborative religious coping skills identified by Pargament. It can be a mistake to assume that all Christians pray regularly. Furthermore, many Christian clients have a limited knowledge of prayer. The anxious client may benefit from an expanded knowledge of prayer. For example, *centering prayer* is an ancient Christian contemplative practice that strives to still the mind in order to listen to God. It often results in a deep state of relaxation that creates a strong sense of peace and closeness to God.

Spiritual Readings

In distress, many devout Christians turn to the Bible for consolation. It is helpful, then, when the therapist can direct clients to passages that address anxiety. There is also a wealth of daily meditation books and other religious readings that reinforce key spiritual themes related to anxiety such as letting go and radical trust. These readings can create a positive focus to start a day, help a client refocus in the midst of stress or bring a measure of comfort in the evening.

Congregational Support

Support from the congregation for the anxious Christian takes many forms. *Prayers* from the faith community through prayer chains or prayer partners can provide comfort and strength. Some Christians find comfort by increasing their participation in *worship.* As with prayer, many Christians are unaware that there are varied types of worship services. For anxiety, *healing services* and *taize*, a very peaceful, meditative worship experience, can provide consolation. Many congregations offer *trained listeners*, sometimes called Stephen's Ministers or Deacons, who can provide individual support. Finally, many faith communities offer a variety of small group experiences that can offer strong spiritual support for the anxious Christian.

Spiritual Leadership

Many anxious Christians receive strong spiritual and emotional support from the pastors of their faith community. In addition, a faith community may have leaders with the spiritual gift of discerning divine guidance. These spiritually sensitive individuals can be invaluable for anxious Christians seeking new direction for their lives. Finally, Christians seeking intensive spiritual growth may choose to work with a Spiritual Director who is a spiritually mature individual specifically trained to guide this growth.

Spiritual Formation Groups

A spiritual formation group is a small group experience with the intentional focus of creating intimate community to facilitate individual spiritual growth. One example is a *Renovare* group, which encourages its members to practice a rich array of spiritual growth exercises (Smith, 1999). At their best, a spiritual formation group becomes a primary group experience where members take one another seriously, creating strong bonds and exerting significant influence with one another. Such an intimate group has the potential to create the "wombish" spiritual environment that enables its members to make and sustain significant change.

Retreats

Retreats can be a refreshing time away from stress, a spiritual growth experience and/or a life-changing event. Retreat centers exist throughout the country where individuals can experience renewal through quiet reflection or learn spiritual skills such as centering prayer. One type of retreat is an international, inter-denominational movement led primarily by laypersons known by various names such as Cursillo, The Great Banquet and The Walk to Emmaus. This weekend retreat is often a moving experience that can provide a powerfully intimate experience of God's compassion. Many find this retreat to be a life-changing experience. I have often found that this retreat is very effective in conjunction with therapy.

A MODEL FOR INTERVENTION

This model integrates spiritual resources and spiritual dialogues into the clinical treatment of anxiety. Spiritual dialogues are used *within* therapy to address the critical spiritual concerns raised by anxiety. These dialogues strive to utilize spiritual wisdom to facilitate significant change. This intervention model also suggests that Christian clients may engage spiritual resources *in conjunction* with therapy in order to activate Pargament's religious coping mechanisms and/or to develop the intimate relationship with God that can engender radical trust. The most coherent way to present this model for spiritual intervention is to organize it around my clinical construct for the treatment of anxiety. The focus of this presentation, however, is on spiritual, not clinical, intervention. Furthermore, I recognize that many readers have a different clinical protocol for anxiety. It is my belief, however, that the following ideas for spiritual intervention are readily adaptable to varied clinical approaches.

The Distress Phase

Since clients often enter therapy in serious distress, the initial clinical goal of treatment may be the reduction of this high level of anxiety. Mustering spiritual support for the client can be a valuable component of alleviating this distress. Thus, it is beneficial to assess the client's spiritual support system including their individual spiritual practices and their involvement in the faith community. It is also helpful to evaluate the client's current use of these resources since it is not unusual for Christians in distress to abandon these practices. As a result of this assessment, the therapist may recommend activating support from the faith community, perhaps through prayer or pastoral leadership. Furthermore, the therapist may invite the client to initiate individual spiritual resources such as daily prayer or spiritual readings that can bring a measure of comfort. These spiritual interventions can help reduce serious distress by developing the congregational support and spiritual support coping mechanisms.

The Coping Phase

This phase of treatment focuses on the development of an anxiety management plan to help clients cope with anxiety. This plan may include daily activities designed to reduce stress and a strategy to prevent the escalation of distress. Spiritual resources can be an effective component of the anxiety prevention plan. For instance, individual spiritual practices such as daily prayer or spiritual readings and group spiritual activities like a support group or the taize service can contribute to the reduction of stress. Furthermore, spiritual practices such as prayer, remembering a treasured passage of scripture, Christian music or calling a prayer partner can be effective tools in blocking the escalation of anxiety.

Christian clients often raise issues in the coping phase that can be addressed through spiritual dialogue. One example is the devout Christian client who may wonder what the Bible has to say about anxiety. This question affords the opportunity to introduce major spiritual themes such as control, letting go and radical trust, which may engender a desire to work on these spiritual concerns. The equation of anxiety with a lack of faith is another spiritual issue raised by clients familiar with the Lilies of the Field passage. It can be helpful if the resulting spiritual dialogue *normalizes* the experience by sharing key biblical passages on anxiety. Christian clients are often comforted to discover that many biblical writers have struggled with profound anxiety. Furthermore, this dialogue may be an opportunity to present an understanding of the statement "O you of little faith" as a spiritual diagnosis rather than a statement of condemnation.

Finally, many clients will experience both clinical and spiritual recommendations as impractical in the face of their current anxiety. For instance, a client already excessively busy and/or over-committed may balk at the recommendations to take time to relax or to pray. Such resistance often expresses the client's trust in controlling attitudes and behaviors while the interventions of relaxation or prayer introduce a solution of letting go. As a result, this resistance can initiate a spiritual dialogue that directly addresses the key issue of the relationship between the need to control and the challenge of letting go. Since the process of letting go requires a significant level of trust, the spiritual concept of radical trust may emerge from this dialogue.

The Transformation Phase

Treatment for anxiety may reach a crossroads when clients experience a reduction in distress and an increase in their ability to cope with anxiety. Feeling strengthened, many clients choose to leave therapy at this point. For other clients, the experience of handling anxiety in a different manner has provided a hint of the possibility of significant change. At this crossroads, the spiritually sensitive therapist can invite devout Christian clients to enter into in-depth spiritual dialogues with the goal to move from mere coping with to freedom from anxiety. The response to this invitation may have a significant impact on the client's long-term physical, emotional, relational and spiritual health since opting to leave therapy may result in a vulnerability to repeated cycles of anxiety whenever life becomes sufficiently stressful.

With reduced anxiety, some Christian clients may be puzzled or intrigued by this invitation to enter in-depth therapy. This can lead to a spiritual dialogue that introduces the potential spiritual fruits, the long-term antidote to anxiety that can result from an intimate relationship with God that engenders radical trust. This dialogue may produce a vision of serenity that creates a hunger to seek this peace through the process of transformation. As a result, these clients may choose to enter into the transformation phase of treatment in order to pursue significant psychological, relational and/or lifestyle changes. The work of transformation builds on the foundation of the client's successful navigation of the Distress and/or Coping Phases where he/she presumably experienced spiritual support. At this point, the use of spiritual resources and spiritual dialogues strives to develop the radical trust needed to risk making these changes based on a spiritual perspective.

Since I have argued that radical trust rooted in intimate relationship with God is foundational to freedom from anxiety, it now appears crucial for the Christian client to seek this intimate relationship through intensive spiritual growth activities in conjunction with therapy. These practices may build on the spiritual resources used in the Distress and Coping Phases of treatment or may be new activities designed to facilitate change. In my experience, a focus on personal prayer, involvement in a spiritual formation group and participation in a profound retreat experience can be especially valuable in the process of transformation.

Within therapy, the process of transformation often begins with a spiritual dialogue focused on discerning the message in or the meaning of a client's anxiety. In the context of spiritual intervention, discernment is understood as sensitivity to divine communication. Wrestling with the question, "How is God speaking to me in the midst of this distress?" can reveal a client's unique form of slavery to the "broad way" of control and security. It may unveil deep-seated fears, distorted beliefs, poor boundaries or maladaptive behaviors. It also may clarify attitudes, beliefs and/or behaviors that betray a deep-seated trust in values contrary to the spiritual perspective. In effect, this dialogue produces a spiritual "hypothesis" about the meaning of a client's anxiety that can guide treatment throughout the Transformation Phase.

Implicit in this process of discernment is the question of if and/or how to respond to this divine message. Thus, the focus of spiritual dialogue may shift to address this question. Specifically, a client may discern a call to let go of control, set firmer boundaries, develop new perspectives, change maladaptive patterns, alter priorities and/or make bold new decisions. There are times when this dialogue leads to a serious evaluation of priorities that may discover a painful disparity between cherished values and actual lifestyle. This discovery may create difficult decisions that require significant strength and courage. Finally, this dialogue may foster a heightened concern for others that may lead to a personal sense of call to some type of discipleship. While a thorough discussion of this call is beyond the scope of this article, it may be helpful for a therapist to be sensitive to this possible outcome of transformation.

Nurturing Radical Trust

The call to make significant personal changes, to alter one's lifestyle based on new priorities and/or to act on a heightened sensitivity to others, can ignite a very challenging process. This challenge may result in paralyzing fear and other homeostatic forces that block the path to transformation. As a result, the focus of spiritual dialogue becomes addressing these fearsome barriers to change. Facing these barriers and moving ahead puts radical trust to the test.

Acting on radical trust appears to require both strength and courage. It is helpful for the client to mobilize their spiritual support network to provide strong encouragement while facing these challenges. The therapist seeks to guide the client through the process of acting on radical trust. From my viewpoint, this process begins with the *decision to act*. When therapy is stuck in this decision making process, the therapist can help a client *count the cost* of remaining static. People often see the danger of new ways of acting very clearly while being blind to the cost of homeostasis. Understanding the cost of not changing may create the energy to face the dangers of a new path. After a decision to act, therapy endeavors to identify *new trusting behaviors*. Once identified, it may be helpful to break these behaviors into manageable steps. With each step taken, the therapist journeys with the client, providing encouragement through difficult times while framing or reframing the consequences experienced through this new behavior. It is ultimately hoped that the successful implementation of each new behavior will serve to engender radical trust by reinforcing the *trustworthiness* of God.

A Spiritual Lifestyle

Ideally, clients will choose to integrate spiritual resources into their lifestyle whether they leave therapy after the completion of the Distress, Coping or Transformation phases. These ongoing spiritual practices have the potential to help clients maintain the gains they made in therapy. Furthermore, they may lead to a deepening sense of intimacy with God that opens the door to additional spiritual growth.

CLOSING

The prophet Jeremiah compares the person who trusts in God with a tree by a stream (Jeremiah 17:7-8). The tree thrives by being very close to the source of its nourishment and by putting down its roots deeper each day. Due to these factors, the leaves of that tree stay green and it continues to bear fruit *even when* a drought dries up that stream. In the same manner, radical trust can grow in devout Christians when they endeavor to establish deep roots through an intimate relationship with their source. This relationship can produce the spiritual fruit that provides the strength and courage to thrive even in the midst of great anxiety.

REFERENCES

Borg, M.J. (1987). *Jesus: A New Vision*. San Francisco, CA: Harper Press.

Buber, M. (1958). *I and Thou*. New York, NY: Charles Scribner's Sons.

Doherty, W.J. (1995). *Soul Searching*. New York, NY: Basic Books.

Kaczorowski, J.M. (1989). Spiritual well-being and anxiety in adults diagnosed with cancer. *The Hospice Journal*, 5(3/4), 105-116.

Koenig, H.G. (1997). *Is Religion Good for Your Health?* Binghamton, NY: The Haworth Press, Inc.

Koenig, H.G., Ford, S.M., George, L.K., Blazer, D.G., & Meador, K.G. (1993). Religion and anxiety disorder: An examination and comparison of associations in young, middle-aged and elderly adults. *Journal of Anxiety Disorders*, *7*, 321-342.

Krasner, B.R., & Joyce, A.J. (1997). *Truth, Trust and Relationships: Healing Interventions in Contextual Therapy*. New York, NY: Brunner/Mazel Publishers.

Pargament, K.I. (1997). *The Psychology of Religion and Coping*. New York, NY: Guilford Press.

Smith, J.B., & Graybeal, L. (1999). *A Spiritual Formation Workbook*. San Francisco, CA: Harper San Francisco.

Altar-Making with Latino Families: A Narrative Therapy Perspective

J. Maria Bermúdez
Stanley Bermúdez

SUMMARY. This paper explores the uses of making altars in family therapy. Offering artistic expression in the form of altar-making can serve as a creative resource for clients, especially for many Latinos/Hispanics familiar with Catholicism, altars, and/or folk healing beliefs. Altar-making can have many uses. Specifically, altar-making can help people explore spiritual themes in their lives, cope with bereavement and grief, help clients remember their loved ones (White, 1997), memorialize the living, unify families, help families and couples learn to work collaboratively, and strengthen blended families. Suggestions for creating an altar are discussed from a narrative therapy perspective. A case illustration and an artist's perspective are also provided. *[Article copies available for a fee from The Haworth Document Delivery Service: 1-800-HAWORTH. E-mail address: <getinfo@haworthpressinc.com> Website: <http://www.HaworthPress.com> © 2002 by The Haworth Press, Inc. All rights reserved.]*

KEYWORDS. Narrative family therapy, altar-making, Hispanics/Latinos, spirituality, art in family therapy

---

J. Maria Bermúdez is a PhD candidate at the Marriage and Family Therapy doctoral program, Virginia Polytechnic Institute and State University, and Visiting Professor, Texas Tech University.

Stanley Bermúdez is a fine artist working independently.

Correspondence regarding this article may be sent electronically to J. Maria Bermúdez at <mbermudez@hs.ttu.edu>.

[Haworth co-indexing entry note]: "Altar-Making with Latino Families: A Narrative Therapy Perspective." Bermúdez, J. Maria., and Stanley Bermúdez. Co-published simultaneously in *Journal of Family Psychotherapy* (The Haworth Press, Inc.) Vol. 13, No. 3/4, 2002, pp. 329-347; and: *Spirituality and Family Therapy* (ed: Thomas D. Carlson, and Martin J. Erickson) The Haworth Press, Inc., 2002, pp. 329-347. Single or multiple copies of this article are available for a fee from The Haworth Document Delivery Service [1-800-HAWORTH, 9:00 a.m. - 5:00 p.m. (EST). E-mail address: getinfo@haworthpressinc.com].

There is no denying that religion and/or spirituality are important to many of the people we see in therapy (Patterson, Hayworth, Turner, and Raskin, 2000). However, spirituality and religion have long been neglected within the mental health arena due to the tradition of separating psychotherapy from religion. The marginalization of spiritual beliefs by therapists has lead most clients to edit out the spiritual dimension of their experience (Walsh, 1998). When clients do not feel comfortable discussing spiritual concerns with therapists because they perceive it inappropriate to do so, the therapist will inevitably ineffectively assess, diagnose, and treat the people they are trying to help. They will also miss tapping into potentially significant religious and spiritual resources for the client. Not only is it important for therapists to feel comfortable addressing spiritual beliefs, it is also increasingly important for therapists to be sensitive and aware of culturally relevant spiritual beliefs and practices. In this paper we address how therapists can use altar-making as a therapeutic tool, especially when working with Latino/Hispanic clients. We use the terms Latino and Hispanic interchangeably, although we are biased toward the term Hispanic. The authors are both Hispanic and have combined their ideas as an artist and family therapist to suggest the use of altar-making as a therapeutic resource.

SPIRITUALITY AMONG LATINOS

Traditionally, Latinos have espoused a strong sense of spirituality (Ho, 1987). Although the number of practicing Catholics is beginning to decrease (Cobas & Duany, 1995; Rogg & Cooney, 1980), Catholicism is still the predominant religion for Mexican Americans, Cubans, Puerto Ricans, and Central and South Americans (Falicov, 1998; McGoldrick, Giordano, & Pearce, 1996). Many Latinos view Catholicism as part of their cultural heritage, regardless if they attend church on a regular basis. Hence, sacraments such as Baptism, Confirmation, the Holy Eucharist, and matrimony are seen as normal life events (DeBlassie, 1976; Grebler et al., 1970) that influence the meanings given to life cycle transitions and values affecting marital and family life (Falicov, 1998). Many Hispanic Catholics are converting to evangelical religions such as Pentecostalism, Jehovah's Witnesses, or Fundamental Protestantism (McGoldrick et al., 1996). Nevertheless, it will be important for therapists to assess the significance religion may have on the life of individual family members and use their religious network as a resource. In addition to Catholicism, many Hispanics espouse other spiritual beliefs, such as folk healing practices, which may play an important role in their lives (Falicov, 1998; Ho, 1987).

Folk healing practices and beliefs may coincide with Catholicism or they may be the sole focus of spiritual and religious practices and beliefs. There are many ways in which folk healing is practiced among Hispanics. For example, "Santeria" is a folklore that combines the heritage of Spanish Catholic medical and religious values with those of an African and Native American belief system. Catholic saints can represent African deities. This practice is also seen as "white or black magic." The practice of "espiritismo" is also prevalent throughout Latino communities (Morales-Dorta, 1976). This is a belief that the spirits of the dead communicate in various ways to people, usually through an "espiritista" or medium (Caninio & Spurlock, 1994; Delgado, 1988). In addition, those who treat Mexican Americans and other Latin Americans should understand "curandismo." This is a system of folk healing that uses medicinal herbs and potions. A "curandero" is a folk healer that is consulted for many maladies, especially those with psychological components (McGoldrick et al., 1996). Curanderos and espiritistas frequently perform "limpias," which are cleansing rituals often using plants, perfumed waters, religious images and candles. These rituals take place near altars, which are decorated with objects, candles, incense, and images of saints, among other things (Falicov, 1998). Although many Hispanics do not use a particular form of folk healing, many are familiar with people praying to spirits, saints, and deceased loved ones. Therapists should understand the ways in which folk healing and other beliefs may potentially affect the lives of their clients and considered these beliefs as possible therapeutic resources. Instead of viewing these practices as an unconventional alternative, folk approaches have their own wisdom and effectiveness that can play a complimentary role along side conventional healing methods (Falicov, 1998). Offering an artistic expression in the form of altar making can be a creative therapeutic option, since many Hispanics are familiar with Catholicism, altars, and/or folk healing beliefs.

RELIGIOUS AND SECULAR ALTARS

Throughout many of the Spanish speaking, mainly Catholic regions in Latin America, the custom of altar-making is common and reflects a cultural amalgamation of European, African and Indigenous elements (Tomás Ybarra Frausto, 1987). Catholics in countries such as Cuba, Colombia, and Mexico, among others, believe that altars are an effective method of worshiping and many people make home altars or shrines.

Definitions of Altars

There are several definitions of altars and shrines. According to the *American Heritage Dictionary* (1989), an altar is any elevated structure upon which sacrifices may be offered or before which other religious ceremonies may be enacted. In *Larousse's Diccionario de la Lengua Espanola* (1994), the word altar has a similar meaning. However, this is not how the term altar is being used here. Most home altars are never used for the intention of sacrificing. They may be used to enact small ceremonies, but nothing like a priest would do during a Roman Catholic Mass. We use the term *altar* to mean homemade shrines. The *American Heritage Dictionary* (1989) defines a *shrine* as a container for sacred relics, the tomb of a saint, or a site or object revered for its associations. Both definitions are closer to what most Hispanics refer to as "altares." Therefore, we will continue to refer to them as altars since this is what is most familiar, even though they might more properly be called shrines. Altars can also be described as a physical structure that enables one to communicate with the gods, functioning as a doorway through which the physical approaches the spiritual and the spiritual acknowledges the physical (Page, 1994). We add that not only can you communicate with the gods through altars, but also in the case of many Hispanic Catholics, you can communicate with a variety of Catholic saints, angels, ancestors, and sometimes with recently deceased relatives. I (M. B.) have also found that when working with non-Hispanic and/or non-Catholic clients, the term shadow box is more appropriate. Clients will choose which term they are more comfortable with, which will often depend on their spiritual and religious beliefs and the purpose for making the altar in therapy.

Universality of Altar-Making

In one form or another altars have been a primary component of worship throughout history (Page, 1994). For example, during the Spanish colonization of Venezuela, the Spaniards introduced African slaves, who brought their beliefs and customs with them. Roman Catholic beliefs began to mix with the traditions of Africans and indigenous peoples. In countries such as Venezuela, Cuba, the Dominican Republic, and Puerto Rico, many religious altars have a strong African flavor to them. "The Africans have made of Christianity a more effective, sentimental, and irrational religion, by seasoning it with superstitious and magical beliefs" (Pollak-Eltz, 1991, p. 49). In his essay, *Private Reflections of Public Life*, he writes:

> Home altars have formed a part of personal devotion in Europe, Africa, and North America since well before the encounter of these cultures in the wake of the Columbus voyage. At least dating to Roman times, families in the Mediterranean basin had home altars to the household gods, the Lares. At least dating from the rise of the Bantus, western African peoples maintained domestic relics. At least dating to the Toltec peoples, families in the Mexican central valley had personal shrines to deities. (Salvo, 1997, p. 91-107)

In any case, regardless of their origins, altars seem to be a common denominator in many different ancient, as well as more recent cultures of the world. For many, an altar is a little spot of remembrance that has been arranged with tenderness, love, and thought, to honor an absence, a loss, or a grief. It is a very special small space filled with a variety of images, objects, and words that have specific or distinct meanings. This definition can be more useful for clients in therapy.

Functional Altars

Unlike art altars, real working altars or functional altars are continually evolving and changing in appearance. For example, most people add new candles, add more images of Saints or the Virgin Mary, or photographs. They also frequently relocate the altars from one part of the home to another. In the last six years my grandmother (S. B.) has moved her altar about five or six times. This practice is not exclusive to a particular Hispanic Catholic culture. In *The Buena Vista Social Club* (a documentary film about Cuban music), Ibrahim Ferrer, one of the singers in that documentary, had a homemade altar in his house. Every day he sprays his altar with perfume before he leaves the house and he also places a small shot glass filled with rum for the saint in his altar to drink. In Mexico, altar makers change their homemade altars every day according to the seasons and the harvest. They also move them from one part of the house to another. Nonfunctional or art altars do not necessarily change with time. Once the altar has been assembled, the client does not need to add images, objects, or words to them after the altar is completed.

Real altars are working altars. By working altars we mean that they serve a function for the religious or spiritual people who make them.

For many they are like a telephone for talking to God, Jesus, The Virgin Mary, Saints, family members, friends, or deceased loved ones. People pray in front of them, light candles, do petitions, or kneel in front of them. They can serve other functions such as a means to idolize, memorialize, and immortalize people or events in life, especially one's family. Altars can also be used as a way to communicate one's heritage. Clients can decide for themselves if they want to make a working altar or an art altar merely for expressive and therapeutic purposes. Some similarities between real working altars and art altars are that they all use images, found objects, manufactured objects, or words. Making an altar invites the participant to experience an artistic process that allows them to decide the meaning it will have for them.

ALTAR-MAKING FROM A THEORETICAL STANCE

Altar-making is an experiential process. Experiential therapists believe that the way to emotional health is to reveal deeper levels of experiencing that may lead one toward individual and relational growth (Nichols and Schwartz, 1991). However, using altar-making in therapy is an experiential approach that can be used in combination with a variety of other theoretical approaches. For example, the Structural Family Therapist can use this tool as a means to unify or realign certain subsystems. By asking the children to make a shrine of their deceased grandparents and the parents make one of their own, they are able to create a rich and healing experience together while still reinforcing the parent's authority and explore their experiences of their deceased family members from various perspectives. On the other hand, the Bowenian Therapist might use altar-making as a way to help family members explore emotional cutoffs, triangles, the multi-generational transmission of customs, beliefs, and patterns as well as explore ways to stay emotionally connected (differentiate without leaving the system), while developing an ability to individuate.

In my practice (M. B.), I have used Narrative Therapy Theory as my guide when helping families make shrines/altars in therapy. Experiential therapy and Narrative therapy can be integrated very easily. The goal of therapy would be to co-create an experience with clients so that they can relive, reinvent, or experience for the first time an event or relationship that does not pertain to their dominant story. This would be a unique outcome that pertains to their "preferred self." By experiencing this event in therapy, the client will have experienced a new and preferred aspect of their self that they can take home and continue to experience in their lives long after their therapy sessions have been completed.

NARRATIVE THERAPY AND ALTAR-MAKING

As a therapist, what I find most useful with the Narrative Therapy Theory is that I am able to work with an individual, couple, or family to deconstruct old ways of thinking about a person, life style, and/or a problem, and reconstruct a more preferred and healthy perspective. Narrative Therapy, as suggested by White and Epston, (1990, p. 83) enables therapists to:

a. encourage a perception of change by plotting or linking lived experience in time,
b. invoke a subjective mood by triggering opinions and beliefs, examine personal meanings, and generate a multiple perspective,
c. invite a reflexive posture,
d. encourage a sense of authorship and reauthorship of one's life and relationships by the telling of one's story.

We are suggesting the integration of art and Narrative Therapy to make altars in therapy. Art has already been combined with Narrative therapy to enhance therapeutic possibilities (Carlson, 1997). The following is an integration of the work of White and Epston (1990) and Freedman and Combs (1996) with our work in altar-making in psychotherapy.

CREATING THE ALTAR IN FAMILY THERAPY

Most Family Therapy theories and models do not delineate specified steps for the therapy process. However, we thought that it might be beneficial for the reader to see how we have experienced altar-making and then take the liberty to make adaptations.

There are several steps or phases involved in this creative and therapeutic process: The client/s choose altar-making as a therapeutic resource, decide on the theme or topic of the altar, gather information about the topic, collect images and objects (made or found) related to the altar, assembling the altars, and finally punctuating the process with a ritual or ceremony. We will describe how we integrate the altar-making process from a Narrative Therapy stance.

Step 1: Choosing Altar-Making as a Treatment Modality: Deconstructive Listening

Our first priority is to provide opportunities for clients to make decisions about the therapeutic process. One way to do this involves providing descriptions of ways in which the clients and we could work together. By providing alternatives, the clients can decide what sounds best to them and can choose altar-making as a therapeutic resource, if it is a good fit for both the client and the therapist. This means that the therapist should be knowledgeable and flexible enough to provide several options and the client should have as much input as they can provide. Offering alternative therapy modalities is a first step toward egalitarian therapy (Prouty and Bermudez, 1999). Once the options have been presented and the client decides that making an altar or shrine is a useful and creative therapeutic resource, then the topic or theme can be discussed.

In Narrative Therapy the beginning phase of therapy involves the deconstructive process. As the therapist is deconstructing the problem, it becomes apparent to the therapist that making an altar or shrine may be of therapeutic value. The therapist begins to deconstruct the dominant or problem saturated story in order to loosen the grip of restrictive stories, examine the various possible meanings, look for gaps in our understanding, and ask the client to fill in the details. As they tell their story, we can interrupt at intervals to summarize our sense of what they are saying. Our hope is that the process of making an altar continues to generate new meanings about themselves and/or their family.

Step 2: Deciding the Theme: Externalization

As mentioned previously, altars can have religious and/or secular meaning. Most likely the client will want to make an altar related to the presenting problem or therapeutic issue. For some, the theme can relate to memorializing a deceased loved one, a celebration of one's life, or a means to externalize a problem/trauma or resource. The altars can also be about popular religious celebrations, one's family, or about the personal history of meaningful life events. The most important thing to remember is that the client decides on the theme, not the therapist.

Using Narrative Therapy Theory as a framework helps us see how altar-making is a form of externalization. By assembling and dedicating a shrine to another person or to their self, the client can separate their self from the person or persons being memorialized. This type of physical externalizing helps the client to visually see personal artifacts, pictures, and objects assembled in a way that creates an illusion of the memorialized person being present in the room. This can be especially healing for those coping with bereavement or an estranged relationship. If clients are a couple or a family, then making an altar or shrine can be a symbolic externalization in which they can discuss their feelings, concerns, and strengths, while focusing on an external object.

Sometimes it may be therapeutic for a client to make an altar related to a presenting problem or a traumatic experience. If this is the case, then the externalization process can also serve more traditional functions in Narrative Therapy:

1. encouraging persons to objectify and personify the problem or experience that they believe to be oppressive,
2. see the problem as a separate entity,
3. portray the problem and the person's relationships with the problem, as the problem,
4. use externalization as an attitude or perspective rather than a technique,
5. help a person take responsibility for how she interacts with the externalized problem.

Step 3: Understanding Themes

After deciding what an altar is going to be about, it will be important for the client to start doing some research on the specific theme of the altar. The information for making family altars, for example, can come from personal memories of one's family, family photographs, and conversations brought about by questioning family and friends about issues related to the altar. Additional research and materials can be obtained by reviewing newspaper clippings, magazines, the Internet, old letters and cards. Once the client has done her/his/their research on the theme chosen for the altar, the therapist will then start to understand the theme using deconstructive questioning.

The first step in this process is simply to take the language the person uses to describe the problem, modify it so that the problem is objectified, and ask the person questions about it. In Narrative Therapy, it is more important to ask questions to generate experience rather than to gather information. Deconstruction questions address the beliefs, practices, feelings, and attitudes of the client's history of the relationship, contextual influences, the effects or results, the tactics or strategies, and the interrelationship with other beliefs, practices, feelings, or attitudes. These questions are asked within the context of an externalizing conversation.

Step 4: Collecting Images, Words, and Found Objects

After a theme is chosen and the client has done some research, she/he/they start collecting as many things as they can that are related to the theme. Things can include photocopied images, original photographs, poems, prayers, writings, plastic figurines, found objects, toys, candles, coins, silk flowers, store bought objects, and many more. Let the client's creativity and resourcefulness take flight. The client can also include objects that are hand made. These may be things such as jewelry, cross-stitch, drawings, crochet, paintings, small sculptures, etc.

Step 5: Making the Altar and Using Assemblage: Unique Outcomes

Once the materials have been gathered for the altar, the actual altar/shrine/shadow box can be made. Among the materials that can be used to assemble the altar is a cardboard or wooden box, wood, fabric, tacks, a hot glue gun, and glue. The altar can resemble a shadow box with many things glued or placed inside of it. With a wooden box, the wood is cut into strips to make the frame or a shadow box. The frames are best held together with nails. However, many craft stores sell wooden boxes already assembled. These shadow boxes or frames serve as a skeleton for the altars. After getting or assembling the box, then the client can decide where all the elements of a particular altar will fit. The client can move things around and play with the composition until she/he/they are visually, emotionally, and conceptually satisfied. The pieces can be attached as the process unfolds, or all at the same time, once all the materials have been brought together. By assembling the objects in or on the altar, the therapist is able to discuss the new stories that emerge from the process.

By externalizing the problem, people are able to identify previously neglected but vital aspects of lived experience. These aspects, referred to as "unique outcomes," can not be predicted by listening to the dominant story. The therapist can ask questions about unique outcomes that have occurred, use hypothetical experience questions, ask questions that ask about different points of view, and future oriented questions. Since making an altar is a new experience in itself, it is inevitable that new stories and experiences will emerge. It will be up to the therapist to punctuate the new experience and tie in the unique outcomes that stem from this new experience.

Step 6: Discussing the Meaning the Altar Has for the Client: Reconstruction

In my view (M. B.) this is the most exciting part of Narrative Therapy. The reconstruction of a preferred story begins with discussion of a unique outcome. I will usually ask clients to tell me about what meaning the altar has for them, what feelings emerge as they look at it, and what important memories are triggered that they had forgotten. The unique outcome will most likely be the new experience invoked from talking about the altar. The therapist can also ask about events that do not fit with problem-saturated stories, such as referring to the times or places when the new experience might have occurred. For example, if a client is making an altar for her deceased mother, whom she remembers as absent and non-caring, then maybe the therapist can ask the client to remember a time when her mother was there for her and showed tenderness and care. By asking questions that track actions, behaviors, thoughts, awareness, and that link the unique outcome with the present and that extend the story into the future, the therapist is then able to help co-construct a new reality with the clients.

Step 7: Creating a Ceremony or Ritual to Amplifying the New Story (Thickening the Plot)

White and Epston (1990) also suggest circulating the story through tapes, letters, documents, and ceremonies. Creating a ceremony or ritual in therapy, using the altar or shrine made by the client, can be an excellent way to perform a ritual to punctuate the therapeutic outcome desired. For example, for clients using altar-making as a tool for the bereavement process, they can have a session in which a small ceremony is performed to memorialize the deceased person and in the process, amplify their new experience of him or her.

A ceremony, for example, can create an experience that enables people to experience their lives and themselves in new ways as they focus on previously neglected and unstoried aspects of their experience. The preferred story is amplified by asking detailed questions that invite people to slow down an event and notice what went into it and by asking questions relating to time, past, present or future, actual or hypothetical. Questions about context can anchor a story to a particular place and situation, and can invite people to extend stories into new places and new situations, which help solidify the changes made while in therapy.

Step 8: Taking the Altar Home: Spreading the News

As White and Epston (1990) point out, identifying and recruiting a wider audience is essential for the preferred perspective or story to take hold. Sometimes a new way of thinking or being can be tenuous and needs the support of others to get stronger. The client can free themselves from the constraints of the old story as she, he, or they recruit others to their new way of being or thinking. For example, if someone were to make an altar dedicated to a life free from the oppressive influence of drug addiction, then invite others to see and talk about their altar, the process could amplify the new story about how the client was able to overcome the dictatorship of addiction. Ultimately it is the client's decision to share their altar with others. Sometimes they may feel it is a personal, sacred, and/or private process or it may be something that they may want to share and celebrate with others. It will depend on the client's purpose and rationale for making the altar. However, once the client takes the altar home, then the opportunity is there for the client to share the experience of making the altar and discussing the meaning it has for her/him or them.

CLINICAL USES FOR ALTAR-MAKING

Altar-making can be a therapeutic resource for anyone: for individuals, couples or families in therapy, for people of various ethnic or religious backgrounds, or for people with differing presenting problems in therapy. However, in this article we have focused on it being especially beneficial for Hispanic families because of their familiarity with altars and shrines, especially in their homes and churches. Making an altar in therapy can serve many therapeutic functions. There are many benefits for clients creating a shrine or altar. Here we will delineate a few; however, the list could be endless.

Bereavement/Grief and Remembering

Perhaps the most obvious therapeutic resource is making an altar to memorialize a deceased person. I have found this to be an excellent tool for people coping with the loss of a loved one. Making an altar helps them to reconnect and obtain a greater sense of peace and closeness. By bringing in their personal objects, pictures, and making art for the deceased person, clients are able to bring the person into the room and talk about the significance the person has in their life. This process can be healing and comforting and the outcome can serve a constant reminder of the person they lost.

From a narrative therapy perspective, altar-making can be a powerful remembering practice. Remembering is a fairly new practice in narrative therapy (White, 1997) and is based on the work of Barbara Myherhoff (as quoted in White, 1997). Myerhoff refers to remembering as a:

> special type of recollection . . . calling attention to the reaggregation of members, the figures who belong to one's life story, one's own prior selves, as well as significant others who are part of the story. Re-membering then, is a purposive, significant unification . . . (p. 22)

The purpose of remembering is to help persons experience a return to membership with key figures in their lives that have helped to shape their preferred identities as persons. One of the reasons that the pain of losing a loved one is so acute is because the person experiences more than the loss of the person; from a narrative perspective, they also experience a loss of their self identity. While traditional notions of grief work involve encouraging a person to move on and create a new identity separate from the loved one, narrative therapists, through the use of remembering practices, encourage persons to remain "in membership" with loved ones who have died. When a person experiences the loss of a loved one, they often experience a dislocation from their membership with the loved one. Remembering is a practice that allows persons to once again be remembered with the loved one.

Altar making can be a powerful tool to give life to the remembering process. Normally remembering involves using questions to invite persons to experience the presence of the loved one. From a narrative therapy perspective questions are used as a means of generating experience for the persons involved. While remembering questions are used with this purpose in mind, using an experiential activity such as altar making can help persons experience the presence of loved ones more fully. Also, when persons have something tangible that they can keep with them like an altar, it helps them to maintain the presence of the loved one in their daily lives more easily.

Memorialize the Living

Making altars in therapy can also help clients to re-member or reconnect with living people in their lives. Sometimes people feel disconnected by people they were once close to or with people that no longer live in close proximity. Scattered families and a loss of connectedness with extended family seem to be more the norm than the exception. This can cause extreme anxiety, especially with Hispanic families that are accustomed to having their extended family near by. Most Hispanic families have a strong sense of loyalty and commitment to their family. The cultural attribute, called "familismo," is said to be the core value of Hispanic Americans (Ho, 1987).

Familismo is a cultural value and belief that the family is central in the life of the individual. It is thought to be the basis of the Cuban family structure (Bernal & Flores-Ortiz, 1982), the Mexican American family structure (Falicov, 1996; Mindel, 1980; Mirandé, 1985), the Puerto Rican family structure (Comas-Díaz & Griffith, 1988; García-Preto, 1982), and Central and South American family structure (Hernández, 1996). There is a clear image of Hispanic families being cohesive, sometimes enmeshed, and that the majority of an individual's life will revolve around his or her extended family. Familismo is a cultural attitude and value of family interdependence. Hispanics have a "deep awareness of and pride in their membership in the family" (Ho, 1988, p. 124), and they are the means by which an individual's confidence, self worth, security, and identity are determined (Abalos, 1986; Ho, 1987). By making an altar to memorialize the living, a Hispanic person or family can continue to feel connected with family members and honor and celebrate the significance that person has in their lives.

Unify Families

Altar-making in therapy can help families feel closer together by giving them a shared activity and a common goal. Rarely do the families seen in therapy report doing artistic activities together. Endless possibilities can emerge when family members make an altar of their own family. They can use pictures, show important dates and names, and make or bring meaningful objects. This experience can serve to punctuate certain experiences and amplify their strengths. The altar can be hung in the family room or kitchen and can serve as a reminder of their experience in therapy. It can also be a symbol of their renewed sense of family cohesion and family pride.

Help Families Learn to Work Together

The process of building an altar requires teamwork and cooperation. This process can be an excellent resource for families, groups, or teams. As a group they have to decide what the theme or purpose will be, what will go into the altar, and who is responsible for obtaining the objects that will go inside the altar. They will also need to decide on the tools necessary to build the altar (i.e., hot glue, nails, paint, etc.) and who will be responsible for bringing everything needed to the session. Building an altar can help a family or group discuss the reasons for making an altar and hear multiple perspectives in terms of what meaning the altar may have for them individually. I think this process can be useful for anyone who wants or needs to learn how to work together to obtain a common goal and a shared positive experience.

Strengthen Blended or Stepfamilies

Altar-making can be especially useful for a newly formed blended family. They often struggle with the issues mentioned above. Making an altar of their new family can give them a structured, shared activity that can help them discuss important issues, share feelings, begin to solidify a sense of family, increase cohesion and belonging, and amplify strengths. This process can be especially beneficial for stepsiblings who feel thrown together to form an instant family.

Unify Subsystems Within a Family

This process can be helpful when certain members of a family want to be greater aligned. Sometimes the children in a family need to work together to feel closer, fight less, have meaningful shared experiences or get a sense of who they are within their family. Sometimes parents need work together to solidify their strengths, discuss parenting styles, discipline, and their roles as parents, among other things. Even though I am more aligned with Narrative ideas in therapy, it is hard being a family therapist and not thinking in terms of Structural Family Therapy. This is especially evident when the goals for therapy are to strengthen the parents' role in the family, help them strengthen their sense of authority as parents, or help them provide loving, safe, structured, and consistent parenting for their children.

Couples Therapy

Couples can also benefit from making an altar in therapy. This could be helpful to all types of couples; premarital couples, newly married couples, couples celebrating an anniversary, couples trying to overcome particular problems (such as excessive arguing, emotional distance, or infidelity) or for couples coping with illness or loss. The dialogue that can emerge from this process can be healing and informative as well as help them co-create something sacred that symbolizes their relationship.

CASE ILLUSTRATION: ALTAR-MAKING IN THERAPY

Therapeutic Goal

The goal in therapy was to help a 9 year old girl and her mother cope with the loss of their father and husband, who died 5 years ago. Claudia's mother brought her to therapy to address her misbehavior in school, poor school performance, inability to sleep alone, feelings of sadness, and rebellion. After a few sessions of addressing her school performance, it became evident that she was needing to address the unresolved grief she had been experiencing since her father's death. I asked her if she would be interested in making an altar in honor of her father. I described the process and she agreed it would be a fun thing to do. Her mother agreed and we began the process.

Process

First, I asked Claudia if her mother could be in the room to help with making the altar. She could be there to answer questions and tell stories about Claudia's father that she may not remember or know. She agreed. Then I asked them to get the supplies needed and to bring all the objects belonging to him that she wanted to include in the altar. A few sessions later she brought her materials, which included photographs of herself and her father together, his belt and belt buckle, pins he had won, stickers related to his club membership, his identification card from work, and she also colored pictures of animals since he enjoyed fishing and hunting. She also glued a silver fish and a cross and wrote son of God inside. Those and other meaningful items were glued into a shadow box, which we called a shrine.

Outcome

In the end, Claudia had created a visual reminder of her father and their relationship. This bright box had colorful beads glued on the top with all the objects glued inside and on top of her shrine. I asked her to write him a story, prayer, or poem, and to put it inside the box. I thought she was going to do it at home; however, she quickly wrote something, said it was a special prayer, rolled it like a scroll, made a ribbon out of tissue paper and put it around it and glued it inside the box. I asked her how she would remember what was inside it, and she said that she would. She told me she was going to hang on her wall at home and was very excited about what she had created. Ultimately, it was important to me that she was in charge of creating the altar, asking for help when she needed it. When she did, I asked her mom to help her, but in the end, she knew it was her altar that she made. She wrote at the top, "Daddy's shrine, keep out!" I asked if there was anything else she wanted to say about her father or their times together and she said no. We had a moment of silence, her mother cried, and we brought the session to a close. She seemed proud of what she had accomplished and was able to keep a visual reminder of her relationship with her father. In the process, she continued to experience her grief and make connections about her father that she could not have earlier due to her age at the time of his death. Making an altar can be a spiritually powerful process for anyone involved.

AN ARTIST'S PERSPECTIVE

Creating a series of altars for my Master's Thesis project was a wonderful and positive experience for me. I am a Roman Catholic, originally from Venezuela. Therefore, I fit many of the points made earlier about Familismo, Catholicism as a cultural heritage, folk healing, and others. As an artist, it does not surprise me that a high percentage of my artwork is both religious (related to Catholicism) and family related. Throughout the years I have created paintings and sculptures about family members and about Christ. My Master's Thesis project was about what I call contemporary memory and religious altars. After struggling with finding a topic, the idea came to me from watching an exhibition of Russian Icons, where metal work was combined with painting. I wanted to create art that would allow me to combine mediums and also be meaningful. Altars were the answer. I grew up exposed to Catholicism, in combination with many folk, African, and Indigenous beliefs. I created altars with religious themes, like Altar to San Benito, Altar to Dr. Jose Gregorio Hernandez, Altar for Christmas, and Altar to the Virgin Mary of Bethany.

However, more meaningful than those were the altars that I created about my family. As mentioned earlier, altars can be used to memorialize, idolize or immortalize the dead. In my case, I did not want to wait until many of my family members were deceased to memorialize, idolize, and immortalize them. I wanted to do it while many of them were still alive. I wanted to say thank you for being my family. The process of creating altars to my parents, grandparents, brothers, sisters, and wife was positive and therapeutic. I felt very close to them–more than before, even though we were all miles away at the time. I had to go through many family pictures and recollect childhood memories and stories. I even went as far as going to Venezuela for two months to spend time with my family and research altars and other Venezuelan cultural beliefs and practices. I believe I accomplished what I set out to do, which was to memorialize them in life and to show my gratitude towards my family for their love and support. In turn, I created a meaningful body of work and had a wonderful experience.

CONCLUSION

Currently, there is a need for spiritual interventions that are culturally relevant. In this paper we have offered altar-making as a spiritual resource for clients, more specifically for Hispanic/Latino clients. It is our hope that creating altars in therapy may offer clients an avenue in which to experience a preferred story about their selves, lives, and relationships in a creative and artistic way.

REFERENCES

Abalos, D. T. (1986). *Latinos in the United States: The sacred and the political.* Notre Dame, IN: University of Notre Dame Press.

Bernal, G. & Florez-Ortiz, Y. (1982). Latino families in therapy: Engagement and evaluation. *Journal of Marital and Family Therapy*, 8(3), 357-365.

Berude, M. S. (Ed.). (1989). *The American Heritage Dictionary* (5th ed.). New York: Dell Publishing.

Canino, I. A. & Spurlock, J. (1994). *Culturally diverse children and adolescents: Assessment, diagnosis, and treatment.* New York: The Guilford Press.

Carlson, T. D. (1997). Using art in Narrative Therapy: Enhancing therapeutic possibilities. *The American Journal of Family Therapy*, *25*, 271-283.

Cobas, J. & Duany, J. (1995). *Los Cubanos en Puerto Rico: Economia, etnia, e identidad cultural.* San Juan: Editorial de la Universidad Puerto Rico.

Comas-Díaz, L. & Griffith, E. E. (Eds.) (1988). *Clinical guidelines in cross-cultural mental health.* New York: John Wiley & Sons, Inc.

DeBlassie, R. R. (1976). *Counseling with Mexican American youth: Preconceptions and processes.* Austin, TX: Learning Concepts, Inc.

Delgado, M. (1988). Groups in Puerto Rican spiritism: Implications for clinicians. In C. Jacobs & D. D. Bowles (Eds.), *Ethnicity and race: Critical concepts in social work* (pp. 34-47). Silver Spring, MD: National Association of Social Workers.

Diaz, R. E., & Foronda, E. P. (Eds.). (1994). *Larousse: Diccionario de la Lengua Espanola* (1st ed.). Mexico: Larousse Planeta.

Falicov, C. J. (ed.) (1998). *Latino families in therapy: A guide to multicultural practice.* New York: The Guilford Press.

Freedman, J., & Combs, G. (1996). *Narrative therapy: The social construction of preferred realities.* New York: W. W. Norton & Company.

Garcia-Preto, N. (1982). Puerto Rican Families. In M. McGoldrick, J. K. Pearce & J. Giordano (Eds.), *Ethnicity and Family therapy* (pp. 164-186). New York: The Guilford Press.

Grebler, L., Moore, J., & Guzmán, R. (1970). *The Mexican American people: The nation's second largest minority.* New York: Free Press.

Ho, M. K. (1987). *Family therapy with ethnic minorities.* Newbury, CA: Sage Publications, Inc.

McGoldrick, M. (Ed.). (1998). *Re-visioning family therapy: Race, culture, and gender in clinical practice.* New York: The Guilford Press.

McGoldrick, M., Giordano, J., & Pearce, J. K. (Eds.). (1996). *Ethnicity and family therapy* (2nd ed.). New York: The Guilford Press.

Mesa-Bains, A. (1993). Curatorial Statement. In J. P. Pierce (Ed.), *Ceremony of the Spirits: Nature and memory in Contemporary Latino Art* (pp. 9-17). San Francisco, CA: Marquand Books.

Mindel, C. H. (1980). Extended Families among urban Americans, Anglos, and Blacks. *Hispanic Journal of Behavioral Sciences*, 2(1), 21-24.

Mirandé, A. (1985). *The Chicano experience: An alternative perspective.* Notre Dame, IN: University of Notre Dame Press.

Morales-Dorta, S. (1976). *Puerto Rican espiritismo: Religion and psychotherapy.* New York: Vantage.

Nichols, M. P. & Schwartz, R. C. (1991). *Family Therapy: Concepts and methods* (2 Ed.). Needham Heights, MA: Allyn and Bacon.

Page, J. (1994). The Face of the Gods: Art and Altars of Africa and the African Americas. *Art Papers, 18*, 32.

Patterson, J. E, Hayworth, M., Turner, C., & Raskin, M. (2000). Spiritual issues in Family Therapy: A graduate-level course. *Journal of Marital and Family Therapy, 26*, 199-210.

Prouty, A. M., & Bermúdez, J. M. (1999). Experiencing multiconsciousness: A Feminist model for therapy. *Journal of Feminist Family Therapy, 11*(3), 19-39.

Rogg, E. M., & Cooney, R. S. (1980). *Adaptation and adjustment of Cubans: West New York, New Jersey.* New York: Hispanic Research Center.

Walsh, F. (1998). *Beliefs, Spirituality, and Transcendence: Keys to family resilience*, In McGoldrick, M. (Ed.), Re-visioning family therapy: Race, culture, and gender in clinical practice (pp. 62-77). New York: The Guilford Press.

White, M., & Epston, D. (1990). *Narrative means to therapeutic ends.* New York: W. W. Norton & Company.

White, M. (1997). *Narratives of Therapists' Lives.* Adelaide, South Australia: Dulwich Centre Publications.

Index

